INSIGHT GUIDES

The world's largest collection of visual travel guides

BURGUNDY

Edited and Updated by Rosemary Bailey
Photography by Lyle Lawson
Editorial Director: Brian Bell

APA PUBLICATIONS
Part of the Langenscheidt Publishing Group

CONTACTING THE EDITORS: Although every effort is made to provide accurate information in this publication, we live in a fast-changing world and would appreciate it if readers would call our attention to any errors or outdated information that may occur by writing to us at Apa Publications,
P.O. Box 7910, London SE1 1WE, England.
Fax: (44) 20 7403-0290.
e-mail: insight@apaguide.demon.co.uk.

First Edition 1992
Second Edition 1996, updated 2000

Distributed in the United States by
Langenscheidt Publishers Inc.
46–35 54th Road, Maspeth, NY 11378
Fax: (718) 784 -0640

Distributed in Canada by
Prologue Inc.
1650 Lionel Bertrand Blvd., Boisbriand
Québec, Canada J7H 1N7
Tel: (450) 434-0306. Fax: (450) 434-2627

Distributed in the UK & Ireland by
GeoCenter International Ltd
The Viables Centre, Harrow Way
Basingstoke, Hampshire RG22 4BJ
Fax: (44) 1256-817988

Worldwide distribution enquiries:
APA Publications GmbH & Co. Verlag KG
(Singapore branch)
38 Joo Koon Road, Singapore 628990
Tel: 65-8651600. Fax: 65-8616438

Printed in Singapore by
Insight Print Services (Pte) Ltd
38 Joo Koon Road, Singapore 628990
Fax: 65-8616438

This guidebook combines the interests and enthusiasms of two of the world's best-known information providers: Insight Guides, whose titles have set the standard for visual travel guides since 1970, and the Discovery Channel, the world's premier source of non-fiction television programming.

Insight Guides' editors provide practical advice and general understanding about a place's history, culture and people. Discovery Channel and its website www.discovery.com help millions of viewers to explore their world from the comfort of their homes and also encourage them to explore it firsthand.

This book is just one of nearly two dozen in Insight Guides' French series. The region of Burgundy as it is defined today bears only a token resemblance to the original Burgundian empire. But, had history taken a different course, Burgundy could have become a separate country. Europe's national boundaries have always had a delightfully arbitrary nature to them, and it was this aspect of Burgundy that especially intrigued project editor **Rosemary Bailey**. "I felt the fate of Burgundy was a key to appreciating the more flexible frontiers of Europe we are working towards," she says, "and I thought we might learn a great deal from Burgundy's positive regional identity."

Bailey

Bailey is responsible for this new updated version of the guide. She has specialised in regional Insight Guides, having previously edited *Tuscany, The Loire Valley* and *The Côte d'Azur*. She now divides her time between London and Southern France, where she continues to write guidebooks to France and other Mediterranean countries. She also contributes articles on a wide range of subjects to *The Sunday Times, The Guardian* and other publications.

The stunning photography which illustrates this guide is mostly the work of **Lyle Lawson**, an American based (when she isn't travelling the globe) in England. She has brought her keen eye to many Insight Guides, and was photographer of Insight Guides to *Normandy, The Loire* and *Waterways of Europe*. She is passionate about ballooning and barges, and

Lawson

Gerard-Sharp

Graham

Miles

Ardagh

Carter

Rutherford

has contributed articles on both activities in Burgundy. Despite the quantity of camera equipment crammed into her MGB sports car, she also managed to load up an astonishing number of bottles of Pouilly-Fuissé.

Bailey assembled an impressive team of writers who know this part of France well. First to be recruited was **Lisa Gerard-Sharp**, a European-based travel journalist and broadcaster, and a regular contributor to the Insight series. While living in Brussels, she found time to explore the old Burgundian empire, which used to include most of Belgium. She has produced a thought-provoking analysis of the Burgundian character and life in the region today, as well as a comprehensive and illuminating guide to the northern *départements* of the region, sampling some fine Chablis on the way.

Peter Graham is also a frequent contributor to Insight Guides, and here he rises to the challenge of explaining the complicated topic of wine in Burgundy. He also gives a tantalising description of the cuisine of the region and a guide to the Côte d'Or. Graham is an established journalist and an author – his *Classic Cheese Cookery* was a winner of the André Simon Memorial Prize.

For author **Barry Miles**, who also came to Bailey's aid, Burgundy combined two great passions: wine and Romanesque architecture. He writes on the region's architectural heritage, explaining how and why the great churches and monasteries were built, and bemoans the fate of the greatest of them all, Cluny, lost to an early breed of property developer.

John Ardagh is a familiar name to Francophiles, as the author of many books on the country, including the perennially popular *France Today*. His portraits of writers Colette and Lamartine capture their profound attachment to the Burgundy landscape and the literary inspiration they drew from it.

Rowlinson Carter is another frequent Insight contributor, and his dramatic history of the Valois dukes and their court fleshes out the tortuous history of the period with a wealth of detail and gossip.

Ward Rutherford is a broadcaster and author of numerous history books, including a popular account of Celtic mythology. Here he brings his knowledge of the period to the early history of the first Burgundians.

Journalist **Caroline Bailey** participated in the religious community of Taizé, and has given a thoughtful description of its role today.

This Insight Guide combines Burgundy's history with a detailed guide to the region, enriched by the personal observations of the people who live there. It begins with an exploration of the character of the province, tracking the forces that have shaped it. After establishing the historical context, we look at contemporary Burgundy, its local politics and its provincial life. The hugely important subject of food and wine is dealt with next, including interviews with food producers and winemakers.

The Places section journeys round the region, describing in detail the sights to be seen and providing essential background information. Although recommendations are often made about restaurants and especially wine, basic factual information, listing hotels, restaurants, museums, activities, and a wealth of travel advice, is reserved for the Travel Tips section, found at the back of the book for easy reference.

The exhaustive listing of information was compiled by **Jill Adam**, who wrote the Travel Tips sections for the *Brittany, Loire Valley,* and *Côte d'Azur* Insight Guides. She edited the *French Farm and Village Holiday Guide* for some years and welcomes any chance to spend time in her house in southwest France. **Jane Sigal**, a Paris-based food writer, has contributed a knowledgeable survey of restaurants in the region, including some of the finest cuisine in France and many good-value humbler establishments.

Jill Anderson guided the text skilfully through a variety of Macintosh computers in Insight Guides' London editorial office. Proofreading and indexing were completed by **Carole Mansur**.

CONTENTS

Introduction

The Glory of Burgundy
by Lisa Gerard-Sharp **21**

History

The Lost Kingdom
by Ward Rutherford **31**

Brunhilde
by Rowlinson Carter **36**

Decisive Dates
by Ward Rutherford **38**

The Romanesque Tradition
by Barry Miles **43**

Cluny
by Barry Miles **50**

The Grand Dukes of the West
by Rowlinson Carter **55**

Jousting
by Rowlinson Carter **60**

From Renaissance to Revolution
by Lisa Gerard-Sharp **71**

Bussy Rabutin
by John Ardagh **74**

The Twentieth Century
by Lisa Gerard-Sharp **83**

Mitterrand's Morvan
by Lisa Gerard-Sharp **89**

Features

Provincial Life
by Lisa Gerard-Sharp **93**

The Wine Business
by Peter Graham **105**

Wine Confraternities
by Lisa Gerard-Sharp **108**

The Vigneron
by Peter Graham **112**

A Burgundian Feast
by Peter Graham **119**

Snail-Hunting
by Peter Graham **122**

Places

Introduction
by Rosemary Bailey **135**

The Yonne
by Lisa Gerard-Sharp **139**

Colette Country
by John Ardagh **142**

Pierre Larousse
by Peter Graham **152**

The Heartland
by Lisa Gerard-Sharp **169**

Ballooning
by Lyle Lawson **180**

The Nièvre
by Lisa Gerard-Sharp **195**

Burgundy by Boat
by Lyle Lawson **202**

Faïence
by Lisa Gerard-Sharp **212**

Dijon
by Rosemary Bailey **221**

Cooking for the Dukes
by Rowlinson Carter **226**

Mustard
by Rosemary Bailey **232**

The Côte d'Or and Chalonnais
by Peter Graham **240**

Hospices de Beaune
by Peter Graham **248**

Southern Burgundy
by Rosemary Bailey **264**

Taizé
by Caroline Bailey **272**

Mâcon and Beaujolais
by Rosemary Bailey **289**

Lamartine
by John Ardagh **294**

Beaujolais Nouveau
by Peter Graham **302**

Maps

Burgundy in 1477 .... **64**
Chablis Wine Region **106**
Côtes de Nuits Wine
Region; Côte de Beaune
Wine Region **110**
Mâconnais and Beaujolais
Wine Region **113**
Burgundy **134**
The Yonne **140**
Auxerre **147**
The Heartland **170**
The Nièvre **197**
Nevers **211**
Dijon **222**
Dijon Region **230**
Côte d'Or **243**
Southern Burgundy **266**
Mâcon and Beaujolais **290**
Bourg-en-Bresse **292**

TRAVEL TIPS

Getting Acquainted

The Place 310
Climate 310
The Economy 310
Government 310
The People 311

Planning the Trip

What to Bring 311
Entry Regulations 311
Customs 311
Animal Quarantine 312
Health 312
Emergencies 312
Currency 312
Public Holidays 312
Getting There 313
By Air/Sea/Train 313
By Channel Tunnel 314
By Bus/Car 314
Language Courses 315
Disabled Travellers 315

Practical Tips

Emergencies 316
Weights & Measures 316
Business Hours 316
Media 316
Postal Services 317
Telecommunications 317
Embassies & Consulates 317
Tourist Offices 318

Getting Around

Public Transport 318
Private Transport 319
On Foot 320
Hitchhiking 320
By Boat 321

Where to Stay

Bed & Breakfast 322
Self-Catering/Gîtes 322
Camping 322
Hotels 323

Eating Out

Restaurants 328
Wine 333
Wine Tasting 334

Outdoor Activities

Excursions 336

Sites

Places of Interest 336
Museums & Art Galleries 336

Festivals & Nightlife

Live Arts/Diary of Events 342
Nightlife 343

Shopping

Shopping Areas 343
Markets 344
Buying Direct 345

Sport

Participant Sports 345
Spectator Sports 347

Language

Words & Phrases 347

Further Reading

General/Other Insight Guides .. 352

Art/Photo Credits 354
Index 355

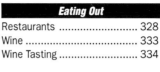

THE GLORY OF BURGUNDY

Burgundy has been called *un état d'esprit*, a state of mind. It is the invisible bridge between northern France and the Midi, a transition from the cerebral north to the earthy south, from adulthood to a fantasy French childhood. Every Parisian is a born-again Burgundian at heart.

Henri Vincenot, traditionalist and professional Burgundian, equated northern Burgundy with *la zone parisienne*. In French eyes, Vincenot's books have done for Burgundy what Pagnol and *Jean de Florette* did for Provence. Full-bodied wine, glittering fish-scale roofs and Romanesque churches suggest a semblance of unity in a subtle province. Burgundian hallmarks exist but are elusive, belonging to character rather than to architecture. Burgundy in the blood presumes an irrepressible spirit. It is tinged with religiosity and nostalgia but tempered by mischievous gaiety and wit as sharp as Dijon mustard.

Even in the 15th century the region was reputed for its climate and rich living. Philip the Bold's family came to Burgundy "to enjoy better air and nourishment unavailable in Flanders". The region officially designated Burgundy today encompasses the *départements* of Yonne, Nièvre, Côte d'Or and Saône-et-Loire, but this area bears only a passing resemblance to the Burgundy of yore, which at various stages extended as far as Provence, and included most of Belgium, as well as parts of the Netherlands and Switzerland. In the Middle Ages the original Kingdom of Burgundy established in the 5th century was always looked back on as a legendary home: the "lost kingdom".

The classic image of Burgundy is of golden vineyards and gentle slopes. But real Burgundy is a patchwork of prosperous wine country and fertile pastures interspersed with poorer plains and woodland. Each view has its chauvinistic champions and evokes a dreamy nostalgia for a childhood never-never

land. Madame de Sévigné, that indefatigable letter-writer, was born in the Auxois and loved the lush countryside and air "which you have only to breathe to get fat". Her grandmother, Jeanne de Chantal, owned the Château de Bourbilly, a short ride from fattening Époisses, the village which produces Burgundy's best cheese. "I have just arrived in the château of my forebears," she marvelled. "Here are my beautiful meadows, my little river and my magnificent windmill, just where I left them."

The hilly Mâconnais is a landscape famously sentimentalised by Lamartine. The Romantic aristocratic poet lived in rural bliss near the village of Milly. As a child he loved his creeper-clad manor and "the sweet and melancholy voices of the little frogs that sing on summer evenings". As an adult, Lamartine owned local vineyards but regularly returned to his childhood home to relive his boyhood.

This landscape remains an inspiration: the Rock of Solutré, a prehistoric site, was always the object of a Whitsuntide pilgrimage by François Mitterrand and his followers. The descent naturally ends in the Pouilly-Fuissé vineyards at the foot of the cliffs.

Preceding pages: *Habit de Vigneron* by Bonnar (17th century); flying the flag; Beaune market; grape-picking; wedding at Auxonne. **Left**, snail-farmer, Jean-François Vadot. **Right**, 18th-century wine merchant's sign.

Less celebrated is the secretive landscape of the Puisaye, with its lakes, neat hedges and slender trees. As Colette's childhood home, its fate is sealed as Colette country. Born in 1873 at St-Sauveur-en-Puisaye, on the edge of Burgundy, this self-appointed *reine de la terre* describes her rural childhood in the *Claudine* books. "If you came to my home on a fine summer's day, you would find a dark garden devoid of flowers, and in the distance, would watch the mountain turn bluish, its slopes covered with pebbles, butterflies and thistles tinged a dusty mauve – you would forget me." However, as Burgundy's best-loved writer, her presence is most pervasive.

literary champions, it remains remote, as do the misty marshes and valleys of La Bresse. To the west, the rolling countryside around Charolles is home to placid white Charolais cattle, an export second only to wine.

Yet to outsiders, the Burgundian landscape is forever linked to wine. The Côte d'Or, named for the rich colour of the earth, is a narrow ribbon stretching south from Dijon. The buff-stone villages in the vineyards have a pampered look, in keeping with the cosseted proprietors. Comtesse de Loisy, for example, belongs to an old family of *vignerons* in Nuits-St-Georges. The canny countess recently traded 12 bottles of Clos de Vougeot Grand Cru 1947 for an Alfa Romeo.

When Shakespeare spoke of "waterish Burgundy", he visualised Flanders, then part of Burgundy, but the image remains apt in the watershed of France. The Yonne is the traditional waterway to Paris; the Loire marks the western border of Burgundy; and the Saône wends its way through the southern vineyards. With 1,100 km (700 miles) of navigable rivers and canals, the region is a veritable paradise for barging.

A third of the territory is forested, from the watery Puisaye to the northern plains of the Châtillonais. The Morvan is the dark heart of Burgundy, a rugged interior dominated by mountains, forests and streams. Devoid of

"The buyers pleaded. I told them the wine was too old to travel, but finally I gave in." Even so, she kept a bottle back, claiming its fragrance of mushrooms and autumn leaves epitomised a Burgundian childhood. As Colette wrote: "My homeland enchants me, intoxicates me, but leaves an after-taste of bittersweet nostalgia".

The Côte d'Or offers rich civic architecture and champagne-coloured villages in serried ranks of vines. Clos de Vougeot and La Rochepot are sumptuous châteaux at ease with their surroundings but the Hôtel-Dieu in Beaune draws the deepest admiration. On leaving Beaune, Henry James remarked: "I carried away the impression of something mildly autumnal – something rusty yet kindly, like the taste of a sweet russet pear."

The sensuous and spiritual landscapes complement one another perfectly. Burgundy may keep its feet on the earth but has its head in the clouds. The Romanesque churches are hymns to the spirituality of the province, as is the proliferation of religious foundations.

If the landscape is deeply civilised it is thanks to the monastic tradition that swept Burgundy in the Middle Ages. Until the construction of St Peter's in Rome, Cluny was the largest church in Christendom, and enjoyed phenomenal power for hundreds of years. Corruption and laxity were, however,

As a leader he was a fanatic, embroiled in every controversy, and launching the doomed second crusade at Vézelay. But to his credit 500 Cistercian abbeys flourished in his lifetime and 3,000 a century later. Simple monastic estates like La-Pierre-Qui-Vire survive in Burgundy today, living the contemplative life and producing the Zodiaque series on Romanesque architecture.

Burgundy has always been characterised by a universal religious impulse, and today shelters a wide spectrum of religious foundations. Roger Schutz founded Taizé here in 1944; it is now a huge flourishing community. Burgundy is also home to the Buddhist monastery at Dettey, the largest in Europe,

inevitable and eventually the reforming figure of St Bernard appeared on the scene.

He was a young nobleman born near Dijon in 1090 who joined Stephen Harding's Cistercian community at Cîteaux. While Harding ran Cîteaux, St Bernard roamed France, preaching, debating and founding abbeys, including Clairvaux and Fontenay. As a monk he adhered to the original Benedictine precepts of obedience, silence, contemplation and penitence, preaching a pared-down Christianity, a reaction against Cluniac excess and luxury.

Left, *en famille*. **Above**, Clos de Vougeot chefs.

while 1992 saw the opening of France's first Islamic theological institute nearby. Not for nothing is Burgundy known as *le toit du monde occidental*, the religious roof over the Western world.

Churches provide the natural stage for Burgundy's procession of master craftsmen. In Autun, the presence of Roman remains inspired church sculpture, imbuing the figures with harmony and a haunting sense of loss. Gislebertus d'Autun's *Eve*, captured at the moment of temptation, is one of the most vibrant Romanesque sculptures ever made. Luckily, medieval sculptors ignored St Bernard's admonitions against ornament: "In

God's name, if you are not ashamed of these idiocies, why at least are you not sorry to incur such expense?"

Nor was expense spared in the time of the Grand Dukes, when the Flemish influence was paramount. Arts and crafts were the acceptable face of cultural imperialism. Sculptor Claus Sluter left his mark in Dijon with his magnificent *Moses*. Roger van der Weyden, another Flemish master, painted a poignant *Last Judgement* to adorn the Hôtel-Dieu at Beaune. The golden triangle of Beaune, Brussels and Bruges grew opulent under lavish Burgundian patronage. The Italianate châteaux of Ancy-le-Franc and Tanlay boast exquisite Renaissance marque-

tion between *douceur de vivre* and *joie de vivre*. Contrary to this rollicking image, Gaston Roupnel defines his fellow Burgundians as "those who pause on their journey, with the time and inclination to marvel".

"Burgundian" may be a byword for opulence and excess but the regional temperament is quieter, more perceptive, patient and pragmatic. Artists tend to be unsentimental and robust. Colette was never self-consciously a "writer" but turned her hand to anything; Vincenot was also a sculptor and carpenter; even Lamartine, the precious poet, was an amateur *vigneron*.

Humour is typically understated, teasing or ironic, occasionally delighting in the mis-

try, a decorative talent which survived the passing of the Dukes. Even at the end of the Ancien Régime, classical châteaux, including Versailles, continued to benefit from Burgundian good taste.

The Flemish inheritance colours the Burgundian character. The stereotype is of a red-faced, simple-minded, hot-blooded womaniser. This *Joyeux Bourguignon* (Jolly Burgundian) is a stock figure in racy 16th-century literature. Such satirical and scatalogical tales echo Rabelais, the product of a similarly merry wine-growing region, the Loire. But this flamboyant temperament owes much to astute public relations and to a simple equa-

fortunes of others. An air of detachment masks a quiet faith, a closeness to nature and a sense of continuity. Burgundian lore stresses that a new thing succeeds only if it is deeply rooted in tradition.

An epicurean image is confined to the Côte d'Or. Yet even here it is muted: conviviality is reserved for visitors or festivals. Beaune is Burgundy's wine capital but its cellars are synonymous with secrecy.

Writer Jean-François Bazin, a Burgundian born and bred, believes that the wine-growers are discreet by nature. They are tolerant on all matters – except for the superiority of Burgundy: "Bordeaux is often prescribed for the sick but our wines are for the healthy." Such caustic humour is a common link throughout Burgundy, best reflected in stories. Equally typical is a sceptical, irreverent tone of distant mockery. In the words of writer Jules Renard: "We're put on earth to laugh. We won't be able to laugh in purgatory or hell and laughter wouldn't be fitting in heaven." Bussy-Rabutin, the author of a satirical novel about Louis XV's court, was a true Burgundian in his witty mischief-making. As Robert Speaight remarks: "A country which produced both St Bernard and Bussy-Rabutin may claim to have reconciled within its borders the extremes of human nature."

(people would rather take it for granted than go and see for themselves).

Chauvinism is justified by the richness of the province yet even famous Burgundians are modest, from Nicéphore Niepce, the inventor of photography, to Gustave Eiffel whose tower dominates the Paris skyline. Eccentrics are rare in such a balanced region. Nonetheless, the transvestite Chevalier d'Eon made his mark in Louis XV's employ and even fooled Casanova about his true sex. This diplomat, spy, swordsman and *bon vivant* allegedly introduced red Burgundy to Britain. Xavier Forneret, Lamartine's contemporary, lived in a Gothic tower near Beaune and slept in a coffin. When not

St Bernard aside, Burgundians are no saints, even in the church. St Bernard himself had selective compassion, railing against spendthrift abbots and scantily clad women alike. In modern times, Chanoine Kir best exemplifies the priest who is more spirited than spiritual. As mayor of Dijon after 1945, he was a truculent, caustic character remembered both as a war hero and as the populariser of Kir. A Burgundian expression holds that *"On aime mieux y croire que d'y aller voir"*

Left, firemen's fête at Ligny-le-Châtel. **Above**, bandsmen at the Bague festival, Semur-en-Auxois.

playing the violin, he wrote poetry which later inspired the French Surrealists.

Burgundy also boasts Pierre-Athanase Larousse, a fitting son for a place so preoccupied with language. Larousse pored over his famous dictionary, "my brain and heart swelling with Burgundian sap". The language is as soft as the landscape. In Burgundy, Auxerre is rolled as "Ausserre" and Auxois melts into "Aussois". The dialects reveal Celtic and Flemish influences. *Tu es un vrai bourguignon* has been a Flemish expression for a *bon vivant* since the days of the Grand Dukes. Despite the trend towards *cuisine légère* most Burgundians still favour *cuisine traditionelle*, food enriched by wine, wine enhanced by food. Henry James relished the "poetry" of Bresse butter: "'*Nous sommes en Bresse et le beurre n'est pas mauvais*,' the landlady said, with a sort of dry coquetry."

Burgundian appetites are nothing if not robust. Jugged hare, *jambon de Morvan*, *boeuf bourguignon*, *poires Dijonnaises* and Burgundy-drenched *coq au vin* are traditional fare. Henry James also gorged himself on eggs in Bourg-en-Bresse: "*La plus belle fille du monde ne peut donner de ce qu'elle a*; and it might seem that an egg which has succeeded in being fresh has done all that can be reasonably expected of it." The region prides itself on being *bien dans son assiette*,

at ease with its soul and stomach. The hearty attitude to food reflects an equally earthy approach to life.

Even the mystical writings of Romain Rolland are suffused with sensuousness. He describes an idyllic country childhood in which "the taste and smell of the resin, of the honey, acacia and warm earth have entered my flesh and bones forever". Sensuousness and sensuality often merge. Réstif de la Bretonne, a friend of Madame de Staël's, supposedly kept a calendar of his mistresses, one for every day of the year.

Earthiness is arguably a Gallic legacy. Certainly, there is a Celtic flavour to Burgundian folklore. Vercingétorix fought the Romans all over Burgundy but was crushed at Alésia, a defeat spelling the end of Gaul. Despite the conquest, the deities of the Roman pantheon did not obliterate Gallic cults. Vercingétorix' misty-eyed appeal is to Celtic sensibilities. There are plans to turn Bibracte, the Celtic camp in the Morvan, into a theme park: Ancient Gaul by way of Asterix.

The archetypal Celt was Henri Vincenot, whose moustache recalls both Vercingétorix and the Jolly Burgundian of yore. The storyteller lived in the fertile farmland of the Auxois until his death in 1985. He used Burgundian settings and his peasant stock as a source for his novels. This modern folk hero defied the Romanisation of France, calling himself "a Celtophile, Celtomane and above all, a Celt". His *Livre de Raison de Glaude Bourguignon* is a work of Burgundian resistance to all colonisation. Vincenot's novels show that the native character has survived the loss of Gauls and Grand Dukes.

In *Pape des Escargots*, his best-known work, Vincenot tells the story of a snail-breeder in the tiny village of Saffres on the Côte d'Or. The biggest snail is fattened up and then ceremoniously eaten on the family feast day. Not for nothing is the snail the regional symbol, occupying church capitals, and decorating Dijonnais town houses, as well as one's plate. It is modest, sensitive, shows its horns from time to time, but mostly goes quietly about its business. The snail is the soul of Burgundy, a province *bien dans sa peau*, happy in its shell.

Vincenot coined the phrase *civilisation lente* to describe the snail's pace of the province. Those visitors who are sensible travel at the speed of the slowest canal boat, indulging in a leisurely wine-tasting, with plenty of time to discuss vintages and note the recipe for *gougères*, crusty cheese pastries that are Burgundian specialities. Trails around Romanesque churches and Renaissance châteaux create an appreciative Burgundian appetite. Henry James "came away with a strange mixture of impressions – of late Gothic sculpture and thick *tartines*". Colette's advice is as sound as ever: "Burgundy is like a pig: some parts are more memorable than others but every bit is edible."

Left, traditional *sabotier*. **Right**, *sabotier* Romain Doré in St-Père-sous-Vézelay today.

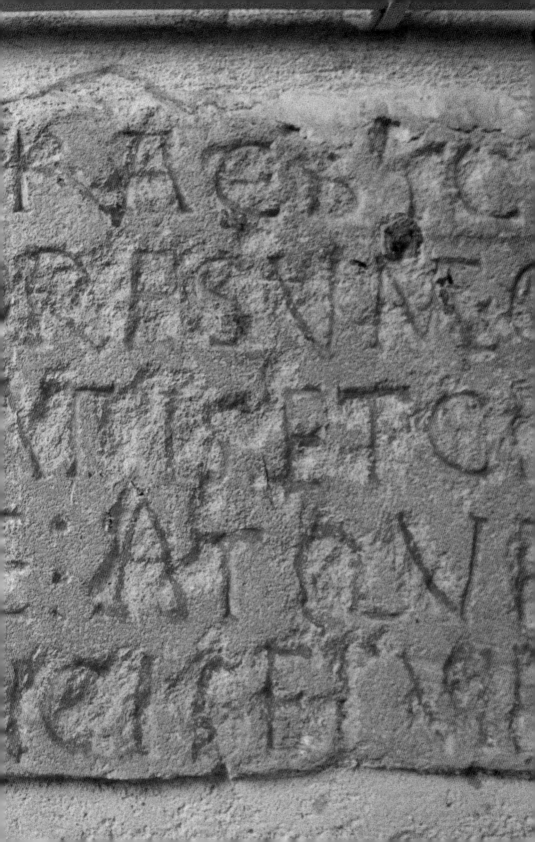

Julio cesare imperante · A theodoto diuisa · nominatur pars tercia
Sed uere est quarta · nā asia et inde partes duas ꝯ affrica tciā europā ē
Habet europa maria XI · Insulas XL · prouincias XX · oiatos gēs ·
autē opida CXX · flumina XXI · Gentesꝗ diuersas numero XXVI
Regna ū que st colore rubeo circūscripta ad romanos grecosꝗ prince̅t reg̅ū
EVROPA dicta ē ab europa filia agenoris regis lybie · uxoris iouis ·

THE LOST KINGDOM

The historical boundaries of Burgundy may have wavered but its devotion to wine has not. The Romans first discovered the symbiosis of wine-grape and Burgundian soil, as one vineyard, the Vosne-Romanée, famous for its high-quality reds, still recalls. But it was earlier occupiers, the Celts or Gauls, who could be said to have been its first serious oenophiles. Ferocious warriors, prodigious lovers and voracious eaters with a weakness for roast boar, the Celts were so addicted to wine that it was said they would swap a slave for a jugful, a servant for a single swallow.

The region had, of course, been inhabited long before the arrival of the Celts in the 1st millennium BC. Indeed, the Rock of Solutré near Mâcon has lent its name to the Solutrean Culture which flourished 23 centuries ago. Distinguished for its jewellery and cave paintings, its craftsmen invented the technique of pressure-flaking of flint, enabling them to produce arrow and lance heads as delicate as the laurel and willow leaves after which they were named.

The Celts continued this love of the beautiful. With their productive farms yielding grain in abundance, they were able to exchange the surplus not only for wine, but for works of art from all Europe, as grave-goods found in a burial chamber on the hill of Vix and now in the Châtillon-sur-Seine museum testify. Besides Baltic amber work, silver cups and bronze wine jars from Tuscany, they included the remains of a funerary chariot. In it was the skeleton of a Gallic princess, adorned with bracelets and pearl necklaces and crowned with a gold diadem.

Most sensational of all was the Vase de Vix, a magnificently decorated bronze krater or urn from Greece large enough to hold at least five fully grown adults. Though its function may have been decorative, it might equally have had a ritual purpose since one Celtic method of human sacrifice was to hold the victim's head down in a container of water until they drowned.

Preceding pages: Roman inscription, Cluny. Left, Burgundia at the centre of a medieval map of Europe. Right, statue of Vercingétorix.

Always a loose and quarrelsome confederation of tribes, the Celts were capable of temporary unification to launch some military adventure. In 390 BC, the Senones, whose capital was at Sens, were the prime movers in an invasion of Italy in which Rome was seized and held to ransom for seven months.

The Vix princess belonged to the Sequani tribe and in 60 BC their neighbours, the Aedui, believing themselves under threat from her people and their allies, the Helvetii,

appealed to the Romans for support. That they gave it was due solely to their fear that Gaulish inter-tribal strife might jeopardise their possessions in southern France and Spain. And what ensued was to change the course of European history.

In a lightning campaign in 58 BC Julius Caesar, the Roman commander-in-chief, defeated the Helvetii outside the Aeduan capital, Bibracte (now Mount Beuvray, near Autun) and seized the Sequanan capital, Vesontio (now Besançon).

However, Caesar was profoundly distrustful of his Aeduan allies and particularly of Dumnorix, younger brother of the king who was making a bid for leadership. During the winter of 53–52 BC he decided on the total subjugation of Gaul and, in the early spring, began the redeployment of the limited forces at his disposal.

Before its completion his fears were confirmed. At a secret conclave in the Aeduan capital the most powerful of the Gaulish chieftains had banded themselves into an anti-Roman league led by the young Vercingétorix, king of the Arvernians (what is now the Auvergne).

The first assault came while Caesar's vastly outnumbered soldiers were on the march. The defeat, which seemed inevitable, was turned into victory by superior organisa-

tion and discipline and a badly mauled Vercingétorix was forced to pull back to Alésia (Alise-Sainte-Reine) where his statue now stands. Pursued and besieged by Caesar, he held out for six weeks only, forced to surrender when an Aeduan relief column failed to reach him. He was taken to Rome in chains, paraded by Caesar at his triumph, then secretly strangled.

Despite the devastating blow dealt to the Gauls' morale by the failure of this, the biggest and most promising of all their revolts, the country remained turbulent, and total subjugation was not achieved until the reign of Augustus, who succeeded Caesar in

45 BC. Razing Bibracte, he built a new capital called Augustodunum, in his own honour. Although the name has since been eroded to Autun, its remains, including a 15,000-seat amphitheatre, testify to a past when it was "sister and rival to Rome".

The next four centuries saw Rome's conversion to Christianity while, at the same time, its hold on its dominions grew feebler. It was now that those who were to give their name to Burgundy entered the scene. From original homelands on the southern shores of the Baltic, the Burgundi had been pushed westward by a variety of enemies finally to reach the easternmost borders of the Roman Empire. Here a century and half of contact had so conditioned them that they spoke of themselves as Romans and had adopted Christianity. The Romans, believing the Burgundi might form a buffer against the hostile Huns and Germans, encouraged them to settle along the banks of the Saône, thus laying the foundations of modern Burgundy.

There was to follow a period of several centuries in which Burgundy passed through different hands and, like a patch of oil tossed on an ocean, would sometimes expand, sometimes contract, sometimes split into several parts. The first expansion, in the 5th century, took its borders to the west bank of the Rhine. Then, in the middle of the century, a rash quarrel with Rome led to almost total annihilation and the massacre of the ruling dynasty, a disaster recounted in the medieval German Nibelungenlied, later used by Wagner as the basis of his *Ring* cycle.

Those who survived were deported to an area round Lake Geneva in what is now Savoy. Nonetheless, they were soon expanding once more, this time north and west and into the Rhône and Saône valleys.

It was during this period that there occurred what may have been the precursor to the later alliance between Burgundy and England. To the north the British – led, according to legend, by King Arthur – had just established a defensive line against the invading Angles and Saxons. The Burgundian king, Gundioc, is known to have numbered among his allies one Riothamus from "over the water". Geoffrey Ashe in *The Discovery of Arthur* argues that "Riothamus", roughly "Great King", was none other than Arthur himself. After a defeat at the hands of Goths in about 470, Riothamus (or Arthur) withdrew to Burgundy where he died. Ashe suggests he was buried at Avallon near Vézelay, rather than in England at the traditional "Avalon" usually identified with Glastonbury in Somerset.

What came to be known as the Second Burgundian Empire reached its peak under Gundioc's son, Gundobad – an achievement which, however, involved him in the murder of his brother, Chilperic, and his wife. Forced, for his own safety, to shut their two teenage daughters up in a convent, a chance encounter by one of them, the spirited Clothilde, with Clovis, the legendary 20-year-old king of the neighbouring Franks, led to romance. Eventually Clothilde es-

crucifixion. The fact that a number of experts have asserted that it was probably a refectory bread knife failed to save it from seizure centuries later by Adolf Hitler, convinced that his own destiny was bound up with it.

The links between the Burgundian and Frankish royal families were strengthened when one of Clovis's four sons married Sigismund's daughter. But, as was inevitable in such a union, it was the more powerful partner, in this case the Franks, who were to dominate and much of the future was to be a struggle by Burgundy to free itself from Frankish domination.

When Clothilde's last surviving son Lothar, king of the Franks from 558, died in

caped and married Clovis in AD 493. Clovis was converted to Christianity and helped establish the powerful link between church and state which dominated so much of the Middle Ages.

In 516 Gundobad was succeeded by his son Sigismund, canonised for his endowment of the monastery of St-Maurice d'Agaune which acquired an international reputation as the home of the lance supposedly used to pierce the side of Christ at the

Left, coin with head of Caesar, Mt Beuvray museum. Above, Celtic pottery, Châtillon-sur-Seine.

561, his empire was divided among his five sons, with the fourth, Guntram, receiving Burgundy. This would eventually be extended to include territories in Provence, Italy and northern central France.

In 570 Guntram's younger brother, Siegebert, married the daughter of the Visigoth king of Spain, Brunhilde. Renowned as a beauty, her ambition and iron will were to make her enemies who, in her old age, subjected her to a cruel and humiliating death. With only one brief intermission, the Frankish occupation of Burgundy lasted 150 years when the torch of independence was raised once more. Its bearer was St

Leodegar (or Léger), Bishop of Autun, who, in 675, fought an epic battle on his people's behalf against the Frankish chief minister, Ebroin, before being tricked into giving himself up to be blinded and beheaded.

Had he survived six years more he would have seen his homeland free, although, like most of France, faced with a new threat from the Saracens. With their advance temporarily brought to a halt at the gates of Sens in 731, Charles Martel defeated them decisively at Poitiers the following year. However, for the Burgundians, relief was tempered by their re-subjugation to the Frankish kingdom a year later.

But their overlords were not without problems of their own. Although in 771 their domains were consolidated into the Holy Roman Empire by Charles Martel's grandson, Charlemagne, who was responsible for the Carolingian "renaissance" of art and learning, territorial quarrels among heirs followed his death. These were partially resolved when his grandson, a second Lothar, inherited the title of Holy Roman Emperor. Resonant as the title was, in practice he was master of only one of the three strips into which Charlemagne's empire had been divided, the one that included Provence and Burgundy. Even his permanent possession of this was doubtful as, to the west, he was faced by a covetous step-brother, Charles, surnamed the Bald.

Charles's territorial hunger had temporarily to be curbed by the common need to meet the menace of the increasingly bold Norman raiders. The truce ended in 878 after a legendary figure in the independence struggle, Gérard of Roussillon, governor of Burgundy and Lothar's chief minister, defeated them. Charles promptly returned to the attack. Gérard vanquished him at Vézelay, only to be defeated himself at Vienne a year later.

However, the family squabbles which had fragmented the Holy Roman Empire persisted so that when Charles's brother-in-law Boso succeeded Gérard as governor in 879, though proclaimed king of Burgundy, he was actually ruler only over the area from Autun to the Mediterranean which came to be known as "Lower Burgundy".

Its counterpart, "Upper Burgundy", from 888 ruled by Boso's brother-in-law Rudolf Guelph, included what is now Savoy as well as a considerable portion of Switzerland. From about 931 Upper and Lower Burgundy were merged, but the Burgundian kings still found they had little authority over one group of their nominal vassals, the counts in the area north of the Rhône in what was called Cisjurane Burgundy.

In 888, Boso's brother Richard the Justiciar had been given command of the forces fighting the invading Normans. Returning victorious, he so reorganised the administration of Cisjurane Burgundy as to make himself effective ruler. In 923 his son, Raoul, who had succeeded him two years earlier, became king of France, giving the dukedom to his younger brother, Hugh I.

Most of what had been the united kingdom of Upper and Lower Burgundy passed into other hands through marriages to become the Kingdom of Arles. At about the same time one of the rebellious Upper Burgundy counts, Raynald III, by refusing to do homage to its king, was finally acknowledged as a "free count" (*franc comte*), thereby giving his territory the name of Franche-Comté.

The region which the world was to know as Burgundy, though it was subject to further additions and subtractions, had come into existence as an independent French dukedom, its throne occupied by Capetian royal family dukes until the 14th century.

Its close relationship with the French crown notwithstanding, Burgundy preserved a surprisingly large measure of independence. The period was one of political stability in which Burgundy could be said to be participating in international events. Hugh I led a crusade against the Saracens in Spain, taking Toledo in 1084, and, in 1146, St Bernard of Clairvaux preached the second crusade at Vézelay.

At the same time, the arts and especially architecture, expressed in the building of the great churches, were flourishing. During the period which became known as Romanesque, roughly 10th–12th centuries, Burgundy's great Romanesque abbeys were created and spread their influence far and wide.

The peace and stability of the Capetian rule provided the opportunity for such developments. The Capetian line came to an end with the death of Philip of Rouvres in 1361, but under the Valois dukes who now acceded the fortunes of Burgundy were renewed.

BRUNHILDE

In 570, two daughters of the Visigoth king of Spain, Brunhilde and Galswintha, left home betrothed to the King of Burgundy. Fortunately for all concerned, there happened to be two kings of Burgundy, but even so the girls were entering what historians subsequently described as the "Merovingian nightmare".

The nightmare is the rich backdrop to a wealth of legend, literature and music, everything from parts of *Beowulf* to the Anglo-Saxon poem *The Wanderer*, from William Morris's epic *Sigurd* to Ibsen's *The Vikings at Helgeland*, and to Wagner's monumental opera, *The Ring of the Nibelung*.

According to Wagner, the people among whom the sisters were to settle were a tribe of dwarfs called the Gibichungs whose king, the Nibelung Alberich, had stolen the Rhine gold during their migration to a new homeland. Wagner was doing the first Burgundians (because that's who they were) an injustice, and it seems he was influenced by a 5th-century description of an altogether different Germanic tribe. "A foul, stunted, misshapen tribe, scarcely human, with a fearful swarthy aspect, shapeless lumps for heads, pinholes for eyes, and the cruelty of wild animals."

Above, Brunhilde, played by Norwegian soprano, Kirsten Flagstad. **Right**, monastic culture.

If the true Burgundians were in any way remarkable, it was owing to their habit of smearing themselves with rancid butter, which they found powerfully attractive, and bleaching their long hair with lime. Where Wagner comes closer to historical reality is in his evocation of a vanquished tribe clinging to its former identity in the shape of ancient regalia, specifically a lance, a sword and the signet ring which is the resounding motif of the opera.

The tribe split, and it was to the respective kings of the two halves, Siegebert and Chilperic, that the Visigoth sisters were married. Both brides experienced immediate difficulties. Chilperic, whom Galswintha married, had a mistress of long-standing named Fredegund who was not about to be usurped. Galswintha bore the king a son but was strangled soon afterwards. And, according to one of the sagas, Brunhilde's loss of virginity simultaneously robbed her of certain supernatural powers.

No matter: Brunhilde had plenty of determination left, and her attempts to avenge her sister's murder led to 40 years of warfare. On the death of Siegebert, Brunhilde's husband, she was forced very much against her will into marriage with her nephew Merovech, Chilperic and Galswintha's son.

Brunhilde had a son of her own who succeeded to both Merovingian thrones but died soon after. The thrones then passed separately to his infant sons, Theodoric and Thierry, with Brunhilde acting as regent to both. She was forced to surrender Theodoric's regency but remained with Thierry in the Époisses château, about 13 km (8 miles) from Semur and one of the oldest fortified sites in Burgundy. Life with grandson Thierry at Époisses was said to have been so depraved that Columban, an Irish monk called in to bless the collection of royal bastards, refused to eat with the ménage. Pressed to say why, he merely stood at the table in silence, whereupon every vessel on it spontaneously exploded.

Despite grave doubts about her private life, Brunhilde the regent ruled with a firm hand. In 613 she was back at war, leading her army in battle on the shores of Lake Neuchâtel in Switzerland. At age 63, she was taken prisoner by the Franks and tortured for three days, tied by an arm and a foot and her long white hair to the tail of a stallion, which was then whipped into a gallop with the unfortunate Brunhilde in tow. In Wagner's version of events, it would seem she got off relatively lightly. ∎

21000–17000 BC: The Solutrian Era (named after the Rock of Solutré near Mâcon).

58 BC: The Celtic Aeduan tribe seek Roman help against the Sequani and Helvetii.

59 BC: Caesar defeats Helvetii near Bibracte (Mount Beuvray), the Aeduan capital.

52 BC: Vercingétorix's rebellion against Romans ends with his surrender at Alésia (Alise-Sainte-Reine).

AD 1–3: Augustodunum (Autun) replaces Bibracte as Aeduan capital.

AD 3–4: First Christian missionaries.

AD 443: Burgunds from the Baltic settle in Saône valley under Roman protection.

457: The County of Burgundy, with Geneva as capital, established by King Gundioc.

474: Reign of Gundobad. Second Burgundian Empire reaches its peak.

534: Franks occupy Burgundy.

616: Burgundy, under Clothar II, separated from Frankish empire.

657: Forced reunion with Franks by Ebroin.

720: Saracens reach northern Burgundy.

737: Charles Martel defeats Saracens and makes himself master of Burgundy.

843: Lothar I becomes ruler of Burgundy and Provence.

856–858: Raids by Normans.

859: Normans are defeated by Gérard of Roussillon.

868: Gérard defeats Charles the Bald.

871: Gérard defeated; succeeded by Boso.

880: Richard the Justiciar, his brother, given title of duke of Burgundy.

888: Rudolf Guelf becomes King Rudolf I of Transjuran Burgundy.

919: Magyar invasions.

923: Raoul, eldest brother of Richard the Justiciar, becomes King of France. Hugh, his younger brother, becomes Duke of Burgundy.

933: King Rudolf II reunites the Kingdom of Burgundy.

936: Separation of Duchy of Burgundy and Duchy of France, which includes Paris.

937: Magyars ravage the Lyonnais.

940: Foundation of Cluny abbey.

951: German influence increases after marriage of Conrad's sister to Otto I.

955: Otto routs Magyars, ending incursions.

973: Majolus, abbot of Cluny, begins expulsion of Saracens.

987: First Capetian king ascends throne of France.

1006: Holy Roman Emperor Henry II captures Basle from Burgundy.

1015: Robert Capet of France takes Burgundy.

1021: Robert Capet's second son, also Robert, becomes hereditary duke of Burgundy.

1078: Hugh I, Duke of Burgundy, leads crusade to Spain.

1084: Burgundian troops take Toledo from the Saracens.

1098: Order of Cistercians founded at Cîteaux.

1146: St Bernard preaches the second crusade at Vézelay.

1164: Hugh III, Duke of Burgundy, does homage to king of France.

1178: Frederick Barbarossa becomes King of Burgundy.

1186: Struggle between Duke Hugh III of Burgundy and Philip Augustus of France.

1193: Holy Roman Emperor Henry VI awards crown of Burgundy to Richard the Lionheart.

1281: Anglo-Burgundian alliance thwarts attempts to restore peace between France and Burgundy.

1315: French retreat from Burgundy.

1346: French defeat at Crécy.

1348: Burgundy ravaged by Black Death.

1361: The death of Philip of Rouvres ends the Capetian ducal line.

1364–1477: The four Valois dukes bring Burgundy to the height of its power.

1415: Decisive English victory at Agincourt turns Hundred Years' War in their favour.

1429: Joan of Arc passes through Auxerre on way to relieve the siege of Orléans.

1430: Joan of Arc captured by Burgundians at Compiègne.

1431: Joan of Arc is burnt at Rouen.

1477: Charles the Bold marries his daughter Mary to the Holy Roman Emperor. Beginning of Habsburg dynasty. Louis XI of France seizes most of old Burgundian kingdom.

1480: Margaret of Bourbon vows to build the monastery at Brou but work does not begin until 1506.

1513: Troops of the Holy Roman Emperor invade Dijon.

1526: Charles V briefly recovers the duchy.

1567: Auxerre invaded by Protestants.

1600: Henry IV invades Burgundy.

1602: Duchy of Burgundy annexed to France and enlarged by addition of Bresse, Bugey and Valromey.

1642: Briare Canal and Rogny lock-system completed.

1723: Burgundy Académie founded

1750: University of Burgundy founded.

1787: Second Lieutenant of Artillery Napoleon Bonaparte posted to Auxerre.

1789: Outbreak of French Revolution. Rioting in Champagne spreads to Burgundy.

1814–15: The Allied nations invade Burgundy when Napoleon I rejects conditions of

1906: Abbey of Fontenay, turned into paper mill during Revolution, restored.

1914: On 5 September, from his headquarters at Châtillon-sur-Seine, General Joseph Joffre, commander-in-chief of the French armies, issues the order which launches the Battle of Marne and brings the first major German reverse of World War I.

1934: Brotherhood of the Knights of Tastevin founded at Clos de Vougeot to promote wines of Burgundy.

1940: Ecumenical religious community founded by Father Roger Schutz at Taizé.

1940–44: French resistance fighters use the forests of the Châtillonais as a base.

14 Sept 1944: Troops of General Leclerc's

the Congress of Châtillon-sur-Seine.

1815: First wine auctions held at Hospice de Beaune.

1832: Burgundy Canal opened.

1836: The works at Le Creusot by Joseph-Eugène and Adolphe Schneider become an important iron-founding enterprise.

1841: Steam hammer invented at Schneider factory.

1871: Burgundy occupied by Prussians.

1880: Vines destroyed by Phylloxera insect.

1890: Briare canal-bridge is constructed.

Above, a Crucifixion retable in the Salles des Gardes, Dijon.

division and the army of Lattre de Tassigny make contact.

1949: Schneider factories amalgamated as the Société des Forges et Ateliers de Creusot, which amalgamates with Compagnie des Ateliers et Forges de la Loire in 1970.

1970: The Morvan Regional Nature Park is designate.

1974: Tibetan monastery opened at Château la Plaige, Luzy.

1981: François Mitterrand becomes President, from his base in Château-Chinon. TGV begins service to Dijon.

1996: Mitterrand buried in Jarnac where he was born in 1916.

& Filio & Spiri- tui fan-

cto. ℞. Chri-ſtus.

Poſt Reſp. dicitur Profa Victimæ, ut in die Sancto
Paſchæ, ad Veſperas. Pagina

IN ASCENSIONE DOMINI.

IN PRIMIS VESPERIS.

Ant. Cant. & Succ.

VEnit hora. Pf.

VNisi Dominus ædificaverit domum; I. f.

Ant. Subd.

DEus. Pf. Beati omnes qui timent Dominum. 7. a.

THE ROMANESQUE TRADITION

It is quite a feat of the imagination to picture how the small medieval French towns (for there were no great cities) looked before the building of the great cathedrals. The roads were muddy tracks, for the most part not even levelled, and the people lived in rude mud and wood shacks.

Towering over the hovels and the small Carolingian churches were the massive, overgrown ruins of long abandoned Roman towns: vast amphitheatres, triumphal arches and colonnaded temples covered with weeds and undergrowth, and gigantic aqueducts bigger than the towns themselves, spanning valleys with ease. The Romans built to last and during the great period of building known as the Romanesque, from about AD 950 to 1150, a huge number of Roman buildings were still standing.

In fact the very building of the great medieval churches resulted in the demolition of these Roman edifices and the reuse of their conveniently dressed stone. This had always been common practice; for example, in Carolingian times, Charlemagne used the columns from Ravenna in the cathedral of Aix-la-Chapelle. Nor was it just columns and dressed blocks they plundered; these early builders were not averse to reusing the occasional Roman capital, particularly in the construction of smaller, country churches.

Only one architectural manual has survived from Roman times, *The Ten Books on Architecture* by Vetruvius, in which he explains the proportions of columns, the floor plans of basilicas (an aisled building with a clerestory level for light) and the techniques of buttresses. After the Dark Ages, this was our only key to Roman construction. It was inevitable that medieval builders were influenced by the architecture surrounding them, and that their own work should become known as Romanesque.

The Middle Ages were fantastic times. Though the threat of barbarian invasion was not over, relative political stability enabled agriculture to flourish and the population to

Preceding pages: medieval manuscript, Auxerre. **Left**, Vézelay, central aisle. **Right**, the founding of Cîteaux.

grow. The way was prepared in the late 5th century when Clovis, king of the Frankish settlers, built an enduring state from the ruins of the Roman Empire, but it was Charlemagne who ushered in the new age.

He created an orderly political system and enlarged the boundaries of Christendom by his military conquests, establishing strong ecclesiastical and political links with Rome wherever he went. He recognised that the Roman church was perhaps the greatest surviving inheritance from antiquity and it

could be said that his coronation as Roman Emperor at Christmastide AD 800 marked a new beginning for Europe. His tremendous energy and flair for innovation encouraged Carolingian art and architecture to flourish, merging the best of the old with new ideas.

His church architects developed many brilliant new ways of building, anticipating many Romanesque characteristics, but scholars hesitate to say that Romanesque architecture began during the Carolingian Renaissance, preferring to date Romanesque proper from the time of Otto the Great of Germany (936–73). This is because Carolingian sculpture, manuscripts and painting differ more sharply from the later Romanesque work and they prefer to group all Carolingian art and architecture together. However, because the Roman component in Carolingian architecture is very strong, the term Carolingian Romanesque is often used to describe their buildings.

Central to the growth and stability of French society was the spread of Christianity and the development of monasticism. The Benedictine order, founded in Italy at Monte Cassino in 529 by St Benedict of Nursia, spread at amazing speed throughout Europe. In the early Middle ages the stable monastic community acted to establish international order at a time when temporal government was to reform the Benedictine order and bring a civilising influence over much of Europe. Cluniac monks spread throughout the continent and within only a few years had established 1,450 houses and dependencies, bringing order and stability to a brutal and feudal world. Solving the problems caused by the construction of this many monasteries brought about a considerable advance in building technique in western Europe.

The monasteries had other civilising effects on their surroundings: they imposed the rule of law and gave the people a unified Christian world view. By implementing the feudal system of government they established new hierarchies of power which ena-

had broken down. An important monastery often consisted of 1,000 or more people, bigger than most towns of the time. The architectural problems involved in planning and building were on the scale of whole towns but even more monumental and integrated. The sophisticated solutions to building on this scale laid the groundwork for the great age of the cathedrals.

After Saracen, Norman and Magyar raids ended the Carolingian Renaissance, the Benedictines became corrupt and lax. However, at the beginning of the 10th century, William the Pious, Duke of Aquitaine, founded in the small village of Cluny, a monastery which bled them to extend their influence and beneficence into every area of society. In Burgundy, to feed the mother house of Cluny required 40 farms, each with its own chapel, and this brought about great advances in animal husbandry and farm management. It was the monks of Cluny who selected and planted the Chardonnay and Pinot Noir grapes in Burgundy, which today make some of the finest wine on earth.

Cluny organised pilgrimages to Santiago de Compostela and encouraged the Christian re-conquest of Moorish-occupied Spain. In pursuit of this cause Cluny built or enlarged vast basilicas all along the pilgrimage route, though they were not the only order to do so. Cluny was also responsible for the first crusade to drive the heathen from the Holy Land: Urbain II, who preached the first crusade in 1096, was from Cluny.

This was the greatest period of religious building France has ever known. In the three centuries between 1050 and 1350, several million tons of stone were quarried in France to build 80 great cathedrals, 500 large churches and tens of thousands of parish churches. More stone was quarried than in ancient Egypt during its entire history. The foundations of some of the cathedrals were as deep as 9 metres (30 ft) below ground, in certain cases forming a mass of stone as large

talism, that passed down the centuries and was responsible for the great scale of medieval church buildings.)

Not surprisingly, the first people to revive the old Roman ways of building were the Italians; in fact, *Lombardus* became the word for a mason in the early period. Until the monasteries and towns grew larger, masons, bell-founders, glass-makers and fresco painters worked as travelling bands. All across Europe bishops were calling out for skilled masons for their new churches, and craftsmen from Lombardy spread out from Milan, bringing their particular local interpretation of Romanesque with them. Burgundy was one of their destinations: William

as that above the surface. The buildings rose to astonishing heights, 30 or even 40 storeys, high even by today's standards for a small town.

Eventually there was a church or chapel for approximately every 200 people in the country, and in many of the towns, the entire population could attend the same service. (Early Roman Christianity provided only one church for each city in which the whole community was expected to meet. It was this traditional idea, and the notion of monumen-

Left, monks carrying relics. **Right**, cultivating the world.

of Volpiano, who began work on the abbey church in Dijon in 1001, brought craftsmen from his native Lombardy.

The Treaty of St-Clair-sur-Epte in 911 finally put an end to "Norman fury" and laid the foundations for the great Norman duchy. In the ensuing peace an architectural and intellectual revival began in the northwest, in Aquitaine and in Burgundy. Because of its rivers, Burgundy was uniquely situated to receive and exploit the new ideas and to select the best of the old: it had easy contact by way of the Loire with the architectural school of Western France; it was connected to the Empire by way of the Saône and knew about the Lombard First Romanesque style by way of the Rhône. There was a cult of relics with its consequent flow of pilgrims bringing new ideas, and monastic developments were growing apace.

Until the middle of the 12th century Burgundy was, comparatively speaking, the safest part of France. To the east were the Huns and to the north the Normans, while the Saracens kept up the pressure from the south. As a consequence, monks brought the relics of their saints from outlying parts of the country to the safety of the interior: Mary Magdalen was brought from St-Maximin to Vézelay, where her cult later brought riches to the abbey and town. Lazarus (who, legend

has it, brought Mary Magdalen in a rudderless boat to Marseille) was taken to Autun where he is buried behind the high altar; the church still possesses the oriental cloth in which his body was wrapped. St Baudèle was brought from Nîmes to Beaune; St Philibert's relics made a long journey from Noirmoutier to Tournus; St Médard, the 5th-century bishop of Noyon, was brought from Soissons to Dijon.

The peace of Norman France did not stop the pyromaniac Hungarians from visiting in 937 and 955, stirring the Burgundians to think seriously about fireproof vault construction. St-Philibert in Tournus was one of the monasteries which suffered most from the Hungarian invasion. The monks rebuilt it, however, and the new crypt was dedicated in 979. The ambulatory of their new church was derived from St-Martin in Tours, which had the first ambulatory, radiating chapels in procession behind the altar. It was the beginning of specifically French development in Romanesque architecture.

The plan and structure of Tournus shows a marked influence from the west of France, except in the St Michael chapel and the original belfries which were Lombard First Romanesque in style – the Burgundians were picking and choosing as they pleased. The result, after 150 years of labour when conditions were still very primitive, was an advanced church of the greatest importance to the history of medieval achitecture.

What Kenneth John Conant (the medieval scholar responsible for excavating Cluny earlier this century) called "the most spectacular of the Burgundy accomplishments in the Early Romanesque style, a very instructive example which summed up the progress of church architecture in the 10th century", was the Cluniac abbey church of St-Bénigne in Dijon. It was an entirely vaulted church, 95 metres (305 ft) long, begun in the first year of the new millennium.

Like Tournus, it was a *summa* of what had thus far been created in church architecture: the east end had a highly elaborate three-storey rotunda, essentially the same scheme as the Holy Sepulchre in Jerusalem, built over Christ's tomb, and probably copied from the Early Christian St-Pierre in Geneva, built around the year 600, which uses the same scheme. St-Bénigne had nine towers and turrets, which is a Carolingian arrangement, and was vaulted, which was Roman. Only the crypt remains of this amazing structure but it is well worth visiting.

The main problem facing the medieval architect was getting enough light into the building without weakening the walls. It was always a hit-and-miss business – we marvel at how long these buildings have remained standing only because we never knew the ones that fell down, often within a few years of being built.

The prototype of all Romanesque churches is the Roman basilica or hall – originally a very simple structure consisting of a central space, or nave, with collatorals or aisles on either side. A light wooden roof topped the building. No light could reach the central nave directly, since only the aisles had light from the outside walls. In Italy, with its strong sunlight, this was not much of a problem and small windows pierced in the outside walls provided all the light needed, reaching the nave through the triforum, the upper level of arches above the columns.

In order to light the nave directly, the next step was to raise the roof of the nave higher than the aisles so that windows could be pierced in it, creating a clerestory (literally "clear storey"). Since the nave only had to support a wooden roof, the loss of strength involved did not compromise the solidity of

which collapsed shortly after, or even during, construction. The vertical downward thrust caused by the tremendous weight of the stone roof tended to make the walls bulge or thrust outwards as soon as openings were made in the clerestory.

The problem was the barrel or tunnel vault (*berceau*) which is the main characteristic of early French Romanesque churches, and particularly those of Burgundy. Unfortunately it makes the building top-heavy. This was the chief, if not the only, architectural difficulty that the builders of these early churches faced. Different parts of the country approached the problem in different ways: the Normans opted out and used

the building to any great extent and the roofs of the aisles now became lean-tos, preventing the walls from bulging.

In the northern, greyer climate of France, however, the problem was much greater. The builders wanted their churches to be fireproof, an important consideration in an age when enemy invasion was a constant threat. This, as well as the climate, dictated that they should vault the basilica in stone, not wood, posing a difficult structural problem as evidenced by the number of naves

wooden roofs but the Burgundians took such risks that in some of their experiments the stability of their churches was very seriously threatened; the nave of the great church at Cluny, for example, fell down on more than one occasion.

Finally, after 200 years, it was the innovative Burgundian architects (or builders, for that was what they were) who solved the problem when they discovered rib-vaulting and the flying buttress – inventions which paved the way to Gothic with its unbroken columns soaring toward heaven and huge windows beyond the wildest dreams of Romanesque builders.

Left, capital from Cluny. <u>Above</u>, tympanum at Vézelay.

The builders of Cluny III were determined to achieve direct lighting of their nave at all costs so they made their barrel vault as light as they dared, pointing the arch to diminish the outward thrust, a feature which later became one of the hallmarks of the Gothic style. They were never tempted to abandon the barrel vault, however, because the Cluniac psalmody, which was admired and imitated throughout western Europe, sounded its most beautiful when sung in a tunnel-vaulted church.

Another new feature, peculiar to the churches of Burgundy, was the narthex, or entry vestibule, built on to the west end of the nave. This can be open, as in St-Benoît-sur-

Loire, or closed as at Vézelay or Tournus. It was used as an antechamber where pilgrims waited their turn for admission. (These were all abbey churches, not generally open to the public.) The narthex alone at Cluny was five bays long, bigger than most parish churches. In some churches they were used as a prætorium where the abbots held their court, so they had a civic as well as an ecclesiastical use. At both Paray-le-Monial and Tournus, the narthex is double-storeyed. In fact, at Tournus the upper storey is a complete church in itself, called the *église supérieure*, originally intended for use as a sanctuary in times of danger.

Burgundian churches are of an unusual spaciousness but often have an unassuming barn-like exterior, relieved only by elaborate portals. Autun is often thought the most beautiful Burgundian church, provided you face away from the ugly 15th-century choir. Paray-le-Monial is cited for the airiness and beautiful proportions of its nave. All of these churches can be seen as forging towards the Gothic order as they strive to unify the interior into an orchestrated space.

Burgundy is also famous for its stone carving: the magnificent tympani at Autun and Vézelay; the capitals at Cluny and Sanlieu are considered national treasures; the wall-paintings at Berzé-la-Ville are possibly the best in France.

Under the puritanical strictures of St Bernard of Clairvaux and the Cistercians, Romanesque architecture took a more ascetical turn, producing the stark unadorned beauty of the abbeys of Fontenay and Pontigny. The Cistercian order banned the use of coloured glass, decorated floors, towers and carved capitals. St Bernard criticised his Cluniac brethren for their cloisters covered with "horrible beauties and beautiful horrors… disgusting apes, ferocious lions and monstrous creatures".

One of the daunting things about visiting these buildings is the business of Romanesque and Gothic. While it is generally true that if it has a round arch it is Romanesque, and if it's pointed it's Gothic, it is more useful to bear in mind the age of the building. There was a huge difference between a mid-11th-century church and a 13th-century one.

The differences are in the hundreds, or even thousands, of small technical advances made by the builders and incorporated in the next generation of buildings – a 250-year span of innovation and discovery which was to be followed by a further 250 years during which practically no progress was made at all in building construction.

During the course of their labours the Burgundian masons invented most of the features – the flying buttress, the pointed arch and the rib vault – which gradually combined to create the Gothic style, and paved the way for the great airy cathedrals of the 13th century.

Left, vaulting at St-Philibert, Tournus. Right, Paray-le-Monial, east end.

CLUNY

In 1132, the citizens of Cluny watched awe-struck as a procession of 1,212 monks, their voices raised in song, passed down the wide staircase from the abbey gates and entered their great abbey church. The monks entered the nave beneath the huge polychrome tympanum of Christ in glory, its brilliant colours now protected from the elements by the newly constructed narthex (or porch) after 20 years in the open. A double avenue of columns, 56 in all, led the eye to the high altar, and beyond that, painted on the half dome ceiling of the apse, a huge figure of Christ against a background of gold.

The greatest artists in Christendom had been assembled to paint these walls with scenes from the lives of the saints, all in glowing Byzantine colours of deep reds and blues. The capitals were carved by the unknown "Master of Cluny" a medieval genius whose work influenced countless other sculptors; a man capable of taking risks, of carving figures in motion, their clothing billow-ing in the wind, of making stone live. Like all the other stonework, the capitals were brightly painted, shining in the direct light which poured in from the high clerestory level.

Each day and night, for hundreds of years, the great church echoed with massed male voices as the 138 psalms of the day and night services were sung and the hours were recited by the two to three hundred monks always in attendance. The eight modes of Gregorian chanting, which was held in high esteem at Cluny, are shown on the eighth and ninth capitals of the choir; four to each capital and each represented by a musician. Each musical tone had religious as well as musical symbolism to the medieval mind and the Gregorian capitals are justifiably famous, though they suffered greatly at the time of the demolition. The chanting at Cluny was so important that the barrel vault was always employed in new Cluniac establishments because it provided the best echo for the chant. It was, said the monks, "as though Easter was celebrated every day in the abbey."

The monastery of Cluny was once the greatest power in Europe, deferred to by popes and kings, controlling the lives of tens of thousands of people, able to start crusades, and, though not possessing an army of its own, armed with the ultimate deterrent: excommunication. It had a fabulous income and controlled much of western Europe from a huge monastery built around the largest and most beautiful abbey church in the world, Cluny III, the pinnacle of Romanesque artistry and technical achievement. In fact, if the church had been any more advanced in its techniques, it would have been Gothic – as it was it already had flying buttresses and its barrel vault was slightly broken (both definitions of the Gothic order).

Cluny controlled more than 10,000 monks in over 1,600 monasteries, from Germany to Spain, Scotland to Switzerland, Italy to the Vistula in Poland, as well as more than 800 daughter houses in France including the great churches of Vézelay and Moissac. There was a saying, "Wherever the wind blows, there is rent for Cluny abbey."

Cluny was founded and endowed as a Benedic-tine monastery on 11 September 940 by Duke Guillaume of Aquitaine in the grounds of one of his houses. It was a good location, at the centre of a road network and yet surrounded by a great forest, parts of which survive to this day. Guillaume made it subject only to the Pope, a vital decision because interference by civil powers was common at the time.

Of the first church, Cluny I, built in 926, nothing remains. The second, Cluny II, was consecrated in 981 while the monastery itself was being rebuilt, but this, too, proved to be much too small to accommodate the growing numbers of monks. We still have its ground plan, part of which is marked out in a remaining chapel of · Cluny III.

It was St Hugues of Semur (1049–1109) who conceived and began the stupendous building programme of the abbey church of Cluny III. He was the sixth abbot of Cluny and during his 49-year rule Cluny reached the apogee of its influence. In England William the Conqueror offered to pay in gold for the honour of having Cluny-trained monks as members of his clergy. Hugues refused the offer but a number of monks from Cluny were placed in English abbeys, notably Lewes and Wenlock. The Cluniac plan, utilising a double transept, appealed very much to the English and was used in many of the great British cathedrals even though no further exam-ples were built in France.

In 1083 St Hugues visited the famous monas-tery of Monte Cassino, home of the Benedictine order of which Cluny was a part. Cluny was already too small for the size of its congregation and the vast size and sumptuous Byzantine paintings and mosaics of Monte Cassino inspired him to rebuild Cluny on a monumental scale.

From 1085 onwards the abbey became a building site; the design of the new building was carefully worked out, and combined the most advanced ideas of architecture from all over Christian Europe. The work began on 30 September 1088, and in 1095 Pope Urbain dedicated the five altars in the choir; by 1100 both transepts had been completed except for the towers. At the time of Hugues's death in 1109, the entire east end, with its radiating chapels and towers, and half of the nave had been completed. The nave vault was completed by about 1120 but it collapsed soon afterwards and had to be rebuilt. The church was finally consecrated in 1130 by Pope Innocent II, and it was two years later that 1,212 monks processed through the magnificent building.

down more than 4 metres (13 ft), was a monumental labour in itself. Cluny survived the Revolution, and the painting of Christ on the apse was apparently still fresh and brilliant on the day it was blown to pieces by early 19th-century property developers, 700 years after it was painted. Now all that remains are a few fragments; the south tower of the transept, a gateway and a few capitals in the museum. It is possible to piece together how it must have looked by visiting other buildings in the area which were profoundly influenced by Cluny; this is best done by first visiting Paray-le-Monial, which, though smaller, is very similar to Cluny III in everything except the length of its nave. It gives a good sense of the architectural form of the original abbey.

It took just over 40 years to complete; an immense edifice 187 metres (608 ft) long, with four major steeples, two towers and double aisles in decreasing height. It was the longest building in Christendom for 500 years until the construction of St Peter's in Rome, which is only 1.5 metres longer. The organisation of building such a structure, the opening of quarries, making of scaffolding, recruiting and housing the workmen was a formidable task. The scale of the work itself was much larger than anything that had gone before it; just digging the foundations, which go

Above, the high altar at Cluny's new church is dedicated by Pope Urbain in 1095.

The abbey at Tournus, the sculpture of Vézelay, and the paintings at Berzé-la-Ville, give some indication of the richness of the decoration.

Most of what is now known about Cluny comes from the indefatigable work of the American archaeologist, the late Kenneth Conant, who painstakingly excavated the site and did many drawings reconstructing how it must have looked.

Imagination is necessary fully to appreciate its lost glories. But in Cluny today the massive abbey church, though long destroyed, still exerts a tremendous power. It is like an ancient ruined skyscraper, immensely larger than anything built in Cluny since, still controlling the lives of the townspeople who tore it down. ■

THE GRAND DUKES OF THE WEST

Another great flowering of art and architecture was seen under the Valois dukes, self-styled "grand ducs de l'Occident", who ruled Burgundy for the next century and a half. After petering out at the death of the last Capetian incumbent Philip of Rouvres in 1361, the Duchy of Burgundy was revived as a reward for the youthful petulance of Philip, fourth son of King John the Good of France. The 14-year-old prince had fought stoutly at his father's side during the Battle of Poitiers in 1356 and was not in the least overawed when taken prisoner, along with the king and half the French nobility, after a crushing English victory. He slapped the face of an English knight who in his opinion did not show due deference to the King of France, disregarding the outcome.

Father and son were bundled off to England. The terms of their captivity observed the courtesies of a chivalric age, and indeed Edward III laid on a banquet to honour their arrival. Philip's stand on dignity was as vigilant as ever, and when a butler presumed to put food in front of the King of England before a King of France, he was given a sharp lesson in priorities with another resounding slap in the face. "Truly, cousin," sighed Edward, "you are indeed Philip the Bold." A famous 13th-century French king had been so called, and the nickname stuck. Philip's father promised that he would reconstitute the Duchy of Burgundy and give it to him.

In so doing, he created the illustrious line of Valois dukes, who were to become synonymous with the peak of Burgundy's glory. There was hardly any substance to the title or the duchy when the promise was made good. The whole of France was in a pitiful state, and not only because of the disastrous run of the Hundred Years' War with England, Poitiers being just one of a series of defeats. To make matters worse, the Black Death was raging, Paris was ungovernable, peasants everywhere were in open revolt, and gangs of disaffected mercenaries had taken the law

into their own hands. The Kingdom of France had not yet achieved any degree of ascendancy over the principalities, duchies, baronies and counties which made up the patchwork of feudal Europe. It was only a modest part of modern France and was overshadowed by many if not most of its neighbours, like Normandy. The kingdom was so short of money, in fact, that John was unable to meet the instalments on the ransom agreed with England. True to the spirit of the age, he dutifully returned to England and surren-

dered his person. Replying in kind, Edward laid on another banquet, an occasion marred by a wholly unexpected development. It seems, if some sources are to be believed, that John acknowledged the gesture too fulsomely and at the height of the celebrations dropped dead of drink.

With the French kingdom passing to Philip's elder brother Charles V (1364–80), Philip's only chance of making his inheritance, the Duchy of Burgundy, more than a name was through judicious marriage. Margaret, daughter of the Count of Flanders, and the former fiancée of Philip of Rouvres, was a candidate with mixed qualifications.

Plain to the point of wincing ugliness, she was nevertheless extremely rich, or would be when her father died. Her inheritance encompassed large parts of what are now Holland and Belgium as well as Franche-Comté. The count had justifiable misgivings about Philip's prospects, but these were adequately met by the French king who, if unable to help with money, was at least able to declare the Duchy of Burgundy hereditary. Philip and Margaret were married in Ghent in 1369 to the ultimate satisfaction of all concerned. They could have moved into any one of a number of suitable ducal residences, but Philip was particularly keen to establish Dijon as a dynastic capital. The

COURONNE de l'effigie des Funérailles DU DUC PHILIPPE LE HARDIT (1404)

town had existed in Roman times and grown in importance under the Capetian dukes. Philip himself had been living in Dijon for five years prior to the wedding.

The population of Dijon at the time numbered only a few thousand, and the skilled labour required to realise Philip's ambitious plans for the town was brought in from Flanders. He renovated and enlarged the Capetian residence, whose focal point was a massive square tower, some of which survives and is the oldest part of what is now the Palais des Ducs.

Philip's other major undertaking was to build outside the city walls the Chartreuse de

Champmol, a monastery which he envisaged as a dynastic mausoleum. Margaret's contribution was to build a ducal bath-house. The cauldron for heating water eventually had a capacity of 23,000 litres (5,000 gallons). It took six men three days' work and an enormous quantity of wood to bring the water up to the required temperature, a task performed once a month.

Ordinary living conditions, however, were squalid. Drainage was practically non-existent so, in keeping with the times, all manner of rubbish and waste was simply dumped in the street. Philip called the town council together to discuss pavements and drains, but the finance was not forthcoming. Trenches filled with stones and covered with sand were dug down the centre of the major thoroughfares; paving did not materialise until the end of the 17th century.

Noble houses had roofs of coloured tiles in geometric patterns such as may still be seen on the Hôtel-Dieu in Beaune (founded 1443) and many architectural flourishes, introduced by the craftsmen brought in from Margaret's Low Countries. Lesser houses were wooden and thatched. The greatest contrast of all, however, was between the incredible extravagance of the knightly tournaments which went on for days, and the menace in the alleys of the town when darkness descended. A great number of traders were constantly passing through Dijon, and their presence attracted a floating population of "thieves, gamblers, adventurers, and scoundrels of all kinds", as described in William R. Tyler's lively account, *Dijon and the Valois Dukes of Burgundy*.

Nevertheless, Dijon prospered. The marriage of Philip and Margaret had effected a potent mixture of Burgundian ambition and Flemish wealth. Dijon became established as one of the major cities of medieval Europe and the centre of the most glorious period of Burgundian history. Philip the Bold was revered as a statesman and great patron of the arts. The junior line of the House of Valois was soon in a position to challenge its senior, the future kings of France proper. King Charles V, who had sanctioned Philip's marriage, died prematurely, suceeded by his 11-year-old son Charles VI. The boy was undoubtedly stupid and very likely mad. His uncle the Duke of Anjou showed what he thought of the future under the boy-king by running off with the contents of the treasury and the royal jewels. He had to be bribed with the promise of a fair share to bring the rest back. The compromise seems to have been satisfactory because the duke lent his influential voice to an arrangement which installed Philip of Burgundy and another of the king's uncles as regents.

Any hope of Charles being capable of ruling without regents receded as years went by. He started seeing and hearing things, with unpredictable results. He was once travelling with his entourage when he got it into his head that they were all traitors. Flailing at them with his sword, he was subdued with difficulty and taken home in

tinely pocketing half the revenues destined for the royal treasury. Philip had to wait until 1384 to get his hands on Margaret's colossal inheritance. While her father was still alive, he created a good impression by dealing efficiently with sedition in the Flemish towns, especially in Ghent. On the count's death, his responsibilities widened and he proved to be an excellent administrator with a special interest in the arts, manufacturing and commerce.

The one blindspot throughout Philip's career was the management of money. Neither the money he expropriated from King Charles nor the liquid element of Margaret's inheritance lasted long as change in his

disgrace. "His debaucheries, his violent passions, and the intoxicating influence of royal power," it was noted, "predisposed his weak head to an attack of madness which was brought about by sudden excitement and by sun-stroke." His incapacity was put beyond doubt when he decided he was made of glass. Acting as regent, Philip cannot have been too disappointed. What little money he had, plus a huge loan, had gone towards the cost of his wedding. As Charles's regent he could at least draw a salary, a euphemism for routinely

Left, crown of Philip the Bold. Above, Order of the Golden Fleece, Palais des Ducs.

pocket. He died with lands of inestimable value but absolutely no cash. His gold and silver plate were sold to pay for the funeral.

Philip's son and successor as duke of Burgundy appeared to be a chip off the old block and was dubbed John the Fearless (1404–19). He rushed off to the crusade of 1396 and launched himself at the Turks "with a total disregard of all the rules of tactics". It was nearly his undoing. He escaped the fate of 10,000 French troops who were captured and beheaded only because of the sultan's rather naive assumption that his family could and would pay a handsome ransom. The money was raised somehow, and John returned to France with undiminished ambition. There was a struggle for power between the Burgundians and the Armagnacs, led by the Duke of Orleans, who was Charles VI's brother and ruled France during Charles's periods of insanity. John had the duke assassinated. He was followed into a dark alley by John's hirelings and knocked senseless.

The same gang had previously botched a similar assignment, so they took the precaution of lighting a wisp of straw and holding it to their victim's face to satisfy themselves that he was dead. There must have been some doubt because one of the chronicles is quite specific about what happened next: "The right arm was cut in two places, at the elbow and at the wrist; the left wrist was thrown to a distance, as if from the violence of the blow; the head opened from ear to ear; the skull broken, and the brains scattered all over the pavement."

The murder of the powerful and popular duke caused an uproar which persuaded John that he had better retreat to Flanders, which of course formed the larger part of his inheritance. From there he issued statements which sought to justify the murder. He also despatched a priest, one Jean Petit, to preach sermons in his defence. The duke's death was necessary for ten reasons, the priest told congregations, and he ticked them off. They included heresy, plotting against the throne and having tyrannical tendencies. The wretched Charles was wheeled on to add his seal of approval. The murder, he agreed, was for the common good.

John returned to Paris to play the worthy saviour and to be "most affable to all sorts and conditions of men". At the same time, however, he secretly recruited a private army of thugs among the butchers of Les Halles. Confident that his back was covered, he made speeches promising the poor a reduction in taxes. To the upper classes he gave assurances that their privileges were secure and that he would increase the number of noble fiefs. In modern parlance, John was running for king and as such was throwing down a challenge to the old feudal party whose figurehead had been the murdered Duke of Orleans. The Orleanists consolidated their alliance with the Armagnacs and prepared to do battle under the Count d'Armagnac. Armagnacs and Orleanists versus Burgundians pitted the west and the

south of France against the north and the east. The former wore white scarves, the latter blue caps with the cross of St Andrew and a fleur-de-lys in the centre. The Burgundian slogan was "*Vive le Roy!*" Having fortified himself in Paris, John opened proceedings by ordering his butchers to root out any Armagnac supporters in the city.

Across the English Channel, Henry V watched these developments with pleasure. A divided France was an opportunity to seize the whole of Normandy and to consolidate the provinces he had already conquered. The English crossed the channel and laid siege to Harfleur. Under this provocation, the French factions dropped their differences to mount a challenge. The ensuing battle was fought famously at Agincourt.

Although the combined French armies heavily outnumbered the English, the result was a rout. "Never was there a more complete, or more humiliating, defeat," said a contemporary French account, "the proud French knights had been vanquished, not by English noblemen and gentlemen, but by merely archers on foot, by mercenaries five times less in numbers." The number of French knights killed was put at 8,000.

Curiously, John the Fearless seems to have kept his distance, although he expressed disgust at the outcome and "announced loudly his intention of chastising the English, and of restoring the king to the full enjoyment of his power". Actually, says a contemporary in a terse aside, "his only desire was to reconquer his own authority". Exploiting the disarray among his French rivals, he sent his army into Paris to continue the purge of Orleanists and Armagnacs. The Provost of Paris tried to stop the carnage but was brushed aside. "In the devil's name," the butchers protested, "plead no more for them." One of the chronicles pictures the provost turning his head aside in sad resignation and saying: "Do what you please."

In the meantime, the English advance swept through Normandy. The French lords again appealed for unity, and John was specifically given guarantees of personal safety if he presented himself at Montereau to plan the next phase of resistance. The assurance came from Tanguy Duchâtel, one of the king's advisers, and when John stepped on to the bridge at Montereau on 10 September 1419 it was Duchâtel himself who crept up behind him and buried an axe in his head. "The unfortunate duke," says one account, "fell on his knees and was immediately despatched." After this treachery, the Burgundians allied themselves with the English. Philip the Good (1419–67), son of John the Fearless, became the new Duke of Burgundy, and attended the treaty of Troyes which in 1415 recognised Henry V of England as King of France as well. The feeble-minded King Charles, still soldiering on, was demoted to dauphin and ordered out of the palace and into the Hôtel St Pol to make way for Henry. Charles was one of those held responsible for the murder of John the Fearless, and at his trial he was found guilty and

Burgundy and the controversial Isabelle of Bavaria, Charles's widow, were among those who swore allegiance to the babe. In 1429 Joan of Arc emerged to defend the dauphin, Charles VII, and determined to drive the English from France. She was captured at Compiègne by the Burgundian army, then in alliance with the English.

Philip the Good handed her over to the English in 1430 for a vast ransom, and she was subsequently burnt at the stake. However, the English had by then been reduced to a toe-hold in Calais and possession of the Channel Islands. France emerged from the period of English occupation with Charles VII (1422–61) as king. Philip, Duke of Bur-

Above, Detail of retable of Saints and Martyrs, Palais des Ducs.

sentenced to be paraded through the streets of Paris in a cart. Perhaps he did not understand what was required of him, but in any case he failed to appear for the parade on the appointed day and was stripped of his residual rights to the French crown.

Henry V and Charles VI died within six weeks of one another in 1422. The heir to both English and French crowns was Henry's grandson Henry VI, who was all of nine months old. Few people thought the dual kingdom would last, although the Duke of

gundy, abandoned the English cause and did well out of tortuous negotiations which saw Charles installed on the throne. In effect, he demanded and received 400,000 crowns to recognise the arrangement. His deal with the French king meant that the Duchy of Burgundy now became an independent principality encompassing part of Holland, nearly all of Belgium, Luxembourg, Flanders, Artois, Hainault, Picardy and the land between the Jura and the Loire.

The relationship between king and duke was uneasy, representing as it did a new twist in the struggle for supremacy between monarchy and the old feudal order. Instead of

JOUSTING

In 1442, a general challenge was issued to the knights of Europe to assemble at the village of Marsannay-la-Côte on the road between Dijon and Nuits-St-George for a tournament of arms at dawn on 11 July the following year. Such tournaments were the opportunity for knights to show off their martial skills, and this promised to be the grandest ever staged.

Knights had the choice of mock battle, on foot with pairs of carefully matched battle-axes or swords or mounted, when the knights charged at one another from either side of a fence in suits of armour weighing about 100 kg (200 lb).

The Marsannay tournament was a battle for an ancient tree known as "*l'arbre de Charlemagne*". The home team, 12 knights hand-picked by Pierre de Bauffremont, Lord Charny, were in possession of the tree, and the outsiders had to wrest it from them. Rather than a general mêlée, the rules specified a succession of single combat in the tradition of champions.

The identity of the challengers was the subject of much intense speculation, especially when one of the newcomers was revealed as being Pedro Vasco de Saavedra, a Spaniard whose great prowess was legendary. If any of the local knights were to stand a chance against him, it would have to be Charny himself.

The Duke of Burgundy, then Philip the Good, invited the Duke of Savoy and the two of them and their entourages spent the night of 10 July at Nuits-St-George. They were up early enough to be at the tree at sunrise for the preliminaries, when the challenger's champion chose his method of fighting, signifying by a touch on one of two shields whether to fight on horses or on foot.

The champion Saavedra rode up. He approached the shields, leant forward and touched first one, then the other. To choose to fight on horseback and on foot was almost unprecedented. At 8am Saavedra reappeared for a formal introduction to the duke. He wore a short tunic and hat and was dressed wholly in black. Charny then presented himself. Compared with the understated Spaniard, he cut an amazing figure. His horse was decorated with his coat-of-arms; six others were caparisoned with gold-threaded crimson satin. The first contest, at 9am, would be with battle-axes.

The armour developed specifically for tournaments had, in the interests of safety, deviated considerably from its military origins. At the cost of mobility, it was made heavier to resist the thrust of a lance and the pounding of sword, mace and battle-axe. The tips of lances were blunted, and in some cases the horses' chests were protected with a kind of mattress filled with straw. The contestants crossed themselves and laid into one another with their battle-axes. The flurry of blows quickly added up to the quota under the rules, whereupon the duke threw down his white stick to end the contest.

The tournament continued for six weeks and over the course of several encounters the two knights developed such respect for each other that Charny offered the Spaniard the position of chamberlain in his household. The umpire's verdict at the end of contests involving all the knights was that the home-side had successfully defended the Tree of Charlemagne.

Ten years later – in 1435 – Burgundy and the Christian world in general were devastated by the news that Constantinople had fallen to the Turks. Philip the Good was at the forefront of the clamour for a crusade, and a series of tournaments like that at Marsannay were quickly arranged to drum up enthusiasm for the cause. Knights were only too eager to test their tournament skills in earnest and it became a matter of inescapable honour to do so. Almost to a man they signed up and set off. What they were left to discover was the reality of warfare against a ferocious, mobile enemy. Few came back. ∎

having to "borrow" armies from the feudal lords in times of need, Charles VII found the money to raise an army that was exclusively loyal to him. By appealing straight to the bourgeoisie and peasants, he diverted the chain of feudal allegiance. It was totally new for people to look for leadership beyond the confines of the estates to which they owed their livelihood. The Count de St Pol was one of the nobles who sensed that they were being usurped and he complained. The king had him sewn into a bag and dumped in a river. At this even the Duke of Burgundy, it was said, "felt the necessity of keeping quiet".

Philip's only recourse was to keep the king's enemies simmering, and in this he

provinces and Dijon in particular flourished under Philip the Good; the population doubled in size and the court was famous for its luxury and culture. But Burgundy had become far too rich for the king's liking, and the hostility between Burgundy and France boiled over when Philip died and was succeeded by his tempestuous son Charles le Téméraire (1467–77). His name is translated sometimes as Charles the Bold and sometimes as Charles the Rash, and there is a case to be argued for both.

As the contest between Louis and Charles lifted the Duchy of Burgundy to the apogee of its power and as swiftly to its destruction, it may be worth quoting Sir Walter Scott's

Above, Knights tilting in full armour.

was supported by the king's son Louis. The son's intrigues so greatly tormented Charles that eventually, convinced that Louis was out to poison him, he could not bring himself to eat anything at all and quite literally starved to death.

Philip and Louis found a *modus vivendi* to begin with, although rigorous protocol was required to keep their relationship on an equitable footing. The civility between them was shattered on the former's accession as Louis XI. The Duchy of Burgundy had grown stupendously rich on its Flemish

assessment of the two protagonists. Louis, he wrote, "was by nature vindictive and cruel, even to the extent of finding pleasure in the frequent executions which he commanded. But, as no touch of mercy ever induced him to spare, when he could with safety condemn, so no sentiment of vengeance ever stimulated him to a premature violence. He seldom sprung on his prey till it was fairly within his grasp, and till all hope of rescue was in vain; and his movements were so studiously disguised, that his success was generally what first announced to the world the object he had been manoeuvring to attain."

Sir Walter clearly had his preference, and he described Charles as one who "rushed on danger, because he loved it, and on difficulties because he despised them. As Louis never sacrificed his interest to his passion, so Charles, on the other hand, never sacrificed his passion, nor even his humour, to any other consideration." Louis and Charles began to circle one another like gladiators.

With wholly uncharacteristic naïvety, Louis was the first to fall into a trap. He accepted an invitation to a conference with Charles in Péronne, which was in Burgundian territory. Of all their various difficulties, the most pressing was Liège, where the king had blatantly been urging the popu-

lation to cut themselves off from Burgundy and come over to him.

In Péronne, Philip greeted Louis "most cordially, embraced him, and led him to the castle, where lodgings had been prepared for his reception". He gave no intimation that the lodgings in question were in fact the tower, a doom-ridden place notorious as the place of execution of an earlier king known as Charles the Simple. Louis was securely locked up before he knew what was happening. Ignoring the advice of aides who wanted Louis put to death there and then, Charles had devised a strategem which would cause Louis more discomfort than a quick death.

He was made to wear a cap emblazoned with the Burgundian cross of St Andrew, dumped in a cart, and driven through the streets of Liège. To add a note of piquancy, and no doubt to the puzzled amusement of the citizens of Liège, the king was required to keep up a cry of "*Vive Bourgogne!*" throughout. Feeling very pleased with himself, Charles then released the king. He was free, a chronicle records, "to depart wherever he wished to go, having spent the three most anxious weeks of his life".

No sooner was he back in the relative safety of France than Louis replied in kind. Cardinal Balue and the Bishop of Verdun, both staunch Burgundy supporters, were locked up in iron cages, where they remained for 10 years. They were still in their cages, and Louis and Charles were still at loggerheads, when Charles received a letter. It was from Frederick III, the Habsburg Holy Roman Emperor, and it contained the fascinating proposal of marriage between his son, Maximilian, and Charles's only child, his daughter Mary. The proposal was not without flaws, but Charles saw it as the chance to settle scores with Louis at a stroke.

Frederick III was the most glorious figure in Christendom. A Habsburg duke by birth and therefore ruler over vast domains, he was also the elected King of Germany and Holy Roman Emperor, ordained by the Pope in Rome and regarded as semi-divine. Beneath the trappings, however, Frederick had to contend with appalling personal, dynastic and financial problems. The Turks were threatening his borders, he was plagued by a belligerent brother, he had lost Hungary and had twice been besieged in his palace by his own furious subjects. During the second siege, he had been reduced to eating the palace pets and then the vultures which settled on the roof with a view to eating him. Above all, he was broke.

Charles, on the other hand, had taken to flaunting the Duchy of Burgundy's wealth, most of it derived from the Flemish provinces. The cloaks he wore were generally made of gold thread and his favourite sword was embedded with diamonds which spelt out the Pater Noster in full. Charles understood perfectly well that in proposing marriage between Maximilian and Mary the emperor had designs on his money, but he would happily part with money in exchange for something which the emperor could give him. Charles believed that as emperor Frederick was empowered to make him a king, and in a broad sense that was true. Frederick could create a kingdom out of thin air if he wished, but Charles needed one that would put him on at least a level pegging with the hated Louis XI of France. Frederick might even agree to make him King of the Romans, the formal status of the heir-designate to the imperial throne and one next to which the Kingdom of France could not hold a candle. If Frederick baulked at conferring a suitable kingdom, Charles was confident that a brisk review of his financial situation would change his mind.

A meeting between Frederick and Charles was arranged in Trier for 30 September 1473, and in their different ways both were playing for psychological advantage. Charles arrived on a black horse draped in gold cloth. He wore gleaming armour and a short cloak dripping with diamonds and rubies. He was accompanied by 14 heralds-at-arms, 100 heavily-muscled bodyguards and a band of trumpeters. Fastidious to the last degree, his fingernails were as long as talons and manicured to perfection.

Frederick had to borrow money simply to make the journey. His robe was dotted with pearls but had clearly seen better days. Frederick was not too concerned about such details. He believed that his whole persona exuded dignity and that he was a direct descendant not merely of Augustus Caesar but of King Priam of Troy. He had done the genealogical research himself and no one dared to contradict him. All his possessions were engraved with the letters A E I O U, and while these might have appeared to be just the vowels of the alphabet they were actually an acronym (a secret not uncovered until his death) for *Austriae Est Imperare Orbi Universo* – "Austria (by which was meant the House of Habsburg) is Destined to Rule the Whole World". He arrived in Trier with the 14-year-old Maximilian in tow.

When they came face to face, Charles begrudgingly made token submission by bending a knee, but in case Frederick got the wrong idea he then pointedly snubbed the emperor's invitation to ride alongside him.

Left, Philip the Good and the Order of the Golden Fleece. **Right**, Charles the Bold and Louis XI.

Frederick was welcome to think he was descended from King Priam; Charles preferred to model himself on Alexander the Great, son of Philip of Macedon. He attached some significance to the fact that his father was also a Philip.

Although Charles was technically the guest in Trier, he took care of all the arrangements. Frederick, who could well recall eating vulture, was given a place at a table festooned with 800 pieces of silver and gold plate which Charles had brought along. Dukes of Burgundy, he explained, were not comfortable eating off anything less. Charles was so confident of the outcome of the marriage negotiations that he had already

seen his jewellers and had his head measured for a suitable crown.

The negotiations lasted two months. They were prolonged by issues with wider implications than marriage. Pope Pius II, who tended to regard the emperor as his military right-hand man, was keen to see a Habsburg-Burgundy alliance, without which Frederick could not afford to mount a campaign against the Turks who had captured Constantinople in 1453 and were threatening not to rest until they stabled their horses in the Pope's palace in Rome. The Pope hoped to secure a commitment from Charles which would enable Frederick to lead another crusade. With

| Boundary between Holy Roman Empire and France |
| Territory at the accession 0f Charles the Bold 1467 |
| French Royal Domain placed under Burgundian Control in 1435 |
| Territory added by Charles |
| Ecclesiastical Lands |

FRIESLAND

ZUTPHEN

Utrecht

HOLLAND

ZEALAND

GUELDERS

BRABANT

*HOLY
ROMAN
EMPIRE*

Calais

FLANDERS

LIMBURG

Liège

ARTOIS

HAINAULT

NAMUR

Abbeville

Péronne

Amiens

LUXEMBURG

Paris

RETHEL

Nancy

Orléans

Rhine

Seine

LORRAINE

*KINGDOM
OF
FRANCE*

BRISGAU

UPPER
ALSACE

DUCHY OF
BURGUNDY

Dijon

COUNTY OF
BURGUNDY

NIVERNAIS

Nevers

SWITZERLAND

Burgundy in 1477

80 km / 50 miles

Charles making it plain that there were plenty of better-heeled suitors for Mary's hand, Frederick played his cards carefully. He was determined to hold the Kingdom of the Romans in reserve for young Maximilian, so he suggested instead that Charles consider becoming King of Burgundy, a defunct kingdom which shared only its name with Charles's existing duchy. Frederick proposed a reconstituted kingdom along the lines of the "Middle Kingdom" as envisaged at Verdun in 843 when, following the collapse of Charlemagne's empire, it would have served as a buffer between Germans and Franks.

Added to the considerable territory which the Valois dukes of Burgundy had acquired by various means, the kingdom under discussion would have given Charles dominion over a solid mass of territory from the northern tip of the Netherlands to the Italian Riviera and a sizeable portion of modern Switzerland as well. Ironically, it would not include the nuclear Duchy of Burgundy itself. As Charles did not need reminding, that was technically subject to Louis of France and therefore not within Frederick's remit.

Charles liked the idea. A lot of proverbial water had passed under the bridge since the Middle Kingdom had originally been outlined, and while the inhabitants might at first ask questions about being arbitrarily bundled together as his subjects, he was confident that he had the arguments, and if necessary the force, to make them acquiesce. It might not be the Kingdom of Rome, but it was undoubtedly a kingdom which would put the loathsome Louis to shame.

Agreement was reached in principle and Charles, mindful of the Pope's interest, promised to put 10,000 troops at Frederick's disposal to fight either the Turks or, even better, Louis XI. With that he ordered his craftsmen to prepare the abbey church of St-Maximin for his coronation. He wanted two thrones, one for himself and one for the emperor, who would of course place the crown on his head. Benches for distinguished guests would be arranged in tiers on scaffolding around the church.

For his part, Frederick was quietly congratulated by a Habsburg cousin for having pulled off "the greatest piece of luck that had

for long befallen the house of Austria". The date for the coronation would be set as soon as Frederick had consulted his astrological charts. He settled on 25 November and Trier went into a frenzy of activity for the great occasion. As the preparations neared completion, something began playing on Frederick's mind. He never revealed what it was. Some of the chroniclers thought that he detected in his charts a warning that Charles was riding for a fall. Others suggested that he took a personal dislike to Charles. Whatever the real reason, in the hours of darkness of the very morning on which the coronation was due to be held, Frederick slipped out of Trier and took Maximilian with him.

Charles was thunderstruck by the discovery that Frederick had walked out. He was stuck with a town full of important guests, a redundant crown, and a betrothed daughter facing an indeterminable future. The only message Frederick left for him was that he might be willing to reconsider the matter sometime in the future. The Archbishop of Trier was none too pleased either: Frederick had left word for his numerous creditors that all bills should be sent to him.

Reconstituting the ancient Middle Kingdom as the Kingdom of Burgundy had taken root in Charles's mind, and it was not long before the disappointed dignitaries who had

Above, *Philip the Good* by Roger van der Weyden.

filed out of Trier were reconvened, on this occasion in Dijon. He treated them to a magnificent banquet on the same gold and silver plate which had seen service in Trier and then announced his intentions: he would unilaterally create the Kingdom of Burgundy and, if necessary, crown himself.

High on Charles's list of priorities was to declare war on Louis, and to this end he proposed to engage the support of England. Edward IV of England was his brother-in-law (Charles had allied himself with Edward by marrying his sister, Margaret of York) and the proposition which Charles put before him had at least the virtue of simplicity. If Edward would help him defeat Louis, he

could become King of France while Charles proceeded with his plans to become King of Burgundy. The only condition was that Edward would cede to him unfettered sovereignty over the Duchy of Burgundy which, as we have seen, was still, painfully, part of the French kingdom as then was. The duchy could then take its place at the heart of the new Kingdom of Burgundy.

The scheme did not work. In fact, everything that Charles attempted fell to pieces, leading to speculation that he had lost his senses. As he stumbled from one futile military campaign to another, it was said that his troops completely lost sight of where they

were and whom they were supposed to be fighting. One of his troops was reputed to have approached an officer for enlightenment. "This war, I think," the officer is said to have replied, "is over some sheepskins."

The chroniclers confessed to being at a loss. "If only he could have tempered his greatness of spirit with moderation and prudence," wrote Thomas Basin. "But, as it happens often with princes, he prided himself on his own judgement and listened only to his own wisdom, rejecting good advice most of the time or listening to it little, and making up his mind according to his view of what he wanted done."

In 1476 the string of débâcles caught up with Charles and left him a broken man. Edward of England, initially not unwilling to go along with Charles's plans, had been bribed to abandon him. Louis employed Swiss mercenaries to inflict punishing defeats. Charles achieved what many would have considered practically impossible: he exhausted the Duchy of Burgundy's wealth. The Emperor Frederick, who had unwittingly set the train of disaster in motion, chose the nadir of Charles's despair to pop up again. Was Mary still free and willing to marry Maximilian, he asked. He could have her, Charles replied, on any terms he liked, in fact unconditionally.

A few days later, Charles was with his troops at Nancy trying to forestall an attempt by Lorraine to secede from his domain. His forces were overwhelmed and in the mêlée Charles went missing. The following morning, his naked body, stripped of its armour, was dragged out of a frozen lake. It had already been half-eaten by wolves and could be identified among the pile of dead only by the remarkable fingernails.

The postscript is that Maximilian and Mary duly married, and with that the Duchy of Burgundy ceased to have a history to call its own. Part of the Duchy passed to the Habsburgs and Louis XI occupied the remainder, which consisted of Burgundy, Mâconnais, Auxerrois and Charolais. In the space of just two years, the wealthiest state in Europe crumbled, its identity lost to the Habsburgs and to France.

Left, chapterhouse window, Palais des Ducs. **Right**, the book of hours of Mary of Burgundy, 15th century.

After the glories of the Grand Dukes, Burgundy was cut down to size by the upstart French kings. For the Burgundians, there was no question of redrawing the map of the world but rather of remoulding the province into a comfortable shape, and of ensuring independence within the new frontiers.

More a retrenchment than a dilution of Burgundian identity, the period still produced leaders of national stature. The Condé dynasty helped shape the Wars of Religion and the *Frondes*, the struggles against absolutism. The radical province also claims St-Just, the ideologue of the French Revolution, not to mention Napoleon's greatest generals, and, more recently, wartime Resistance heroes such as François Mitterrand.

The duchy ended with the death of Charles the Bold near Nancy in 1477. Even if this defeat spelt the end of the Burgundian empire, the Valois dukes could bask in royal connections. Burgundian glory embraced Edward III of England and anticipated François I, the Renaissance King of France. Emperor Charles V, his equal on the world stage, also claimed Burgundian blood and planned to recapture the lost province before being buried in the Chartreuse de Champmol, the traditional tomb of the Grand Dukes. It was not to be.

Repeatedly humiliated by the Burgundian dukes, Louis XI eagerly desired the fall of the duchy. Louis wasted no time in informing his new Burgundian subjects that they were *"de la couronne et du royaume"*. The dynastic marriage of Charles's daughter, Marie de Bourgogne, to Emperor Maximilian of Austria in 1478 temporarily foiled plans for French hegemony: Flanders and many Burgundian enclaves went to the Empire. However, in 1479 Louis invaded Burgundy and, after occupying Dijon and Beaune, built fortresses to secure his kingdom. Dijon's Palais des Ducs became the Logis du Roi.

In 1493 the Treaty of Senlis formalised the dismemberment of the Burgundian empire:

Preceding pages: interior, **Château of Bussy-Rabutin. Left,** Marguerite de Brou. **Right,** Drapers' Guild window, Semur-en-Auxois.

Artois, Flanders and the Franche-Comté would stay in the emperor's hands while Burgundy fell to Louis XI. Both leaders wished to settle the succession with a marriage between the emperor's daughter, Marguerite d'Autriche, and the dauphin, the future Charles VIII. Instead, Charles married Anne de Bretagne while Marguerite, a pawn in the political power game, married Philibert le Beau of Savoy. Sadly, Marguerite's stay in Bourg-en-Bresse, her ancestral estate, was as short-lived as her marriage.

On the death of her brother in 1504, she moved to Mechelin as Regent of the Low Countries and the Franche-Comté. There she brought up the future Emperor Charles V, Maximilian's grandson. As the last heiress of the Burgundian dukedom, Marguerite made the luminous monastery at Brou into her memorial. The craftsmanship is a tribute to her Burgundian heritage – a monument created by French and German masons, under the guidance of Flemish and Burgundian sculptors. Her enigmatic motto adorns the church: *"fortune infortune fort une"* ("through good and bad fortune, one woman remains strong").

Yet the territorial sharing of the spoils had serious consequences: Burgundy became a buffer between the French crown and the Empire and remained so for two centuries. As a royal precaution, Avallon, Beaune and Chalon were heavily fortified by successive kings. In 1513 Dijon was besieged by the emperor's Swiss forces, and again in 1636. Much to the crown's displeasure, Burgundy exploited its mastery of the borders. Spanish and French coinage were both in circulation so currency deals were rife, as was fiscal fraud, smuggling and the training of mercenaries. Profiteering was rampant in Bresse, Charolais and Château-Chinon, enclaves controlled by the emperor. Only Louis

that continued until 1914. Navigation along the Saône fostered trade from Rheims to Lyon while the Loire linked Nevers with Orléans and Tours. In Nevers, the Duc de Gonzaga established luxury industries, a glassworks and factories for faïence, fine pottery still made today.

Despite assimilation by France, Burgundian towns defended their privileges. The region still clung to fragments of foreign policy, purchasing Bresse and Bugey in 1601. Even so, Burgundy was reduced to the status of a province ruled by a governor, a crown appointee. The governor, intendant and bailiffs, drawn from the ranks of the nobility, created an administrative caste that

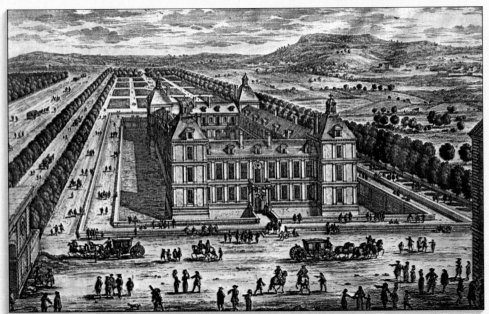

XIV's annexation of the Franche-Comté in 1678 ended Burgundy's buffer role and ushered in an era of peace and prosperity.

Not that Burgundian merchants were strangers to prosperity. At the turn of the 16th century, the wool merchants of Semur-en-Auxois vied with the drapers of Dijon and the wine merchants of Beaune. Iron foundries flourished in the Châtillonais and the fairs at Chalon and Dijon attracted traders from as far afield as Flanders and Italy.

By the middle of the century, the wooded heart of Burgundy began to be exploited: paper mills were created while the rivers were used to float firewood to Paris, a trade

survived until the Revolution. The ruling class accepted the king's authority on condition that he allowed considerable autonomy. Self-government and lenient taxation were the price for peace in the province. Yet, against its will, Burgundy became embroiled in the Wars of Religion, providing national leaders on both sides.

The first Huguenot centres were Dijon and Nevers but the new faith soon spread to Chalon and Mâcon. In 1547, the inspirational preacher Théodore de Bèze resigned his priory at Vézelay and joined Calvin in Geneva. After succeeding Calvin, Bèze was a calming influence over his compatriots.

Protestants dominated the professional and artisanal classes while the nobility, bourgeoisie and the rural population clung to the Catholic cause. Significantly, the regional administration, the *Parlement* and the *États*, were staunchly Catholic. However, moderate Catholics spared Burgundy a bloody St Bartholemew's Day Massacre.

Prince Louis de Bourbon, the Protestant leader of the Burgundian Condé family, was killed at Jarnac in 1569, the climax of a series of Catholic victories. But the tide turned the following year when the Huguenot Henri of Navarre won at Arnay-le-Duc. Led by the Duc de Mayenne, Governor of Burgundy, the Catholic League met in Dijon Parliament gaining control of Dijon in 1595, Henri routed the Catholics at Fontaine-Française. This decisive victory over Mayenne and his Spanish troops was the turning point of the war. The King converted to Catholicism but not before his supporters had desecrated Auxerre Cathedral and destroyed the châteaux belonging to prominent opponents.

Luckily, most Burgundian châteaux survived the onslaught. Politics aside, Tanlay is a tribute to a less troubled age. Like the refined châteaux of Ancy-le-Franc and Sully, it is a product of the Renaissance, shaped by Italian painters and Burgundian master craftsmen. These moated châteaux have mullioned windows, sculpted fire-

while the Protestants plotted in the Château de Tanlay, the home of their leader, Gaspard de Coligny. Tanlay remains a political commentary on the troubled times: the Tour de la Ligue, a turreted tower, contains witty mythological representations of the contemporary protagonists.

In 1589, despite royalist sympathies, Burgundians sided with the Catholic Duc de Mayenne. Henri IV responded by besieging Autun and other Catholic strongholds. After

Left, château of Ancy-le-Franc, a 17th-century engraving. **Above**, a 17th-century etching, Cormatin Château.

places, frescoes and busts of Roman emperors. In Nevers, the Gonzaga's Italian court provided a channel for Renaissance ideas. Not for nothing does the city boast "the first Loire château".

On a smaller scale, the region abounds in Renaissance *hôtels particuliers* typified by the Hôtel de Crôle in Auxerre, with its sculpted facade adorned with pilasters and ornamental gargoyles. Above all, Burgundians excel in the decorative arts, particularly sculpture. In Montréal, the church stalls reflect a Burgundian earthiness, matched by a daring pulpit: bare-breasted Bacchanalia at play in the vineyards. In Dijon, the talent of

BUSSY-RABUTIN

The handsome old Château of Bussy-Rabutin, 40 miles northwest of Dijon, enshrines one of the oddest sagas of the 17th century – as you can see from the bizarre satiric frescoes in its main rooms. Here the outrageous and flamboyant Roger de Rabutin, Count of Bussy, was exiled to his country seat by Louis XIV for lampooning court life, and then took a lonely revenge by decorating his walls with bitchy cartoons and comments on his ex-mistresses and other celebrities of the day. Few stately homes remain so expressive of the personality of their former owner – in this case, a witty, womanising renegade.

LA CAUSE EN EST CACHÉE

Secluded in a narrow valley, amid majestic trees, the château itself is quite striking. Part 17th-century, part much older, it has pepperpot towers, a moat, a fine Renaissance courtyard, and a terraced garden with pools. The Bussy-Rabutins, a leading Burgundy family, bought it in 1612 and then rebuilt it.

Roger, a cousin of Madame de Sévigné, led a life of lurid melodrama. As a soldier, he kept changing sides in civil conflicts ("The best officer in my army – for songs," said Marshal de Turène, who hated him). In 1659 he took part in the notorious "debauch of Roissy", near Paris, where gays and libertines sang obscene songs to hymn-tunes and a priest baptised a frog. Bussy's role was to improvise lyrics poking fun at Louis XIV's love-life. The young king was not amused and sent Bussy on a first exile to Burgundy. Here he wrote his *Histoire Amoureuse des Gaules* (a pun, for *gaule* can also mean stick, or phallus, in slang): this stylish novella was a wickedly accurate portrayal of certain ladies at court, thinly disguised, and their adulteries. A copy found its way to Paris, where Louis was prevailed upon to send Bussy to the Bastille, although he had just been elected to the Académie Française.

Released after a year, Bussy then returned to exile, and set about turning his château into a sardonic memorial to the follies of his age. Few of the murals he commissioned are of much artistic quality, but they shed fascinating light on his quirky character, and on the decadent times of the Sun King.

The château today is State-owned. The guided tour will take you first to the Salle des Dévises, which has a remarkable mural of Versailles – then half-built – as well as allegorical paintings with Latin inscriptions. One is devoted to Madame de Sévigné who had formerly rejected his bid to become her lover: she is depicted as a jug pouring cold water on hot coals, with the tag, "She is cold and enflames me."

The Salon des Grands Hommes has 65 paintings of military leaders, many caustically captioned. Cromwell is there, "condemned by his great crimes to eternal notoriety". But Bussy's scorn falls most fiercely on his faithless mistress Marquise de Montglat whose desertion hurt him deeply; she is shown as the moon, "with more than one face". His bedroom is decorated with portraits of mistresses of French kings, clearly an obsession with him, including such famous beauties as Agnes Sorel and Diane de Poitiers.

The Tour Dorée in the west tower has the château's most ornate decor, including a ceiling that Bussy called "*le ciel somptueux d'un lit d'amour*". Round the walls are portraits of ladies of the court, tartly captioned – the Marquise de las Baume ("she would have been the prettiest and most lovable, had she not been the most unfaithful"), the Duchesse de Choiseul ("very well informed, notably about other people's faults"), and others.

Here Bussy-Rabutin died in 1693, aged 75. He had a nasty character, arrogant, hot-headed and malicious, but he also had style and candour. Perhaps the clue to this rebel and *provocateur* lies in the family motto, "*Et si omnes, ego non*" – "If others are for it, I'm against." ∎

Hugues Sambin enlivens the door of the Palais de Justice, the former regional Parliament. Inspired by Roman statuary, the master craftsman sculpted a riot of garlands and lions but couldn't resist adding a final flourish with the humble Burgundian cabbage. Sambin was a quintessential Renaissance man: a military engineer, art historian, court entertainer and imaginative sculptor as well as a committed Protestant.

After the Wars of Religion, Burgundy's convalescence was slow, hindered by creeping centralisation. The *Parlement*, although unelected, acted as a barrier between the people and the king, protecting Burgundians from excessive royal demands. The province

With royal authority, they kept the peace, dispensed positions and favours. As leader of Louis XIV's army, Le Grand Condé crushed the first *Fronde* uprising in 1648 but after a clash with Mazarin, switched sides and led the second *Fronde* revolt in 1650. He was aided by La Grande Mademoiselle, the king's cousin, who also detested Mazarin. After inciting Orléans and Paris to rebellion, she stood on the towers of the Bastille and fired the cannon on royalist troops.

Perhaps fortunate only to be exiled to St-Fargeau, her desolate Burgundian château, she is recalled in a *son et lumière* that recreates these momentous events. Despite popular support for Condé, his Spanish forces

was largely self-governing yet suffered from increasingly heavy taxation. In 1630 Dijon's *vignerons* rebelled against a centrally imposed wine tax. The *États de Bourgogne* acted as the royal tool for tax collection yet could also be stubbornly independent. In 1659, after Dijon had failed to ratify the royal taxes, Louis XIV exiled the *États* to loyalist Noyers-sur-Serein and then severely curtailed the power of Parliament.

The Princes de Condé, already local lords, became governors of the province in 1631 and remained in power until the Revolution.

Above, Revolutionaries: Paris Tribunal 1792.

overstepped the mark; the uprising was quelled and the Prince subsequently exiled.

Condé was, however, spared the expense of life at court. Madame de Sévigné complained that the *noblesse d'épée* were burdened by debts. Courtiers like Marigny, one of her witty correspondents, were ruined at Versailles and slunk back to Burgundy in disgrace. Nor was Madame de Sévigné's cousin Bussy-Rabutin forgiven for his satire on court manners. Exile to Burgundy at least enabled Bussy to decorate his château with veiled allegorical insults to Louis XIV, his former master. But the courtly ambience, defined by Bussy as *"une société de prudes, cocottes, sottes et hommes galants,"* was at odds with the spiritual tenor of the times.

The 17th century saw a religious revival and renewed church building. Bussy himself had studied with the Jesuits in Autun but the Order was also well established in Dijon. Jeanne de Chantal, Madame de Sévigné's grandmother, founded the Order of the Visitation while Anne de Xainctonge, a Dijonnaise, established an Ursuline convent in Dôle. In Paray-le-Monial, St Marguerite-Marie Alacoque had heavenly visions, a prelude to the cult of the Sacred Heart that suffuses the city today.

Yet, apart from a Carmelite convent in Dijon and a church in Nevers, Burgundy

sponsible for Versailles. In Louis XV's day, Burgundian cabinet-makers were valued at court; rococo ornamentation and lacquered *chinoiserie* were *de rigueur*.

On the eve of the Enlightenment, Dijon came into its own as an intellectual centre. An *Académie* and law faculty were founded in 1723, followed by the Université de Bourgogne. In the 1750s the Academy was at the forefront of French thought, introducing Rousseau's revolutionary ideas to a wide public. The President of the Parliament had the largest library in Burgundy, a collection ranging from illuminated manuscripts and chivalric tales to the latest scientific works. This formed the basis of the first public

CLUNY – Affiche du XVIIIᵉ siècle

avoided the baroque. Instead, the province threw itself into classical architecture, from the abbey at Chalon to the reconstruction of monastic buildings at Cluny.

Burgundy might have lost its political independence but it flourished artistically. Louis XIV's reign saw the triumph of French classicism. Dijon created the Place Royale, fit for a king, belatedly adding a statue of Louis XIV in 1721 to curry royal favour. As for châteaux, few rival the formal grandeur of St-Fargeau, partially rebuilt by Le Vau, the architect of Versailles. Bussy-Rabutin's château has classical elements and a garden landscaped by Le Nôtre, the designer re-

library, opened in 1701. Perhaps as a reaction against such edification, the bourgeois were nostalgic for a pastoral fantasy: travel books and paintings indulged the fashion for sweet shepherdesses and cowhands in *scènes galantes*.

The provincial aristocracy mingled with the enlightened *haute bourgeoisie*. Comte de Buffon, the naturalist and royal gardener, had a residence there and designed Dijon's botanical gardens. The city offered free classes in anatomy, chemistry and astronomy, with particular encouragement to *sages-femmes*, the blue-stockings once mocked in Molière's plays.

76

Encyclopédistes like Diderot mixed with Jean-Philippe Rameau, Bach's contemporary, and the major French classical composer. The new drawing academy later educated François Rude, the Romantic sculptor. For the moment, however, classicism was in the ascendant. Symmetrical mansions took the place of half-timbered medieval houses. Soufflot, from the Auxerrois, left the region with a classical legacy, including his grandiose hôtel in Irancy, his home town.

One of the most colourful figures of the period was the Chevalier d'Eon, Louis XVI's roving ambassador and enigmatic secret agent. His spying activities in England and Russia led him to dress as a woman,

trolled by the *noblesse* while the *États* represented the nobility, clergy and the urban bourgeoisie. The Third Estate rallied to the revolutionary flag, supported by the *petit-bourgeoisie*, peasants, rural clergy and intellectuals. St-Just, born near Nevers, was the great philosopher of the Revolution. The Nivernais remains the most radical region in Burgundy. The storming of the Bastille was followed by uprisings in Dijon and Beaune. Dijon's newly-finished États de Bourgogne was abandoned until it was rechristened as the Hôtel de Ville. Yet thanks to widespread support for the Revolution, the region was spared the bloodshed that occurred in the Vendée. Still, in radical Mâcon a bonnet

aided by his feminine Christian names and build. He so liked his disguise that "his sex was sometimes open to speculation in Paris or London but never in Tonnerre". The Quentin Crisp of his age retired to Tonnerre during the Revolution and later died in London, after having made Burgundian wines as celebrated as his sex.

The Revolution was generally welcomed in Burgundy. It was as much a reaction against Burgundian authoritarianism as French absolutism. The *Parlement* was con-

Left, sale notice for the stone of Cluny. **Above**, Cluny before it was torn down.

decorated with *fleur de lys* was enough to invoke fears for "the safety of the Republic". While reactionary Catholic farmers in Charolles protested, the merchants and small landowners on the Côte d'Or took advantage of the forced sales to consolidate their gains. As émigrés' estates came under the hammer, land speculation was rife. However, close ties between the nobles and the local people meant that châteaux changed hands but were spared. In Époisses, for instance, the owners had long allowed local merchants to store their grain and wine in the castle cellars. As a result, the *châtelains* kept their heads and several wings of their home. However, in keeping with events, the château was later sold as a *Bien National* to the highest bidder. If most châteaux escaped lightly, churches were not so fortunate. While Fontenay Abbey was converted into a paper mill, most monasteries were destroyed. Cîteaux Abbey was vandalised while Cluny was gutted and sold off for building material.

The monks at Lugny expressed the resignation of many: "Since our misfortunes aid the prosperity of France, let our losses enrich the common good." But the Revolution also built. Writing from Saulieu in 1790, Abbé Courtépée praised the enlightened authorities for "street lighting, paved roads and the covering of medieval moats". The Burgun-

so did Carnot and Junot, Napoleon's patriotic Burgundian generals. In Fixin, near Dijon, is François Rude's romantic statue of *Napoleon Awakening to Immortality*, a tribute to a local hero.

In 1870 the province swarmed with German troops: there were 8,000 in Semur-en-Auxois alone. Enlistment faced the town's weavers, tanners, millers, wine merchants, horse-breeders and hemp-gatherers. Despite such a motley crew, Burgundy inflicted some of France's only defeats on the enemy in Dijon and Nuits-St-Georges. Fittingly, Maurice de MacMahon, from Semur-en-Auxois, became president of the Third Republic after the demoralisation of the

dians did not allow revolution to affect business. *Faïences patriotiques*, Revolutionary pottery, did a roaring trade. On the designs, an anchor symbolised hope, an oak meant moral strength, a mirror truth and a snake prudence.

Départements were artificially imposed in 1791 and the last shreds of Burgundian autonomy faded. However, the *Ancien Régime* was not mourned and few citizens supported the Restoration. Burgundians were largely in favour of Napoleon, seeing him not as an enlightened despot but as the spirit of the Revolution. Just as the great Vauban had distinguished himself in Louis XIV's wars,

Franco-Prussian War. After 1830, depopulation was Burgundy's biggest problem, only partially stemmed by industrialisation. In keeping with its industrial heritage, the region was a pioneer. The Grande Forge, set up by the Comte de Buffon in the 18th century, was one of the biggest French foundries of its day. A period sketch shows dignitaries in fine frock coats holding lanterns over grimy foundry-workers. While visiting monarchs enjoyed the spectacle as pure theatre, the workers compared it to hell.

Buffon's foundry was near Montbard but later industry centred on the south, between Nevers and Chalon-sur-Saône. The names are atmospheric enough: Le Creusot, Montceau-les-Mines and La Machine. Adopting British techniques, Le Creusot steelworks introduced coke-fired production and prospered by building machines, cannon and other armaments. Eugène Schneider took over the factories in 1836 and quickly produced the first French steam engine. After his first sale to Britain, the triumphant Schneider was congratulated in Parliament. Selling trains to the British in 1865 was as rare as selling planes to the Americans in the 1990s. A town square displays the famous Schneider power-hammer, claimed to be sensitive enough to crack a walnut without damaging the kernel.

Burgundy's prime Charolais cattle. The vineyards, once the preserve of the monks and nobles, became the property of the bourgeoisie and, after the Revolution, were sold to the highest bidders. Even so, many of the most famous wine estates remained intact. Clos de Vougeot belonged to a single proprietor until the end of the 19th century. But from 1870 Phylloxera devastated the region, leaving only the *grands crus* to build from.

Despite such troubles, the period was far from fallow. The landscape near Lamartine's village of Milly was celebrated by the Romantic poet. Our pleasure in the rolling countryside also owes much to the invention of photography by a fellow Burgundian,

At its height, Schneider rivalled Krupps, employing over 10,000 workers. But such industrialisation would have failed without excellent communications. The opening of the Canal du Centre, linking the Saône to the Loire, coincided with the expansion of Le Creusot in 1794. The advent of the railway meant that Dijon's population grew from 20,000 in 1800 to 70,000 by the end of the 19th century. Yet Burgundy remained agricultural at heart. The flight from the land was slowed down by the successful breeding of

Nicéphore Niepce. The spiritual landscape was shaped by Lacordaire, the leader of the liberal Catholic movement. His Dominican foundation still survives in Flavigny-sur-Ozerain while his birthplace in the Châtillonais, ancient Templar country, is now a convent.

From the *Frondes* rebellions to the Revolution, regional ties counted for more than national loyalty. The writer Edme Bardet puts it thus: "Burgundy, like all places off the beaten track, resembles a family. Although separated by rank and fortune, the family members are united by deeper bonds." In short, still backwaters run deep.

Left, industrialisation at Le Creusot, 1847. **Above**, 1858 foundry-workers.

THE TWENTIETH CENTURY

"Une Tradition de Tradition" is the region's slogan, a faith rooted in radical politics and pragmatic economics. Burgundy's republicanism has survived into this century. In 1914 the region was awash with patriotism while 1941 saw the emergence of France's most active Resistance cells. The end of the 20th century saw the election of smooth socialist stars, much in their master's mould. Yet this passion for politics is tempered by an old mercantile spirit. Even at the height of World War II, the region kept the Reich supplied with fine wines. The land knows how to exploit its natural charms; today's tourist trade is merely an extension of traditional Burgundian hospitality.

On the eve of World War I, Burgundy's radicalism and early industrialisation aligned it firmly with the left. An influx of refugees to the industrial south led to the expansion of Le Creusot and Monceau-les-Mines, aided by a burgeoning arms industry. While the war was fought elsewhere, Burgundy contributed arms and men. The aftermath brought inflation and strikes in the mines, steelworks and railways.

The inter-war years saw a political polarisation: Dijon, the Châtillonais and Charolais harboured Conservative pockets but the Saône-et-Loire was, after Marseille, the most left-wing region in France. The Catholic response to communism was politicised priests, such as Canon Bélorgey in Dijon. His spiritual successor was Chanoine Kir, an impassioned priest turned journalist who remained a formidable political force for 30 years. Kir's partiality for wine and *cassis* is celebrated in the Burgundian liqueur that bears his name.

The region had a special significance for the Nazis, not merely as a strategic border zone with munitions factories. Himmler formulated the idea of a Burgundian state with its own army, currency and laws – the hub of a mythical empire formed by the Franche-Comté, Benelux and Switzerland.

He tried to revive a spirit of Burgundian nationalism, saying, "What have the French ever done for Burgundy except pickle it in wine?" This "return" to the Teutonic fold failed to inspire Burgundians.

It took the Wehrmacht only five days to occupy Burgundy in June 1940. Most towns were declared *villes ouvertes* to deflect the wrath of the invading troops. Over half the population fled south, joining a stream of Belgians, Dutch and French in search of security. A mythical sense of safety beyond

the Loire led hordes of refugees to block the bridges at La Charité and Nevers. One fleeing dignitary, the Grand Duchess Charlotte of Luxembourg, lost her retinue near Château-Chinon and was swept onwards alone.

The remaining citizens quickly learnt to protect their property with a *Haus bewohnt* (house occupied) sign. There was no organised resistance but stranded French forces and rash individuals did battle in Saulieu and Sens. Cavalry officers from the military school at Autun daringly charged an armed convoy. In Tonnerre a lone *ancien combattant* donned his fireman's uniform and guarded the city gates until he was shot

Preceding pages: early mechanical threshing. **Left,** World War I memorial, cathedral window, Semur-en-Auxois. **Right,** World War II Resistance monument, Quarré-les-Tombes.

down. Paul Meunier, a farmer near Vézelay, helped the mayor burn a list of *garde civile* members before rushing to Mass to warn his neighbours of the approaching tanks.

According to the terms of the Armistice, Chalon bounded the demarcation line between Occupied and Vichy France. Chalon and most of Burgundy therefore remained under tight control, with the industrial might of Le Creusot and Monceau-les-Mines harnessed to the German war machine. Dijon stayed as the administrative centre, with military bases at Auxerre, Autun and Nevers. By contrast, Cluny, Charolles, Mâcon, Tournus and Bresse lay in Vichy France. They enjoyed a more liberal regime

until full occupation of Burgundy in 1942 rendered any distinction meaningless.

As elsewhere, Maréchal Pétain commanded massive support at first. On 17 June 1940 Madame Lemaire shot a German officer in Cosne-sur-Loire, traditionally taken to be the first act of resistance against the occupying army. However, other individual gestures soon followed, from feeding deserters and hiding arms to forging documents and helping Jews cross the demarcation line. When Pétain's "peace with honour" degenerated into shortages, round-ups and deportations, Burgundian resolve stiffened. By the end of 1940, the first *Résistant* cells

emerged in the Nièvre. These included communist steel workers in Nevers, socialist teachers in Charité-sur-Loire and clandestine Gaulliste supporters in the Morvan. Maréchal Leclerc was helped to flee Avallon disguised as a priest. At the same time Michel Debré, de Gaulle's future prime minister, escaped from a German camp at Autun. Hairdresser Georges Moreau from Clamecy insisted that a Nazi officer wait his turn so his salon was closed. In response, he set up Le Loup *maquis*, a network which came to control much of Burgundy.

Robert Morlevat, mayor of Semur-en-Auxois since 1937, was one of the few officials to play an early role in the Resistance. In 1941 the Vichy government appointed its own mayors but Morlevat had his council reinstated. He later limited deportations and turned a blind eye to arms caches. After refusing to swear an oath of allegiance to Pétain in 1943, he and the council were removed. They left the chamber carrying a bust of Marianne and swearing to return. They had to wait only until September 1944, when Semur was liberated by the Resistance and Morlevat returned as mayor.

Naturally, first-hand stories of collaboration are scarce. Insofar as generalisations are possible, Dijon and the Yonne harboured more *collaborateurs* than the rest of the province. After Liberation, it was here that revenge killings were widespread. Profiteering was the more acceptable face of collaboration. The day Dijon surrendered, one astute wine merchant stood in the deserted city centre, waiting to sell crates of Burgundy to the victorious troops.

Other Dijonnais started a factory to produce German side-cars. Elsewhere, profiteers supplied Champagne to officers' favourite bars or to private beaches on the Saône. Yet life for most citizens was both fraught and tedious, with painful daily compromises and grim acquiescence. There were petty regulations on everything from the etiquette of pedestrians to obligatory attendance at military bands and the correct temperature for serving apéritifs.

The war was not without its ironies: Nazis unsuspectingly gave lifts to grandmothers struggling home to feed clandestine rebels on their farms. The station master at Luzy spent the day repairing trains and tracks that he had sabotaged the night before.

The *maquis* at Luzy was operated by a Scottish teacher and an English parachutist. The British SAS established close links with such networks and parachute drops brought vital arms as well as fishing rods, pipe tobacco and other odd items. In return, the locals claim that Michel Hollard saved London by warning the Allies of a secret base with 15,000 flying bombs intended for the British capital. Burgundy provided ideal camouflage for the Resistance, from the forested plains of the Châtillonais to the mountainous Morvan. The *Résistants* often ignored the demarcation line. Roland Champenier, a celebrated leader, travelled between the Nièvre and Paris, hiding in abandoned farms

Resistance centre it is fitting that France's Resistance museum should be in St-Brisson, a hamlet destroyed along with Dun-les-Places.

In Cluny, Danielle Gouze, later Mitterrand's wife, was so horrified by the Jewish deportations that she joined the Resistance as a nurse. Allied success elsewhere aided the freedom movement but in Burgundy, unlike most of France, it was the *Résistants* themselves who secured their liberation.

Both the Battle of Cluny and the liberation of the first Burgundian town took place in August 1944. The latter was followed by the Battle of Autun and the merging of the French army and Resistance forces. The French and Allied forces travelled up the

or on sandbanks in the Loire. The effectiveness of the Morvan Resistance brought fierce reprisals, from hostage-taking to deportation. In 1944, the villages of Montsauche and Planchez were torched.

In June, the SAS-aided *maquis* murdered troops and sabotaged plants so the Germans responded with the massacre of civilians in Dun-les-Places. Mitterrand attended the memorial service every year, and made it his first engagement after his election as president in 1981. Since the Morvan was the

Left, the Nazis in Dijon. **Above**, 11 September 1944, Liberation; the first tanks roll into Dijon.

Saône corridor, catching the retreating German army in Burgundy.

The liberation of Dijon occurred in September, followed by the integration of French regular and Resistance forces at Châtillon and the historic meeting of the Allied armies from Normandy and Provence. Where the French forces failed in June 1940, the *Résistants* succeeded in summer 1944, bringing a revival of national pride. There were mixed feelings towards the Allies.

In Nevers and Le Creusot, hundreds of civilians were killed in Allied bombing raids, while the historic heart of Nevers was gutted. Historian Jean-François Bazin comments wryly: "The building of British and American planes often outpaced the training of Allied pilots."

Nièvre was formally attached to Burgundy in 1945, echoing its "annexation" under German rule during the war. In Dijon, Chanoine Kir's victory speech compared the Liberation to the Burgundian defeat of the Swiss on the same day in 1513. Since the Mayor of Dijon had fled in 1940, Kir was elected and ran the city for 23 years.

Politically, Dijon remains ambiguous. As victim of Parisian magnetic power, it is one of the most isolated French cities, with a sparsely populated hinterland and confusing political links. In elections, Dijon favours

sions or cultural status. Elsewhere, the Mitterrand connection brought better cultural and educational facilities. New colleges and *maisons de culture* have been designed to curb the young brain drain to Paris. As a supreme tactician, Mitterrand remained "Sunday mayor" in the Morvan until the presidency. At the end of his 14-year term as president, his protégés were secure in this socialist fiefdom.

Mitterrand's successors at Château-Chinon are also *amis du Nivernais*, designer socialists with the popular touch. Whether out of loyalty or cunning, while in the Elysée Palace Mitterrand remained on the Château-Chinon electoral register. For a decade and a

the right while the left wins in its immigrant suburbs. The Yonne and the Côte d'Or are broadly centrist but become increasingly conservative in the wine belt. By contrast, however, the Nièvre and the Saône-et-Loire, the other two *départements*, tend to vote for the left. The industrial belt around Montceau-les-Mines remains resolutely communist, whereas Nièvre votes socialist. In recent elections, the Nièvre has been the sole French region in which every *canton* (constituency) voted socialist.

While its suburban soul is ridiculed by Henry Miller, Dijon remains the only Burgundian town with any cosmopolitan preten-

half, the Mitterrand Mafia, the so-called *fraternité nivernaise*, had influence stretching far and beyond Burgundy. Friends in the Elysée Palace are absolutely essential if a politician is to attract heavy state subsidies to his region. The major figure was Pierre Bérégovoy, mayor of Nevers who as finance minister and then prime minister, brought an economic rigour to the region, though his sudden suicide in 1993 was a most extraordinary and unexpected tragedy which greatly divided the party. Henri Nallet, Mayor of Tonnerre, was derided as the Justice Minister implicated in the Socialist Party's slush-fund scandal, but as mayor, was praised for attracting new industry to his depressed little corner of the Yonne.

As the crossroads of France, Burgundy offers a confusing choice of directions. Sens, Auxerre and Nevers fall under the Paris spell while Chalon and Mâcon identify with Lyon. Only Autun and Beaune clearly look towards Dijon. As a result, Burgundy's four *départements* have differing outlooks. The Côte d'Or and Saône-et-Loire are the most popular, with good communications, a balanced economy and a share of the wine wealth. By contrast, the Yonne suffers from depopulation and the Paris effect. But this rural exodus is most marked in the Nièvre: the Morvan averages only 10 inhabitants per

cores for nuclear reactors while in Salives, near Dijon, nuclear arms are designed. Chalon also works in the nuclear and electronics fields. The steel industry along the Loire is in decline but metallurgy is still Burgundy's most important sector, based in the triangle of Montceau-les-Mines, Chalon and Le Creusot. The Schneider firm grew rich on arms manufacture but now makes the bogies for TGV trains.

While Monceau is home to Michelin, Avallon has its own tyre company, Pneu Laurent, which was founded in 1945. Burgundy has maintained its reputation for craftsmanship and design: Semur produces accordions and harmonicas while Nevers

kilometre. New industry is concentrated in the Saône-et-Loire, leaving the Nièvre to cope with the reconversion of outmoded plants. Naturally, the Saône-et-Loire's per capita income is 25 percent higher.

Burgundy's trading vocation has been bolstered by the high-speed TGV trains. The region is rarely associated with industry yet is at the forefront of nuclear research. More humbly, Burgundy boasts the invention of the egg-timer. The old industrial heartland has gone high-tech: Montbard manufactures

Left, technology: the TGV comes to Burgundy.
Above, prosperity: château and Jaguar.

and the Puisaye are renowned for pottery. Kodak has a research centre in Chalon near to where Nicéphore Niepce invented photography. Peculiarly, Beaune boasts the world's biggest factory for casino chips. As for tourism, Romanesque architecture and wine are the twin attractions. Only French visitors outnumber the British and Germans. While the British have pioneered canal barging, Germans favour green tourism in the Morvan.

Dijon is primarily a commercial and administrative centre, aided by its proximity to Paris. However, the city is justly proud of its food industry: mustard, gingerbread, *cassis* and chocolate vie with dairy products, ham and snails. Burgundy still lives off the fat of the land, even if farmers account for only 11 percent of the workforce. Cereal covers the Châtillonais plains, while fruit, especially cherries and pears, grows near Auxerre. Forestry is still the Morvan's major industry: Christmas trees supply Paris, solid oaks end up in Autun's furniture factories. Further south, the Nivernais and Charolais are cattle country while the Bresse has unique *appellation contrôlée* chicken. But to the wine-lover, the Côte d'Or epitomises Burgundy.

Burgundian wines have every reason to get drunk on their success. Vineyards represent only 1 percent of land yet generate 25

Burgundy's cheaper wines suffer competition from the Midi while the fashion for white wine risks eclipsing the reds. However, the finest vineyards remain priceless and rarely change hands. Even so, institutional investors are tempted by the profits: wine is safer than houses, more interesting than shares and most suitable for corporate hospitality. As a result, prices soared, tripling throughout the 1990s. To local approval, AXA, Auxerre football team, had acquired prize Romanée vineyards. But Beaune's prestigious Maison Jadot was bought by Americans, including part of the sacred Clos de Vougeot estate. Japanese investments are also bitterly resented in Bur-

percent of agricultural revenue, with over 50 percent of wines exported. The creation of the Confrérie des Chevaliers du Tastevin in 1934 helpfully coincided with the start of the *appellation contrôlée* system. Since then, wine professionalism and profits have gone hand in hand. Dijon University was the first in France to offer courses in oenology, including a highly-valued degree in wine.

Local celebrities can also affect the wine trade. In Tonnerre, Justice Minister Henri Nallet recently established a major replantation programme while actor Gérard Depardieu's buying into Burgundian vineyards caused other stars to follow suit.

gundy. Takashimaya department store now controls a third of the top producers in Auxey-Duresses. Not that resentment is ever a bar to business. Centrifugal forces suck the region towards Paris but Burgundian identity survives. Visiting civil servants are constantly surprised by the commitment to the old province by politicians and citizens alike. Mayors happily define themselves as *un ami du Nivernais* or *un vrai Bourguignon*. If regionalism is a French religion, it finds its purest form in Burgundy. This is provincialism raised to an art form.

Above, promotion: buglers at Clos de Vougeot.

MITTERRAND'S MORVAN

Thanks to its Celtic roots and bitter climate, the Morvan often goes against the mainstream. The natives are wary of outsiders, and are as tough and inflexible as their granite mountains. But one outsider, François Mitterrand, became a legendary part of this austere landscape for half a century. In his book, *L'Abeille et L'Architecte* (The Builder and the Bee), Mitterrand declared: "I love the forest: my path in life often brings me back to the forests of the Morvan."

Mitterrand was born in Jarnac, cognac country near Bordeaux, and it was here that he was buried. His career, however, belongs to Burgundy. As a *Résistant* untainted by Vichy, he was "parachuted" into the Nièvre to fight a parliamentary seat. In 1946, at the age of 30, he was elected a *député* of the Morvan and this remained his political power base until the presidency. His wife, Danielle, had a family home in Cluny and a background in the Resistance so this tied the Burgundian knot. The president's pilgrimage to Solutré, the great rock near Mâcon, became an annual reward for his disciples.

After being made mayor of Château-Chinon in 1959, Mitterrand became Président du Conseil Régionale and cultivated a brand of consensus politics. In local posts, as in the presidency, he was a wily pragmatist, with a team characterised by personal loyalty rather than shared ideology.

Beaten by de Gaulle, Mitterrand cultivated the political backwoods and fought again in 1981. It was in the Hôtel du Vieux Morvan in Château-Chinon that Mitterrand learnt he had become the first Socialist President of the Fifth Republic. Ginette Chevrier, the manageress, cried with delight. Mitterrand had stayed in Room 15 for 22 years, and in May 1991, Chevrier was one of the first Morvan friends invited to the Elysée to celebrate his golden decade.

Despite his mythological ascension from *Tonton* to *Dieu*, Mitterrand remained loyal. "*Bonne chance pour demain,*" reads the president's postcard to a Morvan mayor in the 1989 local elections. Marchand, the mayor of Gouloux, had been elected unopposed since 1954 so luck was a mere formality in a tiny village with little more than a waterfall and a clog-maker to its name. The mayor first met Mitterrand in 1949, following an illegal wolf cull. A councillor had been killed in the chase and the *commune* fined 7 million francs. Mitterrand fought the case and the fine was reduced. Marchand returned to clog-making while Mitterrand went on to the presidency, an office he held for 14 years. But in 1984 Marchand was in hospital in Chalon and forbidden phone calls, despite insisting that one was from the Elysée. "The nurse took me for a lunatic until I showed her a presidential letter."

Mitterrand was renowned for sending postal greetings to Morvan folk from all over the world. He never wrote addresses but sent his "*fidèles pensées*" care of "Nièvre, France". Little love was lost between the former president and Nevers. Mitterrand always found the Morvan "*une terre de fidélité*" compared with the "shifting sands of Nevers". Mitterrand's greatest fans are at Château-Chinon. His former deputy, Simone Bondieux,

TONTON révolutionnaire

says: "We always called him President – we knew he would succeed." Wine merchant André Emery confirms local legend: "He never had any money on him and didn't wear a watch; his house was insignificant – he would never be rich." But a *gendarme* gives Mitterrand the highest accolade: "Not once did he try to get out of a speeding fine."

Mitterrand's views of his adopted home matched his penchant for nature imagery and purplish prose. "My roots remain here – my writing contains the breath of the region as an accent would the speech." In September 1995, four months before his death, he acquired 10 square metres of Mont Beuvray for a burial plot. This was where Vercingetorix was made king of the Gauls. ∎

Clochemerle, the archetypal provincial village, belongs to Burgundy. Writer Gabriel Chevalier said he based it on Gueugnon, his childhood haunt in the Charolais, although other villages also claim the honour. "Part agricultural village, part industrial town, Gueugnon was where I learnt about provincial life." There he found his inspiration for a social satire centred on the installation of a public lavatory. The cast included a ruined *marquise*, a vicious hunchback, a lecherous widower, bosomy haberdashers and an old maid madly in love with the local priest. This Burgundian soap opera may be drawn with a broad brush but the provincial theme strikes a chord with visitors. Real life is less scandalous but equally robust.

The small-town atmosphere is captured in photographers' studios all over Burgundy. The portraits in the window provide a projection of the town's self-image. Avallon may offer chaste maidens attending first communion yet, in Chalon, carnival revellers are caught in full flood.

But spontaneity is rarely part of the picture. Nevers focuses on the unexpected formality of a family picnic. Paray-le-Monial shows scenes of Sunday best while Charolais farmers pose awkwardly at a rural wedding. In Toucy, potters display their wares for a publicity shot. In Châtillon, weekend fishermen hold aloft a stuffed salmon. Dijonnais new graduates boast the bourgeois sophistication of bankers. Clamecy's enthusiastic canoeists are a contrast to the shots of chic wine merchants in Beaune. In Chablis, a dignitary looks smug in his wine confraternity costume. In Auxerre, a stolid couple celebrate a life of mutual boredom.

Burgundy prides itself on its provincialism, its claim to the mythical status of *France profonde*, deepest France. The social composition supports Burgundy's singularity. Compared with the rest of France, there is a higher proportion of farmers, wine growers, craftsmen, traders and family-run enterprises. Salaries are below the national average and *cadres* (executives) are few and far between.

Preceding pages: grape-picking, Santenay. Left, off to the fields. Right, a winning smile.

This social mix fosters traditionalism and political moderation, a pattern broken only by the impoverished but radical Nièvre.

Demography also plays a part: Burgundy is underpopulated, particularly in the rural Yonne and Nièvre. Here too, Burgundians are growing old gracefully. The population is considerably older than elsewhere: 18 percent are over 65 compared with a national average of 13 percent. But this already high figure doubles in rural areas, especially in parts of the Puisaye, Bresse and Morvan.

Mitterrand was always seen as highly typical of the region, sharing a faith in the sanctity of provincial life. His 1981 presidential campaign presented an avuncular sage with *France profonde* in his soul. According to Alain Schrifès, an acerbic French journalist, "Giscard might read the *Financial Times* but only Mitterrand could tell you when it was going to rain. A hat on his head, a rose in his hand, roots underfoot, the president would let time find its own solutions." Cottage-garden socialism was the essence of *la force tranquille*, the slogan which shaped the region to his own peculiar rustic image.

"*Une ville quelconque*," remarked Zola of "Anywhere-ville". Burgundy has its share of tedious towns, from Gueugnon and Clamecy to Montceau and Tonnerre. But behind the brickwork beats a provincial heart. Tonnerre is a slice of local life, from petty politicking to the "Paris effect", the economic blight caused by the escape of the young to Paris. This crumbling town in the Yonne is not grand enough to attract buyers of second homes and is too shabby to tempt tourists. Instead, it is left to the locals to manufacture sofa beds and video recorders, telling occupations for a sedentary population.

Burgundy is a pawn in the game of political patronage. A notable tendency is to mere *sale affaire parisienne* (dirty Parisian scandal) which mattered only if it cost Nallet his ministerial post. More important was the mayor's impact on the economy, from welcome state subsidies to the setting up of new firms and clubs. He has encouraged the replanting of vines, both Pinot Noir and Chardonnay. The prestigious neighbouring vineyards of Chablis benefit from having a friend at court and appreciated a visit from Nallet in their hour of need in the frosts of 1991. Complaints about an absentee mayor are outweighed by the prestige of having a personal grandee in Paris. As a local accountant says: "Up there, they play politics. Down here, we just balance the books."

parachuter (inject) the president's man into local politics. Usually a powerful national figure, the "parachutee" is rewarded with a secure political base while his mentor bolsters a regional fiefdom. Tonnerre, an insignificant town of 6,000 people, was amazed to receive a minister as its mayor in 1989. A presidential commitment to consensus still allows scope for imposed appointees.

Henri Nallet, Minister of Justice and mayor of Tonnerre, has recovered from a bumpy landing. Despite allegations of the minister's involvement in a slush-fund scandal, the local consensus was that Nallet revived sleepy Tonnerre. But to most locals the affair was a

A typical town council meeting in April 1991 approved a pay rise for the firemen and the replacement of obsolete fire extinguishers in the town gym. After agreement on how to spend a citizen's bequest to the town, the mayor and councillors retired for a drink. The bar discussion ranged from the effects of unemployment to the lack of street lighting in Rue Fosse-Dionne. After brooding on the impact of disastrous spring frosts on the wine trade, Nallet was soundly beaten at table football. The mayor's limousine then swept him off to the Parisian bright lights and his more lucrative weekday job as France's Minister of Justice.

The mayor, priest, lawyer, school-teacher and merchant were once notables, stock figures in provincial society. The old order may have faded but the mayor and the priest still have symbolic importance in the countryside. In 1987 Senator Signé replaced François Mitterrand as mayor of Château-Chinon. He is a seasoned politician as Machiavellian and as enigmatic as his mentor.

Priests command little political power and summon only wavering respect in the provincial heartland. Religion is a thorny issue in Burgundy so spirituality is accompanied by scepticism or anti-clericalism. Mitterrand's 1981 campaign poster set his face against the backdrop of a cosy village, which

tions. The Charolais farming families have always been devout while Paray-le-Monial, a pilgrimage centre second only to Lourdes, is linked to the cult of the Sacré Coeur and has a long tradition of mysticism. It is no coincidence that this pocket is sandwiched between Autun and Lyon, the two most powerful medieval bishoprics.

Elsewhere, the Yonne is the least Catholic part of Burgundy, not that the full-blooded enthusiasm for religious festivals reflects a *déchristianisé* image. In Vézelay, the July Fête de la Madeleine draws vast crowds. While St Bernard's hairshirt principles are not shared by his fellow Burgundians, the Bernard de Clairvaux spectacle is moving.

would have been cosier still if Mitterrand, fearful of clerical overtones, had not insisted that the church tower be airbrushed out.

Perhaps, not surprisingly, the places with the greatest number of practising Catholics are those once dominated by the abbeys of Cîteaux, Cluny, Fontenay and Pontigny. Cîteaux remains a working Cistercian community where Trappist monks have time for contemplation and the production of the celebrated Cîteaux cheese. But Paray-le-Monial and the Charolais have the largest congrega-

Left, Bresse chickens; off to market in Bresse. **Above**, village café.

Held at the reconstructed monastery of Clairvaux, "the passion that shook Europe" is re-enacted by a local cast every summer. Nevers draws pilgrims to the tomb of St Bernadette of Lourdes. But the greatest congregations materialised for Pope John Paul's pastoral mission in 1986. His tour, to Taizé, Paray-le-Monial and Vézelay, touched upon the sacred spots of Burgundian heritage.

In trading terms Burgundy seems a bastion of traditionalism. The region was renowned for its hardy peasants: Burgundian cowboys, known as *galvachers*, who roamed France; *flotteurs*, who supplied the capital with firewood, floating convoys of logs downstream;

and *nourrices morvandelles*, who nursed orphans in Paris and the provinces. These trades may have died out by 1914 but cheese-makers, clog-makers and thatchers stlll survive.

In the Morvan, many traditional trades appear in different guises. The woodcutters remain but forestry is a sensitive issue, dividing technocrats, ecologists and local people. The ancient forests of birch, beech and oak are struggling to survive against the intrusive planting of conifers. Christmas trees and pine furniture are big business in the Morvan.

However, provincial Burgundy moves with the times, its artisans adapting traditional skills to tourism and popular taste. Survivors of the rural recession include the Pierlot

family of potters in the Puisaye, a region known for its stoneware. In the sandstone Château de Ratilly, the family exhibit rustic pots and run a summer school to supplement their income.

Further south, in the tiny village of St Pères-sous-Vézelay, Romain Doré works as a *sabotier*, a clog-maker. He is proud of belonging to the eighth generation, an authentic tradition matched by his medieval workshop. He uses ancient tools and carves only wood grown on the slopes of Vézelay: walnut, oak, elm and ash.

Sylvie Julien, a traditional glass-maker, also works in the shadow of Vézelay. Unlike the instinctive Romain Doré, she waxes lyrical about "the relationship between light and matter", and rails against the modern world: "who will be left to adorn the cathedrals of the future?"

Benoît Andriot in Monthélon, near Autun, combines cattle-breeding, his first love, with work as a *chambres d'hôtes* host. The cost of producing beef has doubled in the past 15 years without a commensurate rise in farm prices. Despite slender profit margins, he abhors the trend towards mechanisation and the excessive use of hormones in meat production. By contrast, his cattle "live a balanced, natural life", free to graze wherever they wish. Looking like a caricature of the ruddy-faced farmer, he relishes sheepdog trials and recently led a delegation of Charolais farmers on an export drive to Canada. Yet his joviality masks a passion for regional history and folklore. Andriot regrets that his children will not follow in his footsteps but realises the drawbacks of the rural life. Although a member of a dying breed, this modest and cultivated farmer is the quintessential Burgundian.

Lifestyles are changing in traditional wine-growing regions, from the patrician Côte d'Or to the poorer Beaujolais. Claude Carlier, the director of Clos de Vougeot, is the epitome of a sophisticated *gestionnaire*, as smooth as his prized product. In the Beaujolais, ruddy-faced peasants in berets have given way to white-coated oenologists with a wine degree, the *licence de la vigne* from Dijon University. Technologist Olivier Venot typically tastes 77 different wines to determine the blend of Gobet's Beaujolais Nouveau.

William Fèvre led a Chablisien delegation to confront their Californian competitors on enemy soil in the Napa Valley. "Chablis of California must stop taking our name in vain," fumed the French growers. At stake is both Burgundian prestige and the lucrative Japanese market. Still, Chablis has cornered the Vatican market – Domaine Defaix supplies Pope John Paul and Vatican officials with Chablis vintages.

Provincial life is a hotbed of petty rivalries and *problèmes de voisinage*, quarrels among neighbours. Ever meddlesome Burgundians are in their element. Disputes over inheritance are the bane of provincial life, with offspring squabbling over the division of spoils, often one tiny smallholding. A bourgeois couple complain about the grasping *mentalité paysanne* that covets a neighbour's success. After selling honey as a sideline, they were shocked when neighbouring farmers followed suit. But this "peasant mentality" is common sense in its purest form.

Marc Meneau, chef at the famous L'Espérance, in Vézelay, arouses mixed feelings. He is admired as the local boy made good, the star who attracts celebrities in helicopters; others begrudge his success. Meneau's fans point to his investment in projects like the restoration of St-Père church. The chef himself is more interested in promoting Burgundian cuisine: "It's just as much part of our culture as is our artistic heritage."

sense of solidarity pervades the vineyards of the Côte d'Or.

To outsiders, the sumptuous tiled roofs of the Côte d'Or overshadow the simple slates of the Morvan. But Burgundy is also the lichen-covered cottages of the Puisaye, low brick houses of the Bresse and stone farms of the Charolais. To pessimists, gentrification spells the end of true rural life. Yet it saves villages from a slide into lethargy, with cafés replaced by video shops. Clamecy, once the centre of the logging trade, is a village in decline. A cheery welcome can't hide the cultural void and grim unemployment.

No such fate has befallen the wine-growing communities. Gevrey-Chambertin is sleepy

Culinary matters are also uppermost in Chaumard, a lakeside village in the Morvan. Each of the three restaurateurs advises against eating elsewhere: "They use nothing but frozen food down the road." Yet Burgundy is neighbourly in the warmest sense of the word, from its political leaders downwards. Mitterrand's postcards expressing *sincères amitiés* are highly treasured by citizens of the region. Wine-growers will help rivals with a troublesome harvest, either as an individual gesture or through the wine associations. A

Left, farmers near Saulieu. **Above**, postman discusses the news of the day, Sacquenay.

and smug – typical wine country. Four hectares (10 acres), the average patch, produces a very good living. The sleek cars outside *vignerons'* homes in Nuits-St-Georges and Fixin are proof of what the Fisc, the tax office, terms *signes extérieurs de richesse*. Traditional market towns thrive, such as the earthy yet highly appealing Charolles. At the Wednesday market, tough farmers bid against each other for the prized white cattle as well as pigs, sheep and chickens. Farmers gossip below the orange-tiled roofs while, between the canals and the scruffy allotments, bustling traders sell every form imaginable of pâté and sausage. Pragmatism and continuity are a recipe for success in the land of plenty. Charolles's setting, within the spiritual triangle of Taizé, Cluny and Paray-le-Monial, means that the church is central. There are summer concerts in Romanesque chapels, and folklore festivals, often followed by a rich *entrecôte charolaise*.

Leisure is equally robust. Fans of AXA Auxerre, the best regional football team, flock to matches. Canal and river banks are generally lined with motionless fishermen hoping to tempt perch, carp and even catfish. Oddly, Burgundians prefer cycling along canal towpaths to barging itself. Quiet pursuits include mushroom-picking or hiking near Solutré.

is in the tradition of Flemish burlesque, with wise fools offering a witty commentary on modern manners. Satire aside, it is also a Mardi Gras release, an excess of licence before Lenten abstinence.

The Fête de la Vivre, held in Couches every 20 years, parades a mythical beast, part dragon and part snake. The creature, a sorcerer's familiar, was blamed for destroying the crops in medieval times and so is ceremonially burnt. Burgundians are susceptible to magical, pagan tales.

Celtic beliefs and Christianity coexist. On Shrove Tuesday, the village near the abbey of Pierre-Qui-Vire re-enacts a Gallic ceremony: broth is sprinkled on houses to ward

Burgundy has a reputation for conviviality and spontaneity, best appreciated at festivals. The water jousting ceremony at Clamecy recalls the region's former dependence on the river trade. In industrial La Machine, citizens celebrate the Fête de Sainte Barbe, the patron saint of miners. The goose fair at Toucy and the snail festival at Blaisy-Bas confirm the Burgundian fixation with food. In Semur, the Fête de la Bague is the oldest horse race in France, run since 1639. It takes its name from the prize, a gold ring engraved with the city arms. Even more significant is Chalon-sur-Saône carnival, second only to that of Nice. As a medieval Fête des Fous, it

away spirit-snakes, the evil woodland masters. Montréal sees the survival of an ancient spring rite. Bundles of twigs, known as *mais*, are propped against doorways. Left by amorous boys, these sexist signs suggest that the young girl inside is ripe for matrimony.

Ancient superstitions linger, especially in the marshy Bresse and the austere Morvan. In the 19th century, the Morvan was known as "a land of savages, witches and wolves", myths perpetuated by storytelling shepherds and woodcutters. In the 1950s witchcraft was still practised in rural Morvan, linked to animal sacrifice and the cult of wolves and black hens. Nowadays, feasts for the dead, a legacy of Gallic rites, are still offered in some parts. A belief in herbal remedies is widespread in the mountains, although roast lizard is no longer considered an effective cure for epilepsy.

The Bressans are born storytellers, conjuring up images of white ladies swirling in the dense mists over the marshes. An owl's cry heard during the day predicts a pregnancy in the neighbourhood. After the christening, the godfather and godmother must pray that the baby "be neither a simpleton, brat, dribbler nor stammerer". In the past, mothers put a collar of wolf's teeth around the baby's neck as spiritual protection. The loss of the child's first tooth was a rite of passage: the child tossed the tooth into the fire, promising to reclaim it on Last Judgement Day. After a death, the clock, windows and television screen are covered; even vases are emptied "in case the departing soul drowns". Folklore still lurks below the surface.

Burgundian regionalism is renowned, touching émigrés and residents alike. *Régionalisme* is one of the biggest sections in local bookshops; schoolchildren even study an anthology of Burgundian literature. A wariness of outside influences underpins provincial society: in this respect, the Japanese have recently replaced the Americans in local demonology. Regional identity reinforces provincialism, as does the cultivation of rural dialects, customs and festivals. The Burgundian paradox lies in its spiritual passion for earthly pleasures and its pragmatic approach to spiritual matters.

Scratch the surface and literary peasant roots are unearthed. Vincenot's *La Billebaude* is a portrait gallery of modern peasants and a homage to a gamekeeper grandfather who taught him *l'art de chasse et l'art de vivre*. During his childhoood, peasant costumes and beliefs were common in the Auxois. Paul Meunier, a self-styled peasant storyteller, records the folk history of Asquins, near Vézelay. As the great-grandson of the village miller, he recounts the cherry harvests, labours of the month and the slaughter of the family pig. Proverbs are revealing: "Labour is a gypsy child who doesn't obey any law." At its most pretentious, Burgundy indulges in a *mitage du paysage*, an idealisa-

tion of pastoral living and provincial life. At its truest, it is a rootedness in the region that comes before all else. Burgundian roots are essential to provincial status, no matter how humble. Certain *vigneron* families trace their ancestry to the days of the Grand Dukes.

Vineyards are a fertile source of superstition. Spring vigils chill the workers to the bone, bringing the most dangerous moments for frost just before dawn. Given the sacredness of wine, incantations against hail are not unknown. In Chablis, April moons symbolise destructive power so *vignerons* may still resort to Faustian pacts with nature.

Superstition and religion are natural allies in Burgundy. La Chablisienne, the wine co-

operative founded by the Curé of Poinchy, controls a third of the local trade. In 1990 the Archbishop of Sens blessed the harvest and officiated at the St-Vincent wine festival. On a smaller scale, Noyers also pays its religious dues: a Madonna on a medieval gateway is hung with grapes in grateful thanks for a successful harvest.

In 1952 the Burgundian wine confraternities played hosts to their rivals from Bordeaux. Clos de Vougeot witnessed an unprecedented display of pageantry, with a grand Mass and processions of trumpeters, heralds, archers and singers. But the role of the orders is not limited to camaraderie and

Left, folk dancing in Dijon. **Right**, adding a fresh lick of paint.

public relations. Their solemn duty is to spread Burgundian culture and maintain the traditional wine festivals.

Les Trois Glorieuses describes a trio of harvest festivals. The first is the Chapitre de la Confrérie des Chevaliers du Tastevin, a banquet held at the Château de Clos de Vougeot. The following day is the Vente des Hospices de Beaune, the wine auction treated as a benchmark for Burgundy wines. Then comes *La Paulée* at Meursault, a literary banquet at which *vignerons* present their finest bottles. *La Fête des Vins* follows a week later. By contrast, *St Vincent Tournante* is a January procession, based in a different wine village each year. *Tastevinage* is also a

spring event, held in the Cistercian cellars of the Clos de Vougeot. The wines are put before a jury of 200 wine writers, growers and brokers. The jury then assesses each bottle's *honnêteté, caractère et qualité*.

Historically, Beaujolais was Burgundy's poor country cousin but the popularity of Beaujolais Nouveau is changing that. The *Clochemerle* series was filmed in Vaux-en-Beaujolais but *vigneron* Gérard Texier remarks: "The cast came to drink our wine but we've never seen the series." Still, visitors feel the convivial *Clochemerle* effect. Michel Déflache attributes any jollity to Beaujolais: "The people are extrovert and so is the wine."

Even a shy Japanese importer was found clog-dancing in front of Vaux's lavatorial tourist attraction, naturally inscribed as "*La Pissotière de Clochemerle*".

Dijon is Burgundy's window on the world, a city that has grown without sacrificing its soul. Outsiders would say that its soul was always resolutely provincial. As a dormitory town of Paris, Dijon attracts a shifting population and also appeals to Swiss and German property speculators. Still, only Dijon has any cosmopolitan pretensions, with its clutch of Parisian intellectuals and sizeable foreign community. At best, its status as regional capital makes it a magnet for the arts. A lively student population ensures an experimental attitude to culture. Recently, a fashionable crowd gathered in a deconsecrated church to watch a play by Lacarrière, who lives in nearby Sacy. His reveries on passion and mortality held the audience spellbound.

But at heart Dijon is bourgeois and conservative, a city of civil servants, academics and office workers drawn to the Burgundian good life. Dijon's gastronomic fair is a byword for Burgundian sumptuousness as well as cuisine. Its bustling ethnic markets seem untypical of Burgundy: Italian and Algerian traders jostle for space; a gypsy has trained a mongoose to sit on a pony and beg. Yet behind the exoticism are Burgundian signs and symbols. La Petite Flamande sells snails beside stalls stacked with jars of mustard; nearby, bourgeois students join Dijonnais matrons in browsing for junk. They are bound by a mercantile yet convivial approach that embodies the spirit of this countrified capital, and of Burgundy itself.

Immersion in provincial life is one of the chief pleasures of Burgundy. A balloon flight over rolling countryside reveals gilded roofs, pointed weathervanes, fields of sunflowers and Charolais cattle. A smooth descent may alight upon a boldly painted barge, a bicycle race or a Burgundian wedding. Such cameos may be glimpsed from the ground as easily as from a hot-air balloon. "Good wine is an inward emotion," said Henry James; so is provincialism. Behind the lace curtains are cultured farmers and cunning *vignerons*. Burgundy has its finger on the pulse of provincial France.

<u>Left</u>, wine-maker, Côte d'Or. <u>Right</u>, taking shelter in Tanlay.

"No wine is as earthy as red Burgundy... And no wine accompanies dusk as intimately, and is such a friend of the night, as the wine of Nuits-St-Georges, which is nocturnal in its very name, dark and twinkling like a summer evening in Burgundy. It shines blood-red on the threshold of the night like the fires of the setting sun on the crystalline rim of the horizon. It kindles red and deep-blue glints in the purple earth, in the grass, and in the leaves of the trees, still warm with the tastes and aromas of the dying day. With the arrival of night, wild animals go into their dens deep in the ground; the boar crashes noisily through the dense undergrowth; the pheasant, with its short and silent flight, swims in the twilight already floating above the woods and fields; the nimble hare slides on to the first moonbeam as though on to a silver tightrope. It is the hour of Burgundy wine."

— Curzio Malaparte, Kaputt.

This paean to Nuits-St-George is entirely typical of the lengths writers will go to in order to express their passion for Burgundy wine. And it inspires not only passion but deep confusion in anyone attempting to understand the fiendishly complicated business of growing and selling Burgundy.

Who, for example, declared that "Burgundy, and in particular Côte d'Or, is... excruciatingly difficult to comprehend," and "to a large extent... an unfathomable mystery"? A novice wine buff? Or maybe a chauvinistic Bordeaux château-owner? Neither: it was none other than Robert Parker, one of the world's greatest experts on Burgundy (and Bordeaux, for that matter). You have been warned.

Before looking at why some Burgundy wines pose such a problem, let's first define what we are talking about. The *appellation contrôlée* wines of Burgundy (Grande Bourgogne), come from five areas: Chablis and the Auxerrois, Côte d'Or (Côte de Nuits and Côte de Beaune), the Chalonnais, the Mâconnais and Beaujolais. Beaujolais, then, is technically a Burgundy, though rarely referred to as such. Despite its adjective,

Preceding pages: Pinot Noir grapes. **Right,** tasting the vintage, Côte d'Or.

Grande Bourgogne produces only about half as much wine as Bordeaux (excluding Beaujolais, only a quarter as much).

Beaujolais is the easiest to understand of all the Burgundy *appellations*. It has only three categories: Beaujolais, Beaujolais-Villages and 10 named growths – the Institut National des Appellations d'Origine (INAO) allowed Régnié to join the club in 1988; it comes in a single colour (red) and is made from a single grape variety (Gamay).

The relatively recent marketing success story of Beaujolais, and more particularly Beaujolais Nouveau, is well known. It is alleged that Parisian journalists marooned in Vichy-run Lyon during the Occupation re-

quality and price. This is the result of a syndrome which has also taken its toll, though to a lesser degree, in Chablis and Côte d'Or.

It works like this: your vines produce say 50 hectolitres per hectare (about 500 gallons per acre) of excellent wine, which you lightly chaptalise to make it smoother (chaptalisation consists of adding sugar to the fermenting must to boost its alcoholic content); it sells like a bomb; demand outstrips supply, so you put up your price; but you are also tempted to cajole your vines (by pruning techniques, selection of clones and so on) into producing ever greater yields; the quality of the wine automatically goes down, as does its alcoholic

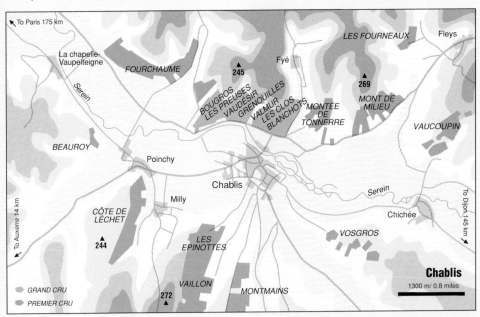

turned to the capital after the war with stories of a deliciously light and fruity red wine they had discovered called Beaujolais. But even without the hacks' efforts to publicise the wine, it is doubtful whether any advertising copywriter could have come up with a more alluring brand-name than Beaujolais (with its suggestions of *beau* and *joli*). Many of the growth names, too, are melodious (Brouilly, Chiroubles) or full of sensual (Saint-Amour, Juliénas) and visual (Moulin-à-Vent, Fleurie) associations.

In recent years, though, Beaujolais sold to consumers outside the Beaujolais area has tended to be distinctly less attractive, in both

content; your consumers are accustomed to a certain strength, so you chaptalise a bit more. The resulting wine is an undrinkable brew that produces instant migraine.

In 1988, the French consumer magazine *Que Choisir?* caused a bit of a scandal when it was able to prove, through nuclear magnetic resonance tests, that chaptalisation had boosted the alcohol in some Beaujolais wines by as much as 4°, way above the permitted level of 2°. There has since been a swing back to non-chaptalised or less chaptalised wines on the part of some more intelligent growers. If buying Beaujolais on the spot, try to track them down, or invest in a reliable up-to-date wine-buying guide (such as the Gault-Millau or the Hachette). And steer clear of all but the most reliable *négociants* (Pierre Ferraud, Louis Tête, Georges Duboeuf).

The Mâconnais area, like Beaujolais, which it adjoins to the north, is also relatively straightforward to understand. Its most prestigious wine – many would say it was overrated and overpriced – is the white Pouilly-Fuissé, a Chardonnay that sells well on the US market. Otherwise the Mâconnais produces an ocean of unpretentious, largely white wines under the Mâcon *appellation régionale* which vary widely in type, depending on grape variety and soil, as well as

Middle Ages on, by Chablis and the Auxerrois. That this was once one of France's principal wine-growing areas can be seen from the adjective *vineux* in some place-names. In the 19th century the railway, which opened up the capital to cheaper wines from the Midi, and the arrival of Phylloxera, together caused wine-growing in the region – which for climatic and geological reasons was never an easy option – to go into serious decline. Many vineyards were grubbed up and put to other uses.

It is only in the past few decades that the trend has been spectacularly reversed, mainly as a result of vineyard extension. Production of Chablis, for example, rose 16

in quality. Mâconnais wines, like Beaujolais, benefited from shrewd advertising, though at a much earlier date. In 1666, a giant of a man called Claude Brosse decided to take two barrels of his red Mâcon to Paris on spec, shipping it by oxcart. He somehow managed to sing the praises of his wine to Louis XIV in person, and immediately received an order from the royal cellars.

Because of easy waterway communications via the River Yonne and the River Serein, a substantial share of the Paris wine market was cornered, from the end of the

times between 1945 and 1990, and could increase further if more vineyards are planted (as they are legally entitled to be).

Those interested in lesser-known, recently replanted *appellations* should sample some of the red and white wines of distinct character and reasonable price that are dotted all over the Yonne *département*, They include Irancy, Epineuil, Saint-Bris-le-Vineux, Chitry and Coulanges-la-Vineuse.

These wines, however, are dwarfed in quality and price by the area's most celebrated name, Chablis. At its best, this Chardonnay can be a superbly intense wine. But recently it has been in such demand,

<u>Above</u>, mechanical grape-picker, Chalonnais.

WINE CONFRATERNITIES

The vinous motto "*Jamais en Vain, Toujours en Vin*" belongs to the *Confrérie des Chevaliers du Tastevin*, the most celebrated wine confraternity in France. The tradition of bacchic brotherhoods goes back to the Middle Ages when *confréries vineuses* abounded in Anjou, the Bordelais and Burgundy. They provided practical support and camaraderie, under the banner of St Vincent, patron saint of *vignerons*.

After the Revolution, Burgundy's loss of political power whittled away regional pride; the wine confraternities were relegated to folklore. As a result, most wine-tasting orders date from the

20th century. The success of Burgundy's *Chevaliers du Tastevin* has spawned countless imitators. In the 1930s, Burgundian wines were not selling. Desperate wine-growers at Nuits-St-Georges revived the festival of St Vincent, citing an old saying, *Si nos caves sont pleines, nos coeurs débordent* (If our cellars are full, our hearts are overflowing). In reality, their hearts were far from overflowing. The growers hit upon an inspired idea: invite their friends to drink Burgundy wine. "They will then discover that, as in St Bernard's day, these are the finest wines in Christendom".

The idea was perfect public relations, soon robed in chivalric splendour and housed in a dreamy château. In 1934 the *Chevaliers du Tastevin* acquired

Clos de Vougeot, a walled wine estate built by St Bernard's Cistercian monks. Its 50 hectares (124 acres) are shared by a total of 70 owners, making it a symbolic spot for such a joint venture.

The *Chevaliers du Tastevin* organise 17 chapters a year and during the grand *disnées* (banquets), folkloric rituals initiate newcomers in Burgundian ways. The colourful ceremony, inspired by Molière, uses dog Latin and archaic French. The dinner is a homage to Burgundy, from *oeufs en meurette*, eggs poached in red wine, to vintage Meursault and Montrachet. Merry drinking songs include the refrain, "*Toujours buveurs, jamais ivrogne*" (ever drinkers, never drunk).

The *intronisation* (initiation ceremony) requires the postulant to swear an oath of fidelity to Burgundian wines and to make a speech. As initiates, Princess Grace of Monaco, General de Gaulle, François Mitterrand, Ronald Reagan and George Bush have all drunk from the *tâtevin*, the traditional wine-tasting cup.

As far as such anachronistic rituals are concerned, "*le nouveau c'est l'ancien*" remains the rallying cry. In Racine's day, *confréries* had no compunction about adopting the ceremonial of an ancient religious or chivalric order; it was a respectful nod to history, with no trace of mockery. The *Chevaliers* likewise plundered the past: their costumes resemble the academic gown of Rabelais; titles such as *Chef du Protocole* and *Grand Chambellan* are redolent of another age.

The *confréries vineuses* also play an essential part in protecting the quality and reputation of Burgundy wines. In 1950 the pioneering *Chevaliers du Tastevin* formalised this in *Tastevinage*, an annual *dégustation*. More quality control than competition, it judges whether the Burgundy is typical of its *appellation* and, more subjectively, whether it is a wine fit to offer friends. The dual aim is to reward the grower for high quality wine and to signal the symbiotic relationship between producer and consumer. The successful bottles are pronounced *tastevinées*, strictly numbered, and labelled with the prestigious *Tastevinage* seal.

The hushed atmosphere could not be more different from the boisterous initiation ceremonies. One celebrates Burgundian verve while the other honours the mystical nature of wine, with praise such as "*il est grand, le mystère de la foi*".

Purists might wince at the fake folklore and public relations but beyond the bold pastiche, a genuine Burgundian spirit prevails. Clos de Vougeot is the shrine of wine, symbolising its central importance to the region. ∎

especially outside France, that it has suffered from the Beaujolais syndrome. To avoid nasty surprises, you can to some extent trust the INAO classification of Chablis.

But there is more than meets the eye to the INAO categories and their respective qualities. It is here that we start moving into the forest of complications that bedevil comprehension of top Burgundy wines. To understand the problem, one needs to know a little about their history. While it is known that there were vines in Burgundy when the Romans left Gaul (they may even have been introduced there by Julius Caesar – an old grape variety used in Irancy is called César), the development of wine-growing in Chablis

detect its characteristics by tasting the soil. The Cistercians divided up what is now Clos de Vougeot, in Côte d'Or, into three separate entities, which they called, in ascending order of quality, Cuvée des Moines, Cuvée des Rois and Cuvée des Papes. So it has been known for centuries that distinct wines can be produced by different parcels of a single vineyard, depending on their orientation, altitude, exposure, slope and soil (recent research has shown that in the Côte de Nuits alone there are 59 different types of soil).

Matters were further complicated by the French Revolution. The church's vast estates in Chablis and Côte d'Or were confiscated and sold off in small lots. Two centu-

and Côte d'Or was largely the work of medieval monks, particularly the Cistercians. Despite their concern with matters spiritual, they displayed great temporal sophistication when it came to wine-making. They also realised the value of great wine as a bargaining counter or diplomatic tool.

The monks naturally needed to know the "market" value of wine from this or that vineyard. So they initiated the lengthy process of classifying parcels of land that is still being continued by the INAO today. It seems they were so skilled that they could even

ries later, intermarriage between winegrowing families and the Napoleonic law which requires property to be divided up equally between all progeny have together resulted in a pattern of vineyard ownership in Chablis and Côte d'Or that forms a gigantic mosaic of tiny, often widely separated, parcels of land. Some are owned by individual growers, who may market their own wine, or sell all or some of it to *négociants*; others are in the hands of *négociants*, who may blend the product of one vineyard with wine from another of the same *appellation*. When the mosaic of ownership is superimposed on the intricate pattern of appellations and growths,

Above, Grape-picking, Moulin-à-Vent.

the result looks like a scrambled TV picture. If you add to the equation the fact that not all wine-growers or *négociants* are equally interested in getting the best out of their vines because in many cases they are certain of selling all their wine at a good price, irrespective of its quality, then buying Burgundy starts looking like a lottery. Even the INAO classifications are not always a model of clarity. About half the 40-odd *premiers crus* in Chablis can replace their actual name with that of a more famous neighbour. Thus the 20-hectare (50-acre) Chablis Premier Cru Chapelot is entitled to masquerade under the name of its more highly ranked 5-hectare (12-acre) neighbour Montée de Tonnerre.

a *grand cru* on their territory by simply annexing its name to their own. Thus, the villages of Aloxe-Corton, Chambolle-Musigny, Vosne-Romanée, Gevrey-Chambertin, Chassagne-Montrachet and Puligny-Montrachet, for example, were once simply called Aloxe (pronounced *Alosse*), Chambolle and so on.

With the possible exception of Clos de Vougeot, whose multiplicity of ownership (70 growers share 50 hectares) makes for a certain irregularity of quality, you are unlikely to be disappointed by any of the *grands crus* – always supposing you are able to lay your hands on, and afford, a bottle or two. Two of the finest wines of them all are

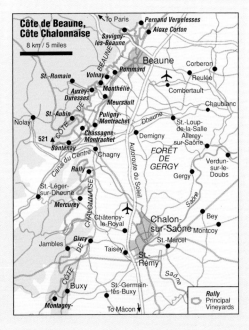

The situation in Côte d'Or is even more confusing, even if there is no blatant name substitution as in Chablis. It divides into Côte de Nuits, which produces mainly reds, and Côte de Beaune, where both whites and reds are found. The area has no fewer than 32 *grands crus*, scarce and expensive wines that are viewed as being among the very finest in the world. Even their names conjure up sensations of a vinous nirvana – the French singer and bon viveur Pierre Perret wrote a song consisting almost wholly of names like Richebourg and Corton-Charlemagne.

Historically, *communes* have tried to extract maximum benefit from the presence of

generally thought to be the white Montrachet (pronounced *Mon-rachet*) and the red Romanée-Conti.

Where buying becomes more complicated is in the next two categories down, the *premiers crus* and the *appellations communales*. In general, mention of a *premier cru* on the label provides a certain guarantee of quality. However, a wine which simply calls itself Chassagne-Montrachet, for example, is an *appellation communale*, which means that it will have come from any vineyard in that large *commune* and may not necessarily be worth the hefty price that is being asked for it.

Communes less prestigious than Chassagne-Montrachet, in that they have no *grand cru* on their territory, are often a better bet. Some very good Burgundies can be picked up, in both the *premier cru* and *appellation communale* categories, in Fixin, Pernand-Vergelesses, Savigny-lès-Beaune, Beaune, Volnay, Monthelie (also spelt Monthélie; pronounced *Mon-tli* by locals), Auxey-Duresses, Saint-Aubin and Santenay. Greater caution is needed when it comes to Pommard, Meursault and Nuits-St-Georges, because of their high reputation, particularly on export markets, and correspondingly steep prices. Greed and the law of supply and demand are responsible for

Beaune and St-Romain. Wines from the hills of Côte d'Or, which go under the *appellations régionales* of Bourgogne Haute-Côtes de Nuits and Bourgogne Haute-Côtes de Beaune, are also good.

Although the wines of the Chalonnais cannot compete with the finest of the Côte d'Or names, they have been steadily improving, and now provide some of the very best value to be found in Burgundy. They include some *crémants* (lightly sparkling wines) which can rival lesser champagnes and are around 50 percent cheaper. Since 1990, wines from the Chalonnais that do not come from its four *appellations communales* (Rully, Mercurey, Givry and Montagny)

Burgundy's spectacular price hikes in some years (such as 1989). These are usually followed by much talk of crisis and an easing of prices. But, even allowing for inflation, the figures for Burgundy exports between 1975 and 1990, for example, look good: they rose by 68 percent in volume and by 622 percent in value.

Probably the best value for money in Côte d'Or is provided by lesser-known *communes* which cannot even boast a *premier cru*. They include Marsannay (which got its *appellation communale* in 1987), Chorey-lès-

Above, 1983 Aloxe-Corton *premier cru*.

have been entitled to the *appellation régionale* Côte Chalonnaise. For the time being at least, it would seem that the ethos of the enthusiastic Chalonnais growers is "we try harder". One feels that a Chalonnais wine might have been the kind of thing James Thurber had in mind when he wrote his celebrated cartoon caption: "It's a naive domestic Burgundy, without any breeding, but I think you'll be amused by its presumption."

In Burgundy, as in Beaujolais, a wine-buying guide is a vital asset. Not all growers are equally meticulous about the sanitary conditions of their equipment or equally prepared to invest in expensive new oak

THE VIGNERON

S t-Romain is one of the least-known of Burgundy wines and perhaps for that reason it is very good value. It got its *appellation communale* only in 1947 and has no *premier cru*. Its geographical location also sets it apart: it is higher up and farther west than any of its fellow Côte de Beaune *appellations*.

The road leading up to the village of St-Romain from Auxey-Duresses runs along a deeply gouged valley dominated by grandiose cliffs – a foretaste of the landscape of the Côte d'Or hinterland. The upper part of the village, St-Romain-le-Haut, is a secluded cul-de-sac of warm-

coloured old stone houses and a 15th-century church, with the vineyards beyond. On the left stands the handsome 17th-century home of one of St-Romain's top growers, Alain Gras.

Gras, a small muscular man with a weatherbeaten face and melodious voice, is not one to waste time on pleasantries: he immediately suggested a visit to his *salle de dégustation*. Out came the bottles and glasses – Burgundian growers, unlike *vignerons* in some other areas, are notable for their willingness to pull a cork on a finished wine rather than siphon out a sample from the barrel. After attending the Lycée Viticole in Beaune,

Above, Alain Gras and his daughter Clémentine.

Gras worked as a home help before doing his military service. Then his father gave him a tumbledown house he had acquired through the ancient and rather macabre system of *viager* (whereby the buyer acquires a property by paying the seller an annuity for as long as the latter lives).

"In those days – the late 1970s – St-Romain wines were even less known than they are today," Gras said. "And the two hectares of land that came with the house, although entitled to the *appellation*, were being grazed by cows. I put vines there instead, bought up parcels of other vineyards here and there, did up the house, and then in 1982 made my first wine."

He pointed to a photograph of his *vigneron* great-grandfather. "He lived to be 100, and my grandfather is still going strong at 93. Perhaps it has something to do with the fact that we never drink *vin ordinaire*, just our own wine!"

Gras's 4 hectares (10 acres) of St-Romain vines, which are located at an average altitude of 380 metres (1,250 ft), produce about 16,000 bottles of wine a year, half of it white (Chardonnay) and half red (Pinot Noir). He also owns 2 hectares (5 acres) lower down in the Auxey-Duresses *appellation*, which yield about 6,000 bottles of red. Every Burgundy grower has his or her own wine-making techniques, partly out of personal inclination and partly because of differences in soil, altitude and so on. Gras prefers fairly traditional methods. They are – for the technically minded – 25 percent new oak barrels; 100 percent de-stemming; 12–14 days' maceration; fermentation at about 73°F/23°C (white) and 86°F/30°C (red); chaptalisation if the year has not been particularly sunny; malolactic fermentation in vats (white) and in barrels (red); and fining with infusorial earth. Gras bottles his wine almost a year after the harvest, in August (white) and September (red).

Gras has never had any problem selling his wine – in fact, rather the reverse – because St-Romain in general, and his St-Romain in particular, is considered such good value. In the days when the dollar was strong, a group of 18 American importers once came to sample his wine. They had been doing the rounds of a large number of prestigious Burgundy growers. "A fellow from Florida said my St-Romain would make a nice picnic wine," Gras recalled drily. True, both his white and red St-Romains are lightweights compared with a good Meursault or a Volnay. But they have such breeding that the best place for them to be brought out of a picnic hamper would be the lawns of Glyndebourne. ■

barrels – and some have even been known to use oak shavings to flavour their wines.

Nor will even reputable growers necessarily agree on what is the best method of vinification. Some de-stem all their grapes before pressing, others a certain proportion, yet others none. They have different opinions on such questions as yields per hectare, maceration before fermentation, fermentation temperature, filtration and fining. Those more interested in quick profits go for big yields, bottle early, and both fine and filter in order to save time. A badly made Burgundy can be disgusting, particularly when a certain quinone forms in the wine which, with age, gives it a nose that has been variously described as "almost decaying" or reminiscent of "dead mouse" and even "faeces".

In the 1980s, the consulting oenologist Guy Accad set the cat among the pigeons by recommending up to 10 days of cold maceration before fermentation, to give the wine a darker robe; he also urged the use of old-fashioned organic fertilisers. Over a dozen growers use his services and put him in the same league as such legendary Burgundy wine-makers as Henri Jayer and André Porcheret; others call him "a sorcerer", which is not a compliment in Burgundy country. But there is a growing awareness among the more intelligent growers and *négociants* (such as Leroy and Leflaive) that too many insecticides, fungicides and modern fertilisers damage not only the balance of the soil but the actual taste of the wine.

The reliability of Burgundy *négociants*, most of whom both own vineyards and buy in wine, is a vexed question. Historically, partly as a result of the Flemish connection, they have always been skilled exporters. Exports went up by 50 percent in the 1980s and 1990s, and today nearly half of all Burgundy finds its way abroad.

This has not always worked in favour of quality: some *négociants* tend to produce heavier wines that go down better on export markets. Where the handful of good *négociants* (Leroy, Leflaive, Jadot, Faiveley and Roux, for example) score over the growers is that because they are not so vulnerable to climatic accidents, they can guarantee supply of a given wine. The variation in wine-making methods from one Burgundy grower or *négociant* to another is far greater than in, say, Bordeaux. The only respect in which the great Côte d'Or *appellations* are more straightforward than their Bordeaux counterparts is in the vine varieties used: Pinot Noir (a notoriously difficult grape to grow and vinify) for red wine and Chardonnay for white. The differences with Bordeaux do not end there. Visiting a top Bordeaux château is often a much more formal affair and it is not always possible to taste the wine you may wish to buy.

Burgundian *vignerons*, whatever their wealth – and it may be considerable – prefer casual dress or even overalls; they are fully prepared to let you sample their wares (in a few cases asking for a nominal payment), sometimes opening a bottle of vintage wine

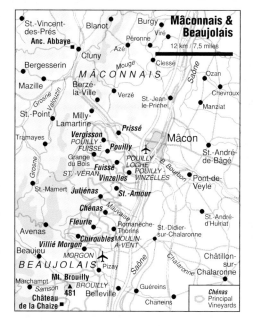

for you which they do not bother to decant. When the tasting is over, they may then inform you that they have no wine to sell.

Stendhal's description, in 1837, of the Burgundians as being "small, wiry and ruddy-faced" still holds today. They often live to a ripe old age (this may have something to do with the excellence of their everyday drinking wine). They are loud, bluff and fiercely individualistic people, who in their transactions still use pre-Revolutionary land measures, the *ouvrée* (428 sq. metres/512 sq. yards) and *journal* (8 *ouvrées*). They are not very good at pulling together, and it was not until the mid-1980s that they got round to forming the Bureau Interprofessionnel des Vins de Bourgogne, a trade association covering the whole of Burgundy with the exclusion of Beaujolais.

The Burgundians are also very chauvinistic about their wine. For them, and many would agree, there can be no better wine than a *grand cru* Burgundy. They will have to keep on their toes, though: at the 1991 Olympiades du Vin, a blind tasting organised by the wine fair Vinexpo, it was no surprise when the Chardonnay category was won by a 1986 Montrachet from Domaine Ramonet; but sharing second place with another well-known Burgundy came a 1988 Coldstream Hills from Rising and Shantell Vineyards, Yarra Valley, Australia.

For the time being, though, the Burgundians see claret as their greatest rival. Their motto might almost be "*Bordeaux, connais pas!*" Or they may say, dismissively, "I think Bordeaux is often prescribed for the sick… Our wines are for the healthy."

Their dismissive attitude is heartily reciprocated. The Bordeaux-born novelist Philippe Sollers wrote in 1986: "Burgundy is not wine, but a beverage to make sauces with. When you drink Burgundy you have the awful feeling you're drinking something that has bled; what's more, you can taste the appalling heaviness of the soil. In my view, then, anyone who likes Burgundy (or Beaujolais for that matter) is – not to put too fine a point on it – a nerd."

Describing the glorious sensations produced by a really big Burgundy is notoriously difficult. Wine writers resort to a huge variety of associations; these range from grilled and marinated meat, Arab mare, toast, tobacco, cinnamon, clove, lavender honey, dead nettle, mignonette and hawthorn blossom to the more familiar winespeak terrain of vanilla, mango, almonds, cherry (wild, raw or cooked), plum, raspberry, blackcurrant and so on.

Hyperbole is a distinct temptation; Chambertin, for example, has been memorably described as "the good lord himself sliding down your gullet in a pair of velvet trousers". And Roald Dahl once remarked that drinking Romanée-Conti was like having an orgasm in one's mouth and nose at the same time.

Right, The wine harvest.

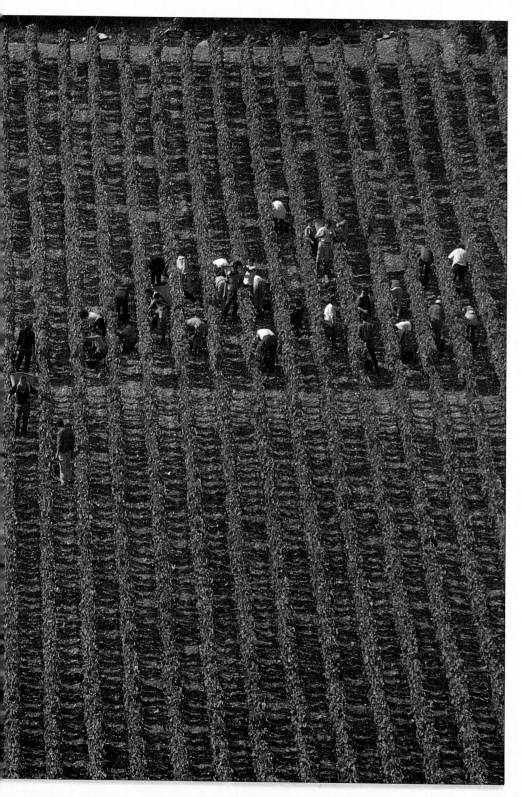

A BURGUNDIAN FEAST

"We went as often as we could afford it to all the restaurants in town, and along the Côte d'Or and even up to Morvan, to the Lac de Settons, the Avallon… and down past Bresse. We ate terrines of pâté ten years old under their tight crusts of mildewed fat. We tied napkins under our chins and splashed in great odorous bowls of *écrivisses à la nage*. We addled our palates with snipes hung so long they fell from their hooks, to be roasted then on cushions of toast softened with the pâté of their rotted innards and fine brandy. In village kitchens we ate hot leek soup with white wine and snippets of salt pork in it."

> – M.F.K. Fisher, *Long Ago in France.*
> *The Years in Dijon.*

Burgundy's near-religious devotion to food has not diminished since the legendary food writer M.F.K. Fisher's pilgrimages in the region in the 1930s. Open the Michelin guide at the restaurant map of France, and you will find that Burgundy has a concentration of one-, two- and three-star establishments unparalleled elsewhere in France, except for the Paris area. They cluster like metal filings, as if magically attracted there by some invisible gastronomic magnet. The restaurant map in the Gault-Millau food guide shows a similar pattern.

The excellence of Burgundian restaurants is nothing new. Towns and cities such as Sens, Auxerre, Avallon, Saulieu and Dijon have always been staging posts on the main route south from Paris to Lyon and Geneva. Competition for travellers' custom on such a well-frequented route was inherently likely to spawn inns of repute. When travel by motor car became popular during the inter-war years, chefs including Jean Parizot of the Buffet de la Gare in Dijon and Alexandre Dumaine of La Côte d'Or in Saulieu became nationally famous and triggered off a self-perpetuating tradition of gastronomic excellence: once a restaurant gains a high reputation under one chef, this often creates extra motivation for the next chef to perform equally well in the kitchen.

Preceding pages: Marc Meneau's restaurant, Vézelay. Left, the ingredients for *matelote d'anguilles*. Above, tomato and mustard tart.

The Burgundians themselves will tell you that the high quality of their region's cuisine is the natural result of their innate gourmandise. They will point to ancient culinary inscriptions in the Dijon archaeological museum and talk of a mysterious conjunction of the invading Burgundian tribes and the Gallo-Romans in the 5th century which produced a unique gift for gastronomy.

That is as may be – other regions of France would probably dispute the right of Burgundian cuisine to a special place at the

top of the tree. The fact remains that the dukes of Burgundy gave considerable priority to matters culinary. This is evident from the size of their kitchens, as Curnonsky reminded us: "Whereas other sovereigns built a hearth in a kitchen, the dukes of Burgundy designed a kitchen in a hearth; in other words, the four walls of the chamber were simply an enormous machine for cooking, spit-roasting, boiling, grilling, casseroling and frying. Bustling squads of scullions worked away in the middle of the vast room, hemmed in by revolving spits, seething cauldrons, sizzling pans, puffing casseroles and bubbling soups."

It was Philippe le Bon who is thought to have been responsible for the first written "menu", when, for a banquet he held in 1457, he displayed an "*escriteau*" (placard) listing the dishes to be served. The Bishop Princes of Sens certainly enjoyed their food and liked to eat in comfort: they made indentations in their dining tables to accommodate their bellies. The tradition of good food has been kept alive by the numerous gastronomic clubs that flourish today in the region, and by Dijon's important international food fair. Dijon's two main culinary specialities, *pain d'épices* and mustard, have long historical roots. *Pain d'épices* (a cake similar to gingerbread) was introduced to the area from

French Cheeses (the definitive work on the subject) Patrick Rance tells us that the creamy Chaource and the marvellously rich-smelling Époisses, which is regularly washed with *marc* or white wine, were probably first made in the Abbaye de Pontigny and Abbaye de Fontenay.

The making of proper unpasteurised Époisses almost died out recently, but has started up again. Cîteaux, a delicate Reblochon-like cheese made in the Abbaye de Cîteaux, is in such short supply that it is available only from the monastery itself and in local restaurants. Abbaye de la Pierre-Qui-Vire produces a similar, more recently devised cheese, La Pierre-Qui-Vire.

Flanders during the reign of the dukes of Burgundy. Mustard, brought to Gaul by the Romans, was particularly appreciated by Philippe le Bel, who would give away barrels of the condiment to guests, so they could make it known elsewhere. This no doubt helped to create Dijon's reputation as a mustard producer. Dijon mustard is made from mustard powder and verjuice (the juice of unripe grapes) or white wine.

Several of the cheeses of Burgundy also have a long history: they have been made in monasteries since medieval times by monks whose diet was restricted to fruit, vegetables and dairy products. In his highly readable

When Rance asked one of the monks there if they washed their cheeses in *marc*, he replied: "No, we prefer to drink that separately." Burgundy also produces several goats' cheeses of various shapes and sizes, one of which, Bouton de Culotte ("trouser button"), is little more than a mouthful. Cheese (Gruyère) goes into a Burgundian choux-pastry speciality called *gougère*, whose delicate, unassertive flavour makes it a wonderful accompaniment to wine.

Burgundian cuisine, like all cuisines to a greater or lesser extent, was shaped by the availability of certain ingredients. It is the wide variety and the excellence of those ingredients, combined with a frequent use of red wine, that made Burgundian cuisine what it is today.

Although vegetable dishes are often imaginative (cardoons with bone marrow, for example, or kidney beans in red wine), the predominant ingredients are meat and fish. Wild produce is especially prized, and there are numerous recipes calling for freshwater fish, crayfish, frogs, snails, pigeon, quail, thrushes, boar and venison, as well as wild mushrooms (morels, cèpes, chanterelles and fairy-ring mushrooms).

Domestic animals have long been carefully bred for their culinary qualities. The off-white Charolais cattle that are a familiar

that out of gratitude to the Marquis de Treffort the council voted that he should be made a gift of two dozen fatted poultry." When Henri IV conquered Bresse in 1600, he remarked on the delicacy of the chicken he had tasted.

Two centuries later Brillat-Savarin – never one to be at a loss for a pat apophthegm – gave his reckoned verdict: "Queen of poultry, poultry of kings." By the 1920s its fame had spread throughout France and it began to command increasingly high prices. Fraudulent Bresse chickens appeared on the market, so in 1936 a special *appellation contrôlée* was created (the only one for a meat product in France).

sight in the fields of Burgundy produce renowned beef. Elsewhere in France they are often crossed with other breeds to enhance the latter's culinary qualities.

Poultry from Bourg-en-Bresse has long been highly esteemed. Four centuries ago it was already a prestigious enough product to be thought worthy of being offered as an official gift. According to the Bourg-en-Bresse archives for 12 November 1591, the people of the town were "so joyous at the departure of the Romans [the Savoyards]

Left, varieties of onions and shallots. **Above**, Dijon specialities: mustard and cassis.

Bresse chickens are free-range white Beny poultry reared in a strictly defined area and fed on a diet of maize and whey only. They have an aluminium ring on one foot, and a stamp on the base of the neck. Their flesh is indeed remarkably flavoured (this is especially true of Bresse capons, France's most expensive poultry product). But care has to be taken, before cooking a Bresse chicken, to remove the wads of yellow fat from its stomach cavity and to prick the fatty areas of skin. The nickname of the people of Bourg-en-Bresse, *ventres jaunes* (yellow bellies), may derive from the yellowish tinge of their poultry.

SNAIL-HUNTING

The French name for the edible snail (*Helix pomatia*) is *escargot de Bourgogne*. It is so named because it was once particularly common in the vineyards of Burgundy. Nowadays the use of weedkillers has largely driven snails out of the vineyards, and three-quarters of all edible snails consumed in France are imported from Eastern Europe. In the 19th century, however, there were still battalions of snails in Burgundy, if local writer Henri Vincenot is to be believed. He claims that engineers building the Paris-Lyon railway line toyed with the idea of sending trains up and over the ridge west of Dijon separating the

Rhône and Seine river basins. When they worked out how steep the incline would be, requiring trains to climb 200 metres (650 ft) in only 2 km (1.5 miles), they feared that the thousands of snails which were bound to be squashed would make the rails so slippery that locomotives would slither to a halt. So they decided to drive a tunnel through the ridge instead.

The *escargot de Bourgogne* is a pretty good traction engine itself. Scientific tests have shown that a single individual can carry a weight of up to 250 gm (9 oz) on top of its shell. When it comes to dragging rather than carrying, the creature is capable of shifting a weight of 4 kg (9 lb). The snails' other great forte is munching and they are as happy munching hemlock as cabbage leaves, which means they may be poisonous unless they are starved ("purged") for a week or two before being eaten.

Once in the kitchen, the poor creatures are covered with salt, to make them give up their slime, and then washed. They are now ready for cooking, usually for an hour or two in a *court-bouillon* before being finished off in any number of ways. Usually they are put back into their shells with lashings of garlic butter and heated in the oven. This preparation, which is called *escargots à la bourguignonne*, is extremely popular. The first recorded *escargots à la bourguignonne* recipe dates from 1825 and calls for *fines herbes*, which might at that time have included a little garlic, among other things. The delicate flavour of snails is brought out in several interesting recipes from other French regions. Ingredients can include: parsley and aniseed; sausage meat, onion, tomato and slivered almonds; raw ham, anchovy, spinach and walnuts; onion, tomato, orange peel, savory, fennel and saffron.

Burgundy has given *Helix pomatia* its official French name. But the snail goes by an impressive number of local names elsewhere in France: *carnar* (Lorraine), *egorgo* or *carcalou* (Auvergne), *bavou* or *luma* (Poitou), *ekerbo* (Normandy), *escarabotte* (Limousin), *cagaraulau* (Languedoc), *cagouille* (Charente), *cantereu* (Comté de Nice), *tapada* or *carago* (Provence) and *carsaulada* (Roussillon). Even Burgundy itself has a local name: *canigo*.

Although the French are very much identified with the eating of snails, this has not always been the case. The first known French recipe for snails is given in an anthology known as *Le Ménagier de Paris* (*c.* 1390), which says that "*escargolz*" are "for rich people". But Philip Hyman, who has researched snail recipes exhaustively, suggests that, at Parisian tables at least, the mollusc suffered a virtual eclipse for two centuries.

Several other peoples have eaten snails at various times – the Romans (who were the first to farm them), the Italians and even the British (18th-century Newcastle glass-makers and now day-trippers to Calais). The Swiss, however, are not noted for their fondness for the mollusc, perhaps out of embarrassment that their national characteristic is perceived by the mercurial French to be slowness. Hence the joke about the Frenchman who goes snail-hunting with a Swiss friend, who catches only one snail. "Didn't you find any others?" asks the Frenchman. "Yes. One. But it got away." ∎

The charcuterie of the Morvan, and in particular its lightly smoked raw ham, is highly prized. Farther south, in the Chagny area, a succulent and very thick sausage called *judru* is made. Pork marinated in *marc* and cut up into chunks, rather than minced, goes into the sausage, which is matured for six months. Traditionally, the meat for *judru* comes from pigs that are sent out into the woods round Chagny to feed on acorns and the occasional viper, which, it is alleged, lends their flesh a special flavour.

Three Burgundian pork-based specialities only rarely encountered on restaurant menus are *rigodon*, *ferchusse* and *gruotte*. *Rigodon*, from southern Burgundy, a curious dish of

bowl and held together with aspic mixed with liberal quantities of garlic and parsley. When cut, it presents an attractively appetising mosaic of red-pink ham and dark-green parsley. Some modern chefs inexplicably prefer to mash the ingredients together, thus robbing the dish of its visual effect. *Jambon persillé* is often oversalted by charcutiers and restaurant chefs. It is easily made at home, however, where that particular pitfall can be avoided.

Because of Dijon's reputation as the mustard capital of France, any dish with the epithet *dijonnais* implies use of the condiment. One of the best marriages of the cooked mustard taste (which is more aro-

salt pork or ham baked in a mixture of milk, eggs and a little flour, is reminiscent of the medieval *lait lardé*; in times when bread was baked at home it would be put in the oven after the loaves had been taken out. *Ferchusse* is also linked to a specific event in the calendar of the domestic economy, the killing of the pig. It is a stew consisting of the pig's heart, liver and lights. *Gruotte* is similar, but made from wild boar. The best-known pork-based dish from Burgundy is *jambon persillé*. It consists of roughly-cut pieces of cooked ham pressed down into a

Above, Burgundy bistro meal.

matic and less pungent than its raw flavour) is with kidneys, in *rognons à la dijonnaise*.

Perhaps the most distinctive characteristic of Burgundian cuisine is its frequent use of red wine. The classic explanation, proposed by Burgundians and non-Burgundians alike, is that this is only natural, given that the region is famous for its wines. Yet the cuisine of other major wine-producing areas, such as the Bordelais, is not similarly vinous in character. It is possibly true that red Burgundy is more suited to the stewpot than the more astringent Bordeaux; but, equally, trying to come up with a neat explanation is probably an impossible task.

However that may be, the list of red-wine-based recipes is impressive. They range from simple dishes such as *trempus* (pieces of toast dipped in sweetened red wine) and the already mentioned kidney beans to the famous and often traduced *coq au vin*. All the recipe books tell you to use the same wine in that dish as you intend to drink at table. The price of really good Burgundy being what it is nowadays, this poses something of a problem, and there is no harm in using an excellent *bourgogne ordinaire* in the dish and putting something much bigger and pricier in your wine glass.

The essential ingredient of *coq au vin* is not so much the wine as the bird, which treated in much the same way as the cock in *coq au vin*. In *saupiquet*, an ancient dish from the Morvan (a recipe for it appears in a 16th-century cookbook by Jean Reynier), Morvan raw ham is lightly cooked and served in a sauce of vinegar, shallots and juniper berries. The Burgundians have a fondness for fish-meat combinations, which produces such interesting dishes as *poularde aux écrevisses* and *poulet en matelote,* in which the chicken is cooked with eel in a red-wine sauce.

The words *en meurette* indicate a red-wine sauce. The most common such dish is *oeufs en meurette*, in which the sauce, slightly thickened with *beurre manié*, accompanies

should be – and this is where many restaurants fall down – neither too young nor too old. When properly made, the dish (which also contains pickling onions, lightly smoked bacon, mushrooms, garlic, *marc* and *bouquet garni*) should have a pronounced but not over-gamey taste. Many chefs insist that it should be eaten only after being re-heated the day after it is made. Alexandre Dumaine always marinated the bird for at least 12 hours before cooking it; his personal touch was to add a tablespoonful of uncooked wine to the sauce at the very end.

Another celebrated dish is *boeuf bourguignon*, in which stewing beef is poached eggs, pieces of bacon and mushrooms. It is usually served with deep-fried croûtons, whose crispness contrasts well with the rich and velvety sauce. Brains and freshwater fish, particularly eel or carp, also thrive *en meurette*.

Pauchouse (or *pochouse*), Burgundy's most famous freshwater-fish dish, uses white, not red, wine. Just as the paternity of the cassoulet is fought over by Toulouse, Castelnaudary and Carcassonne, so *pauchouse* exists in two slightly differing forms, one from Verdun-sur-le-Doubs, and the other from nearby Seurre. Although the two recipes differ little, both villages are adamant that theirs is the "genuine" version.

As often happens in France, their location in different departments (Saône-et-Loire and Côte d'Or respectively) has exacerbated their rivalry down the years. In Verdun-sur-le-Doubs, where there is an active Confrérie de la Pauchouse, the dish is made with eel, burbot, pike, perch, onion, shallot, garlic, *beurre manié* and Bourgogne Aligoté. The amount of garlic employed varies from one clove to a whole head. The Seurre version calls for cream to be added to the sauce at the last moment.

Modern chefs generally prefer to thicken their sauces in a lighter way than with *beurre manié*. Michel Lorain of La Côte Saint-

ingredients that customers at pricey restaurants expect (foie gras, lobster, truffles and caviare), they have on the whole remained remarkably faithful to the spirit of Burgundian cuisine. In particular, they have explored new possibilities of red-wine sauces and fish-meat combinations: *feuilleté de moelle et girolles au vin rouge* (Jean-Pierre Billoux at Digoin), *dorade au vin rouge à la fondue d'échalote* (Loiseau), *carpe au vin rouge aux lanières de queue de boeuf* (Jean-Pierre Gillot at Moulin de Martorey in Chalon-sur-Saône), *gratin de pommes de terre au vin rouge* (Lorain).

But what distinguishes those chefs, like their colleagues Marc Meneau at Vézelay,

Jacques, for example, emulsifies the sauce of his *pauchouse* with cream and egg yolks. Whereas Parizot of the Buffet de la Gare in Dijon used to spend two hours over his *oeufs en meurette* imperceptibly thickening its flour-based sauce, Bernard Loiseau of La Côte d'Or lends it consistency by beating in a fine purée of cooked carrots and butter.

But although there has recently been a detectable trend among the new generation of top Burgundy chefs towards a systematic, and ultimately anonymous, use of the kind of

Left, Colette Girand making chèvre cheese near Saulieu. Above, the finished product.

Jean-Pierre Silva at Le Vieux Moulin in Bouilland, Jacques Lameloise in Chagny and Georges Blanc in Vonnas, is their constant quest for perfection at both the invention and the execution stages.

In that, they are worthy successors to that greatest perfectionist of them all, Alexandre Dumaine. Towards the end of his life he was very ill and suffered fits of delirium. In his moments of lucidity he would talk obsessively of nothing but cooking. According to his wife, he said: "I think I now know how to make a good *coq au vin*." "But you've been making it for 30 years," his wife said. "I was just practising!" Dumaine replied.

A

JOUBERT

LA VILLE DE PONT-DE-VAUX

SA PATRIE

MDCCCXXXII

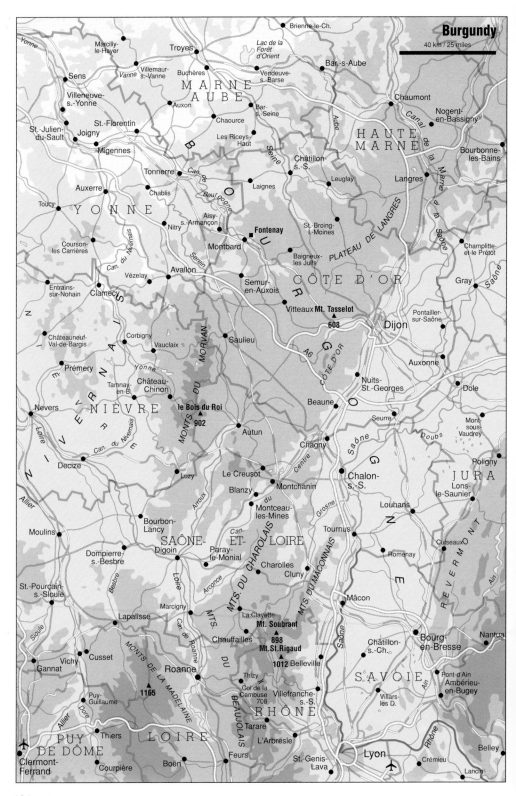

40 km / 25 miles

Brienne-le-Ch.

Marcilly-le-Hayer

Troyes

Lac de la
Forêt
d'Orient

Sens

Villemaur-s.-Vanne

Buchères

Vendeuve-s.-Barse

Bar-s-Aube

Chaumont

Villeneuve-s.-Yonne

Vanne

M A R N E

Auxon

Nogent-en-Bassigny

Yonne

St.-Julien-du-Sault

St.-Florentin

Joigny

A U B E

Bar-s.-Seine

Chaource

Les Riceys-Haut

H A U T E
M A R N E

Bourbonne-les-Bains

Migennes

B

Langres

Auxerre

Chablis

Can. de

Châtillon-s.-S.

Leuglay

Canal de la Marne à la Saône

Toucy

Y O N N E

Tonnerre

Bourgogne

Laignes

Seine

St.-Broing-l-Moines

Champlitte-et-le-Prétot

Courson-les-Carrières

Can. du Nivernais

Nitry

Aisy-s.-Armançon

O

PLATEAU DE LANGRES

Gray

Saône

Entrains-sur-Nohain

Vézelay

Avallon

Serein

Fontenay

Montbard

U

Baigneux-les-Juifs

Pontailler-sur-Saône

Clamecy

Semur-en-Auxois

R

CÔTE D'OR

Châteauneuf-Val-de-Bargis

Corbigny

Vauclaix

Saulieu

Vitteaux ▲Mt. Tasselot
608

Dijon

Auxonne

N

Prémery

Yonne

Château-Chinon

MONTS DU MORVAN

G

A6

CÔTE D'OR

Dole

Nevers

I

Tamnay-en-B.

le Bois du Roi
▲902

Beaune

Nuits-St.-Georges

Seurre

Mont-sous-Vaudrey

Allier

N I È V R E

Can. du Nivernais

E

Autun

Chagny

Saône

G

Poligny

Decize

Luzy

Le Creusot

Blanzy

Montchanin

Chalon-s.-S.

JURA

Lons-le-Saunier

Bourbon-Lancy

Digoin

SAÔNE-

ET-

LOIRE

Montceau-les-Mines

Can. du Centre

Grosne

Louhans

Tournus

N

Cuiseaux

Dompierre-s.-Besbre

Besbre

Paray-le-Monial

Arconce

Charolles

Cluny

MTS. DU CHAROLLAIS

MTS. DU MÂCONNAIS

Romenay

E

St.-Pourçain-s.-Sioule

Loire

Marcigny

Can. de Roanne

La Clayette

Mt. Soubrant
▲898

Mâcon

Châtillon-s.-Ch.

Bourg-en-Bresse

Nantua

Sioule

Lapalisse

MTS.

Chauffailles

Mt.St.Rigaud
▲1012

Belleville

Saône

Ain

Vichy

Cusset

MONTS DE LA MADELAINE

DU

Thizy

Col de la
Cambuse
708

Villefranche-s.-S.

S A V O I E

Pont-d'Ain

Ambérieu-en-Bugey

Gannat

▲1165

Roanne

BEAUJOLAIS

RHÔNE

Villars-les D.

Ain

Puy-Guillaume

Dore

Tarare

P U Y
D E   D Ô M E

Thiers

L O I R E

L'Arbresle

Rhône

Belley

Clermont-Ferrand

Courpière

Boën

Feurs

St.-Genis-Lava

Lyon

Crémieu

Lancin

Burgundy offers a rich and diverse landscape to the traveller. The following pages journey from the Yonne, with its great rivers and wide cereal plains, and Chablis, offering the first taste of Burgundy wine, then head south into the heartland, the religious mystique of Vézelay and the great abbey of Fontenay. Then we go west to the Nièvre and the black granite heart of the Celtic Morvan, with, further south, the ancient Roman remains at Autun, echoed by its magnificent Romanesque cathedral.

Burgundy's capital, Dijon, follows with its great museums, its glittering tiled roofs and fine restaurants, a prelude to the celebrated red earth of the Côte d'Or and some of the finest wines on earth. The trail continues through the wine country of Chalonnais to southern Burgundy and its abundance of Romanesque churches, the earth-hugging wooden houses of the Bresse and the rich pastureland of the Charolais. Finally we encounter the south, heralded by the hilly contours and terracotta roofs of Mâcon and Beaujolais. Traditional Burgundy, which at one time extended over vast swathes of Europe, spills over today's boundaries and we have been equally profligate in our explorations.

Within these generous limits there are treasures to be found. Wine, of course: magic names like Gevrey-Chambertin, Romanée-Conti, Clos de Vougeot. And food, undoubtedly: *escargots*, mustard, fine Charolais beef, *appellation contrôlée* Bresse chickens and pungent Époisse cheese.

Cultural riches abound. One of Burgundy's great gifts to the world is its Romanesque architecture and within its boundaries are some of the finest examples in Europe – from the still thriving shrines of Vézelay and Paray-le-Monial and the great monastic foundations of Fontenay and Pontigny, to the sad emptiness of Cluny and literally hundreds of stunningly simple small chapels. The architectural tradition continues with the extraordinarily preserved Hôtel-Dieu in Beaune, the great Gothic cathedral of Sens, the flamboyant Gothic splendour of Brou, and many sumptuous Renaissance châteaux.

Whether your interests are cerebral, sensual or *sportif*, architectural investigation, wine tours, or rock-climbing, Burgundy supplies a feast for every visitor and rewards many return journeys. For the French, Burgundy is their mythic childhood home, their lost kingdom, and even for a first-time visitor Burgundy can strike a peculiarly nostalgic chord.

<u>Preceding pages:</u> Hospices de Beaune; Romanesque church at Semur-en-Brionnais; choirstalls at Brou; Joubert statue, Pont Vaux.

In a region of rivers, the **Yonne** reigns supreme. The French dispute whether the Yonne or the Seine flows into Paris. Convention favours the Seine but Burgundians are adamant: at the confluence in Montereau, the Yonne is the greater. This is also a pointed reminder that, but for a quirk of medieval history, France would be Burgundian.

As the closest region to Paris, the Yonne suffers rural depopulation yet remains deeply conscious of its Burgundian identity. After all, Colette settled in Paris yet was passionate about her homeland: "I belong to the country I've left behind." Chablis is an equally celebrated ambassador. Just for good measure, Auxerre regularly beats Paris at football.

Rising in the Morvan, the Yonne is known as the *enfant terrible* because of its chaotic flow. By the time it reaches Basse-Bourgogne and its historic heart at Auxerre, it has acquired stature. Burgundian borders are as fluid as the river. Sens is the official gateway to the region but Auxerre is a warmer, more informal Burgundian welcome. Historically, the towns north of Auxerre were not part of the Burgundian kingdom. If geography is any guide, the Yonne's cereal plains should belong to Champagne. If architectural frontiers apply, then Burgundy begins not in Gothic Sens but in Romanesque Pontigny. If wine is a definition of Burgundy's borders, then these should be redrawn at Chablis, Burgundy's first great white wine.

The *département* resembles a Burgundian snail, with Auxerre curled inside a variegated shell. Sens and Joigny join the river Armançon to form an outer circle, embracing Burgundy's châteaux country. On the western rim, watery Puisaye has little in common with these Renaissance glories. Closer to the Burgundian heartland, the placid

Preceding pages: fields of mustard near Chablis. Left, Auxerre from the river.

river Serein forms an inner circle to the east: Pontigny and Chablis are quintessential Burgundy. The lifeblood of the region is the Auxerrois wine route stretching south along the River Yonne. After Auxerre, the rivers Yonne and Cure belong to the Morvan mountains.

Gateway to Burgundy: Orchards and rich cereal plains signal the Sénonais, known as Burgundy's granary. **Sens**, on the right bank of the Yonne, is an ancient city at the crossroads of Burgundy, Champagne and the Île-de-France. The city's heyday was in the 12th century so the rectangular Roman grid has since given way to an oval-shaped medieval nucleus. As a major ecclesiastical centre, Sens welcomed St Bernard, Pope Alexander III and Thomas à Becket. The Archbishop of Sens held sway over northern France, leading the Gothic revolution and inspiring great Gothic cathedrals from Amiens to Chartres, Canterbury to Jerusalem. Sens's pre-eminence only ceased in 1622: Paris became an archbishopric and Sens then lost the primacy.

Leafy boulevards now trace the line of the old city walls, but the **cathedral** still sits at the medieval heart. Given the tradition of Romanesque architecture in Burgundy, Sens Cathedral owes more to the simplicity of St Bernard than to the soaring verticality of High Gothic.

The result is a fusion generally known as Burgundian Gothic: the austerity of a Cistercian abbey allied to the grace of Gothic ribbed vaulting. If it is reminiscent of Canterbury Cathedral, that is only natural: it was William of Sens who later rebuilt the airy choir. Although begun by Archevêque Sanglier, St Bernard's follower, Sens spans five centuries. Yet the cathedral's spirit survives a Renaissance belfry and flamboyant Gothic flourishes. The vivid windows are arguably the finest in Burgundy and they include a glittering tribute to Thomas à Becket, a lasting reminder of the Archbishop's happy exile in Sens.

Le Palais Synodal, adjoining the cathedral, forms part of the Archbishop's Palace, now an ambitious

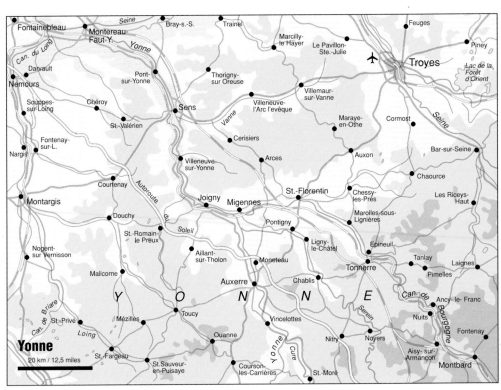

Yonne

20 km / 12,5 miles

museum complex. The building itself is an architectural trail through Sens, with Gothic, Renaissance and classical wings built on Gallo-Roman foundations. The religious and historical collections cover prehistoric times to the present. The siting of exhibits in former dungeons, kitchens and chapels makes an atmospheric whole. The highlights are the Roman mosaics and Le Trésor. Set in a converted chapel, the treasury is the richest collection in France. Byzantine reliquaries vie with Flemish tapestries, altar cloths and ancient silks used to wrap relics.

The cathedral quarter enjoys a market bustle on Mondays and Fridays. Before leaving, wander along the narrow Grande Rue and admire the half-timbered houses between here and Place Victor-Hugo. For a gastronomic feast, try Hôtel du Paris or Le Clos des Jacobins, set in a former monastery. As a Burgundian initiation rite, what could be more apt than garlicky *escargots*, wine-drenched *oeufs en meurette* or *boeuf bourguignon*?

Joigny is a compact medieval town further along the meandering Yonne. Behind the uninspiring riverside rises a golden town covered in jagged brown tiles. Joigny suffered a great fire in 1530 and was rebuilt in stone. The town is full of quiet charms, mostly lurking in tiny squares at the end of steep passageways. A leisurely climb reveals views of the 18th-century stone bridge, an ivy-covered tower, two squat medieval city gates and tumbledown ramparts. Several half-timbered houses escaped the blaze and retain their naive carvings of foliage, grapes and garlands. Joigny offers three Renaissance churches, all rebuilt after the great fire. St-Jean, once the château chapel, has a fine barrel-vaulted nave while St-Thibault presents an equestrian statue of the saint setting off on a hunting trip.

St-André, tucked into the heart of the *vignerons'* quarter, sports a doorway sculpted with vines. The vineyards of Lower Burgundy were ravaged by Phylloxera in the late 19th century and, unlike in the Côte d'Or, the growers here lacked the resources to replant.

However, a revival of the *Vignoble Auxerrois* is underway, beginning with Vin Gris in Joigny. As a gastronomic centre, Joigny boasts À La Côte St-Jacques, one of the finest restaurants in France, which especially prides itself on Burgundian dishes.

Joigny is a traditional Burgundian crossroads: from here, roads lead south to Auxerre, east to châteaux country along the river Armançon, or west to the mysterious Puisaye.

La Puisaye: Despite the fame of Colette, her region remains off the beaten track and singularly unknown. The success of the pottery industry and the cultural events at St-Fargeau have drawn French visitors but few foreigners. Nor are the natives convinced that La Puisaye has a future. On average, the Yonne has fewer than 8 inhabitants per square mile, half that in La Puisaye.

Colette herself did not excel in regional public relations. While *she* loved La Puisaye, "you'll look for it in vain, only seeing a rather sad landscape that casts a shadow over the forests, a quiet

Sens Cathedral sculpture.

COLETTE COUNTRY

Sidonie-Gabrielle Colette (1873–1954), perhaps the 20th century's best-loved French woman writer, spent a magical childhood in a grey stone house in the Rue de l'Hospice in St-Sauveur-en-Puisaye – a house with three small gardens, full of cats, dogs and children. Colette lived here until she was grown up, with her adored mother "Sido" and her father, a former army captain, and she was educated at the local school. Later she moved to Paris, and became known for her very adult and mildly shocking studies of love, jealousy and music-hall life, such as *Chéri* and *Gigi*.

But some of her best work evokes the more innocent world of her Burgundy childhood and that house, which lives on in the pages of two of her most captivating books, *La Maison de Claudine* and *Sido*: "A large solemn house, rather forbidding... that smiled only on its garden side... I shall never be able to conjure up the splendour that adorns, in my memory, the ruddy festoons of an autumn vine borne down by its own

weight and clinging despairingly to some branch of the fir-trees... Both house and garden are living still, I know; but what of that, if the magic has deserted them? If the secret is lost that opened me to a whole world – light, scents, birds, and trees in perfect harmony, the murmur of human voices now silent for ever – a world of which I have ceased to be worthy? It would happen sometimes long ago, when this house and garden harboured a family, that a book lying open on the flagstone of the terrace or on the grass, a skipping-rope twisted like a snake across the path, or perhaps a miniature garden, pebble-edged and planted with decapitated flowers, revealed both the presence of children and their varying ages... it was then, from beneath the ancient iron trellis sagging to the left under the wisteria, that my mother would make her appearance, small and plump in those days when age had not yet wasted her."

These books are above all a portrait of her mother – "the personage who, little by little, has dominated all the rest of my work". From this wise, warm-hearted and unusual woman Colette derived not only her love of animals but her feeling for nature, and her books are full of sensitive descriptions of the rural sounds and smells of her childhood: "No summer, save those of my childhood, enshrines the memory of scarlet geraniums and the glowing spikes of foxgloves. No winter is now ever pure white beneath a sky charged with slate-coloured clouds foretelling a storm of thicker snowflakes yet to come, and thereafter a thaw glittering with a thousand water-drops and bright with spear-shaped buds."

Colette's mother was steeped in country lore, and had remarkable insights into how animals could foretell changes in the climate – a cat digging in its paws tight, or a squirrel hoarding quantities of walnuts and cob-nuts, meant there was going to be a hard winter. Colette's own feeling for animals (especially cats), and her minute observation of their lives, are qualities rare in French literature: Jean Giono and Maurice Genevoix are two of the few French writers who can compare with her in this respect.

And it was a gift that came from her childhood home: "To those who live in the country and use their eyes everything becomes alike miraculous and simple." ∎

The young Colette with cat.

but poor village, a watery valley." Colette's description of her birthplace, **St-Sauveur-en-Puisaye**, is accurate yet tinged with the same quiet charm that pervades the region. At the age of 12 she called herself *la reine de la terre* and later infused her childhood with a sensual nostalgia. Her home remains in Rue Colette, as described in *La Maison de Claudine*. The 17th-century village château now houses a Colette museum, tea-shop and library.

Just outside St-Sauveur, on the road to St-Fargeau, is the **Poterie de la Bâtisse**, which has been running since the 18th century. La Puisaye is justly famous for its simple brown stoneware, called *grès*, and its elegant blue faïence. Just south of St-Sauveur is the **Château de Ratilly**, a chance to glance at a weathered Burgundian château while selecting home-made ceramics. However, the pottery capital is **St-Amand-en-Puisaye**, a quaint village that lives off its ochre-rich clay and where many of its potters are 10th generation. There is a pottery museum in the château.

St-Fargeau, the grandest château in the region, is a reminder that La Puisaye always had more than its fair share of feudal landowners. Anne-Marie-Louise de Montpensier, Louis XIV's cousin, was exiled here in 1652 and recast a feudal hunting lodge as a classical château. The summer *son et lumière* performances are as well-attended as those in the Loire Valley. Nearby is **Guedelon**, an amazing construction site, where a medieval château is being built using only 13th-century materials, methods and equipment.

La Puisaye is a landscape unlike any other in Burgundy: houses made of brick and timber; orchards and meadows bounded by neat hedges; tunnels of greenery; copses of oak and beech; pools and marshes. As well as being home to potters and woodcutters, La Puisaye has sheltered exiles and outsiders, from Jansenist priests to *maquisards*. It is a place of legends: tales of ghostly *dames blanches* and werewolves have not been diluted by an influx of newcomers.

Ratilly Château.

Villiers-St-Benoît has an appealing rural museum representing an 18th-century bourgeois home. In the same village is a Gothic church with a dramatic 15th-century mural, the *Dit des Trois Morts et Trois Vifs*, showing three nobles who encounter three ghoulish spectres while out hunting. **La Ferté-Loupière**, east of Charny, boasts a similar church mural, this time accompanied by a rare *danse macabre*, a cortège of kings and babies, nobles and cardinals, all escorted to eternity by grim skeletons.

The Vanity of Human Wishes need not dissuade one from trying La Puisaye specialities, such as honey and buttercup-yellow goats' cheeses. If you are planning on leaving the region near Briare in the northwest, don't miss **Rogny-les-Sept-Écluses**. There are scenic views of the Canal de Briare's series of seven locks, designed to cope with the falls in water levels on a canal linking the Seine and Loire. This amazing ladder of locks pre-dates Isambard Brunel by 200 years.

Auxerre, unlike much of the Yonne, looks towards Dijon not Paris for its identity. In that sense, it is truly Burgundian, the cultural capital of Basse Bourgogne. The city is pronounced *"Ausserre"* in soft Burgundian tones, a softness in keeping with the view from the Pont Paul-Bert: spires and red-tiled roofs mirrored in the limpid river. As a Gallo-Roman town, Auxerre retains some of its ancient walls. Under St Germain, a 4th-century bishop, Auxerre's spiritual influence radiated throughout Christendom.

Materially, the city owed its wealth to an active port and its prominence on the wine route. After the struggle between Burgundians and Armagnacs, Auxerre joined the French crown in 1477. Peace brought prosperity and renewed church-building. Economic decline was gradual but, in the 19th century, the river lost out to the railways and Auxerre found itself off the main Paris-Lyon trade axis. Auxerre is still an economic backwater, with little industry but a pleasant lifestyle.

La Ferté-Loupière.

144

Recently, however, the well-restored town centre has been pedestrianised, pleasure cruisers have revived the river and the AXA team has brought football fame to the region.

On Rue Joubert is a shabby Renaissance gateway that once signalled an abbey but now introduces the **Église St-Pierre**. The representation of Ceres and other harvest symbols is a reminder that this was the wine-growers' parish. The *vignerons* shared the former church with the monks but, denied the use of the belltower, decided to build a grander church on the same spot. The Gothic tower and Renaissance facades are grimly imposing but the spartan interior is somewhat disappointing. Just around the corner is Église St-Pélerin, containing Auxerre's first church: the chevet and a deep well remain from the 4th-century basilica.

The streets between here and the town centre disclose the city's Roman past. Rue des Boucheries has some remains of Gallo-Roman walls, while Rue Lacurne-Ste-Pallaye is interrupted by an ancient tower. Nearby is the lively heart of Auxerre, **Place Charles-Surugue**, built over the Roman forum. The square has a fountain, half-timbered houses and a jaunty statue of Cadet Roussel, an 18th-century eccentric. He was mocked for "having a home for swallows, a house without rafters or roof". A tiny loggia connected his house to the medieval clocktower around the corner. The **Tour de l'Horloge** remains, with its quaint 15th-century sundial showing the phases of the sun and moon and a Latin motto: "When I die, you die, but in dying, I am reborn."

Place de l'Hôtel de Ville, the other side of the tower, has an imposing classical town hall built on the site of the medieval château. The square is lined with half-timbered houses, all blending brick and beams in a fishbone design. Notice the wizened statue of Marie Noël, a local modern poet whose lyrical *Chansons* were often set to music.

Rue Philibert-Roux has several period mansions including, at number 3, a Renaissance facade topped by gar-

Timber-framed houses, Auxerre.

goyles. On rue d'Egleny is the Musée Leblanc-Duvernoy, with its collection of Beauvais tapestries, faïence and pottery. From here, take Rue Fourier to the Gothic **St-Etienne Cathedral**. Despite the decapitation of statues by the Huguenots, the facade is a delicate Gothic masterpiece. The cathedral's dimensions are not as impressive as Sens but there are compensations. The lightness of the interior is created by an architectural illusion which hides the true function of the support columns. Described as diaphanous, the design gives an impression of grace and weightlessness.

The vivid stained-glass windows, dating from the 13th century, rival those in Chartres and Bourges in their conception and symphony of colours. The high windows in the choir show Christ in majesty, echoing the theme of the frescoes in the barrel-vaulted Romanesque crypt. Denis Grivot, an authority on Burgundian churches, calls these frescoes "an ensemble of unparalleled grandeur". The Christ in majesty is surpassed by an unique fresco of a leader on horseback, attended by angels. Painted in shades of ochre in 1100, the scene has diverse interpretations, a mystery heightened by the penumbra. Once thought to represent the Apocalypse, the fresco is now taken to be the coronation of a Christ-king, a scene inspired by Roman coins.

From the gloom of the crypt, ascend the tower to enjoy a view of steep gabled rooftops and the river. From here, Rue Cochois leads through the riverside quarter to the **Abbaye St-Germain**, a Benedictine abbey with the finest Carolingian crypts outside Poitiers. The abbey was founded in the 6th century to preserve the tomb of St Germain, the bishop who combated heresy in Britain as well as in Gaul. The initial impression is confusing: a sole Romanesque tower standing aloof from a neo-Gothic facade and an archaeological zone. Above ground, the troubled abbey church has a cool Gothic choir, 18th-century cloisters and the newly-discovered tympanum above the north transept. However, the greatest treasure is

Auxerre's pedestrianised place.

146

the series of vaulted underground chapels, containing the most ancient church frescoes ever found in France. Painted in oranges and ochres in 858, they depict the martyrdom of St Stephen. Although naive, the frescoes are painted with vivacity, especially the expressions of hatred and ecstasy. The deepest crypt is a tomb chamber used to conceal St Germain's tomb under mosaics. In this hallowed spot, low barrel-vaulting is supported by Gallo-Roman columns. While the Romanesque church above was pillaged, the double-storey crypts remained intact and, in times of war, sheltered locals. The abbey is now home to a museum complex, covering the archaelogy and history of the region.

Once back in the daylight, take Rue Cochois to the heart of the shipping quarter: Place St-Nicolas is a picturesque square with a medieval fountain. From the river footbridge is a view over the cathedral, with a glimpse of an arcaded Romanesque gallery on the former bishop's palace. Until this century, wines, grain and wood were shipped downriver. South of Auxerre, the Yonne is *l'enfant terrible du Morvan* but is navigable from Auxerre to Paris. In summer, pleasure boats run dinner cruises. Gastronomically, Auxerre is solid rather than spectacular. Le Jardin Gourmand favours such local specialities as *quenelles de truites au Chablis* and *cerises d'Auxerre*, cherry pastries soaked in kirsch. Appropriately enough for the Burgundian heartland, *escargots au chocolat* are common.

River Armançon East: The river rises in the Côte d'Or and winds its way through Burgundy's châteaux country, often entwined with the Canal de Bourgogne. The Armançon's reputation as *mauvaise rivière et bon poisson* is confirmed by the fishermen sitting on the shady banks. St-Florentin and Tonnerre form the Yonne's outer circle; both have a foothold in Champagne and a foothold in traditional Burgundy. Both towns are curious rather than picturesque, and, despite economic blight, are noted gastronomic halts.

St-Florentin, equidistant from Joigny and Auxerre, was a Roman fort, chosen for its hilly site. It has a remarkable church and fine views over the Armançon valley. The church, perched on the hill, is a fusion of late Gothic and early Renaissance. Apart from the rich statuary, the highlights are the windows from the golden age of Troyan glassmaking at the turn of the 16th century.

From here, the scenic Promenade du Prieuré leads up to a grassy square and the remains of a Romanesque abbey and medieval watchtower. Below lie secret passages linking the fortified abbey to the church. From the square are tranquil views over the river, rooftops and flying buttresses encircled by doves. Before leaving, sample St-Florentin and Soumaintrain, the town's reputed cheeses, at La Grande Chaumière.

Tonnerre, a dark stone town, is not immediately appealing but has two unique sights. In the centre of town is the **Ancien Hôpital**, a charitable foundation created by Marguerite de Bourgogne, sister-in-law of St Louis. As Charles d'Anjou's wife, she led a life of luxury in the Loire Valley châteaux yet

Auxerre map — locations shown: to Sens, Joigny; Av. Ch. de Gaulle; R. Faidherbe; Bd. Vauban; Bd. de la Chaînette; St.-Germain; R. de Paris; R. du Lycée (J. Amyot); Pl. St-Germain; Musée Lapidaire; R. Michelet; Rue Française; R. du 4 Septembre; to Aillant; R. d'Egleny; Pl. Robillard; Musée Leblanc-Duvernoy; Pl. L. Bart; St.-Eusèbe; Bd. du 11 Novembre; R. du Temple; R. P. Bert; R. M. des Chesnez; R. Berthelot; R. G. Bénard; R. Briand; Rue d'Eckmühl Davout; R. L. Richard; to Clamecy; Pl. St-Etienne; Cathédrale St.-Etienne; R. Joubert; R. Sous-Murs; R. St-Pelerin; St.-Pierre-en-Vallée; R. du Pont; Boulevard Vaulabelle; Cochois; Quai de la Marine; Yonne; Quai de la République; Q. St-Marien; Rue E. Dolet; Pont de la Tournelle; J. Moreau; Pont J. Moreau; to Tonnerre; to Troyes; **Auxerre** 240 m / 0,15 miles

was also privy to scenes of Sicilian massacres. A widow at the age of 36, Marguerite, Comtesse de Tonnerre, dedicated her life to improving the lot of her subjects. In return, she was buried in the hospital chapel, and a daily Mass was said for her soul until the Revolution. Built in 1293, the hospital is 150 years older than the Hospices de Beaune but lost its glittering tiled roof in the Revolution. The gigantic roof dwarfs the medieval stone building below. Constructed from local oak and Spanish chestnut, the barrel-vaulted ceiling is exactly as it was in Marguerite's day. Her private apartments were reached by a galleried passageway. According to her biographer, she was not above "touching wounds and washing ulcers". However, she had more faith in her cool, spacious barn than in medieval quackery.

For 350 years this hospital healed patients in these alcoves, often stacked six to a pallet. From 1650 the building was used as a church, hence the tombs inside. On one patch of flagging is a

gnomum, an 18th-century sundial designed by an astronomically-minded monk: a hole pierced in the roof lets light through at midday. Before leaving, look at the Mise au Tombeau, a poignant 15th-century *entombement* and masterpiece of Burgundian sculpture. It was commissioned by a rich local merchant and the figure of Nicodemus is not unlike a fat Burgundian *marchand*. The life-sized sculpture was copied from a Mystery play, explaining the realism of the figures and the dramatic intensity of the scene.

Tulip gardens lead to the Église St-Pierre, a Gothic and Renaissance church currently under restoration. On the other side of the hill is Tonnerre's most mysterious sight, the **Fosse Dionne**. An 18th-century *bassin* contains a bubbling blue-green spring, once used as a wash-house. One can see a sharp shelf which disappears into hidden caverns below. Since the 19th century, divers have explored these rocky galleries but deep water, narrow tunnels, strong currents and poor visibility mean that the depths remain unplumbed. Legend has it that a terrifying *serpent basilic* lives at the bottom. With its moss-covered roof and air of abandonment, this secret spring typifies the quaint charm of Tonnerre.

Many shops have been boarded-up since the 1950s, casting gloom on the town. Given Tonnerre's economic depression and elderly population, the locals could do with another Marguerite. Since 1975, Tonnerre has ceased to be a wine-free zone and both white and red grapes have been replanted heralding the revival of the vineyards.

Châteaux country: The Canal de Bourgogne and the River Armançon flow past two of the most sumptuous Renaissance châteaux in Burgundy. The moated **Château de Tanlay** lies slightly east of Tonnerre. It was built in 1553 by Louise de Monmorency, mother of Gaspard de Coligny, the Protestant leader who was murdered in 1572. As a bastion of Protestantism, Tanlay still receives the Dutch royal family, descendants of the de Coligny line. In 1704 Tanlay belonged to the **St-Florentin.**

financier Jean Thévenin, and has been in the same family ever since, currently lived in by another *banquier*, the Comte de la Chauvinière.

A grand gatehouse and bridge guarded by obelisks look across to an Italianate *cour d'honneur*. This was added by Michel Particelli, Cardinal Mazarin's chancellor, as were the classical grounds. Tanlay is a mixture of Renaissance splendour and classical bombast. *Le vestibule des Césars* parades busts of Roman emperors while the upstairs gallery shows a playful *trompe-l'oeil* ceiling, which was inspired by Poussin. Paintings of pastoral scenes are a feature of Tanlay, as are the sculpted Renaissance fireplaces in the bedrooms. *La chambre d'honneur* has a yellow damask canopied bed, which is still employed on visits by the Dutch royal family to their ancestral home. According to the imaginative guide, the shortness of the beds is explained by 18th-century hypochondria: fear of suffocation prompted people to sleep sitting upright.

The quaint corner tower was where the Protestant leaders plotted during the Wars of Religion. A witty frescoed ceiling contrasts the debauched court of Catherine de Médicis with the noble Protestants. In this Olympian allegory, Catherine is an unflattering Juno, elsewhere portrayed as a double-faced sphinx. Diane de Poitiers is a statuesque Venus while naturally the Admiral de Coligny is Neptune. Tanlay's intimate atmosphere springs from such pictorial in-jokes, family portraits and wedding photos. Just outside the château gates is a lively bar, usually full of Pernod-drinking locals discussing the fortunes of the local football team, Auxerre.

Just north of Tanlay are thick woods concealing several minor châteaux in forest clearings. In an isolated spot is the boarded-up **Château de Maulnes**. This solid pentagonal hunting lodge looks more like a medieval castle. It was built in the 16th century by the counts of Tonnerre but was soon abandoned in favour of Ancy-le-Franc. After becoming a glassworks in the 18th century, it

was left to decline until a half-hearted restoration in 1965.

It was this sorry château that inspired the legend of Mélusine, the wicked fairy featured in Jean d'Arras's prose romance and A. S. Byatt's novel *Possession*. Here, the fairy temptress waylaid travellers until she fell unhappily in love and drowned herself in the castle well. Until the 19th century, children threw stones into the well, begging her not to harm them. On moonless nights she is heard to lament her fate: "*Maulnes Maulnes, tant que Maulnes sera, malheureuse serai.*" Since Maulnes may last a little longer, locals hope her spirit may soon rest in peace.

From here, a rural route winds through woodland, hunting estates and sheep farms to **Ancy-le-Franc**, a Renaissance château modelled on an Italian *palazzo*. The Duc de Clermont-Tonnerre wanted it fit for a king: Diane de Poitiers, his sister-in-law, was Henri II's mistress. In 1684 the bankrupt Tonnerre family lost the château to the Comte de Louvois, one of Louis XIV's ministers, but later regained it and kept it until the extinction of the line in 1981. Ironically, the Tonnerre's motto was *Si omnes ego non* (others may abandon you but not I). Ancy is currently owned by an enterprising civil servant who would do well to avoid the Louvois' motto: *Mieux vaut être rompu que plié* (better broken than bent).

This Renaissance château heralds classicism with its restrained, symmetrical forms, its four wings anchored by corner towers. The designs are attributed to Sebastianno Serlio, an Italian architect at the French court. Yet while the cool facade is a magnificent triumph of Corinthian columns, the interior is surprisingly exuberant. Ancy has the most opulent decor in Burgundy, rivalled only by the Château de Bussy-Rabutin. It was probably decorated by Primaticio, a Bolognese artist working at Fontainebleau. It is virtually a royal palace: French kings from Henri II to Louis XIV slept in the gilded *chambre du roi*. The Italian influence prevails in the imperial murals and panelled ceil-

Tanlay Château facade.

150

ings inspired by Pompeian frescoes at the Vatican. From the windows are views of an ornamental pool guarded by two sphinxes. The panelled *chambre des fleurs* is a riot of pansies, roses, tulips and other symbolic flowers. Outside are glimpses of a lakeside folly. Quieter tastes may, however, prefer the green-panelled library with 10,000 ancient volumes.

But for a Burgundian treasure, there is only the chapel, arguably the most authentic Renaissance chapel in France. The life of the apostles, prophets and sibyls appear in 24 *trompe-l'oeil* panels. Above is a soft-hued biblical landscape, reminiscent of Burgundian art in Bruges. Within the grounds there is now a museum of automobiles and horse-drawn carriages. Just south of Ancy-le-Franc is **Nuits-sous-Ravières**, yet another Renaissance château. After a surfeit of châteaux, continue south to the vineyards of the Côte d'Or or return to base at Auxerre.

River Serein South: Just to the north of Auxerre begins the most Burgundian of journeys. The demure River Serein flows past the finest Cistercian abbey in France to the vineyards of Chablis, and leaves the region at Noyers, the Yonne's most authentic medieval town. It is a journey of superlatives: Fontenay may be Burgundy's most complete Cistercian abbey but **Pontigny** is arguably the greatest Cistercian church. In 1114, Stephen Harding, the third abbot of Cîteaux, arrived with St Bernard and 11 monks to found the *deuxième fille de Cîteaux.*

Its location favoured independence, situated on the borders of three counties and three bishoprics. A local adage says that on the bridge at Pontigny, three bishops (of Auxerre, Langres and Sens) and three counts (of Auxerre, Champagne and Tonnerre) could all dine together on home soil. Pontigny used its independence to establish new abbeys and vineyards.

As in Sens, the Canterbury connection looms large. Pontigny forged close links with three English archbishops: Thomas à Becket, Stephen Langton and

Tanlay great hall.

PIERRE LAROUSSE

With sales of just over 1 million copies a year, the Petit Larousse (83,500 entries) is one of the best-selling encyclopaedias in the world, and is to be found in almost every French home. Since it first came out in 1905 it has sold about 25 million copies. Larousse, like Mrs Beeton, is a household name. But the 20th-century version of *Petit Larousse* and its bigger brother, the five-volume *Grand Larousse*, are very different from the extraordinarily idiosyncratic 17-volume, 22,500-page *Grand Dictionnaire Universel du XIXème Siècle* (1866–76) that was largely written by that indefatigable Burgundian, Pierre-Athanase Larousse – "My brain and heart swelling with Burgundian sap," as he put it.

He was the son of a village blacksmith in Toucy in the Yonne. Born in 1817, he showed early promise at school, won a scholarship to the École Normale in Paris and became a teacher. A contemporary remembered him thus: "A short, stocky man with a tawny beard and sparkling eyes,

withdrawn and saturnine, a hard worker who was strongly suspected of harbouring subversive ideas."

By the age of 27 he already had greater ambitions: to become a 19th-century encyclopaedist like Diderot in the 18th. As an admirer of the socialist Proudhon, he wanted "to teach everyone about everything".

Larousse spent several years writing and publishing school textbooks, but still found time to assimilate prodigious amounts of data in public libraries, go to the theatre, write plays, read the literary works of his contemporaries, take notes on the behaviour of his fellow Parisians and even taste unfamiliar dishes, if not test the recipes himself (a task probably carried out by the woman he lived with for 30 years before they married). In 1864, he embarked on his *Grand Dictionnaire*, calling on thousands of contributors (including Jules Vallès, Auguste Vermorel, one of the leaders of the 1871 Paris Commune, and the young Anatole France), but wrote most of it himself. Later editions of the encyclopaedia differ from Larousse's in one major respect: the modern notion of objectivity. One of the joys of dipping into the original work is its Johnsonian idiosyncrasy.

Just as Samuel Johnson defines the word "excise" as "a hateful tax levied upon commodities", so Larousse, after discussing the etymology of a cheese tart called *talmouse* and giving a recipe for it, dismisses it as "an indigestible pastry that could appeal only to unrefined stomachs". He also launches into a lengthy discussion as to whether Cambronne actually uttered his celebrated oath at Waterloo ("*Merde!*"). In the same spirit as the universal exhibitions of the mid-19th century, Larousse firmly and sometimes naively believed in the inexorability of human progress: "Progress is eternal: it pauses, sometimes at a moment of glory, sometimes in the mire, but it never stops."

On his death in 1875, his widow and his nephew, Jules Hollier, completed the publication. Hollier went on to expand the Larousse publishing house and to build the foundations of the present-day corporation. Larousse's ideal of broadcasting the seeds of knowledge to people of all classes was maintained with the motto "*Je sème à tout vent*" (still represented by a dandelion clock on the Larousse logo). ∎

finally St Edmund. Two were exiled here and the third, St Edmund, died nearby. His tomb here still attracts a pilgrimage on 16 November.

Built between 1150 and 1212, Pontigny is Romanesque in design, Cistercian in spirit and Gothic by accident. A line of lindens leads to the sober west porch. Nothing prepares one for the blinding whiteness of the stone inside. The light bleaches out detail and directs the spirit inwards, just as the Cistercians intended. Technically, it is a transitional church. The side aisles and severe transept use Romanesque groined vaulting, as at Vézelay. The elegant choir timidly ushers in the Gothic age. The perspective of the nave is interrupted by church stalls and a baroque choir screen.

Above all, Pontigny is Cistercian. The minimal decoration, mathematical proportions, harmony of mass and line, all induce serenity, not heightened emotions. The retired Curé at Pontigny has firm views on his abbey: "Cistercian abbeys were not made for the public – they were preaching to the converted."

Pontigny, church porch.

Statues, images, colours were all redundant. Religious passion was distilled into prayer. Stark it is, the silent quest for God reduced to the play of light pouring in through tall windows.

A walk in the churchyard allows magnificent views of Pontigny's flying buttresses. Seen from afar, the abbey looks like a great upturned boat adrift in the prairies. Others have compared it to a celestial hovercraft. Sadly, the monastic buildings are now a college so the cloisters, dormitory and abbey farms are out of bounds. It was here that philosopher and pacificist Paul Desjardins founded Décades de Pontigny, a lay monastery for leading intellectuals. For 40 years these encounters drew such diverse spirits as André Gide and Thomas Mann. T.S. Eliot used one visit to seek inspiration for his work *Murder in the Cathedral*.

When not at prayer, the monks fished the rivers for carp and pike, a practice not wasted on the locals today. The sandy banks of the Serein are ideal for picnics. To sample the freshwater fish,

try Le Moulin de Pontigny or a rustic restaurant in neighbouring **Ligny-le-Châtel**. Once there, do not fail to look at the squat Burgundian church with its Renaissance choir.

From Ligny, follow the Serein to **Chablis**, a medieval town snugly nestling in its famous vineyards. A local *vigneron* once punningly pronounced "*À Vézelay, on croit, à Chablis, on a cru*" (Vézelay has faith but Chablis has fine vintages).

Since Roman times, the town has been adept at acquiring special privileges for its vineyards. Chablis has always been rich and even the most modest house exhibits signs of wealth, whether a shadowy Romanesque pillar or a BMW poking out of a solid barn. As a result, the town is only saved from smugness by its tiny scale.

Église St-Martin was founded by monks from Tours in the 11th century. The present Gothic building dates from 1212 and echoes Sens Cathedral but the south doorway is Romanesque, adorned with dove and serpent motifs.

The horse-shoes attached to the south porch were brought by pilgrims en route to Compostela: they implored St Martin to protect their mounts. In medieval times, St Martin, not St Christopher, was the patron saint of travellers. By the chevet is the turreted *Obédiencerie*, an impressive building once owned by the leading monks from Tours.

Clustered behind its medieval town gates, Chablis is a sweet stone town teeming with attractive alleys. Rue des Juifs contains several curious houses, adorned with Romanesque vaults or madonnas in niches. One sculpted Renaissance house is believed to be a former synagogue. Naturally, the creeper-clad wine *domaines* occupy the finest buildings.

Petit Pontigny, in Rue de Chiché, was where the Pontigny monks based their wine estate. These 12th-century stone buildings are now used for the riotous gatherings of the Piliers Chablisiens, the celebrated wine confraternity.

Chablis is the quintessential *vin de luxe* and, as such, restaurateurs feel

Grape-picking in Chablis.

emboldened to over-charge. Even in local bistros, the mark-up is six times the *vigneron*'s retail price. If dinner is still distant, consider Petit Chablis with *gougères*, crusty cheese pastries. At the other end of the scale, a *grand cru* is a perfect *apéritif* in Hostellerie des Clos. This Romanesque Hôtel-Dieu may have lost *dieu* but has kept the hotel and stocked the cellar with 20,000 bottles of Burgundian wines.

This tiny valley is Burgundy's most controversial wine region. Chablis is not only a microclimate but a microcosm of Burgundy's wine trade. Controversy encompasses frost-control methods, the value of oak ageing, the power of the *négociant* houses and fear of foreign competition. The paranoia of Chablis is not unfounded: its fame has long been abused around the world and its name taken in vain.

Chablis is an oddity among Burgundian wines, stranded 100 km (60 miles) northwest of the wine-growing heartland. Cistercian monks at Pontigny first planted Chardonnay on these steep slopes beside the Serein river in the 12th century. The popularity of Chablis soon spread to the royal courts on the Loire and travelled to Bruges with the Burgundian dukes. Its elegance and breeding still make it one of northern Europe's most sought-after *vins de luxe*.

Production and prices depend on the vagaries of the weather – and these are the most difficult wine-growing conditions in France. A cold spring is necessary to produce the wine's acidity but the late frosts of 1957, 1961 and 1991 had a drastic effect on the harvest. This isolated valley attracts pockets of frost as late as May. Still, methods of frost control have improved dramatically since the 1960s. Petrol-soaked torches and oil-burners fight off frost while water-sprinklers spray the vines to give them a protective coating of ice.

Chablis is equally exposed to greedy growers responding to the world thirst for Chardonnay. Chablis *vignerons* fear damage to their *image de marque* as neighbouring wine associations seek to extend the Chablis *appellation*. Local

Sampling Chablis.

growers complained bitterly that Chablis has become a generic term and are outraged that the Americans dare to usurp the Chablis name for their Napa Valley crops.

Local growers have washed their hands of the New World market and now sell mainly to northern Europe. According to *vigneronne* Nicole Adine, Britain leads the Benelux in world demand for Chablis but Italy and Greece are gaining ground. Chablis is an export wine *par excellence*: the French consume only a quarter of the crop. A case of *l'embarras du choix*, perhaps?

The fortune of Chablis is founded on the Chardonnay grape, known locally as Beaunois. The perfect Chablis is described as golden-flecked green, dry, honey-scented, aromatic, with a steely core. It falls into four distinct *appellations*: *petit* Chablis, Chablis, *premier cru* and *grand cru*, grown in a constellation of hamlets around the town. Chablis *premier cru* is produced on the slopes facing east or southeast along the River Serein. Grown in 30 *climats*,

these are the most controversial wines which, depending on taste, can surpass a *grand cru* in sophistication or sink to the blandness of an inferior Chablis.

As for the Chablis *grands crus*, these are grown on the sunny slopes overlooking town. The *domaines*, known as "the magnificent seven", are Blanchot, Bougros, Les Clos, Grenouilles, Les Preuses, Valmur and Vaudésir.

Woodlands and rape fields lead south to **Noyers**, cradled in a bend of the Serein. Noyers is the dreamiest town in northern Burgundy, caught in a medieval time-warp. Its only snag is that this is no secret: classed among *les plus beaux villages de la France*, it is a self-conscious star. The town name comes from walnuts, still common in these parts. In the 15th century the dukes of Burgundy controlled Noyers castle, its hospices and vineyards. Noyers was a border town, dividing the Tonnerrois from the Auxerrois. The approach is charming: an ancient *lavoir* by the river, two pyramids standing sentinel, ramparts and a medieval gateway.

Wood carvings, Noyers; town gate, Noyers.

The streets are as atmospheric as they sound. Place du Marché-au-Blé and Place du Grenier-à-Sel have sloping half-timbered houses and delicate arcades. Petite-Étape-aux-Vins is a tiny square with sculpted facades. Église de Notre-Dame is built in Gothic flamboyant style, with a Renaissance facade. The polished interior looks cosy and well-cared for.

Around every corner are cobbled streets and houses with sculpted Renaissance motifs. Porte Ste-Vérote, a gateway at the end of town, leads out to the fields and quaint wine-growers' cottages. A ruined castle softens up visitors for the inevitable arts and crafts shops. Worth visiting is the Musée d'Art Naïf with its interesting collection.

"From the top of the hill we saw the stone-covered roofs of **Sacy**, a hamlet planted at the meeting of four vales... the landscape inspired such light-headedness that we felt we were the lords of nature." So wrote Réstif de la Bretonne of his home village in 1770. This prolific writer, Jansenist and liber-

tine also set his erotic novels in the Burgundian countryside, and *Le Paysan Perverti*, a cynical portrayal of provincial life, has won him comparisons with Balzac. His birthplace faces the Romanesque church and its octagonal tower. The ivory-hued stone, quarried locally, is the pride of the village. Stretching along a single street are houses enlivened by homely inscriptions carved by *paysans*.

Sacy also has a manor house as well as the Ferme de la Bretonne, an elegant farmhouse on the edge of the village. It once belonged to Réstif but is now owned by another celebrity, travel-writer Jacques Lacarrière. He claims that, apart from television aerials on the barns, Sacy, like its wine, hasn't changed since Réstif's day. In fact, as the grandson of a Burgundian barrel-maker, Réstif de la Bretonne may be best remembered for introducing wine-growing to Sacy. Red and rosé wines are produced, as well as Le Sacy, a dry Sauvignon. However, since the outbreak of Phylloxera in 1905, Frisian

Proud gardener, Noyers.

cattle have reclaimed many of the vineyards. From Sacy, it is a short or long drive back to Auxerre, depending on the appeal of the *route des vignobles*.

The Auxerrois wine route: Until the 19th century, Auxerre was famed for its red wines but le Clos de la Chaînette is the only reminder of the celebrated Côte d'Auxerre. This *domaine*, founded by the monks from St-Germain abbey, made Alexandre Dumas's favourite wines, including one called Migraines. Curiously, the vineyard and *appellation* now belong to the Yonne psychiatric hospital. But the wines below Auxerre could not be in better health. From Vaux to Vermenton, the banks of the river Yonne abound with *dégustation* opportunities. Most of the villages are sweetly set amongst cherry orchards. Several are clustered around Romanesque churches or peer out of medieval fortifications. **Vaux**, a riverside village just south of Auxerre, used to be a wine-growing area but is now awash with fruit. The slopes are covered with apple and cherry orchards. In spring the pastel landscape is an Impressionist's palette, with lilac by the river, cherry blossom overhead, and rape fields edged with bluebells. In passing, notice an elegant manor house and the Romanesque Église St-Loup, topped by a medieval tower. Le Canal du Nivernais flows just beyond the village.

Escolives-Ste-Camille is a wine village beside the Yonne, just south of Vaux. The Romanesque church has a delicate octagonal tower and arcaded porch. Below is a two-storey crypt designed to house the relics of St Camille. The well-restored upper crypt is adorned with early Christian symbolism. The key to the church is with the Borgnats whose wine estate lies down the road. Virtually opposite the church is a typical walled Burgundian farm but the greatest site harks back to earlier civilisations. At the foot of the hill is a rich archaeological zone, with the remains of Gallo-Roman temples, Roman baths and a Merovingian cemetery. Recently, archaeologists have unearthed mosaics and a double-headed Janus, to **Irancy.**

add to the growing collection of sculptures, coins and jewellery. The Gallo-Roman portico is the finest discovery to date, sculpted with mythological scenes. Notice the bas-reliefs depicting grape harvests, a tribute to Escolives' ancient wine roots.

If grape-picking scenes prompt thoughts of wine, combine archaeology and alcohol with a visit to the local *vignerons*. Régine and Gérard Borgnat run their *domaine* from this converted medieval château. They produce reliable rosé and tangy Bourgogne Aligoté in wine cellars which are reputedly the longest in Burgundy. They are also keen amateur archaeologists and the proud possessors of a Gallo-Roman arch. Theirs is a wine marriage made in heaven: his family owned the ancient cellars and hers owned the vineyards.

In **Coulanges-la-Vineuse**, the drunken village next door, wine literally flows like water. When a fire raged here in 1676, the villagers were so short of water that they tackled the blaze with barrels of wine. The ravaged medieval church was replaced by a classical church in the 18th century. In the presbytery is a Flemish *Annunciation*, by Roger van der Weyden. The main street has several fine facades, a sculpted fountain and an old wine-press.

On the other side of the Yonne are equally famous wine villages. The most vinous is the picturesque **St-Bris-le-Vineux**. The Gothic **Église St-Prix** bursts with flying buttresses and Renaissance flourishes. The ornate church contains 16th-century stained-glass windows and a vivid fresco of the Tree of Jesse, painted in 1500. The Renaissance pulpit depicts different natural scenes, from wild boar and snails to corn and wine.

St-Bris is an intriguing blend of styles. Two medieval town gates are all that remain of the ramparts. In the compact centre are Renaissance *hôtels* with mullioned windows, as well as stone-gables, dovecotes and a 17th-century staging post. The post office, once a 12th-century haunt of the Knights Templar, is adorned with a baphomet, a

Wheat fields at harvest.

secret masonic symbol of a head and crescent. Even the classical château has been converted into a combined school and *mairie*.

Running the whole length of the village is a warren of medieval cellars. Given the array of wines and the richness of the vaulting, it is worth returning to the depths.

To disperse the alcohol, one welcome snack is *croquets* – local almond biscuits. Both here and at Irancy, time between wine-tastings can be spent browsing for junk in the *brocante* shops. Just north of St-Bris is **Chitry-le-Fort**, a hamlet with a hulking fortified church, which appears to have been designed for a siege, rather than spiritual peace. Indeed, the hamlet is more riddled with holes than a slice of Gruyère cheese.

Irancy, south of St-Bris, is set in a hollow amongst banks of cherry trees and vineyards. It is the sweetest, most traditional wine-growing village, perfectly captured in the watercolours of Georges Hosotte, a local artist. Over-

looking a cherry orchard is the Église St-Germain, a Gothic church with delicate Renaissance buttresses and a square belfry surmounted by *griffons*. Encircling the church are typical *vignerons'* houses with their characteristic outside staircases.

In medieval times, Irancy was guarded by four gateways but this harshness has given way to Renaissance ease. The main street has a shuttered 16th-century mansion that was the birthplace of Soufflot, the neoclassical architect who has left such a heavy imprint on Paris. On neighbouring facades are opulent Renaissance details, from turrets and mullioned windows to sundials and stone inscriptions. Down below are fossil-encrusted cellars, a reminder that Irancy is home to 25 wine-growing families.

Between Irancy and **Cravant** stretch views of vineyards and valleys framed by cowslips and wild orchids, a fitting end to the wine trail.

River Yonne to the Morvan: Cravant is a crossroads, situated at the meeting of rivers Yonne and Cure. From here one can fork east, following the River Cure to Vézelay or fork west, tracing the Yonne to its wild mountain source in the Morvan. From Cravant to Clamecy, the Yonne is a fast-flowing stream cutting south through woods and valleys. The landscape is as dramatic as any in Burgundy, throwing up sheer cliffs in the face of narrow valleys. Until the 20th century, the Yonne, like the Cure, was used as a route for transporting firewood and wine to Paris. Nowadays, the region provides a healthy break from wine-tasting. Instead, it is a backdrop for boat trips, wooded walks and rock-climbing.

In **Cravant**, the tumbledown towers and medieval gates recall a decisive battle fought in 1423. The Burgundian and English armies finally overcame the French and Scottish forces, leaving the region outside French control for years to come. Today, the fortifications are landscaped gardens but the ramparts remain by Promenade St-Jean. A watchtower guards a sturdy Gothic church: three 15th-century naves and

Rock-climbing, Saussois.

stained-glass windows accommodate an airy Renaissance choir and square belfry. A walk through the narrow alleys reveals medieval houses, a stone manor and a well-preserved *lavoir*.

Mailly-le-Château, many bends south, commands a dramatic loop in the river. The château, built on a rocky escarpment, belonged to the three Mailly sisters who were all Louis XV's mistresses. Set amongst chestnut trees, the picturesque village has a cluster of medieval houses, a Gothic church and attractive views of the river and Canal du Nivernais. From here, cross the 15th-century bridge over the river and, shortly after a canal bridge, **les Rochers du Saussois** loom ahead. These sheer cliffs are often used for rock-climbing.

A little further upriver is **Châtel-Censoir**, a walled medieval village perched on a hill. On the summit is a fortified church beside a ruined château. The church is unusual in combining Romanesque and Renaissance styles without any intervening Gothic. After a fire in 1460, the nave and door-ways were rebuilt in elaborate Renaissance style by Italian craftsmen. The choir is Romanesque, with sculpted capitals representing fire-breathing mythological beasts. Under the church is an austere Merovingian crypt.

On the other bank, just before Clamecy, are yet more cliffs and a charming 16th-century church at **Surgy**. Clamecy itself is a depressing but untypical gateway to the rugged Morvan.

From Surgy, it is well worth making a short detour west to **Druyes-les-Belles-Fontaines**, some of the region's most dramatic ruins. Perched on a bluff, this 12th-century castle once belonged to the counts of Auxerre and Nevers. Comte Philiphe de Courtenay, Emperor of Constantinople, somehow ran his empire from here in the 13th century. A formidable barbican leads to the lower courtyard, now lined by stone cottages. Once through to the roofless keep, there is little to see but the site itself is nevertheless very atmospheric.

At the foot of the hill is **St-Romain**, a harmonious Romanesque church, lying

Barging at Mailly-le-Censoir.

close to Druyes' famed springs and grottoes. From outside, the church chevet resembles a nest of honeycomb domes. Inside, the highlights are the broken barrel-vaulted nave and the carved capitals depicting fighting dragons and devils.

River Cure to Vézelay: This route is not what it seems; the natural landscape conceals a bizarre underworld. Just south of Cravant, vines give way to wooded slopes, heralding the Morvan. The Cure is a brisk mountain stream with weirs that once helped control the Paris firewood supply. **Vermenton**, like Clamecy, is an erstwhile port reduced to green tourism. At the heart of the village is a medieval watchtower and a cluster of 16th-century houses. In the centre is the moss-covered church, with a slender Romanesque tower and a doorway framed by columns of statues. The church is in transitional Romanesque Gothic style with ribbed vaulting, a feature common to churches in the Île-de-France, as is the colonnaded tabernacle below the northwest spire.

From Vermenton to Vézelay, the Cure is a fast-flowing trout stream, often disappearing underground. Across the Yonne from Vermenton is **Reigny**, a ruined Cistercian abbey built beside the River Cure. Now converted into a private home, the scriptorium and luminous Gothic refectory remain, with elegant vaulting supported by slender columns. The dovecote and abbot's house overlook a peaceful scene of grazing Charolais cattle. Just upstream, the mystery begins.

Arcy-sur-Cure's fantastic caves are embedded in limestone cliffs. These caves were discovered in 1666 but have been inhabited periodically since prehistoric times. Buffon, the 18th-century naturalist, regularly came to sketch the animal designs. Over half a mile of galleries can be visited, spanning natural formations and rock carvings. The colours are dramatic, ranging from an emerald green lake to curtains of gold and silver rock. Other chambers contain carvings of mammoths, bison and pilgrimage symbols.

A riverside walk passes caves not yet open to the public, including ones decorated with sculptures of hyenas, bears and wolves. Adjoining galleries contain a medieval burial chamber full of sarcophagi. Just off the shady paths are opportunities for picking strawberries, mushrooms and nuts.

The neighbouring **Manoir de Chastenay** is almost as bizarre as the caves. The Renaissance manor once belonged to the Knights Templar and was a pilgrims' halt on the way to Compostela. As a result, it is adorned with symbols of competing philosophies, from Christian faith to Renaissance mythology and masonic ritual. On the sculpted facade are Santiago cockleshells, a philosopher's stone and a vanitas. The owner delights in explaining this esoteric cocktail of alchemy, numerology and the scriptures. He shows how the medieval mind used divine numbers to unlock the universe. In short, this cryptic visit is reminiscent of a film by Michel Devile or Peter Greenaway. If feeling out of your depth, remember that mystic Vézelay is only a heartbeat away.

Left, St-Germain, Auxerre. **Right**, swan at Tanlay.

THE HEARTLAND

The heartland encapsulates the essence of Burgundy. The region overlaps the Côte d'Or and the Yonne, bordering the great vineyards of the south and the watery landscape of the north. Its châteaux and wines may look like pale imitations but in other respects it rivals or surpasses its neighbours.

The region traces the history of Burgundy, from the Gallo-Roman site at Alésia to the walled medieval town of Avallon. The Forges de Buffon introduce the region's seminal role in the Industrial Revolution while cosy Semur-en-Auxois shows how Burgundy copes with post-industrial society: sleepily.

Sophistication on a small scale is the flavour of the region. Its muted charms have made it the natural home of painters, writers and priests. Flavigny-sur-Ozerain is a tiny village bursting with art galleries, seminaries and celebrity authors in hiding. Not that the region shies away from dramatic set-pieces. The heartland is home to two of the greatest Romanesque treasures in France: the Cistercian abbey of Fontenay and the basilique in Vézelay. Cluny may be a mere shell but Vézelay is the mystic heart of Burgundy.

Perched on a wooded hilltop, **Vézelay** has the allure and self-sufficiency of a Tuscan town. It also has a tradition of painters and mystics that would be equally at home in Siena.

The link is not so spurious as it seems: St Bernard, the Burgundian saint, was equally adored in Siena and his homeland. It was on Vézelay's hillside that he preached the second crusade in 1146. Richard the Lionheart and Philippe Auguste, King of France, followed in his footsteps, inaugurating the third crusade from this spot.

The presence of Mary Magdalene's supposed relics in the basilica made Vézelay a place of pilgrimage. Here, too, Thomas à Becket excommunicated the absent Henry II, King of England. A winding road climbs to the **Basilique**

Ste-Madeleine, a spiritual journey. Medieval pilgrims would have felt a symbolic lifting of the veils, from the uphill toil to the passage from darkness into light. Clustered in the shadowy penumbra of the narthex, medieval pilgrims could ponder the mysteries of the tympanum before flooding into the uplifting nave and rejoicing in the luminous choir. Then as now, the path is crowded, the pilgrims hushed and scepticism suspended. According to the friars who run La Madeleine, the church is designed to be at its most majestic at summer solstice: on 24 June, a funnel of light appears to emanate from the ancient crypt containing Mary Magdalene's relics, acknowleged as genuine by the Pope in 1058.

Vézelay has had many incarnations, first as a 9th-century nunnery founded by Girart de Roussillon at the foot of the hill. It became a monastery in 873 but a Norman attack forced the Benedictines to flee to the safety of the hilltop in 887. Their new foundation was twice destroyed by fire but the present Cluniac

Preceding pages: wheat fields; Semur-en-Auxois. **Left,** *en famille en bicyclette,* Vézelay. **Right,** Vézelay, Ste-Madeleine interior.

basilica dates from 1106. The ochre-tinged basilica is an imposing sight, its groined vaulting and high windows embodying the daring of Burgundian Romanesque builders.

In 1295 the Pope declared that Mary Magdalene's relics had never left Provence. Vézelay's credibility was destroyed and decadence set in. The church was allowed to decline and in 1834 Prosper Mérimée reported a sodden nave overgrown with shrubbery. After his advice, La Madeleine was saved from ruin by Viollet-le-Duc. For good measure, Mary Magdalene's relics were placed in Vézelay's Carolingian crypt in 1876. Curiously, Vézelay has no depictions of the saint.

To the medieval mind, the narthex was Galilee and the choir Jerusalem, a passage from witness to transcendence. The doorway from the narthex into the nave is adorned with the most accomplished **tympanum** in France. An ethereal Christ floats in swirling drapery; around him are the converted and unconverted, a fabulous universe em-

bracing the bewildered apostles, peasants, hunters, giants, pygmies and pig-snouted heathens. Such animation can blind one to the individuality of the Burgundian statuary all around.

The obscurity of the narthex gives way to the joyous nave, an ochre and cream concoction seemingly liberated from earthly constraints. It, in turn, is outshone by an early Gothic choir, radiating a shell-like translucence. Tournus may feel virginal, Fontenay pure, Autun subtle and Paray-le-Monial graceful. Yet of all Burgundy's Romanesque churches, none is as unselfconscious as Vézelay, as fluent in its mastery of spirit and form.

As at Autun Cathedral, the sculpted capitals reach supreme heights but the dense symbolism can be confusing to modern minds. There are more than 100 of them, on a wide variety of subjects. The *Moulin Mystique* capital shows Moses pouring grain (Old Testament law) through a mill (Christ) while the ground flour (New Testament) is gathered by St Paul. This Bible in stone also

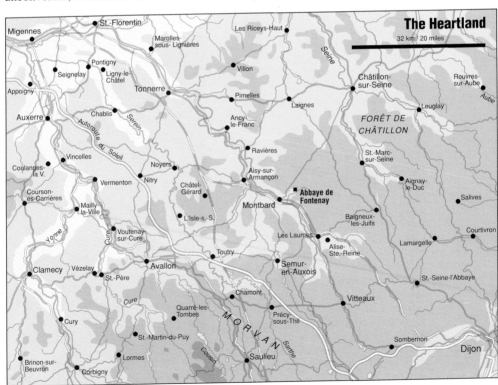

170

presented humanity with moral tales and vivid depictions of greed, despair and lust. *Le Péché Originel* shows an uninhibited Eve passing an apple to a coy Adam. *La Musique Profane*, like several capitals in Cluny, warns against the corrupting influence of dancing.

The town: Vézelay, like the church capitals, is not afraid of earthiness. Rue du Tripot is named after the brothels that once accommodated tired pilgrims. La Grande Rue also shows that the citizens were human: virtually all these medieval houses have vaulted Romanesque wine cellars. The loveliest lie under the Hôtel de Ville, along with two medieval wine presses. The city vines were wiped out by Phylloxera but have recently been replanted. Despite the reputation of *la colline éternelle*, the wines are abysmal.

Opposite the town hall is the turreted Tour Gaillon, a Renaissance *hôtel* in both senses of the word. In the same street are a cluster of historic buildings, including a deconsecrated church and former convents. Rue St-Étienne boasts two 16th-century houses, one of them lived in by Calvin's moderate successor, Théodore de Bèze, who apparently had his Calvinism softened by his Catholic upbringing here.

The ramparts walk is conducive to contemplation. From the wisteria-hung walls are views of woods and vineyards. In keeping with the painterly landscape, Vézelay has a profusion of antique shops, galleries and silk-screen designers. In summer, Vézelay can be unrelenting. The town teems with Danish pastors, Swiss priests *manqués* and *soixante-huitards* in search of New Age philosophies. For religious sceptics, the earthy bars on Champ de Foire, symbolically outside the city walls, provide relief from an overdose of mysticism. For visitors who insist on closeness to La Madeleine, there is Le Pontot, a sumptuous mansion hotel built over well-stocked Romanesque cellars.

Yet, at heart, Vézelay's air of mysticism is not misplaced. Esoteric bookshops specialise in astrology while restaurants dabble in food cults. Even the

Nuns in Vézelay.

dissolute Serge Gainsbourg was affected by the atmosphere. When visiting Vézelay shortly before his death in 1991, he resisted entreaties to enter the basilique. Pressed for a reason, the legendary singer-songwriter merely said, "I am unworthy." Vézelay is suffused with a spirituality that subdues unbelievers. It has long seen itself as a bastion against hostile elements, whether these be heathens or the wilderness below.

While living on the edge of the rugged Morvan, the sophisticated city-dwellers claim it has "*rien à voir avec nous*". In some ways they are right: the Morvan's farming culture is alien to artistic Vézelay; the Morvan has no vineyards yet Vézelay clings to the remnants of its wine-growing industry; the Morvan's low-roofed cottages cannot compete with Vézelay's elegant mansions; even the city's climate is 5°C (41°F) warmer than outside.

At the foot of the hill is **St-Père**, a village in Vézelay's shadow. It was not always so: a Gallo-Roman site once commanded this stretch of the River Cure. The archaeological ornaments on display in the local museum include a Celtic bronze panther and a marble Venus. However, the most curious exhibit is an Iron Age catchment well, made from a hollow oak trunk. Beside the museum is an exuberant Gothic church, studded with cherubs and capped with pinnacles. Although built in 1290, the belltower feels flamboyant, with its riotous decoration of griffin gargoyles and triumphant angels.

As the exterior is restored, the creamy white stone dazzles. The facade depicts the Last Judgement, a reminder that this was built as a funerary chapel for rich benefactors. The church is still noted for its charitable works and carries an inscription saying: "spiritual riches need no material domain." By contrast with the overpowering facade, the sober interior embodies Burgundian Gothic style, with a luminous nave and austere tombs. The restraint is breached only by lively sculpted capitals, one depicting a negroid head.

The pilgrims' route, Vézelay; Vézelay's mystic golden glow.

172

From here, follow the *"sabotier"* signs to the workshop belonging to Romain Doré, one of the last clog-makers and wood sculptors in the region. Watching him carve a boar's head or wooden goblet may generate an appetite for lunch in L'Espérance, one of the finest restaurants in France. François Mitterrand and Jacques Delors are regular guests at this riverside mill. But villagers are blasé about "folk who arrive in helicopters for lunch". Marc Meneau's restaurant is noted for its *foie gras* and roast turbot with *feuilleté de fromages*. An effusive host and a cellar of Bourgogne and brandies confirm its appeal to French celebrities.

It was here that Serge Gainsbourg chose to live the last winter of his life, well away from Parisian debaucheries. According to Marc Meneau, he spent his days composing and his nights propped up against the bar. Unsuspecting diners were delighted by Gainsbourg's spontaneous performances at the piano, accompanied by his tiny dancing daughter, Bambou.

St-Père borders **Fontaines-Salées**, a sacred Celtic settlement which sprang up around magical springs. This wheel-shaped sanctuary was dedicated to the sun god, Taranis. Within the hallowed site, circular baths and temples were used for druid worship. The Romans had a more pedestrian approach, adding conventional baths. The salty, radioactive water was thought to have curative powers, and to be particularly beneficial for arthritis and poor libido.

In medieval times the springs were celebrated in the epic *chansons de geste*. These minstrels' songs encouraged pilgrimages, thus paving the path to sacred Vézelay. The salty springs were only abandoned in the 15th-century. The Gallo-Roman site can still be visited but its obvious finds lurk in St-Père's dingy museum. Delicate amulets, brooches and hairpins were unearthed in the women's baths. Sadly, the museum spirit is more redolent of arthritic Rome than mysterious Gaul.

South of St-Père is **Pierre-Perthuis**, a scenic hamlet with a ruined castle built on a rocky escarpment. Stone bridges span the gorge and the River Cure; in the distance are misty views of Vézelay. Bringing one back to earth are signs for honey and locally quarried minerals. Between here and Avallon is a lush valley carved by the River Cousin. This is rich farmland with grazing for sheep and Charolais cattle. Bordering the river are old washhouses and dreamy watermills, often turned into inviting inns. Since the valley is only two hours from Paris, these manors and mills are fast becoming *résidences secondaires*.

Like the Haut-Châtillonais, this region was once the haunt of the Knights Templar. Their austere *commanderies* guarded the Burgundian borders and pilgrim routes. Humble Templar churches half-heartedly addressed the Gothic revolution that was enveloping northern Burgundy. Compared with the Haut-Châtillonais, however, fewer Templar lodges remain. Even so, Saulce has a sturdy 13th-century chapel, which is the remains of a Templar guard post. In the neighbouring hamlets of Island and Menades,

Bridge at Pierre-Perthuis.

Gothic verticality and bourgeois manors reign together triumphant.

Pontaubert is a welcome return to Burgundian Romanesque. This squat church, once linked to a *commanderie* and hospital, also reflects the Templars' preference for Romanesque. The tiered tower may be Gothic but the tympanum, sculpted capitals and the groined vaulting in the nave reflect an earlier sensibility. Before leaving, notice the medieval polychrome statues of the Virgin and St John.

Like many of the bridges over the Cousin, the village bridge was first built by the Templars. Between here and **Vault-de-Lugny**, the Cousin is a fast-flowing mountain river, popular with trout fishermen. Vault-de-Lugny has a moated medieval château and a 15th-century church with striking frescoes. This 16th-century series represents the Passion: chaotic but artful scenes cover the wide nave and choir. From here, follow the river to Avallon, calling at the romantic Moulin des Ruats for a trout-inspired dinner.

Avallon is twinned with Tenterden in Kent, a similar gentrified market town. But the lofty location and the impressive ramparts are Burgundian enough. Avallon is perched between two ravines and its prominent site has been fortified since Charlemagne's time. The town has a turbulent history, fought over by the early French kings and the dukes of Burgundy. It was occupied by the English in the Hundred Years' War and pillaged in the Wars of Religion.

A walk along the ramparts gives a sense of Avallon's strategic importance. Although several towers have been razed, most of the bastion remains. In between turrets are plunging views over the rooftops and church to the Cousin Valley. (Walking itineraries are available from the tourist office.)

Église St-Lazare was rebuilt in Burgundian Romanesque style, shortly after Vézelay. Intended to house the relics of Lazarus, the church retains its original Carolingian crypt. But the interest centres on the facade. A tower collapsed in 1633, destroying one door-

Avallon rooftops.

174

way but the remaining two are as exuberantly sculpted as any in Burgundy. Despite a battered tympanum, the large doorway reveals the signs of the Zodiac, the labours of the month and musicians of the Apocalypse. The smaller one is lovely, interweaving flowers and foliage in stylised patterns. The sober interior echoes the vegetal theme in its foliated capitals. A Cluniac nave, groined vaulting and a semi-domed apse are enlivened by polychrome statues.

Despite its fraught history, Avallon is almost too calm. A charming clocktower straddles the narrow Grande Rue. Beside it is the 17th-century Couvent des Ursulines. Rue Masquée, off the Grande Rue, is lined with medieval houses and leads to the fine 17th-century Maison du Prévôt.

Beyond these quaint, cobbled alleys, this is a pragmatic city. The 17th-century Couvent aux Capucins is now a cinema. The local *tribunal* has moved into the ducal castle; the great hall is now the courtroom while the vaulted cellars below are used for receptions.

The most atmospheric spot in town is the Hôtel des Sires de Domecy. The delicate turret over the stairwell and entrance is peculiar to Burgundy.

Parc des Chaumes, just outside town, affords views of Avallon's terraced gardens, ramparts and rooftops. From here, a circuitous route leads east to Semur-en-Auxois.

Close to Avallon is St-Jean-des-Bonhommes, a ruined 12th-century priory with a delicate chapel and refectory. The priory depended on the neighbouring village of **Montréal**. As the name implies, this village has a royal past, dating back to Queen Brunéhaut, regent of Burgundy. The walls of her 7th-century *Mons Regalis* have been incorporated into medieval houses. The village prospered under the Burgundian dukes and acquired the artistic reputation it retains today.

The delightful **church** was finished in 1170 and feels early Gothic with its rose windows and ribbed vaulting. However, pointed Romanesque lancets and delicate capitals reveal that this is a

Avallon, gateway and belltower; fine carving, Église St-Lazare.

transitional work. The naive alabaster altar-piece is thought to have been carved by a Nottingham soldier left behind after the Hundred Years' War. But the highlights are the 16th-century choir stalls, made by the local Frères Rigolley. The misericords are a masterpiece of Burgundian wood-carving. Rough scenes from peasant life are mixed with biblical stories.

From the churchyard are panoramic views over the Serein Valley and the distant mountains of the Morvan. Severe gateways mark the upper and lower entrances to Montréal but the lofty stone village spills out of its medieval towers. High-walled houses sprout turrets and mullioned windows. The stone is softened by creeper-covered walls and neat flower beds. In this well-tended village even the Romanesque priory has been turned into a cosy old people's home.

For similar sights, visit **Île-sur-Serein**, a picturesque riverside village just north of Montréal. Well-restored Renaissance houses, a ruined castle, a

medieval church and a former priory provide an attractive setting. Following the River Serein north is the most Burgundian of journeys, but for a direct route to Semur-en-Auxois, follow the D954 through rich farmland. Spare a glance for Savigny-en-Terre-Plaine, an exquisite Romanesque church perched on a windy hill.

Époisses, to the east, is the most welcoming of the châteaux in the Auxois region. The harmonious village nestles amid sloping Burgundian roofs and mellow stonework, its 17th-century houses decorated with elaborate chimney pots and sculpted doorways. The château lies beyond the *basse-cour*, virtually a medieval village in itself. As well as farm buildings and a 13th-century church, there is a dovecote with room for 3,000 doves, a sign of the importance of the feudal estate. Originally a ducal residence, this moated 15th-century château has belonged to the Guitaut family since 1672. The early fortifications remain but several wings were destroyed in the Revolution.

Herding cattle.

A drawbridge leads to the *cour d'honneur* and a well which is decorated with delicate ironwork produced in an early foundry nearby. The château blends medieval towers with Renaissance mullioned windows; rose-coloured roofs are matched by warm stone walls. Inside, a gallery displays portraits of the last four dukes of Burgundy. However, the prevailing spirit is of Madame de Sévigné, a regular 17th-century visitor. Her portrait overlooks a four-poster bed while the library contains her letters. Small wonder that the sparkling marquise preferred this appealing château to dilapidated Bourbilly, her ancestral home nearby.

To the French, however, Époisses means cheese: the local *fromagerie* is the fitting place to sample Burgundy's most famous cheese. Invented by 15th-century Cistercian monks, it is now made by the Berthaut family. Époisses regularly wins the gold medal for traditional cheese at the Concours Agricole de Paris. This creamy cheese requires 2 litres (half a gallon) of milk and is dipped in *marc de Bourgogne* every day for two months. The result is a smoky cheese with the texture of old Burgundian pottery. Époisses, best with a glass of Savigny-lès-Beaune, can also be sampled at the local café.

Château de Bourbilly, just south of the village, was once a fief of Époisses. Set in a clearing, the small white château is surrounded by inquisitive Charolais cattle. In Madame de Sévigné's day, Bourbilly was an austere feudal castle, reflecting the personality of Jeanne de Chantal, her saintly grandmother. Jeanne founded the Order of the Visitation and created 80 convents all over Europe. The château today is a charming pastiche, restored in romantic style in Napoleon III's time. The facade is topped by pepperpot towers and mock-medieval crenellations. Madame Darcy, the *châtelaine*, blames the British: an earlier Darcy fell under the spell of Victoriana and, along with the pepperpot towers, added a "Gothick" library. The chapel is charming, however, decorated with frescoes by a monk

Époisses Château.

from La-Pierre-Qui-Vire monastery. From here, it is a short drive north to **Semur-en-Auxois** and the farmland Madame de Sévigné called "a delicious valley". In its own charming way, Semur remains delicious and is an ideal base, an historic centre enclosed by snug walls. During the Wars of Religion, this military stronghold became the home of the Burgundian Parliament. In 1941 Semur was a symbol of Resistance, led by Maire Morlevat. The initial sighting of the town, glimpsed from Pont Joly, is of a turreted bastion perched on a rocky spur above the River Armançon. Semur is stacked around the four towers of its castle keep and merges into the rose-coloured rock.

Porte Guillier, a medieval gateway, leads through the pedestrianised centre to a square lined by half-timbered houses and **Église Notre-Dame**. This priory church depended on the abbey at Flavigny. Dating from 1218, the eclectic church offends purists but delights others. The north portal bears a tympanum with the legend of St Thomas and, beside it, two snails symbolise the region. The interior borrows freely from Burgundian Gothic churches. A narrow nave and spindly capitals emphasise the height of the vaulting. Yet the mood is intimate, from the piped music to the slender nave bathed in light. It is a church one could almost live in.

Much of the statuary is being restored but a faded polychrome Entombment has the expressiveness of Claus Sluter's work. The medieval panelled windows represent local guilds: in one, a butcher is poised to slaughter a cow; in another, drapers are busy weaving Semur's fortune in cloth. Outside are imposing flying buttresses and devilish gargoyles. The church cloisters have been absorbed by the Hôtel de Ville.

The **ramparts walk** is, unlike Avallon's, a rural experience, encompassing former convents, mills and tanneries. Rue du Rempart winds past towers, including Tour de l'Orle d'Or. Named after its glinting roof, this was the entrance to the town, prior to the building of Pont Joly. From the walled

Fête de la Bague, Semur-en-Auxois.

Place de Montbeillard, Rue Basse follows the river's loops to the weir at Quai d'Armançon. The pink-tinged ramparts are overgrown with heather, broom and climbing plants. The scene is completed by a tiny island, mills and terraced gardens, gradually rolling into open countryside. Soon after the Pont Pinard, Escalier du Fourneau climbs steeply back to the high town and a cluster of friendly bars.

Semur does not rest on its laurels. The main museum, housed in a former convent, has illuminated manuscripts and Burgundian paintings. The *Fête de la Bague* is the French equivalent to the Italian *Palio*. Held on 31 May, the oldest horse race in France has been run since 1639. The victor receives a gold ring engraved with the arms of the town. In summer, Semur presents ballets, concerts and opera, an appropriate range for a town with a *conservatoire* and an accordion industry. With its period lanterns and alleys hung with flower baskets, Semur narrowly escapes tweeness. But the warmth of local hospitality

Fête de la Bague is the oldest horse race in France.

dispels any doubts. In the words of Sebastien Munster, a 16th-century visitor, the citizens are *"paisibles, doux, débonnaires et charitables"*.

From Semur, a country drive leads to Montbard via the **Château de Lantilly**. It is called *le château aux cent fenêtres* because of its profusion of windows. Although originally medieval, the château is largely classical. Lantilly enjoys sweeping views across the Brenne Valley to Mont Auxois. The location is perfect for the summer concerts and exhibitions hosted by the cultured owners.

Montbard, north of Semur, is marked by economic rise and fall. The presence of forests, rivers and a canal made Montbard a natural candidate for industrialisation. However, its success was entirely due to the local Comte de Buffon. The multifaceted count was a royal gardener, botanist, scientist and industrialist. In essence, he was a product of the Enlightenment, with an encyclopaedic knowledge of the sciences and a belief in progress. In Montbard he

BALLOONING

On 21 November 1783 two men were frantically stuffing straw and twigs into a brazier. Their work was vital: the fire *had* to be kept hot; if there were any let-up, disaster might result. One man took a moment from his labours to gaze below; this made his co-worker slightly nervous, and he remonstrated with his friend: "If you look at the river in that fashion you will be likely to bathe in it soon."

Pilatre de Rozier and the Marquis d'Arlandes were making the first manned hot-air balloon flight. Paris, the River Seine and the King and Queen of France, Louis XVI and Marie Antoinette, were below, and this historic flight lasted less than half an hour. Afterwards, the Queen is supposed to have gushed: "It is the sport of the gods!"

The means of ascent that afternoon was a 24-metre (78-ft) high, blue and gold coloured linen-and-rag "balloon" (or "envelope") called a Montgolfière after its inventors, the Montgolfier brothers. Raised by heated air ("fire balloon" was the original name), the earliest models were always in danger of catching fire even before the flight started. Inflation was by hanging the envelope between two poles and building a fire underneath, then achieving the exact mixture of hot-air exhaust and flame height.

The first balloons were almost round with a hole in the bottom. Netting surrounded the balloon both for stability and to hold the attachment lines which kept balloon and basket tethered to one another. Despite technical advances, all flights still begin in much the same manner; the balloon is spread flat on the ground, with the open end nearest the basket, which has several tanks of fuel and a propane burner in it. The basket is tipped on its side with the burner pointing toward the open end of the balloon, and the steel cables at the base of the balloon are attached to the basket supports.

Two people are stationed at the mouth of the balloon to hold it open, with one or two others at the top end. A large fan is set up to blow the heated air into the balloon. The pilot pulls the burner release, and a "whooooooosh" emits from the small black flame-thrower. Nothing seems to be happening, even when the process is repeated several times. But then, magically, the silk-like fabric takes on a life of its own. In undulating waves, it rises and falls, all the while expanding. As the balloon inflates, those anchoring the top-end leads begin to loosen their grip and allow it to rise. This brings the basket upright, and after a few more flame spurts, all is ready.

As the balloon slowly rises, panic subsides, and in exchange comes a feeling of elation and freedom. Except for the occasional bursts of burner flame, and the quiet comments of the pilot, it is a silent world. There is no feeling of an air current because the balloon is going with it. Flight speed and direction are at the wind's pleasure, although by combining burner blasts with manipulations of the balloon's turning vents, the pilot can make the balloon revolve at will. Altitudes will vary from a few feet to several thousand, depending upon passenger requests and wind conditions. A traditional champagne toast follows the flight, since in the early days pilots carried bottles of champagne to placate angry farmers whose crops might be ruined by visitors arriving unexpectedly from the sky. ∎

fostered a metal industry that still survives today.

Landscaped over a ruined château, **Parc Buffon** was laid out by Buffon and remains a tribute to Montbard's greatest son. Bordering the park is Buffon's study, set in a romantic medieval tower. Buffon lived by the belief that "*Il ne faut que du temps pour tout savoir*". Since then, however, ailing components factories have cast a shadow over his legacy. Nowadays, despite the presence of the TGV, Montbard has scant faith in progress. Despite the park, canal views and a cluster of old houses in the town centre, there is little to detain the visitor apart from the local cuisine.

Just downriver is the finest monument to Buffon, **La Grande Forge**. Like all early Burgundian foundries, it required a watery site and massive amounts of wood. Built in 1768, this was one of the biggest French foundries of its day. Until 1866 it produced tools and weapons, including cannon used to attack the British in the Napoleonic wars. Buffon's ironworks were rendered obsolete by the triumph of *forges à l'anglaise*, coke-fired furnaces. The ironworks became a cement factory until 1945 but Buffon's creation has been lovingly restored by Taylor Whitehead and his French wife.

To the modern eye, this industrial complex is delightfully rural. Buffon's main residence was in Paris but his *pied à terre* in Burgundy includes all that a country gentleman would expect: a classical manor, chapel, dovecote and orangerie. As a naturalist, Buffon also installed an aviary and zoo to aid his research on the classification of species. Buffon, like most foundry masters, lived beside his workforce but the master's and minions' accommodation naturally differed.

Four hundred privileged workers lived on-site while the foundry's woodcutters and labourers had to fend for themselves. These spartan 18th-century dwellings represented the model housing of the day. Several workers' cottages remain and, despite being occupied by farmers until recently, are fur-

Buffon forge.

nished much as they were in Buffon's time. The foundry itself is the star exhibit, the showcase of the early Burgundian iron industry. Although later eclipsed by Le Creusot steelworks, the 18th century belonged to northern Burgundy. The visit is enlivened by working models and a witty commentary. The blackened brick chimneys of the blast furnace are real enough, as are the water-driven bellows and the rushing mill-race. In the metal finishing workshop the sounds and processes are recreated; only the heat is missing. Given the plans to turn the foundry into a *forge artisanal*, heat and cast-iron souvenirs are not far away.

The foundry must have presented a dramatic picture of early industrialisation. Buffon would invite honoured guests to stand on a great staircase overlooking the raging furnace below. From this grand balcony Louis XVI first witnessed the reality of the Industrial Revolution. As half-clad figures loomed out of the pitch darkness, the contrast between court finery and grimy workers must have affected the king. At the very least, the spectacle made a change from a comedy of manners by Molière. Not for nothing does the guide call the scene *un théâtre industriel*.

Yet Burgundy's industrial heritage owes more to St Bernard than to Buffon. In these forests the Benedictine monks were medieval forge masters, first at Fontenay Abbey and later at neighbouring priories. **Prieuré de Vausse**, just west of Buffon's forges, was founded by the monks from Montréal. Although now a working farm, the priory is still visible. The church itself has become a charming library; Romanesque cloisters enclose a rose garden, occasionally overrun by recalcitrant ducks.

Abbaye de Fontenay, west of Montbard, is a Benedictine treasure on a greater scale, the oldest Cistercian ensemble surviving in France and now a World Heritage site. Founded in 1118 by St Bernard, Fontenay was named after the many healing springs in this marshy valley. In 1139 the Bishop of Norwich endowed the abbey and, as a **Fontenay Abbey.**

posthumous reward, is buried beneath the choir. But 14th-century prosperity gave way to absentee abbots and 16th-century decadence. After the Revolution, Fontenay became a paper mill until saved by the Montgolfier ballooning family. In 1906 their descendants restored the abbey to its Cistercian simplicity. The Aynard family still lives in the grounds, in an austere house built on the site of the refectory. Rather like the Cistercians, they make their living from fish-farming.

The abbey complex presents a virtually complete view of early Cistercian life. The refectory may be missing but the rest remains, including the kitchens, small prison and an over-restored infirmary. The smoke-blackened *forge* is the best conserved of early Benedictine foundries. For the Cistercians, manual work was a form of prayer, a vocation the Cluniacs had rejected. The self-sufficient monks built a water channel, ran a mill, forge, dovecote and lived off their vegetable gardens and trout-filled ponds; trout even appear on the abbey's arms. Curiously, most manual work seemed to fall to the *frères convertis*, the lay brethren.

Fontenay is faithful to the precepts of St Bernard, at once supremely mystical and functional. But unadulterated by ornamentation, it has no belltower, tympanum, coloured glass or decorated capitals. In fact, unlike magnificent Cluniac churches, it does not boast.

St Bernard accepted the Platonist credo that truth lay in proportion so the architecture reflects mathematical design and Christian numerology. The **church** embodies St Bernard's beliefs. The bare facade is pierced by seven narrow windows, a sacred number, symbolising perfection. Three windows are placed above the rest since four represented the earth and three the heavens. This fusion of heaven and earth is echoed throughout the interior.

A dramatic single-storey nave is sustained by pointed arches. The capitals are only decorated with natural foliage, acanthus leaves and aquatic symbols inspired by the marshy setting. The sin-

Fontenay cloisters.

gle statuary is a 13th-century Virgin, the protectress of the abbey. There was a practical purpose behind the absence of ornamentation: St Bernard did not permit anything that could distract the monks from prayer. Yet St Bernard's vision was broader than mere abnegation. His austerity was softened by a burning faith that manifested itself in light rather than imagery. In Fontenay, the mystical symbolism of light is ever-present. The monks were buried in the north of the church so that they would not see the light until the Resurrection.

Upstairs is the dormitory, covered by a ship-shaped oak roof. The 300 monks slept fully-clothed and ready for prayer; only the abbot had enough privacy to test his vows of chastity. The design of the dormitory and latrines is copied by Fountains Abbey in Yorkshire. Nearby, the chapter house was a place for meetings, penance and the business of monastic life. Only *moines de coeur* were allowed here, no *frères convertis*. Naturally, the vaulted scriptorium was designed to be the lightest room. Although the windows are modern, they reproduce the original abstract designs. Next-door is the *chauffoir*, the only warm room in the abbey. Not that the monks' comfort was uppermost in St Bernard's mind: the room sometimes served to warm the copyists' hands but its primary purpose was to stop precious inks from freezing.

The presence of the white-robed monks lingers in the cloisters, an intimate spot. The midday light was intended to illuminate the rigorous patterns on the columns. A walk around the grounds shows the Cistercians' genius for selecting sacred sites, a gift equalled only by the Romans. The mellow stone complements this watery forest clearing. The last scenes of the 1991 movie *Cyrano de Bergerac* were filmed by the fountain. In the romantic twilight, Roxanne cries, *"C'est vous..."* to Cyrano. In real life, however, the actor Gérard Depardieu says that leaves were added to give summer an autumnal air. St Bernard would not have countenanced such fabrication.

Châtillon-sur-Seine.

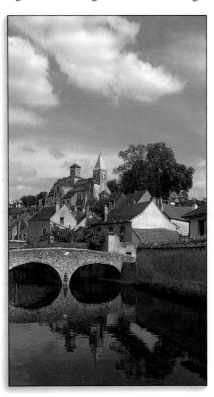

From Fontenay, one can go east to Dijon, south to the Côte d'Or or north to **Châtillon-sur-Seine**, an isolated town with a unique Gallic collection. The journey across the plains was the path taken by the Allies during the Liberation of Burgundy, culminating in the fusion of the French forces. But Châtillon's fame comes from the unearthing of the remarkable **Treasure of Vix** in 1953, found in a Gallic necropolis dating from 6 BC. Celtic tribes then controlled a trade route leading from the Seine to the Mediterranean and lived by barter, trade and patronage. Mont Lassois had already delivered lesser Gallo-Roman finds but the Vix burial chamber was on a royal scale.

The tomb revealed an elaborate funeral litter and the skeleton of a 30-year-old princess, wearing jewels and a gold diadem. Nearby were Attic vases, an Etruscan wine pitcher and the bronze Vase de Vix, the largest yet known from antiquity. Made in Magna Grecia, this *krater* could contain over 1,000 litres (1,760 pints) of liquid. The vase depicts Gorgons' heads, and the snake-like legs which re-occur as a theme in Burgundian medieval sculpture. The treasure is on display in the Maison Philandrier, a Renaissance mansion undamaged in the war. Such Celtic wealth remains a mystery in this forlorn frontier zone.

Alise-Ste-Reine is the site of Gallic Alésia, known to French children through the Asterix books. Adults also associate it with the final defeat of the Gauls in 52 BC, and thus with the founding of modern France. After Vercingétorix was declared leader of the Gauls at Bibracte, he led a surprise attack against Julius Caesar. However, the Roman army, strengthened by German mercenaries, beseiged the fleeing Gauls at their citadel of Alésia. Caesar's double *enceinte* kept out Gallic reinforcements and Vercingétorix surrendered to save his people. This first and last leader of a united Gaul was later put to death in Rome.

High above the village is a statue which has become a shrine to Celtic mythomania. The bronze of heroic

Vix vase, Châtillon-sur-Seine.

Vercingétorix was erected by Napoleon III, who popularised the rediscovery of France's pre-Roman roots.

Alise-Ste-Reine is an odd experience, from the disparate village to the mounds of Gallic earthworks. The windswept village places symbolism before sights. The archaeological zone includes the remains of the forum, Celtic temple and forges. The star finds may be in Paris but the local museum, Musée Alesia, has many objects found in the excavations including spears, coins and silver cups. Nearby is the Renaissance Chapelle Ste-Reine, named after a Christian orphan who was beheaded rather than marry a Roman.

Just outside flows the Source Ste-Reine, said to have sprung up when the saint's head hit the earth. The cult attracted an influx of sick pilgrims so a hospice was built nearby. The 17th-century building still stands, complete with the original pharmacy and library.

Beside the archaeological zone is **St-Léger**, arguably the finest Carolingian church in Burgundy and now restored to its original appearance. The domed basilica dates from the 7th century and retains a Merovingian wall and an altar carved with a Byzantine cross. On a ridge overlooking the church is a modern pastiche of a Gallo-Roman theatre, used for summer concerts. For those still oblivious to Gallic glory, there is a prominent statue of Joan of Arc.

Over the brow of Mont Auxois is a witty link to a latter-day Gaul. **Château de Bussy-Rabutin**, named after its 17th-century owner, is the most absorbing stately home in Burgundy. Virtually every painting and motto symbolises the life of Roger de Bussy-Rabutin. The sardonic count had much in common with his forebears. Mockingly, Bussy even entitled his scandalous account of court affairs *Histoire Amoureuse des Gaules*. The book offended Louis XIV and led to Bussy's banishment to Burgundy. For 16 years of exile, his life revolved around his château, a time enlivened by love affairs and letters.

The moated château, set in gardens designed by Le Nôtre, has a gracious

Bussy-Rabutin painted ceiling.

Renaissance facade and elegant Italianate wings. Inside is a picture of the Burgundy snail which, to Bussy, was a poignant reminder that his home had shrunk to this small shell. "*Je rentre dans mon coquille*," Bussy has noted beside it. But the snail also represents self-sufficiency: the erstwhile courtier and soldier did not waste his time.

Bussy's morganatic wife was banished from the château and paintings of his mistresses soon covered the walls. Most portraits of the Marquise de Montglat, the woman he loved, refer to her inconstancy: "*plus légère que le vent*". But a floral painting contains the plaintive "*Son absence me tue*".

Many paintings are allegorical, both to elevate Bussy's suffering and to disguise key courtiers. A picture of the sun obscured by clouds is clearly a metaphor for the stormy regime of *le Roi Soleil*. A phoenix rising from the ashes refers to Bussy's own fate, although his reprieve happened very late in life. One gallery contains 65 portraits of European soldiers, including Cromwell. In

an arrogant flourish, Bussy portrays himself as a Roman emperor.

One room is devoted to portraits of his real and imagined mistresses, including several shared with the Sun King. According to the guide, "If we showed all Louis XIV's mistresses, the room would explode."

Several paintings show the château and gardens as they looked in Bussy's day. The grounds are being restored to their original glory in time for the tricentenary of Bussy's death in 1993. Echoing Versailles, perspectives should be signalled by classical statues, topiary and fountains.

After leaving the château, visit the lovely Romanesque church in Bussy-le-Grand before going on to **Flavigny-sur-Ozerain**. A dramatic location and history seem a heavy burden for this mild town. As the seat of an 8th-century bishopric, it was the religious centre for the Auxois, with a powerful Benedictine abbey. Flavigny was loyal to the crown and during the Wars of Religion shared the Burgundian parliament with

Wall panel paintings, Bussy-Rabutin.

Semur. Its religious authority remains: in 1848 a Dominican monastery was established, now run by an English priest. Recently, a controversial *seminaire intégriste* has swollen the religious ranks. This right-wing order is fighting for a return to cassocked priests, Latin mass and traditionalism. These rival organisations are Flavigny's bread and butter, but have divided the town.

Flavigny is perched on a rocky spur overlooking two deep ravines. Beyond the severity of the ramparts and medieval gates is an intriguing nucleus. Richly-decorated houses are a legacy of Flavigny's 16th-century prosperity. This mellow stone town reveals Renaissance turrets, mullioned windows, romantic balconies and madonnas in niches. Flavigny's charm lies in its wealth of discreet details rather than in one outstanding site. Even so, the eclectic **Église St-Genest** contains a galleried nave, Romanesque chapel and Burgundian sculptures. But most of the famous 15th-century Flemish choir stalls and misericords have been stolen.

Abbaye de St-Pierre possessed a renowned scriptorium whose manuscripts are now in the Vatican collection. The ruined abbey contains fine 8th-century crypts supported by Roman columns and Byzantine pillars. The abbey crypts, church and remaining buildings have been subsumed by an *anises* factory, *bons-bons* originally made by the Benedictines. A professed interest in aniseed drops unlocks a visit to the crypts. Flavigny retains its religious complexity and traditional craftsmanship. As a chic address for Parisian weekenders and media folk, the village has sprouted an art school and craft shops. Sunday painters and amateur builders help one another renovate their Renaissance arcades.

Flavigny is well-disposed to tourism, seeing it as a chance to reduce the influence of the clergy. On Sundays, the terraces and ramparts witness processions of rival priests of different nationalities and orders. In Le Trop Chaud bar, however, there tend to be sly jokes about defrocked priests.

For a Burgundian departure, one can sip from the **Sources de la Seine** at Chanceaux. As proud *Bourguignons* like to remind Parisians, the capital's river rises here. Napoleon III, a victim of *la gloire de la France*, commandeered the site for the city of Paris. Since the languid nymph Sequana embodies the spirit of the Seine, Haussmann was ordered to create a nymph-encrusted grotto over the springs. An early bronze of the nymph was found nearby but is now in Dijon museum. Even so, the wooded site is more atmospheric than the statuary.

If Burgundy represents religion, Romanesque architecture and wine, then the heartland lives up to its name. Druids, St Bernard, the Templars and traditionalist modern priests have all left their legacy in stone. But quibblers will send wine-lovers south to the Côte d'Or: only a vintage Meursault has the edge over the splendours of Vézelay. St Bernard might disapprove of such indulgence but Serge Gainsbourg would give his blessing before disappearing in a puff of Gitanes.

Left, artist at work. **Right**, Flavigny-sur Ozerain, church interior.

THE NIÈVRE

La Nièvre is the official name for a *département* with a slippery soul, as elusive as its celebrated son, François Mitterrand. This is not the traditional Burgundy of wine and song. The jolly Burgundians of yore are confined to the vineyards of the Côte d'Or. Without wine and rich pastures, there is little good fortune to toast.

Like a black granite heart, **the Morvan** occupies the centre of the region. This is the land of the Gauls, with a separate language and culture. The Morvan is also a central mystery, its myths striking a chord with current French Celtomania. For visiting earthlings, its appeal lies in rustic cuisine, rugged landscape and a chance to flee vintage charts and Romanesque masterpieces. Yet around its black heartland is a cluster of warmer influences. Auxois, to the east, is a generous Burgundian landscape looking towards Dijon. Autun, in the south, is the Roman heart of Burgundy with its Romanesque cathedral an echo of the imperial past. Nivernais, to the west, was for long an independent duchy with the Burgundians only one of many masters.

Significantly, all these regions feel marginalised by the wealthy Burgundian wine belt and vote left, though there are signs that the region may move towards the mainstream. Perhaps then Nièvre's wandering soul will feel *bien dans sa peau*, at ease with itself.

Contrasting influences make this Burgundy's most diverse region. Autun and Saulieu have a rich religious heritage and gastronomic heights. The Auxois and Nivernais prairies are home to Charolais cattle and the occasional château. In summer, the Morvan becomes the green belt of Burgundy while rural canals make Nièvre the ideal barging base. Travelling west leads to the charming medieval towns on the river

Preceding pages: Burgundy Canal at Châteauneuf; Nevers Cathedral. <u>Left</u>, Commarin Château.

Loire. The centre of Nièvre may be a wine-free zone but the Loire's Pouilly-Fumé vineyards amply compensate.

Stretching westwards from Dijon is **L'Auxois**, a soft, watery landscape celebrated by Henri Vincenot, the modern regional novelist. In his tales, truculent farmers are at odds with each other but at one with the gentle scenery. This rich region was once the granary of Burgundy but is now better-known for its cattle and cheese. Made in brown-tiled farms, Époisses cheese joins prime beef on the local menus. Before starring in *boeuf bourguignon*, Charolais cattle laze around lush meadows. This is the watershed of Burgundy: tumbledown mills border the Armançon and Serein rivers; the Canal de Bourgogne runs idly by, silenced by the railways.

Commarin was Vincenot's childhood home and attracts literary pilgrims in search of snails and *douceur de vivre*. *Escargots* are particularly tasty in the area but Vincenot also described the snail as the secret heart of Burgundy. Commarin has a remarkable château which has belonged to the same family for over 600 years. Guarded by stone lions, the château presents a feudal face with classical features. The towers, moats and wooded grounds are a prelude to an opulent interior. Renaissance tapestries and imperial busts are a backdrop to furniture that has been *in situ* since 1750.

A short drive south leads to medieval **Châteauneuf**, with its commanding views over the plains. This crumbling citadel is encircled by Burgundian merchants' houses. From here, follow the Canal de Bourgogne to **Pouilly-en-Auxois**, the point where the canal disappears underground for 1ˇ miles (3 km). Built in 1822, this fine piece of engineering pre-dates Brunel. Now a backwater, Pouilly was then a thriving port supplying Paris with firewood. By the 16th century, Normandy's forests were depleted and Burgundy became the capital's chief supplier until the age of coal. The wood was felled in the Morvan and floated down the Yonne, Cure and, later, along the canals.

Barging on the Burgundy Canal, Châteauneuf.

Just west is **Chailly-sur-Armançon**, best known not for its watery landscape but for its Renaissance château, now Burgundy's most exclusive hotel. Mike Sata, a Japanese industrialist, fell in love with Chailly and after spending £10 million on renovations, persuaded the French Prime Minister to open it in 1990. Since then, the Japanese have supplanted the Americans in Burgundian folklore. Villagers talk in awe of these exotic imperialists, arriving for lunch by helicopter, then sweeping off to examine their vineyards in the Côte d'Or. The keynote is not envy but puzzlement at such a frenetic pace of life. Burgundians rarely sacrifice pleasure to speed: "Don't hurry a good wine" is a motto with wider implications.

After resisting a pampered stay in Chailly, there are further temptations in **Saulieu**, a gastronomic halt since the 17th century. Saulieu owes its prosperity to its position on the old Lyon–Paris trade route. Wine, fish, grain and wood were exchanged at Saulieu's fairs. Merchants then restored themselves with hearty portions of ham and *andouillettes*. The town was at its industrial peak in the 1860s, with clog and tile factories in town and tanneries on the river. In the 20th century, Saulieu was blighted by rural depopulation and war. As the Resistance centre of the Morvan *maquis*, Saulieu experienced fierce fighting, deportations and executions. Recently, the town has waved the flag of green tourism, presenting itself as the gateway to the Morvan.

Cynics say that Saulieu's gastronomic revival stems from the building of the N6 motorway: after an early start, Parisians could make Saulieu for lunch and Lyon for dinner. But the A6 autoroute bypassed Saulieu in favour of the vineyards of Beaune, bons-vivants still flock to Saulieu. Bernard Loiseau's La Côte d'Or rules the roost.

Loiseau is a skilled exponent of *cuisine légère*, a light touch which does not apply to diners' wallets. Typical dishes include snail and nettle soup; rabbit livers; endives in a truffle sauce; pike-perch in red wine; and red mullet with

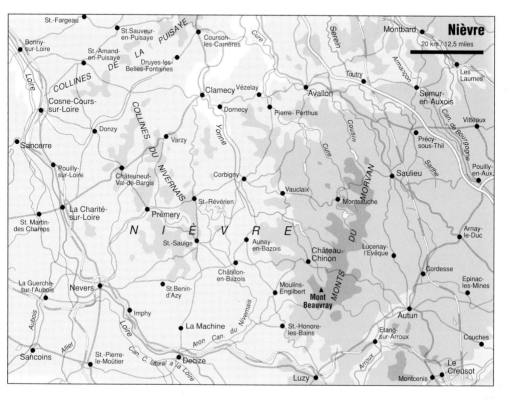

sea-urchins and beans. François Mitterrand invited favoured colleagues here, whilst former EU President Jacques Delors chose this Burgundian inn for his talks with Soviet leaders on the future of the USSR. When the negotiating team withdrew to the Japanese Château de Chailly, the press joked that this was a chance for the Russians and Japanese to settle their age-old territorial dispute.

Saulieu is pleasingly Burgundian in its hearty hospitality, rustic cuisine and Romanesque architecture. **Basilique de St-Andoche**, the town's notable Romanesque church, is best seen on a summer's afternoon. The sombre granite interior is then relieved by light beamed on to the sculpted capitals. The church honours the Greek missionary who brought Christianity to Saulieu before Saulieu brought martyrdom to him. Inside is his 8th-century marble tomb, carved with pagan and Christian symbols. Despite a collapsed Carolingian crypt, 15th-century chapels and an 18th-century choir, the church still feels early Romanesque. The choir and transept were torched by English marauders during the Hundred Years' War but later alterations do not detract from the barrel-vaulted Cluniac nave.

The nave's pictorial capitals contain all the symbolism of Romanesque architecture. An eagle with outstretched wings represents spiritual striving; a phoenix symbolises eternal life; bees build a nest in arum leaves, a sign of solidarity and companionship.

Elsewhere, grotesque heads peer out of acanthus leaves and griffins devour a wolf. Dancing goats and fighting bulls are linked to the signs of the Zodiac. On the remaining space, ferns, acorns, arum and acanthus leaves are entwined. The capitals were carved by a disciple of Gislebertus of Autun, one of the greatest sculptors of the Middle Ages. These distorted, naive shapes are infused with feeling but do not attain the stylistic perfection of the capitals in Autun Cathedral. Before leaving, look at the medieval stalls, carved with inscrutable animal motifs. One features a hunting centaur while another depicts a

Bernard Loiseau's La Côte d'Or, Saulieu.

dog clutching a Camembert in its mouth. The hunting influences are natural in a region famed as a game paradise.

Next door is the **Musée François Pompon**, a chance to view the animal studies made by François Pompon, a local sculptor doomed to oblivion by a silly name. Pompon's sculptures of animals in motion are only too realistic portrayals of chickens and ducks. His 19th-century imagination lacked the poetry of his Romanesque counterparts. But the best works can be seen outside: a bull adorns the square dedicated to the sculptor while a fierce condor guards his grave.

Saulieu dominates a windswept ridge overlooking the Morvan so healthy pursuits are *de rigueur*. The thickly-wooded terrain is dotted with bridle paths and picnic sites as well as a trout-filled lake. A well-marked 4-km (2-mile) walk leads to Lake Chamboux while other trails weave through plantations of Christmas trees to unexpected glades. After such exertions, follow in the footsteps of Madame de Sévigné and indulge in a Burgundian feast – or at least a drink in a workmanlike art nouveau bar.

The Morvan has long been the butt of Burgundian jokes. "*Il ne vient du Morvan ni bonnes gens, ni bon vent*" runs a local expression. The winds are biting and the people reputedly austere and inward-looking. The very name Morvan is a corruption of *montagne noire* (black mountain), a reference to the dark granite slopes. The region lacks rich pastures and vineyards and relies on logging and small-scale farming. As a traditionally poor area, the Morvan is devoid of châteaux, fortified farms and Romanesque churches. Only in the south is the landscape remotely dramatic. Covering 175,000 hectares (435,000 acres), the Morvan is bounded by Avallon, Saulieu, Luzy and Corbigny. **Bas-Morvan**, the area north of Montsauche, is a plateau covered by forests and ponds. **Haut-Morvan**, climbing south, heralds the Massif Central. With fast-flowing streams, high waterfalls and alpine pastures, it is clearly mountainous. On the peaks, snow and rain fall 180 days a year. The Morvan is a sodden sponge leaking into the Cousin, Cure and Yonne rivers.

West of Saulieu is **Pierre-Qui-Vire**, a curious monastic community in the depths of the forest. In 1839 God appeared to Père Muard with the command "*Je veux que vous soyez saint.*" Muard took him at his word, establishing this Benedictine abbey in a lonely spot. The abbey takes its name from the dolmen on a rock that swivels upon the slightest touch. During the war, the abbey was a refuge for Resistance workers. One day the Gestapo burst into the refectory but the reception was so frosty that they quickly withdrew.

The monks have founded similar communities worldwide. The site is atmospheric in winter, with fir trees, silver birches and snow-covered hills. There is a big congregation for Sunday Mass but for the unconverted, curiosity and forest walks justify the visit.

Prayer and penitence form the core of the community's beliefs. Given the Order's requirement for manual labour,

Carved corbel, Saulieu.

the 100 monks also work on their neighbouring farm. In addition, they run the renowned Zodiaque publishing house which produces books on Romanesque architecture and religion.

The books are beautifully illustrated by one privileged monk who roams France, photographing Romanesque churches for posterity. The series, *La Nuit des Temps*, follows in the footsteps of the medieval monks who laboured over illuminated manuscripts.

As to your reception, writer Robert Speaight refers to the "detached and business-like Benedictine demeanour". One can meet a monk upon request but the sombre Benedictines are more relaxed amongst male fellow Christians. Couples are occasionally welcomed on retreats. Female heretics must be content with the bookshop, chapel and the chance to buy cheese and pottery from the model farm. Few visitors leave without a Zodiaque book or a tape of Gregorian chants. But to be shown either the cloisters or the printing works, little short of a miracle is required.

Quarré-les-Tombes, the closest village to the abbey, stimulates spiritual and earthly curiosity. Encircling a severe church are 100 Merovingian tombs, most without lids. Certainly, granite was quarried nearby but opinion is divided as to whether this was a warehouse for sarcophagi or an actual necropolis. The surrounding countryside is dotted with even more ancient remains. The Forêt au Duc shelters La Roche aux Fées, a dolmen linked to druidic rites. Despite the abbey, Christianity is only skin-deep in the Morvan.

Quarré, like most of the Morvan, was a Resistance centre so is dotted with war memorials. Arms and radio transmitters arrived in British parachute drops. By the bridge over the River Cure is a *stèle* commemorating 2,000 *maquisards* who fought here in 1944. To dispel a sombre mood, Quarré offers a couple of rewarding restaurants.

As always in Burgundy, a rustic exterior belies the culinary inventiveness within. Auberge de l'Atre has a local dish for every season: wild mushrooms

A dog's dinner, Quarré-les-Tombes.

in spring; shrimps in summer; truffles and game in autumn; and *terrine de sandre en bourgogne rouge* all year round. If setting off on a hike or canoe trip, call in at La Fontaine, a *pâtisserie* with home-made flans and biscuits.

From here, it is a gentle drive south, past forests and lakes, to Mitterrand's power-base of Château-Chinon. For further information on walks and wild-life, visit the Maison du Parc at **St-Brisson**. This classical mansion, built by a British architect, houses a Resist-ance Museum and exhibitions devoted to the **Parc Naturel du Morvan**. This is a protected zone which, according to local ecologists, is not protected enough. Between 60 and 80 percent of the Morvan is wooded. The traditional trees are oak and beeches but chestnuts are also common. But nowadays the ancient forests are losing ground to massive plantations of conifers. The fast-growing Douglas pines and mini-ature Christmas trees are profitable but unaesthetic and damaging to local flora and fauna.

Just south of St-Brisson is **Saut de Gouloux**, a spot that encapsulates the changing face of the Morvan. A path leads to the waterfall which, in itself, is unspectacular. However, nearby are delightful forest walks. The vegetation runs from willows beside the River Cure to daffodils and wood hyacinths in the copses or foxgloves and willow-herb in the forest clearings. Wild rasp-berries and bilberries grow on the higher slopes. The lush undergrowth of ferns and mosses flourishes – for now. For an original souvenir, visit a *sabotier* (clog-maker) in the hamlet of Gouloux. Alain Marchand is one of the last clog-makers and wood-carvers in the region.

The Morvan's forests have long been the main source of revenue. A harsh climate and poor soil did not favour regular farming so logging kept the re-gion employed for six months a year. In the 16th century, Parisian landlords set up firewood companies on the Cure, Seine and Yonne rivers. In November the wood was sold at Château-Chinon fair and sent downriver in "fleets"

Roadside picnic.

BURGUNDY BY BOAT

In 1787, an American tourist travelling through France penned a short note to one of his compatriots in Europe: "You should not think of returning to America without taking the tour which I have just taken." The writer was Thomas Jefferson, then American ambassador to Paris, speaking of a voyage along the Canal du Midi in southwestern France.

Jefferson's enthusiasm could easily apply to Burgundy, a region rich in navigable waterways. But while the accommodation offered today is more comfortable than Jefferson's crude packet boat, the vistas seen from the boat have changed very little through the centuries. There are still medieval villages, fields in a patchwork of green, rolling acres of cereals and corn, golden vineyards in autumn and, at each lock, the ubiquitous keeper, mistress of her domain, purveyor of foodstuffs from the garden and gossip from along the waterway.

But the most important ingredient of all is the canal that has, through the centuries, bound these gems together. Burgundy's canal system was begun by Henri IV, linking Paris with other parts of the country. One of the earliest efforts was in 1604 in Burgundy, when work commenced on its first artificial waterway, the Briare, which connected the Seine and Loire Valleys.

Other waterways which interconnected with the Briare followed: in 1723 the Canal du Loing was opened; the Canal du Charollais appeared in 1792, and in 1838 the Canal Latéral à la Loire and the Canal de Roanne à Digoin. These five waterways form a system now known collectively as Les Canaux du Centre. The Canal de Bourgogne was started in 1775 and when it was finally completed in 1833, linked Paris to Dijon. The Yonne and Loire rivers were linked in 1785 and in 1842 the Canal du Nivernais was finally opened to traffic.

The use of waterways for recreational purposes is an innovation of the past 25 years. After World War II, when roads became the choice of transporters, lock maintenance on many of the waterways virtually halted and some rivers and canals were closed to navigation. But a hardy band of canal-boating enthusiasts prevailed, and today those canals which were begun almost 400 years ago are still navigable and form Burgundy's 990 km (620 miles) of cruising network. Most pleasurably, all the waterways are linked making it easy to go from one area to another.

Each of the waterways offers its own distinct charm: 470 km (290 miles) long, Les Canaux du Centre courses south from the Seine at St-Mammes, through the eastern Loire valley wine regions to Nevers. It connects with the Canal du Nivernais at Decize and at Digoin for the waterway to Roanne before arriving at the pilgrimage site of Paray-le-Monial. The Canal du Nivernais is considered to be the most unspoiled and beautiful, its 175-km (110-mile) length passing through a countryside of vineyards, fruit trees and châteaux.

The Burgundy Canal begins at Laroches Mignennes on the Yonne and its 240-km (150-mile) length passes some of Burgundy's most elegant châteaux, best restaurants and vineyards, and its capital city, Dijon. No matter which area you cruise, the best thing about seeing Burgundy by barge is that it's a movable feast. ∎

Quiet backwaters of the Nivernais.

steered by foresters with long poles. On the river ports of Clamécy and Vermonton the logs were bound into rough rafts and floated towards Paris. By the 19th century canals were also used and the firewood trade only died out in the 20th century. Artificial lakes and dams regulated the water flow and so helped Morvan's firewood distribution system. At logging time, the reservoirs were pumped into the rivers, swelling the water supply.

Each of the Morvan's main lakes has its own charm, from the wild Lac de Chaumeçon to the mysterious Lac de St-Agnan, hidden in the woods. **Lac des Settons** is the best-known, with all that popularity entails. Out of season, it is bleak but more Cardiff Bay than *Hôtel du Lac*. Until being dammed in the 1830s, Les Settons was a brackish peat-bog but is now a bustling summer resort. When water sports, ice-cream parlours and tourist trains begin to pall, consider a boat trip to the island on the lake.

Alternatively, escape the Swiss chalets by visiting a couple of neighbouring farms, either a *mièlerie* (honey farm) in Corancy or a *chèvrerie* (goat farm) in Ouroux-en-Morvan. It is worth returning to Les Settons for a lakeside dinner of trout, *coq au vin* or shrimps in La Morvandelle. If it is available, try *vin de noix*, a liqueur made from walnuts, red wine, sugar and brandy. *Jambon du Morvan* (home-cured ham) features on most local menus. Pork was once the only meat available throughout the year. Even today, the family pig-killing is a November and February ritual.

Lac de Pannecière, the largest lake, is enticingly rural, especially on the left bank. It feeds into the Canal du Nivernais. Here, fishermen are more in evidence than wind-surfers and sailors. To enjoy locally-caught trout, pike and pike-perch visit **Chaumard**, the village overlooking the lake. The most charming and welcoming restaurant is Les Vouas, run by an ecologist deeply committed to protecting the Morvan.

The breeding of pigs, sheep and cattle ensures that the quality of local meat is good, though beef is not as tender as on

Kayak trip.

the richer Nivernais plains. In the Morvan, rye, buckwheat and potatoes are the staple fare. Traditional dishes include *crapiaux*, bacon-filled *crêpes* and *galette aux treuffes*, a pancake made with potatoes, eggs and cheese. *Meurette de l'Agnès de Civry*, made with onions, bacon and beans, is stewed with eggs and a litre of red wine. Other simple dishes are *soupe aux choux* (cabbage soup), wild mushroom omelette, and duck stuffed with chestnuts.

Before leaving Chaumard, notice the church with a Romanesque belltower and the closed village school, proof of rural depopulation. As a Resistance centre Chaumard was encircled by German soldiers in 1944 and lost most of the village in the ensuing attack. The drive up to Planchez passes several hamlets with traditional houses, including a thatched cottage.

A winding road leads south to **Château-Chinon**. Its November fair was once a medieval labour exchange for farmers turned foresters. More recently, Mitterrand transformed his town, endowing it with worthy socialist facilities, including exceptionally ugly schools and hospitals. Despite its powerful former patron, Château-Chinon is unremarkable, a medieval citadel mangled by modernity. Nonetheless, the hilly setting is appealing, with several wooded walks radiating from the ruined fortifications. The local museum has been restored and houses a Musée du Costume but the star vehicle is still the **Musée du Septennat**, where the president's official gifts are held.

On leaving for Autun, say farewell to Mitterrand in the modest hotel that was his local home before the Elysée Palace. Au Vieux Morvan contains a couple of signed presidential photographs in the bar and, in the noted restaurant, the staff are only too happy to gossip about "Tonton". From here, a circuitous route takes in a hamlet, gorge and Gallic shrine before turning east towards Autun. **Arleuf** is a typical village tucked into the wooded mountains. Until the 20th century, traditional stone cottages were white-washed, thatched

A quiet pool near Mt Beauvais.

and simple, consisting of a living-room with possibly a bedroom and cellar. Attached was a barn and stables. Nowadays, granite cottages are still low-roofed but are tiled. In rough terrain, log cabins with sloping slate roofs and protective stone walls are common. The piles of firewood outside most houses reflect the triumph of the people over the landowners in Revolutionary times: the *Morvandiaux* won the right to exploit the forests without hindrance. Although personal property ownership has now filtered down to this socialist citadel, the locals still raid "their" forests for wood, mushrooms and game.

This area once had the region's most romantic occupation: *la galvache*. The word is a corruption of *voyage*, referring to the journeys made by carters as far afield as Flanders. Known as Morvan's cowboys, these nomadic errand boys delivered minerals, ironwork, tools and even crops. After a grand village farewell on May Day, the carters set off with loads pulled by piebald cows. They only returned for the

Anost fair on 1 December, a fair still held today, 70 years after the last cowboy hung up his boots. However, folklore groups at Château-Chinon keep alive the memory of the *galvachers* in their festivals. The atmosphere and country music faintly recalls a hot day in Nashville.

Until recently, migration was a way of life in the Morvan. Farmers and woodcutters were often away for months while thousands of peasant girls worked as maids or wet-nurses in Paris. These *nourrices morvandelles* have a lot to answer for. In the 19th century, they were prized by Parisians and, after acting as wet-nurses, stayed on as nannies and maids. Their trips back to the Morvan were an economic lifeline, also bringing city fashion and culture to a rural community. In addition, Parisian babies, both working-class orphans and children from *bourgeois* or noble families, were brought up in the Morvan. Known as *les Petits-Paris*, these children established firm ties in the region and later returned, often as owners of

South Morvan.

résidences secondaires. It is no surprise that a third of all houses here are second homes and, in lakeside resorts, the figure rises to 80 percent.

Just east of Arleuf lie the **Gorges de la Canche,** the most scenic valley in the Morvan. While hardly the Grand Canyon, the gorge is striking. Picturesque waterfalls tumble from the top and light plays on the mauve, brown and green rocks. A short but tortuous drive south leads to **Mont Beuvray** and the mountain once inhabited by the Gauls. A path winds through the forest to the summit. To bathe in a brooding Celtic atmosphere, walk up the last stretch alone.

Virtually nothing remains of **Bibracte,** the settlement controlled by the Eduens (Aedui) tribe. In 52 BC the leaders of the Gallic tribes gathered here to elect Vercingétorix as leader in a doomed attempt to stave off the Roman conquest. But the Gauls were defeated at Alésia and Bibracte was deserted on Roman orders. The demoralised farmers and artisans moved to the plains, an area more easily controlled by Rome. Augustodunum (Autun) was created to contain the warring tribes and eclipse the splendour of Bibracte. Expect few visible remains except for some ramparts, and a mysterious atmosphere. Beware of denigrating Gaul: even the sturdiest farmers become misty-eyed over folk memories of Vercingétorix's last stand. There is now a museum on the site devoted to Bibracte and Celtic civilisation.

The drive to **Autun** passes woods, streams and scattered farms. As the forests dwindle and farms seem more prosperous, defeated Gaul gives way to victorious Rome. Autun is not only the Roman heart of Burgundy but also the most Roman city north of Nîmes and Arles. As Augustodunum, it controlled the Agrippa Way, the trade route linking Lyon and Boulogne. The Roman city proffered both an olive branch and a poisoned chalice to the Gauls. *Pax romana* swept in new gods and resident legions. As a window on Rome, it commanded monumental architecture and the greatest Greek scholars.

Roman amphitheatre, Autun.

Autun is the richest yet strangest town in the region. As a cultural tool of Rome, Autun literally re-educated the Gauls, with the creation of a noted Graeco-Roman academy.

Rather like today's *Grandes Écoles*, it formed the French administrative élite for generations. Less a melting-pot than a multi-layered archaeological site, Autun offers Roman, Romanesque, late medieval and classical moods. In the 16th century, Autun was second only to Dijon in importance, with a powerful bishopric. Even then, Autun was referred to as a fusion of Gallo-Roman and Burgundian races.

Roman Autun borders and occasionally overlaps the medieval city. Outside the medieval boundaries, the lunar landscape owes as much to quarrying as to the Romans. Early industrial hillocks and mounds merge with current archaeological digs.

Roman architects had a gift for selecting bold sites. In particular, **Porte d'Arroux** forms a beguiling silhouette when seen from the riverside below.

Built in the 1st century, this gateway is the most authentic, with four sculpted arcades and the Corinthian columns that inspired Cluny. **Porte St-André**, a 4th-century gateway, embodies Roman monumentality in its arcaded grandeur and stern symmetry. Designed with traffic control in mind, it has two low arches for pedestrians and two higher arches for chariots. A Roman sense of proportion is also present in the **Temple de Janus**, an isolated sanctuary to an unknown deity.

The picturesque **ramparts** trace the path of Roman walls while adjoining blind alleys incorporate Roman brickwork. Only the view is more recent: this rolling countryside was formerly dotted with temples. The ruined **Roman theatre** once resounded to the acclaim of 15,000 spectators. But to see Roman Autun rise from the ashes, attend Augustodunum, a summer spectacle held in the Roman theatre. Valiant Gauls, Roman legions and chariot races are presented by 600 eager citizens. Nowadays, however, Burgundian

Autun cathedral, tympanum.

verve tends to triumph over a Roman sense of proportion.

The Romanesque **Cathedral**, built to house the relics of St Lazarus, is influenced by Cluny and Paray-le-Monial. Yet it transcends comparisons thanks to the genius of Gislebertus d'Autun, one of the greatest sculptors of the age. His tympanum is a work of soulful artistry, rivalling Vézelay. This Last Judgement presents the saved and the damned, interweaving biblical stories with fables. André Malraux described it as a "Romanesque Cézanne". Yet this masterpiece was plastered over in the 18th century and returned to its former glory only in 1948. On the lintel, giant pincers clutch the throat of a damned soul while an adulterous woman has her breasts devoured by serpents.

Abbé Denis Grivot has devoted 30 years of his life to watching over the cathedral, rescuing and deciphering the statuary. As *the* authority on Romanesque churches, Grivot is wary of expressing his preference: "Vézelay is more majestic but Autun's sculptures are remarkable, a composite canvas of the medieval mind." Many of the finest sculptures are in the chapter house; an intense Hanging of Judas, a dramatic Flight from Egypt and the wise peacock, symbol of eternal life. The sculptor's sense of fun is apparent in the portrayal of the Three Wise Men asleep in bed, too tired to take off their crowns.

Overlooking the Episcopal Palace is the **Musée Rolin**, one of the most appealing museums in Burgundy. It occupies a 15th-century *hôtel* that once belonged to Nicolas Rolin, the patron forever linked to the Hospices de Beaune. The museum reflects Autun's eclectic past, from Etruscan-style amulets to Gallo-Roman mosaics, expressive Romanesque statuary and vibrant Burgundian oil paintings. The pagan statuary, particularly the magician with a wand, springs from the same impulsion as the surreal cathedral carvings. As for the surprisingly earthy Roman mosaics, the finest is the *Taureau Marin*, an aquatic bull forming part of a tribute to Neptune. Beside it, bathed in

Quiet streets of Autun; clustered rooftops, Autun.

sunlight, is a translucent Gallo-Roman *Tête de Vénus*, carved out of marble.

The most human Romanesque statue is a frank and knowing Eve whose explicit sensuality caused her expulsion from Paradise and, in the 18th century, from the cathedral. Clutching an apple from the serpent's tree, Eve sprawls seductively, showing a gleeful lack of contrition for a fallen woman. The medieval paintings honour Burgundy's Flemish inheritance, with scenes redolent of the golden age of Bruges. But the intimacy, warm colours, expressive faces and realistic landscape belong to a Burgundian sensibility.

The cool elegance of the classical quarter contrasts with the patchwork nature of medieval Autun. Now the commercial centre, it still has a number of grand stone buildings, from an over-restored *mairie* to a baroque Jesuit church, and the Lycée Militaire, a military academy attended by Napoleon. Yet Place du Champ-de-Mars, built by Louis XIV, is a testament to the independent-minded citizens. The square is assymmetrical thanks to the locals' refusal to demolish homes; a gabled inn is a throwback to the late Middle Ages.

To appreciate the texture of Autun, revisit the cathedral. The **belltower** enjoys the most panoramic view in the region. It is worth climbing the steep, dimly-lit staircase to the top of the tower. Below stretches a panoply of glinting fish-scale roofs, intimate medieval courtyards and Roman remains. Above all, there is a realisation that the great Roman city has shrunk to its medieval frontiers, a rusty urban hub encircled by a green swathe beyond. Like an insular Tuscan hill-top town, it defies modernity.

From Autun or Château-Chinon take the D978 across the Morvan to Nevers. En route, Morvan's tiny parcels of land give way to large estates on the prairies. Unsurprisingly, Morvan's more entrepreneurial peasants flocked here after 1918. This is farmland fit for the majestic Charolais cattle and also the gateway to the **Nivernais**, a natural region with low-key charm. The flat countryside

Châtillon-en-Bazois.

stretches all the way to the sandbanks of the River Loire. **Châtillon-en-Bazois**, on the D978, spans both the River Aron and the Nivernais Canal, providing a large canal centre, overlooked by its 16th-century château. Historically, the Nivernais has the distinction of never belonging to the French crown. Even so, this ancient duchy has royal links, providing several Polish queens. This cosmopolitan duchy belonged, in turn, to Rome, Flanders, Burgundy, the Rhineland and Italy.

Nevers, the capital, reached its apogee in the 16th century. By marriage to Henriette de Clèves, Duchess of Nevers, Ludovico Gonzaga brought Italian influence to the region. In fact, Gonzaga's Renaissance Palais Ducal is often called the first Loire château. Nevers was then at the hub of north-south trade routes, a city renowned for its cattle and craftsmanship. It was thanks to the Gonzaga dynasty that Nevers developed its most prestigious industry, faïence. By the 19th century, the pottery industry and the city had fallen into decline. Nevers recovered enough to control the regional railway network, the reason the British bombed the town in July 1944. *Les Anglais* are blamed for the damaged cathedral and gutted town centre. Yet muddled town planning and insensitive restoration are also culprits.

Nevers and the Nivernais re-joined Burgundy only in 1956 so there is no great attachment to this administrative region. Geography has compounded the historical divide: the humble Morvan separates both regions; poor east-west communications mean that Nevers has rarely sought approval from its masters in Dijon. Instead, it looks directly north to the Loire Valley and Paris or south to Clermont Ferrand and the Massif Central.

Nevers shares Dijon's traditional condescension towards the impoverished Morvan. Yet this is not translated into votes. Nevers, in keeping with the region, is a left-wing bastion. The late Pierre Bérégovoy was the city's mayor and France's Prime Minister. Accord-

Nevers from the Loire.

ing to Béregovoy, Nevers's greatest asset is its *savoir-faire*, a provincial sophistication based on a mixture of past grandeur and pretension. In humdrum terms, this translates into excellent shops, hearty cuisine, lush countryside and scenic waterways. Nevers is worth visiting but Charité-sur-Loire makes a more intimate base.

Nevers is an unreconciled hotchpotch of districts. In the west, the pottery manufacturing district is shabby but intriguing. The adjacent cathedral quarter is only half-heartedly restored. The heart of the town is cold: a grandiose square overlooked by the ducal palace and town hall. The pedestrianised commercial quarter lies to the east. The *quartier des faïenciers*, the **pottery district**, nestles between the ramparts and the river. The **ramparts walk** is a chance to sense Nevers as it was before the British bombing. Built into the 11th-century fortifications are some well-preserved towers, of which the crenellated Porte de Croux is the finest. From the ramparts are views of the

Loire and the abbey's ruined cloisters. The Musée Municipal Frédéric-Blandin, housed in an old abbey, has a fine collection of Nevers pottery.

Follow Rue des Jacobins to the musty **cathedral quarter**, dominated by St-Cyr Cathedral. This curious church embraces every architectural style, from Romanesque to Rhineland. The profusion of turrets suggest temporal not religious power, a relic of the old dukedom. A flamboyant Gothic tower is laden with saints and griffins. Inside, a chilly atmosphere prevails, from the dark nave to the garish modern windows. More welcoming are the antiques shops clustered in the narrow alleys.

L'Esplanade, the next big square, features the classical Hôtel de Ville and Renaissance **Palais Ducal**. The mullioned windows and elegant lines recall the great Loire châteaux but the urban setting echoes Bruges, a city with a richer Burgundian heritage. Even on a dull day, the octagonal turrets and sculpted cherubs glisten. Depending on taste, the golden stone facade is over-

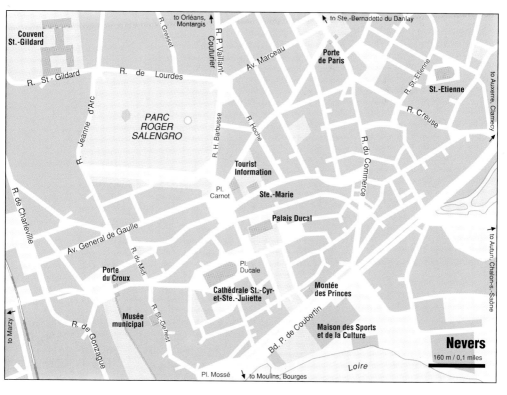

FRENCH FAIENCE

Nevers, like Sèvres, is a household name for fine chinaware. As the cradle of French faïence, it has produced pottery since the 16th century. Yet while Sèvres restricted itself to aristocratic designs, Nevers reflects the full spectrum of Burgundian tastes. In passing, faïence portrays the history of France in miniature, from the Ancien Régime to the Revolution.

Decorative flasks depict the early wine brotherhoods while statuettes of saints symbolise the Wars of Religion. The storming of the Bastille is immortalised in Revolutionary pieces and, in 1783, the first balloon ascent is celebrated in pictorial plates. Then as now, the faïence factories were on the River Loire for easy shipment of materials and pottery. The techniques were imported from Faenza, the Italian ceramics centre with similar soil. In 1566 Augustin Conrade established a French *faïencerie* with Julio Gambin from Faenza. Their elegant style became a model for later craftsmen. While the busy Faenza designs were characterised

by a horror of empty space, Nevers erred on the side of simplicity. Most pieces feature a blue wavy background, inspired by the River Loire, still a stylistic motif.

The golden age of faïence lasted from 1630 to 1730. As China opened up to the West, French potters succumbed to Orientalism. Ming vases inspired ethereal scenes of weeping willows, waterfalls, lotus flowers. Bathed in violet tints, the designs idealised court life. Yet even here Nevers was eclectic, borrowing whimsical cherry blossom scenes from Japan and a shade of deep blue from Persian silk screens. The repertoire of pieces included vases, decorative plates, screens, spice boxes and cherubs.

In the 19th century, there was competition from *porcelaine anglaise*, notably Wedgwood. Napoleon, like the people, preferred porcelain; Sèvres, Saumur and Rouen were happy to oblige. In Nevers, porcelain factories were created but to no avail: the town's future lay in functional white chinaware. Only in 1875 was there a revival of *faïence decorative*, the imaginative creations that typify the town.

Du Bout du Monde, founded in 1648, is the oldest of the *faïenceries* and is still situated by the medieval town gate. The small factory has been in the Montagnon family for five generations. In 1875 Antoine Montagnon relaunched *production artistique*, a reaction against utilitarian chinaware.

Today, Gérard Montagnon uses the same red clay amd white marl as did his 16th-century forebears. Methods are equally traditional and labour-intensive. After a year stored in a damp cellar, the clay is shaped and left to dry. The creations are then fired at 530°C (980°F), a process called biscuit after the colour of the hot clay. The glazing methods are secret: the cobalt blue sheen is the envy of rivals. The pieces are painted and decorated over the glaze before a second firing at 504°C (940°F) fixes the designs.

The soft colours have a metallic base: lead and pewter make white; iron turns red, manganese violet or black, antimony yellow, and copper green. Every piece is unique: replicas of a Loire château, an antique Chinese vase, or a family heirloom. Workaday pieces may depict a city seal, a bourgeois wedding scene, a politician's portrait or a child's first communion. Now, as always, faïence is a mirror of the times. ■ **Du Bout du Monde faïence workshop.**

restored or a model of harmony. The **commercial district** begins on the far side of the square and combines Flemish gables and modern shop-fronts. Visitors in search of antiques, jewellery, china and chocolate could do far worse. At the end of the pedestrianised area is Nevers' loveliest church, **St-Étienne**, a fusion of Burgundian and Auvergnat Romanesque. According to Denis Grivot of Autun, the harmony of the Byzantine domes makes St-Étienne unique. Founded by a 7th-century Irish monk, the church became a Cluniac priory in the 11th century. The bee-hive domes reveal high windows and an austerity softened by the luminous sculpted capitals. By contrast, a visit to the **Couvent St-Gildard** is an unsettling spiritual experience.

The site is a homage to Saint Bernadette. The Virgin appeared 18 times in Lourdes to Bernadette Soubirous, convincing the young girl of her calling. She took her vows in 1866 and stayed in this convent until her death at the age of 35. Her body was discovered intact 30 years later and her presence still attracts 500,000 pilgrims a year, mostly Irish, Italian and Spanish. Despite a tasteless recreation of the Lourdes grotto, Bernadette's waxy face looks eerily real. She was allegedly tormented by an envious Mother Superior but rose above cruelty and sickness. With a humility tinged with resignation, she said: "The Virgin has used me like a broom. When the work is done, the broom is abandoned."

If the cloistered atmosphere is oppressive, stroll down to the **Quai des Mariners**, an old fishermen's path by the Loire. A bracing walk soon prompts thoughts of gastronomic shrines. Apart from *Charolais à la crème*, succulent beef, dishes are inspired by the Loire. Fish specialities include *carpe à la Nivernaise, friture de la Loire* and salmon cooked in local Pouilly-Fumé wine. Auberge de la Porte du Croux is the top gourmet restaurant while Les Voûtes offers elegant cuisine in a Romanesque crypt.

Nevers is also a magnet for those with a sweet tooth. On his visit in 1862,

Nevers old town; Nevers shopping street.

Napoleon III fell in love with *nougatine* and ordered enough for the whole imperial court. It is available from the original maker, Confiserie Edé. *Négus* rivals *nougatine* in pedigree; in 1902 this "racist" chocolate was created to complement the skin tones of Négus, visiting Emperor of Abyssinia. The Ethiopian empire may have melted away but Négus remains in a shop akin to *One Thousand and One Nights* on acid.

The journey north is a gastronomic trail seen through a vinous haze. Although mostly grown in Burgundy, these wines are Loire *appellations*, thanks to the climate and soil. From Nevers, follow the Loire downstream to **La Charité-sur-Loire**, the most entrancing town on this stretch of river. This journey hugs the waterways and the borders, with Burgundy on the east bank and the Cher over the water. The river once carried porcelain, enamel, stone and firewood to Paris. Now, the decorative Loire runs aground on its pale sandbanks while the Canal Latéral makes do with idle pleasure barges.

Poplars and placid cattle fade into this soporific scene, a backwater in every sense. Seen from the 16th-century bridge, La Charité looks much as it did in medieval times. With the only bridge between Nevers and Gien until the 17th century, this fortified town commanded the Loire trade route. La Charité was conquered by the English in the Hundred Years' War and witnessed Joan of Arc's abortive siege. But its original fame stems from the Cluniac priory.

La Charité was one of only five priories honoured with the title of *fille aînée de Cluny*. By the 15th century it was promoted to *première fille* and, as a major Cluniac abbey, controlled 400 monasteries in England, France and Italy. After being pillaged by Protestants, the town later changed its colours to become a Protestant stronghold. La Charité's gentle decline makes it a sleepy tourist centre.

A Gothic gateway leads to **Église Notre Dame**, the priory's soul. Despite clumsy restoration, the church is Romanesque in spirit. The tympanum

Charité-sur-Loire ramparts.

shows Christ blessing the Cluniac Order, a prelude to the airy grandeur within. The luminous transept and choir, decorated with richly-sculpted capitals, represent the confidence of Cluny's sway. Outside, the Romanesque belltower is being restored and excavations are taking place on Square des Bénédictins, behind the church. Even so, the belltower, chapter house, refectory and kitchens can still be seen.

From the front of the church, follow signs to **Promenade des Remparts**. En route, notice the converted abbey outbuildings, especially the prior's lodge and an octagonal tower. Walk up the grassy bank to the fortifications, restored after the English invasion. After climbing up to the Tour de Cuffy, cross a footbridge to the second watchtower. From here, the abbey's delicate proportions fall into place, framed by the sky and the Loire. The Grande Rue, reached by a quaint passage beside the church, is dotted with period houses. For lovers of Art Nouveau and Art Deco, there is a museum with a particularly strong collection from these periods in an 18th-century mansion between the city walls and the Loire. Before leaving the town, sip a glass of Pouilly-Fumé at the *auberge* on Place des Pêcheurs, the atmospheric church courtyard.

Pouilly-sur-Loire, the next town north, is famed for its dry white wines, introduced by the Benedictines. Until phylloxera devastated the region, vineyards stretched from here to Orléans. Today's wine estates are smaller but still slope down to the water. Pouilly-Fumé and Blanc-Fumé, grown from the Sauvignon Blanc grape, are some of the best dry whites in France. Connoisseurs can scent asparagus, nettles, caramel, roasted coffee beans and gunflint. After a *dégustation* at De Ladoucette, sample the wine with Loire fish in Le Coq Hardi, a riverside restaurant.

On the other side of the Loire is **Sancerre**, Pouilly's arch-rival. Although not technically Burgundy, Sancerre is etched in the vinous landscape. At festivals, the towns' competing wine confraternities meet on the bridge over the Loire and chant: "*Eau nous divise,*

vin nous unit" (water divides us, wine unites us).

Once back in Burgundy, continue downriver to **Cosne-sur-Loire**, a busy market town overspilling its medieval ramparts and ruined château. After looking at local ceramics, stroll down to the river and walk along the *levées*, the Loire's raised banks. From here, it is only a short drive north to **La Puisaye**, the watery region celebrated by Colette. But to return to mainstream Burgundy, simply follow the Loire upstream to Decize. One scenic route explores a grand château and priory southeast of Nevers. The other side of the Canal Latéral is **Apremont-sur-Allier**, the finest château in the region. The medieval village lies on the banks of the river Allier and at its heart is the Anglo-Burgundian fortress. The château, belonging to the Schneider steel magnates, has been in the family for 300 years. The grounds are part wild and wooded, part romantically English.

St-Pierre-le-Moûtier, just south of Apremont, is a medieval walled town

St-Pierre-le-Moûtier.

built around a Benedictine priory. The French know it as Joan of Arc's last victory against the English. (Soon after the battle here in 1429, Joan was caught at Compiègne.) The atmospheric medieval towers are matched by a ruined lepers' hospital, converted mills and Renaissance houses.

The chief treasure is St-Pierre, a Romanesque church with a fine sculpted tympanum. Inside, the capitals represent vivid scenes, from admonitory griffins and biblical battles to Cluniac musical notes and dancing bears.

East of St-Pierre is **Decize**, a medieval town also noted for its Benedictine priory, perched on a rocky spur. The craggy old town centre clings to an island in the Loire. Its former defensive function is clear from the moats, circular towers and tumbledown battlements. The priory's Romanesque chapel was recently used as a cinema but is now a peaceful prelude to attractive 17th-century cloisters. Before leaving Decize, visit St-Aré, a partly Romanesque church with a remarkable double Merovingian crypt. From Decize, beat a path back to the heart of Burgundy: Paray-le-Monial and Cluny lie across the rich Charolais plains to the southeast, Dijon and the Côte d'Or further north.

When Henri Vincenot praised Burgundy as *"une civilisation lente"*, he was thinking of his homeland. Here, rivers and speech run slowly; the people appear unruffled, even placid.

Yet these were the people who fought hardest for the Resistance. Insofar as any region explains the early Burgundian heritage, the Nièvre does so. The blend of valiant Gauls, single-minded Romans and rugged Morvan peasants is the darker side of the Burgundian character. But the tough heart of the Morvan will always lose out to the hearty Burgundian wine-belt. The Nièvre suffers from depopulation, from the mountainous Morvan to the lush Loire prairies. Locals joke that even François Mitterrand deserted them to become president in Paris.

Right, herding the goats.

216

DIJON

Kir and mustard are what most people associate with **Dijon** when they stop for a hurried night on their journey to the south of France or ignore it completely as they speed past. But if Dijon is often bypassed by tourists it may well be that the Dijonnais themselves are quite happy with this arrangement.

Although there is plenty of fine art and architecture to see, Dijon's appeal lies as much in its typicality as in its cultural delights. "If you wanted to choose a city to illustrate generic France, you could do much worse than Dijon," advises the travel writer Jan Morris, calling it "one of those grand old middle-sized cities of France that seem largely impervious to fashion".

Henry Miller had a less charitable opinion of Dijon, building up his short stay there as a teacher in 1932 as a humorous passage in *Tropic of Cancer* (though he and his wife, June, had enjoyed Dijon well enough when they bicycled through in the summer of 1928): "Stepping off the train I knew immediately that I had made a fatal mistake. The Lycée was a little distance from the station; I walked down the main street in the early dusk of winter, feeling my way towards my destination. A light snow was falling, the trees sparkled with frost. Passed a couple of huge, empty cafés that looked like dismal waiting-rooms. Silent, empty gloom – that's how it impressed me. A hopeless, jerk-water town where mustard is turned out in carload lots, in vats and tuns and barrels and pots and cute-looking little jars."

While there may be more to Dijon than Kir and mustard, it would be a pity to leave without sampling its famous products. Above all Dijon is a city that is serious about its food, claiming in age-old competition with Lyon to be the gastronomical capital of France.

Of all its recent visitors, the legendary American food writer M.F.K. Fisher captures best the atmosphere of Dijon and the supreme importance granted to food. In her book *Long Ago in France*, she evokes the smells, sights and tastes of Dijon in the 1930s, sampling vast cartwheel apple tarts, fresh plump snails, carefully nurtured for weeks in their crates, and eating in legendary restaurants like Racouchot's Trois Faisans, so famous for its cellar that diners would save for weeks beforehand to sample it.

Of that occasion, Fisher wrote: "I know that never since have I eaten so much... But that night the kind ghosts of Lucullus and Brillat-Savarin as well as Rabelais and a hundred others stepped in to ease our adventurous bellies and to soothe our tongues."

Touring Dijon's wonderful food shops and sampling its famous restaurants is certainly as good a way as any to theme a visit to the town and helps to leaven its grand but sometimes overwhelming architectural heritage.

More than anything apart from food, visiting Dijon means architecture and it is at the Palais des Ducs that the lightning-stop tourist coaches initially

unload visitors. It is, however, vital to appreciate the history of the town before trying to understand its role and the artistic significance of its treasures. Today Dijon, the capital of Burgundy, has a population of 150,000 and benefits, as it always has, from its position as a crossroads of Europe, and a major conjunction of roads and railway routes. The coming of the railway meant big expansion for the town in the 19th century, consolidated a century later by its successful lobbying for a TGV stop.

It is an important airforce base, and a centre for scientific research and higher education. A number of *Grandes Écoles* and the famous University of Burgundy contribute to Dijon's role as the cultural capital of Burgundy. The suburbs accommodate a range of industries including foods, pharmaceutical products, optical instruments, machine tools, light planes and automotive parts, but the absence of heavy industry means the area is relatively unpolluted.

Dijon indeed is extremely proud of its environmental progress (it even boasts the first "scenic" graveyard) and there are a number of landscaped parks just outside the town, including an artificial lake, Lac Kir, created by Canon Kir, who was mayor of the city for 22 years from 1946 to 1968. He is perhaps most famous for his now ubiquitous cocktail, a mixture of blackcurrant liqueur, a Dijon speciality, with white wine – preferably Burgundian aligoté. *Vin blanc cassis* had always been a traditional Burgundian apéritif and the mayor popularised it by serving it at official city receptions.

History: Dijon is an ancient city. It began as a Roman *castrum*, Divio, although scant evidence remains. Part of the Roman wall is visible in the crypt of St-Étienne, now the Chamber of Commerce (to see it, enquiries must be made at the Museé des Beaux Arts). There are carvings in the archaeological museum, and the limits of the original Roman town are indicated on the buildings. Dijon was at the crossroads of many trade routes, including pewter, amber and tin, and the exotic spices that were

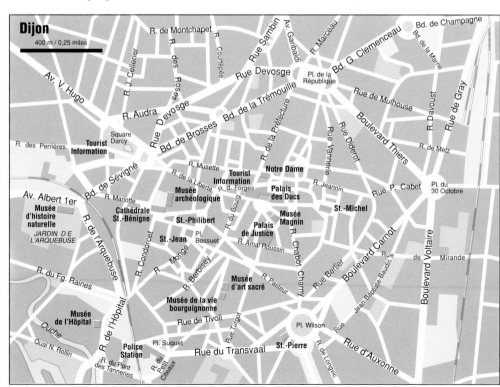

brought here resulted in the production of specialities like mustard and *pain d'épices*.

Dijon was the capital of what was the Kingdom of Burgundy in the 5th century but subsequently became part of Charlemagne's vast empire. It derived some importance at this time from the tomb of St Bénigne, who was responsible for converting Burgundy to Christianity. Pilgrims began to arrive and the Benedictines built an abbey in the 11th century; little remains of the original building but the superb Romanesque crypt of **St-Bénigne** can be visited. It is a good place to start a tour of the oldest part of Dijon and is one of the most interesting things to see there.

After St Bénigne's martyrdom, his tomb became the centre of an extraordinary cult. The original basilica was replaced by a great monastery, little of which now remains except the monks' dormitory and the crypt and Romanesque doorway of the original abbey church. The Revolutionaries who devastated so much of Dijon cannot be held

responsible for all the destruction, however, since the original Romanesque abbey church, which had already been repaired several times, finally collapsed in 1272, leaving only its magnificent rotunda. Regrettably, the Revolutionaries demolished the two storeys above ground but the rubble completely filled the crypt and happily preserved it. It was rediscovered and restored 50 years later. The rotunda is of the greatest interest; built in 1002 by William of Volpiano on the ruins of a previous 6th-century church, it incorporates a mortuary chapel at its east end which dates back to the 6th century, and was originally part of the Gallo-Roman cemetery which extended over the whole area.

When this chapel was built it was above ground but, as in all old cities, the gradual accumulation of refuse over the centuries has raised the ground level and slowly buried it so that it is now completely underground. Excavation has since revealed that the foundations of the Romanesque church remain beneath the present nave, and the current

Dijon's food specialities.

entrance to the rotunda gives access to the crypt and the side aisles with their apsidal chapels and to the place where the remains of the 2nd-century sarcophagus of St Bénigne still lies.

It is a peculiar, dimly-lit maze of closely spaced columns 1,000 years old. The rotunda forms three circles, with an inner circle of eight columns, surrounded by a circle of 16 columns and, attached to the circular outer wall, a final circle of 24 columns, two of which are free-standing. Light originally streamed in from the centre which was open to the floors above, ringed with columns and surmounted by a lofty cupola. Some effort of imagination is required to understand what the original pilgrims saw, with light falling from heaven on to the colonnades.

The Gothic building which replaced the collapsed Romanesque church was begun in 1281 and completed 40 years later. It is cold, bare and featureless – built for monks, not the public and so lacking in any ostentatious display. The spire was rebuilt in 1896.

To the north of the cathedral, on the Rue Dr Maret, is the **Archaeological Museum,** housed in the dormitory of the Benedictine abbey of St-Bénigne. The 11th-century cellar, originally the refectory, has short, thick, powerful columns supporting crossed barrel-vaults. It now houses a fine collection of Gallo-Roman sculpture. The ground floor is 13th-century and two rows of slender columns hold beautiful fan vaults. This room contains the famous head of Christ by Claus Sluter originally belonging to the Well of Moses, which can be seen in the Charterhouse of Champmol. There are also two Romanesque tympana taken from the cathedral. In front of the museum is a large quiet lawn with park benches and shady trees. The buildings of the university occupy the rest of the block.

Across from St-Bénigne is the Romanesque church of **St-Philibert**, now deconsecrated and closed because the building is unsafe – sad, since it is the only example of Romanesque in the city. The spire was added in 1513 and sits somewhat uneasily, as do the unfortunate 18th-century side chapels.

It was originally intended for use by novices of the great abbey church and later became the parish church of the neighbourhood, which at that time gave on to vineyards. Excavations carried out in the transept revealed the remains of an early Christian basilica. A pizza restaurant on the south side of the Place St-Bénigne is also housed in a refurbished monastic building.

In the 12th century much of the town was destroyed by fire, and was rebuilt by the Capetian Duke Hugues III with a wall and 18 towers to encompass a much larger area, contributing to Dijon's later reputation as the city of a hundred towers. It was a prosperous period, as evidenced by the church of **Notre Dame** on the Rue de la Chouette. The street is named after the 15th-century *La Chouette*, the little owl carved on an outside pillar of the church, which is supposed to bring wisdom and happiness to those who stroke it.

Notre Dame was begun in 1230 and took only 20 years to complete. It is a

Sambin carving, Palais de Justice.

masterpiece of 13th-century Gothic, with an amazing facade made up of three ranges of fake gargoyles and slender Italianate columns, the only one of its kind in existence. The front is topped with a mechanical clock, seized as spoils of war by Duke Philip after the Battle of Roosebeck, Flanders, in 1382. The "Jack-o-the-clock" – the Jacquemart – rang the bell alone until the 17th century when he was given a wife. Later, two children came along to help.

There is a huge open porch to the church and the arches above the three doorways were once decorated with over 180 carved figures depicting the story of the Virgin Mary – considered one of the best sets of Gothic sculpture in existence. In the Revolution however, in 1794, a local pharmacist came every day with a ladder and systematically destroyed every one of them. The result is ugly and shocking, 200 years later. Notre Dame also contains a 12th-century Virgin (blackened by the smoke of countless candles) and some finely preserved 13th-century stained glass.

The 14th century was really the heyday of Dijon with the rise of the Grand Dukes who established a glittering court here and turned Dijon into one of the most important towns of medieval Europe. The tower of Philip the Bold, the **Tour de Bar**, named after René of Anjou, Duc de Bar, its most illustrious prisoner, can still be seen, and is the oldest part of the vast ensemble of the Palais. Next to it is the beautiful 16th-century Bellegarde-covered staircase.

Like his elder brother, Jean, Duc de Berry (of the *Très Riches Heures*), Philip was a great patron of the arts, commissioning illuminated manuscripts and tapestries, as well as building and furnishing many sumptuous residences in Flanders, Paris and Burgundy. Philip the Bold also constructed the Chartreuse de Champmol as a necropolis for his family. He commissioned the brilliant Flemish sculptor, Claus Sluter, to decorate the charterhouse chapel and his own funeral monument, which is now housed in the Musée des Beaux Arts.

Hôtel de Vogüé; Maison Millière, Rue de la Chouette.

COOKING FOR THE DUKES

The Valois dukes took food and drink so seriously that one need look no further for the origins of Dijon's reputation as a culinary capital of France. So seriously, indeed, that meals took on the aura of religious ceremonies, with hand-held torches escorting dishes to the duke's table and pointed allusions to the sacramental properties of bread and wine.

The most senior state officials had seemingly menial roles at table. The Grand Master of the Household, whose normal duties were advising on matters of justice and war, was the duke's waiter. On state occasions he led the duke into the dining-hall, a baton held high. The First Master, his immediate subordinate, tasted the duke's food for poison. The wine, too, was tested with a horn which hung by a chain from the duke's silver cup. The officer who carried the duke's pennant into battle and stayed close to him was, at meal-times, in charge of carving.

Four full-time officials, each with a staff of about 50, were responsible for food and

drink. Two of these, the *escuiers de cuisine*, were "kitchen squires" who were given an annual budget to cover the cost of meat, fish and other necessities. The *escuiers* were supervisors; the supremo in the kitchen was, unsurprisingly, the head cook.

The presiding cook commanded operations from a tall chair placed between the serving table and chimney, with a long-handled wooden ladle used equally to taste soups and sauces and to administer summary judgements in kitchen arguments. He was personally responsible for the security of the spice cabinet. When word was received that the duke wished to eat, the cook changed into clean clothes, hung a napkin over his right shoulder and went round tasting everything before it left the kitchen. If it was a very special dish, the cook might present it to the duke personally, in which case he was entitled to help himself to a drink from the sideboard and stand around to gauge the reaction and to receive compliments.

There was a strict division of labour within the kitchen. Unpaid apprentices plucked birds and cleaned fish; roasts, soups and sauces all had their respective experts. Lowest in the pecking order were boys who when not running errands kept the spits turning. One specialist, not strictly speaking a member of the kitchen staff, was the court fruiterer. By a logic which said that fruit came from flowers and flowers nourished bees, the fruiterer was responsible for the supply of wax and candles. The number of candles needed to illuminate the palace was enormous, so the fruiterer alone had a staff of eight.

Records show that the palace regularly consumed about 130,000 gallons (500,000 litres) of wine a year, and in some years double that quantity. There were many mouths to feed in the palace – about 18 aristocrats and their families were more or less permanent residents – but, even so, such quantities can only be explained by widespread court largesse. It seems a fair amount of wine was taken with meals because a chronicler notes with apparent distaste that "Wine carries in itself more greediness than any dish served." As it was thought unseemly for the duke to call out for more wine, an *eschanson* stood in front of him and forestalled any embarrassment by keeping his glass permanently topped up. ■

Banquet scene from the *Très Riches Heures du Duc de Berry*.

Philip the Good, grandson of Philip the Bold, was responsible for building a new palace in the 1430s. His vast **Ducal Kitchens** are particularly spectacular; six giant fireplaces give a good indication of the scale of cooking involved. Also extant is the tower named after him, **Tour Philippe le Bon**, which is 46 metres (150 ft) high, and gives a fine view of the burnished Burgundian tile roofs and the church spires of the old city spread below. The main body of the **Palais des Ducs et des États de Bourgogne** was built between 1450 and 1455, although various alterations and additions continued through to the 19th century, reflecting the complicated history of the building. As well as housing the art museum, it still fulfils its civil function as the Hôtel de Ville; the ground floor makes a particularly splendid marriage room and register office.

The duke's living quarters were on the first floor; the magnificent beamed ceilings and huge fireplaces of the Salle des Gardes (Guard Room) are now part of the museum. Many of the private mansions in the area surrounding the palace were also built at this time by wealthy shopkeepers and financiers.

The death of Charles the Bold ended the Valois rule and the independence of Burgundy, which reverted to the crown of France. The Palais des Ducs became the Logis du Roi. There followed troubled times; the town was ravaged by fire, the Black Death, a wine-growers' revolt and invading Swedes. It was not until the mid-17th century that Dijon regained its prosperity, when it became a thriving academic and cultural centre.

The design of the palace was substantially expanded and altered late in the 17th century by Jules Hardouin-Mansart, the architect of Versailles. It took over a century to create the vast classical ensemble we see today. Mansart was also responsible for the **Place de la Libération**, imposing a graceful semicircle of arcading on the ramshackle medieval buildings that previously surrounded the palace. Today, the symmetry of the arcading is obscured by a busy car-park, and tourist buses.

Facade of Palais des Ducs.

Most of the Palais is now given over to the **Musée des Beaux Arts,** with its vast collection of paintings, the most significant in France outside Paris; much of it acquired during the Revolution from the houses of local nobility, churches and monasteries. There are so many artworks (and so many of them undistinguished) that it would be impossible to appreciate everything. It is probably better to concentrate on selected favourites – either specific artists or periods. Look out particularly for the Dutch and Flemish masters, Vasari and works by Manet, Monet and de Staël. Sculpture is stressed, both Sluter, and Dijon-born François Rude, who was responsible for the sculptures on the Arc de Triomphe in Paris. Rude's statue of Joan of Arc graces the stairway.

No art appreciation should blind the visitor to the architectural splendours of the palais itself; in particular the Salle des Gardes, originally the Banqueting Hall, still conveys all the pomp and splendour of the dukes, themselves encased in giant mausoleums in the middle of the huge chamber, overseen by a gallery accessible by a little spiral stairway. The work of Claus Sluter can best be understood by visiting the Moses Well, but the sculptures that decorate these tombs certainly reward study. His skill lies in an amazing ability to draw real tenderness and humour, even movement, from the stone. Also worth noting in the Salles des Gardes is a fine portrait of Philip the Good by Roger van der Weyden and two magnificent carved and gilded retables.

The old town: Above all it is by wandering through the warren of small streets that surround the palace that one can best appreciate life as it was lived in Dijon. It is especially famous for its *hôtel particuliers*, splendid mainly 18th-century town houses, although in most cases it is only the facades that can be observed.

Most have little wooden doors cut into the double doors large enough to allow carriages into the courtyards and often now accommodating the cars of today's bourgeoisie. As a general rule if

Salles des Gardes, Palais des Ducs.

the door is open don't hesitate to peer inside. According to the local tourist office, if the owners objected they would lock the gates. A few places are open at certain times of the year for concerts or exhibitions, and for the Dijon Music Festival in June, or the Theatre festival in July and August, since many of the concerts and performances take place in the courtyards.

Although these great houses, evidence of Dijon's past grandeur, are scattered all over the city, it would be a mistake to think that there was much contact between the nobility and the common people. The only reason the rich did not build a smart new neighbourhood of their own was that it was safer to remain within the city walls.

They had to buy up a number of humble dwellings until they had enough land to demolish and build a grand house of their own; this is the reason that some of the ground plans are so oddly shaped. Seeing these great mansions, it is hard not to feel a sympathy for the common people whose work enabled

the bourgeoisie to live in luxury and to understand the blind rage of the revolutionaries and the terrible damage they inflicted. The **Rue des Forges** behind the palais was, until the 18th century, the main street of Dijon, named after the goldsmiths, jewellers and knife-makers who had their workshops there. It is now pedestrianised with a series of medieval and Renaissance facades.

The tourist office is here, housed in the **Hôtel Chambellan** at number 34, an astonishing piece of flamboyant Gothic with a stone spiral staircase and wooden galleries round the inner courtyard. The **Maison Milsand** at number 38 was built in 1561 and has an extravagant facade of stone decorations by the celebrated Hugues Sambin, a pupil of Leonardo da Vinci.

Next door, the famous **Hôtel Aubriot**, though originally dating from the late 13th century, was entirely rebuilt in 1908. It has a superb glazed tile roof, best seen from the Rue du Bourg.

The Rue des Forges ends at the **Place François Rude**, a lively square with

Tomb carving in Palais des Ducs.

many outdoor cafés and a charming fountain of a wine-grower crushing grapes in a tub. There is a children's merry-go-round there in the summer months. On rue Vaillant there is a small museum devoted to the work of François Rude. The 17th-century **Hôtel Lantin** on the charmingly named **Rue des Bons Enfants**, houses the **Magnin Museum**, which has a collection of paintings but is worth visiting mainly for its period furniture, giving a very good idea of the elegant life lived in 17th-century Dijon.

Around the corner, the **Palais de Justice**, the former Burgundian Parliament, should be visited. On your way in, look at the doors which were made by Hugues Sambin (actually these are a copy, the originals are in the Fine Arts Museum). Four pairs of columns support a Renaissance porch, but only the central part of the building is 16th-century. Inside is a vast lobby with a fine panelled ceiling. Several of the rooms are open including the richly-decorated Chambre Dorée.

The **Municipal Library** on Rue de l'École de Droit, is housed in a 16th-century college. Its 17th-century chapel is now the reading room. Among the treasures are 12th-century illuminated manuscripts from the Abbey of Cîteaux. You pass the much altered gatehouse to the old Abbey of St-Étienne as you enter the **Place du Théâtre**. Actually on the Place is the abbey church, now used as the Chamber of Commerce.

The wide **Rue Vaillant** leads to the **Église St-Michel**, a strange piece of flamboyant Gothic on Place St-Michel. The church was built over 200 years, beginning in the 15th century. It has an odd front, with a porch extending beyond the main facade. The porch, much older than the towers which rise above it, is famous for its long frieze of foliage and grotesque decorations on all three doorways, which miraculously survived the Revolution.

From here you can follow the **Rue Vannerie**, which extends north all the way to **Place de la République**. Houses

Maison des Cariatides.

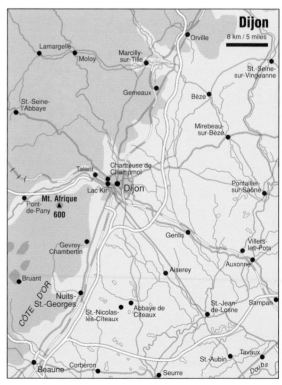

of note include the 18th-century mansion at number 41, and a watchtower built by the ubiquitous Hugues Sambin. A particular highlight on Rue Chaudronnerie is the 17th-century **Maison des Cariatides** at number 28, a beautiful stone house with 10 caryatids framing the windows. The ground floor arches were originally open.

The **Rue Verrerie** is famous for its concentration of half-timbered houses and wood carvings. Numbers 8, 10 and 12 were originally one 15th-century mansion; there is a *pietà* over the door. Number 21 has some fine carving, such as lion heads and Burgundy cabbages (*choux bourguignons*), a local decorative speciality. Numbers 27 and 29 form the 17th-century **Hôtel de St-Seine**.

This section of the old quarter has many important buildings: the **Hôtel de Vogüé** at 8 Rue de la Chouette is a fine 17th-century mansion, built by Hugues Sambin in 1614 for Étienne Bouhier, the first president of the parliament, and has sculpture by Sambin in its inner courtyard. Note the geometric coloured

tiles on the roof, a style introduced from Flanders. Though the courtyard seems symmetrical, the building in fact occupies an odd-shaped site and is very cleverly planned to look bigger than it really is. The doorway is Renaissance. Next door is the **Maison Millière**, a superb example of a 15th-century half-timbered shop, decorated with animals on the roof.

The **Rue de la Liberté** is today the main shopping street of Dijon, extending to the Place Darcy. It has many elegant clothes and shoe shops, and is also the place to find Dijon's gourmet specialites. Here at number 32 is the famous **Grey-Poupon Mustard** shop, with a wide selection of different flavoured mustards, and charming reproduction porcelain mustard jars. At number 16 is **Mulot et Petitjean**, the source for Dijon's *pain d'épices* – spiced breads and cakes in every imaginable form. The only thing Dijon lacks, most surprisingly, are many decent wine shops. Beaune is a much better place to buy and taste regional wines.

Hôtel Chambellan, Rue des Forges; half-timbered houses in the old town.

MUSTARD

The dukes of Burgundy were in the habit of sending their visitors off with a parting gift of a barrel of mustard. In the light of such noble largesse it is not surprising that the name Dijon has become almost synonymous with mustard. The word derives from the Latin, *must*, which refers to *verjus*, the juice of the newly pressed grapes which are mixed with seeds to make mustard. So the plant was named after the preparation.

Mustard has been around for a long time. It was very popular with both the Greeks and Romans, who enjoyed it served with roast meat, and it was praised lavishly by Pliny. Because Dijon was on the European spice route, exotic ingredients became familiar to its citizens, resulting in the popularity of mustard and also *pain d'épices,* the spicy gingerbread for which Dijon is also famous.

The first recorded mention of mustard in Burgundy was in 1336, when the incumbent duke, Eudes III, gave a banquet in honour of the king of France, Philip VI. According to the account book, they consumed 66

gallons of mustard at the banquet. And Louis XI of France was said never to travel anywhere without his own pot of mustard.

In 1390 regulations about the quality of mustard were first established, but it was not until 1630 that the guild of mustard-makers was founded in Dijon. In those days mustard was often made at home and mustard-mills were in common use. All the ingredients – mustard, vinegar and salt – were easily available; mustard seed from the Saône Valley, vinegar a by-product of wine, and salt from the Jura mountains. Mustard could be bought fresh like bread from special mustard shops, and townsfolk would bring their own pots to be filled every day. At first only vinegar was used, but in 1756, Jean Naigeon, a Dijon mustard-maker, first substituted *verjus,* the juice of grapes still green at harvest-time, for vinegar. It is the *verjus* which distinguishes Dijon mustard, and it was this combination which has given Dijon mustard its particular taste and reputation. There is now a mustard museum in Dijon founded by the mustard manufacturer, Amora.

Today mustard is no longer grown in Burgundy and 95 percent of the seeds are imported from Canada, the USA and Hungary. The term Dijon really refers to the manufacturing process rather than the origin of the ingredients but nevertheless Dijon continues to produce about 70 percent of France's mustard. The production process is simple; the seeds are pressed and then steeped in *verjus*, or in slightly fermented wine. Then the mixture is crushed; to create a smooth mustard the resulting paste is centrifugally separated to remove the hulls. For a coarse, grainier mustard the hulls are left in. The darker the mustard seed, the more powerful the mustard.

Today Dijon mustard comes in a wide variety of flavours: tarragon, green pepper, green herbs, shallots. Remember that when cooking with mustard, it loses its sharpness when heated so it is important to add it only towards the end of cooking. Although mustard will not go off, it does lose its pungency once exposed to air, so it is best to buy and use it in small containers (the small reusable glass tumblers sold in supermarkets are ideal). Mustard is of course also famous for its medicinal benefits; from stimulating the appetite to curing headaches, fever and asthma. ∎

Sluter's
carving, Well
of Moses,
Champmol;
statue of
Claus Sluter.

Place Darcy is full of cafés and restaurants and the **Jardin Darcy** gives an elegant resting place in the middle of the city, with tall trees and fountains.

But it is still food which dominates life in Dijon; some of Dijon's legendary restaurants remain, such as the Trois Faisans, and new legends are rapidly being established, notably the Restaurant Jean-Pierre Billoux on Place Darcy, next to the Hôtel de la Cloche.

During November the Foire Internationale Gastronomique takes over the town, an event described by M.F.K. Fisher as "injected with a mysterious supercharge of medieval pomp and Madison-Avenue-via-Paris commercialism". A food event no visitor should miss is the market which takes place three times a week in Les Halles – Friday, Saturday and Tuesday. The great wooden rafters of the market hall echo with the sound of market traders purveying their produce: brightly coloured vegetables, plump sausages, and all the fine ripe cheeses of the region. Fisher recalls the bustle of market days long past, "a kind of whispering pattering rush of women's feet, all pointed one way", and when they returned with "the crooked curls of green beans and squashes, the bruised outer leaves of lettuces, stiff yellow chicken legs... I saw that the women were tired but full of a kind of peace, too."

Chartreuse de Champmol: All that remains of Philip the Bold's monastery, after the ravages of the Revolution, is a chapel doorway and the famous Well of Moses by Claus Sluter, and these are now located, bizarrely, within the grounds of a mental hospital. (Considering the priceless value of the sculpture it is amazing that it is exhibited without any security and only rudimentary protection from the elements. However, plans are under way to create a medieval garden around it.) It is about a mile to the west of the Dijon railway station, and not easy to find, though there are signs if you follow them carefully.

The effort is worth it, however. The well is not really a well, but a huge monument illustrating the theme of the

Spring of Life. It stood in the middle of the monastery cloisters, originally crowned by a Calvary group, but this was broken by accident – before the Revolution. The lower part of the monument was surrounded by water, and between the water and the heavens are six prophets, each carrying a scroll of prophecy. The carving is exquisite, the stone looks so lifelike it is almost warm, and the folds of the garments are remarkably tactile. Sluter is particularly famous for his deep-cut carving.

Environs of Dijon: Apart from the obvious attractions of the Côte d'Or enumerated elsewhere, the countryside around Dijon offers a number of pleasant drives, quiet retreats and interesting architectural highlights; there are no spectacular sights for the hard-pressed tourist to include but instead the opportunity for a gentle ramble through variegated countryside, small villages and little market towns. Heading out of Dijon to the north, perhaps after a visit to the Well of Moses, is the little village of **Talant**. It is high on a hill overlooking

Dijon and Lac Kir and the wooded slopes of Combe la Serpent, a 130-hectare (320-acre) spread of national park, close to the city centre. The view is a good way to get a picture of the evolution of the old city of Dijon and the rapid recent new development evidenced by the tower blocks which surround the old quarter. The 13th-century church at Talant has a rather kitsch rusticated chapel and a good collection of saints, most of them 16th-century, including a Virgin and Child.

If you continue along the N71 you will arrive at **St-Seine-l'Abbaye**; although the Sources de la Seine is actually quite nearby, the town is, somewhat confusingly, named for the saint not the river. It is worth stopping to see the church, which is all that remains of what was once a very important monastery. It looks impressively battered from the outside, but has many interesting features within. The west entrance is at the top of a steep incline with houses either side and appears very imposing. The top two storeys of the south tower no longer **Beaumont Château near Fontaine-Française.**

234

exist and the entrance, set back in an open porch, has also sustained damage. Enter through a tiny old doorway, less than 1.5 metres (5 ft) tall, cut into one of the huge wooden doors. Inside there is a fine life-sized skeleton tomb cover of Jean de Chaudenay-Blaisy in the north transept. The choir has a wall separating it from the transepts, the outsides of which have been covered with fabulous 16th-century frescoes – biblical scenes presented in several dozen panels like a medieval comic-strip, and still very rich in colour, show the legends of St Seine and the Tree of Jesse.

From St-Seine-l'Abbaye follow the D16 skirting the forest of Is-sur-Tille on to **Lamargelle**, **Is-sur-Tille** and **Til-Châtel**, where there is an interesting Romanesque church. It is a quiet, almost empty landscape suffering from the effects of rural depopulation; for the visitor there is plenty of opportunity for quiet hikes through beautiful forest-land. **Lux** has a 16th-century château but it is not open to the public; it should be noted in general that many historic buildings are open for only a few hours a week at certain times of year so strenuous efforts must be made if you wish to be sure of access. A better plan is merely to potter and visit what happens to be open; serendipity often compensates for missing the established tourist trail.

Further to the northeast of Dijon, **Bèze** is a charming place to visit even if you are not interested in the gloomy mysteries of underground caves and rivers. The village itself has the remains of ramparts, a fortified church and several old buildings on the central square.

If you follow the signs to the Sources and grotto out of the village, walk along the side of the River Bèze, a deceptively mature-looking river which comes to a sudden beginning. Its waters run shallow and clear over flowing reeds between the houses, with here and there a little boat bobbing beside a back gate straight onto the river. It really doesn't matter which side you walk along because the river begins here, its wide mature flow springing up as if fully formed from mother earth. You can

Source of
Bèze River.

walk right round the end which is protected by a curved stone balustrade, and watch the waters bubble up in the pool, all overhung with chestnut trees and willows. Just above is the entrance to the grotto where underground river boat rides are possible during the summer.

Further along the D960 is the forest and town of **Fontaine-Française**. The château, which incorporates the walls of the original medieval fortress, was once a famous literary salon, and has some fine Regency furniture and tapestries. **Rosières** is another château worth a detour mainly for the splendid work of restoration which is still taking place. Only the donjon remains of the original 14th-century fortress. The nearby town of **Mirebeau** merits a visit for the 12th-century church of St-Pierre.

To the southeast on the pretty Vingeannes river is the Château of **Talmay** with its original 13th-century tower. The main building is classical 18th-century with formal French gardens and Renaissance interior. The tower provides an excellent view, and it is nearby that poor Brunhilde was apparently tortured to death.

Over to the east of Dijon, **Auxonne**, a comfortable-sized market town on the Saône river, has a number of interesting features. Military connections dominate, evidenced by the statue of the young Napoleon in the main square. He was garrisoned here from 1788 to 1789 and there is a Napoleonic museum in the château. The Arsenal building has two fine stone gateways with cannons carved above the arches, a siege cannon and an artillery cannon. The gateways also lead to a particularly splendid market hall with vast wooden beams.

The church of Notre Dame has a 12th-century Romanesque tower, a nave in the Burgundian Gothic style and a Virgin attributed to Claus Sluter. Steep roofs are characteristic of the town and often have two storeys of dormer windows piercing the slates. Beyond Auxonne, the Côte d'Or and its very particular attractions beckon insistently. They should not be resisted.

<u>Right</u>, Dijon market.

236

The Côte d'Or and Chalonnais

The eminent French historian Fernand Braudel said he thought the Côte d'Or vineyards were the most beautiful in the world. But he added coyly, as if aware that there were several stronger candidates when it came to traditional aesthetic criteria (the terraced vineyards of the Mosel or Hermitage, for instance): "The pleasure of the eye can be combined with certain other pleasures."

When considered objectively, that is to say without interference from the resonance of the name **Côte d'Or** ("Golden Slope") or the glory of its wines, this narrow strip of land where soil, microclimate, vine and human skills combine so magically, is nothing special to look at. Stendhal was probably a bit severe when he wrote in 1837: "Were it not for its admirable wines, I would find nothing in the world as ugly as this celebrated Côte d'Or." But he had a point.

The drive south from Dijon to Santenay via Beaune, along the Route des Vins, takes one through a vast expanse of well-kempt vines that is barely interrupted by hedge or tree or wall. To the left the vineyards are almost flat; to the right they rise – quite steeply until you reach Nuits-St-Georges, then more gently – to a wooded ridge some 100 metres (350 ft) above the road. Vines run right up to the walls of the occasional wine-growers' houses that dot the landscape, for not a scrap of valuable soil – predominantly a reddish-ochre colour (hence the name Côte d'Or) – can be wasted. For the same reason, villages tuck in their skirts.

Yet driving through this rather featureless landscape causes the pulse to quicken: every 2 or 3 miles a sign heaves into view bearing the name of a village of worldwide renown, a commune often pregnant with historical and literary associations, a name excruciatingly evocative of wines once drunk or,

Preceding pages: balloning over the Côte d'Or. **Right,** grape-harvesting.

alas, only dreamt of. Gevrey-Chambertin, Chambolle-Musigny, Vosne-Romanée, Nuits-St-Georges, Aloxe-Corton, Pommard, Volnay, Meursault, Puligny-Montrachet, Chassagne-Montrachet: the mind reels as the great names of Burgundy all succeed each other over a distance of less than 50 km (30 miles).

Côte de Nuits: The first leg of the journey from Dijon consists of the **Côte de Nuits**, an area which runs to a point just south of Nuits-St-Georges and produces mainly red wines. Still within the suburbs of Dijon but an appropriate beginning to a wine tour, is the great 13th-century wine cellar, the *Cuverie des ducs de Bourgogne*, at **Chenôve**. Within are the massive 13th-century wine presses, which continued to function until 1924. The first village with an *appellation communale* is **Marsannay**, which includes some vineyards in the suburbs of Dijon itself. Until World War II, Marsannay supplied Dijon with gallons of cheap Gamay and made virtually the only Burgundy rosé. Some years ago it started to produce classier reds and whites, which earned it an *appellation* in 1987.

Next comes **Fixin**, one of the lesser-known Burgundy *appellations* to contain *premiers crus* (the "x" in Fixin, as in other Burgundy place names, is pronounced "ss"). It produces an earthy red reminiscent of the wine of its more famous neighbour to the south, **Gevrey-Chambertin**, but with less breeding. Fixin village contains a curiosity worth visiting, the Parc Noisot and its little museum. Claude Noisot, one of Napoleon's captains, had a sculpture of *Napoleon Awakening* placed well up the hill in the grounds of his château in 1847 – and had himself buried opposite it. In 1847 Gevrey was the first Côte d'Or village to suffix the name of a famous vineyard located on its territory, in this case Chambertin, to its own. This was understandable, as the nine *grands crus* in the Chambertin constellation, which produce deeply coloured, wonderfully intense red wines, were already celebrated. The best-known *grands*

Clos des Langres, Côte d'Or wine sale.

crus, apart from Chambertin itself, is Clos de Bèze, thought to be the oldest named vineyard in Côte d'Or, apparently planted in the mid-6th century by the monks of the Abbaye de Bèze.

Chambertin is one of the most famous Côte d'Or names, partly because Napoleon made it his everyday drinking wine after his doctors had recommended it. Sacriligiously perhaps, to the modern mind, he watered it down. He took it on numerous campaigns, to Egypt, Germany, Spain and Moscow. After his victory at Elchingen, he repaired for the night at Ober-Falheim, where his Chambertin, among other things, was stolen. He is said to have remarked cheerfully that he had never before had to go without his Chambertin, "not even in the midst of the sands of Egypt".

Chambertin was also much loved by Thomas Jefferson, the German writer and composer Ernst Hoffmann (author of *The Tales of Hoffman*, who called it "the true poetic wine"), and Alexandre Dumas (Athos in *The Three Musketeers* says that nothing makes the future seem so rosy as looking through a glass of Chambertin). But none of the three, as we shall see, was short-sighted enough to restrict his appreciation of Burgundy to Chambertin alone.

Next on the road south is the pretty village of **Morey-St-Denis**. Although not a well-known name, it has no fewer than five *grands crus* on its territory which produce, depending on their altitude, robust or delicate reds of great elegance that many rate more highly than those of its much more illustrious neighbour to the north. One of them, Clos de Tart, has a very long history. Cistercian nuns of the Abbaye de Notre Dame de Tart bought the vineyard in the late 12th century and husbanded it for 600 years until the Revolution.

Just south of Morey-St-Denis is **Chambolle-Musigny**, another attractive and unspoilt village. Its vineyards sweep majestically up towards limestone crags. This is significant because the soil's high limestone content gives its two remarkably subtle red *grands crus,* an additional *goût du terroir.*

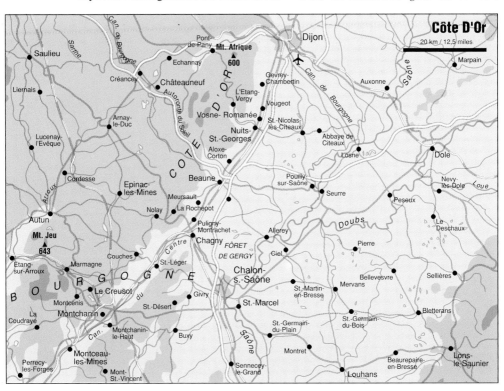

Moving from Chambolle-Musigny down the slope to **Clos de Vougeot** is rather like stepping out of a chamber music concert into the blare and razzmatazz of an American political convention. All the ingredients are there: smooth organisation, selection, ruthlessness, complication. Each year thousands of tourists are shepherded round the Château du Clos de Vougeot as the highlight of their tour of Côte d'Or. People with the right connections are able to wangle an invitation to rub shoulders with the glitterati at the banquet held in the château on the third Saturday in November, the day before the famous charity auction at Hospices de Beaune.

The château is the headquarters of the hard-headed Confrérie des Chevaliers du Tastevin, a guild whose members are mainly *négociants* and growers, with a sprinkling of VIPs who have been persuaded to lend their names in return for plenty of free Burgundy. The Confrérie had lofty ambitions when it was founded in 1934, likening itself not only to the Cistercian community that had created the vineyard but to a smaller-scale version of the League of Nations. It saw its role as one of spreading the good word throughout the world and encouraging peaceful relations. In fact the Confrérie acts as Burgundy's advertising agency and watchdog rolled into one. It has even prevented, through the courts, any use of the word *tastevin* or even its alternative spelling *tâtevin* on the label of any wine other than its own.

But what about the *grand cru* Clos de Vougeot itself (called Clos Vougeot on some bottles), arguably Côte d'Or's most celebrated red wine? Its 50 hectares (125 acres) are divided up among some 70 owners, some of whom possess handkerchief-sized parcels. This makes for enormous variation in quality. At its best, Clos de Vougeot is a full-bodied wine with a remarkably lingering aftertaste. The small amounts of grapes produced by the tiny parcels are difficult to vinify separately, so they are sometimes pressed and fermented along with grapes from other vineyards. A quantity

Harvesting in all weathers, Gevrey-Chambertin.

of wine equivalent to the quantity of Clos de Vougeot the owner is authorised to produce is then drawn off the resulting blend and, allegedly, sold as Clos de Vougeot.

The history of Clos de Vougeot is more interesting than its wine. The vineyard was founded by Cistercian monks from the nearby Abbaye de Cîteaux in the 12th century. In 1371 one of the monks sent 30 barrels of their wine to Pope Gregory XI in Avignon, then seat of the papacy. The Pope duly rewarded his benefactor by making him a cardinal four years later. Not surprisingly, Petrarch claimed in 1366 that the popes so loved Clos de Vougeot they were reluctant to move to Rome, where they would be deprived of that "Olympian nectar".

The château, a fairly unremarkable building lent majesty by being marooned in an ocean of vines, was built in 1551 by Dom Jean Loysier, the 48th abbot of Cîteaux. The massive grape press used by the monks can still be seen in the winery. The châteaux and vine-

Côte d'Or grape-picking.

yards remained in Cistercian hands until 1790, when they were confiscated on behalf of the state by a junior army officer called Napoleon Bonaparte.

Vineyards such as Clos de Vougeot attract legends like flies. Stendhal was told by a fellow traveller in Côte d'Or that General Bisson, en route to join the Rhine army with his troops, told them to halt in front of the vineyard and present arms. According to other sources, his gesture was repeated by Marshal de Saxe, General Galliffet and Marshal Mac-Mahon. Others again claim that no such military posturings ever took place at Clos de Vougeot.

To get to Clos de Vougeot from their base at the **Abbaye de Cîteaux**, to the east of Côte d'Or, the Cistercians had to travel some 13 km (8 miles) across a then marshy plain. So they built a fortress near the vineyard, at Gilly-les-Cîteaux. It was there that they stored their wines. When the building was destroyed during the Thirty Years' War, they replaced it with a finely proportioned château in which they enter-

tained lavishly. The Château de Gilly is now a luxury hotel. The Abbaye de Cîteaux was founded in 1098 and celebrated its 900-year existence in 1998. It is a stark and desolate place, vast in its proportions but, following the ravages of the Revolution, incomplete and lacking in harmony. Nothing remains of the 12th-century church, and most of the buildings that have survived are not open to visitors.

There is, however, a little shop where books, postcards and the excellent cheese, Cîteaux, are for sale. Anyone unaware that the monks made cheese would quickly be enlightened, on entering the shop, by the rich smell within. Interested flies, as well as tourists, slip through the door, but the monk behind the counter is good with a fly-swatter.

The austere, frugal Cistercian community is a very different universe from that of **Vosne-Romanée**, whose church now houses the magnificent wood carvings from the former chapel of the Abbaye de Cîteaux. This sleek little village, which lies between Clos de Vougeot and Nuits-St-Georges, oozes wealth, albeit discreetly. It includes on its limited territory no fewer than eight *grands crus* (Grande Rue was elevated to that status in 1992), several of which rank among the very finest red Burgundies: earthy, spicy and breathtakingly refined Romanée-Conti, with its never-ending aftertaste, deep-flavoured La Tâche, and velvety Richebourg.

Some of these wines are not only horrendously expensive but virtually unobtainable: Romanée-Conti, which is pricier than any other Burgundy except Montrachet, comes from a vineyard only slightly larger than two football pitches and cannot possibly meet demand with its curmudgeonly average production of 6,000 bottles a year. A parcel of its neighbouring *grand cru*, Romanée-St-Vivant, is believed to have sold for nearly 10 million francs an acre in 1990.

The qualities of Romanée-Conti did not escape the beady eye – or should one say quivering tastebuds? – of popes or kings. It is alleged that, like Clos de **Pernand-Vergelesses.**

Vougeot, the wine militated against the papacy moving from Avignon to Rome in the 14th century: Pope Urbain V is said to have been distraught at the idea of being deprived of his supplies. After operating on Louis XIV, doctors recommended he should drink Romanée-Conti. The king remarked that an illness which allowed him to discover a wine like that was a "gift from heaven".

If Vosne-Romanée is the princess of Burgundy villages, **Nuits-St-Georges** is the ugly duckling. It gives its name to the Côte de Nuits, the name taken from the village of Nuits, which then became Nuits-St-George; although it has no *grands crus* on its territory, it naturally acts as the commercial nerve centre for its wines. So one cannot really complain about its industrial sprawl, unsightly warehouses and bleak railway sidings. But it is sad that such a renowned and prosperous place should feel the need to deck itself out with vulgar buntings while allowing some of its public buildings to fall into disrepair. Its late 13th-century Église St-Symphorien is worth

visiting, though, as is the small archaeological museum devoted to locally-excavated Gallo-Roman and Merovingian objects from the Gallo-Roman site of Bolaras nearby.

One great fan of Nuits-St-Georges wine was Ernst Hoffmann. He loved to visit the cellar of his friend Kunz, where they indulged their taste for Nuits wine (it was not yet called Nuits-St-Georges). They made a point of doing so at night (because of the name *nuit*), sometimes sitting astride either end of the barrel and "drinking in no ordinary fashion". Another fan of the wine was the UK politician Ernest Bevin. When asked what he dined on each evening at the House of Commons restaurant, he alarmed his questioner by replying: "Steak and 'newts'." He did not, however, say whether he had ever tried the combination "steak and Beaune".

Côte de Beaune: The town of Beaune gives its name to the second section of Côte d'Or vineyards, **Côte de Beaune**, which produces roughly equal quantities of whites and reds. The area begins

HOSPICES DE BEAUNE

The annual Vente des Vins des Hospices de Beaune in November, which claims to be the world's biggest charity sale, is to the Burgundy wine trade what the spring collections are to the fashion business: both establish the year's trends and, in the case of wine, its prices.

The Hospices sale became a major event due to its bursar in the mid-19th century, Joseph Pétasse, who displayed considerable business acumen in the best tradition of the *négociants* of Beaune. The Hospices' vintages of 1847, 1848 and 1849 sold badly, and the cellars of the Hôtel-Dieu were consequently overflowing with wine. Pétasse travelled round France, Belgium, Holland and Germany and managed to sell off the Hospices' stocks. On his return he told the administrators: "We have established our clientele and our wines are well-known." The Hospices auction was started up again in 1859 and has never looked back.

Wealth in Burgundy has always been synonymous with wine, and when people decided to leave some of their worldly goods to the Hospices, out of gratitude or in the hope of bettering their chances in the afterlife, those goods often took the form of vineyards. The first donation of 0.35 hectares (nearly an acre) in Corton was made by Jehannette Dubois in 1471, 28 years after the founding of the Hôtel-Dieu. The establishment acquired the plural name Hospices de Beaune as hospitals in other communes (and the vineyards they owned) were added to it. By the mid-18th century, the hospitals of Pommard, Volnay and Meursault had swelled the vineyards belonging to the Hospices to about 30 hectares (75 acres).

Today, the Hospices' total area of vineyards is about 53 hectares (130 acres). The value of the wines they produce has soared in value thanks to Pétasse's energy in the 19th century and the marketing skills of the Confrérie des Chevaliers du Tastevin, which in 1934, when it was formed, organised a three-day jamboree, Les Trois Glorieuses, around the annual auction.

Day One begins with a banquet in the Château of Clos de Vougeot; on Day Two comes the serious business of the auction, which, like the banquet, is traditionally held by candlelight. Day Three takes place at La Paulée in Meursault. Most of the diners in this case are growers, who bring along bottles of their finest vintages. La Paulée is rounded off by a literary award.

So much for the folklore. The Hospices auction does serve a serious purpose. The prices paid for the various *cuvées* (which are named after their donors, not the vineyards they come from) are generally inflated — it is after all a charity sale for the Hospices — but they do give an indication of how Burgundy prices are going to move in a given year. The quality of the actual wines is another matter. There is a scramble to produce wines that are presentable by the third week in November, when they will be tasted from the barrel by prospective buyers.

There is no guarantee that the way the wine is treated, during its primary fermentation before the sale, or afterwards, during the cellaring and bottling at the *négociants*, will be up to standard. There is undeniable pageantry, suspense and excitement at the annual Hospices de Beaune auction. But, as with so much else in Burgundy, all that glisters is not gold. ∎

just north of Beaune, at Aloxe-Corton, and gets off to a majestic start with the red and white Corton and the white Corton-Charlemagne, which at its best can rival the queen of white Burgundies, Montrachet. These big, powerful and long-lived wines are produced on the free-standing hill of Corton, which provides a wide range of exposures and altitudes. Ownership is extremely fragmented: there is one tiny parcel which is one and a half times the size of a squash court and produces only about four cases of wine. Past, and bigger, owners have included Charlemagne, Henri II and Charles le Téméraire.

Voltaire did not own any vineyards in Corton but adored the wine. In 1759 (the year *Candide* was published), he revealed an endearing vice in a letter he wrote from Ferney to his supplier of Corton, Le Bault: "The older I get, Sir, the more highly do I value your kindnesses. Your good wine is becoming a necessity to me. I give quite good Beaujolais to my guests from Geneva, but I drink Burgundy in secret."

Tucked away in a valley behind the hill of Corton are the Romanesque church and narrow streets of **Pernand-Vergelesses**, a pretty little village which gives its name to a little-known wine which, for that reason, is often good value. Similar wine – described in a 17th-century inscription as "nourishing, theological and disease-preventing" – is produced, round a bend in the valley, by **Savigny-lès-Beaune**, which huddles beneath the A6 motorway. Despite its sprawl of modern villas (it is now virtually a suburb of Beaune), the village has an interesting church and château with a restored interior and exhibitions of fighter planes, endurance cars and motorcycles in the the grounds.

After such a long succession of vineyards and villages, it makes a pleasant change to enter a real town like **Beaune**. Its tiny centre – a mere half mile in diameter – has hardly changed physically down the years: a circular boulevard runs round its former ramparts, many of which still stand. Within, there is a dense maze of narrow old streets.

Hôtel-Dieu interior.

But don't imagine that you can escape the all-pervasive wine culture: every other shop peddles if not wine, then books on wine, cellar equipment or wine glasses and fancy table accessories; every other café or restaurant proclaims its loyalty to the vinous tradition. The big Beaune *négociants*, who have called the tune in the Burgundy wine trade since the beginning of the 18th century, lure tourists – some 400,000 a year visit Beaune – into their often spectacularly honeycombed old cellars with offers of free tastings. Free they may be, but what comes out of the bottle may unfortunately bear little relation to what the label advertises.

Beaune exudes such affluence today that it is hard to picture the massacres, disease and famine suffered by its past inhabitants as the town was fought over by warring noblemen or blighted by the plague. It was in that context that Beaune was endowed with what is by far its most interesting building, the **Hôtel-Dieu**. This charity hospital was erected in the mid-15th century by Nicolas Rolin, chancellor of Burgundy and one of the wealthiest men of his time, to care for the poor and the sick. His motive, as was often the case at the time, was a desire for prestige. Louis XI, the man who brought down the Duchy of Burgundy, was to remark acidly: "It was only right that he who had made so many men poor during his lifetime should prepare an asylum for them before his death."

From the outside the Hôtel-Dieu has a forbidding, semi-fortified appearance (note the massive knocker on its door, which depicts a salamander about to pounce on a fly). One is therefore unprepared for the Flemish-influenced riot of patterned roof tiles and dainty dormer windows that meets the eye as one walks into the main courtyard. The interior includes the spectacular vaulted Salle des Pôvres (*sic*), which is lined with curtained beds and has a chapel at one end. The beds are now empty – the Hôtel-Dieu served as a hospital until 1971 – but other rooms evoking everyday life, such as the kitchen and phar- **Beaune market.**

macy, contain eerie models of the Soeurs Hospitalières. The highlight of a visit to the Hôtel-Dieu is the splendid nine-panelled altarpiece, *The Last Judgement,* by the 15th-century Flemish painter Roger van der Weyden.

No other sights in Beaune can compete with the Hôtel-Dieu – Eugène Viollet-le-Duc, restorer of Vézelay and Notre Dame de Paris, said that it was so beautiful it made him want to fall ill. But it is also worth taking in the **Collégiale Notre Dame**. Despite its handsome 14th-century porch and delightful Renaissance side chapel, this church is basically Romanesque, to wit its sculpted capitals, which include a particularly dramatic "Stoning of St Stephen".

The **Musée des Beaux-Arts** also deserves a visit. It is mainly devoted to work by local artists such as the 19th-century painter Félix Ziem, whose landscapes are reminiscent of Turner's. The same building houses the **Musée Étienne-Jules Marey**. Marey, another local man, was one of the pioneers of chronophotography, which paved the way for the invention of the cinema. Beaune also has a **Musée du Vin de Bourgogne**, which throws interesting light on such questions as soil and wine-making techniques. Just outside the town, in a motorway rest area, there is another instructive museum, the **Archéodrome**, an historical theme park, which evokes Burgundian dwellings and life from the Stone Age to the Gallo-Roman period, mainly through reconstructions. In the little town of **Seurre** to the east, a smaller version of Beaune's Hôtel-Dieu can be seen, with the same communal arrangement for the sick. There is also a 14th-century church and a number of wooden houses.

Beaune is not just a town but an excellent fruity Burgundy *appellation* of great finesse. Erasmus said he wished he had lived in France instead of the Low Countries, "not to command armies there, but to drink Beaune wine". In the 16th century many Huguenots moved in the other direction, fleeing to the Netherlands and even today Beaune is a favourite tipple of the Dutch.

A successful shopping trip.

Erasmus did not just drink Beaune, but also had a soft spot for its celebrated neighbour Pommard. When charged with drinking it on a fast day, he retorted that, while his heart was Catholic, for a wine like Pommard his stomach was Reformed. In recent years, suspicions of fraud have hung over Pommard. The mass of consumers in red Burgundy-importing countries have always tended to go for long-lasting wines with plenty of tannin. Pommard filled the bill. Despite the considerable size of its vineyards, mounting popularity meant there was never enough of the wine to go round, so it often ended up being blended with another. This unfortunately gave Pommard a bad name among serious Burgundy drinkers – which was unfair, for at its best it is an attractively sturdy wine which goes particularly well with game.

Perhaps in an attempt to improve its image, the village of **Pommard** has planted flowers everywhere, scrubbed its houses and paved its streets. The result is picture-postcard prettiness. Its close neighbour **Volnay** is more demure, though it has more historical associations to boast about. In 1328 its suave and fragrant red wine was served at the coronation of Philippe de Valois, who owned the vineyard Les Cailles du Roi (now the *premier cru* Les Caillerets). Pope Gregory XI liked Volnay (as well as Romanée-Conti), which he said was "much more agreeable than the thick beverages produced by Roman vines". One of the first things Louis XI did when Burgundy fell into his hands after the death of Charles le Téméraire was to get the whole 1477 Volnay vintage despatched to his château near Tours. And Louis XIV was a great fan too – but that is no surprise.

The red wine of Monthelie (also spelled Monthélie), down the road, is the poor man's Volnay – meaning that it is still pretty satisfactory. The village of **Monthelie**, with a 12th-century church, is attractive and remains unspoilt.

Wedged in the deep valley that leads up to St-Romain, **Auxey-Duresses** is another picturesque village that keeps

View of Santenay.

itself to itself. Its church has a fine 16th-century triptych. Before *appellation contrôlée* was introduced (and sometimes, fraudulently, afterwards), its red and white wines were sold as Volnay and Meursault respectively. Nowadays, because it is so little known, it is one of the best buys in Côte d'Or.

The same could be said of **St-Romain**, whose red and white wines are full of character even though they come from vineyards whose altitude (300–400 metres/1,000–1,300 ft) precludes true greatness. The recently excavated ruins of its castle, built on a rocky spur at one end of the upper part of this quiet village, offer a splendid view of the circus of cliffs on the other side of the valley. Down the hill, in the *mairie*, local archaeological finds are on show.

Compared with the calm of St-Romain, the very large and proudly affluent village of **Meursault** seems a hive of activity. It is here that the last of the Trois Glorieuses, a banquet called La Paulée, which culminates with the award of a book prize, is held the day after the Hospices de Beaune sale. Following donations down the years, the Hospices now own large tracts of Meursault vineyards. The village used to have its own hospital, but its patients were transferred to the Hospices de Beaune in the year 1766.

The soft, round and complex white wine of Meursault took Jefferson's fancy when he did a tour of Côte d'Or vineyards in 1787, and two years later he ordered 250 bottles of its *premier cru*, Gouttes d'Or, telling his supplier it was his favourite. A wine-imbibing French prelate, Cardinal Bernis, who was French ambassador in Rome under Louis XV, even went so far as to use nothing but Meursault (from a good year) as altar wine. When surprise was expressed at his practice, he replied quite unabashed: "I wouldn't want our Lord to see me wincing while I take communion."

An almost uninterrupted expanse of vines, with not a building in sight, awaits as you drive the few miles from Meursault to **Puligny-Montrachet** as

well as from Puligny-Montrachet to **Chassagne-Montrachet**. These last two villages have a total of five white *grands crus*, two of whose vineyards they share, including Côte d'Or's most celebrated and most ferociously expensive white wine, Montrachet. Elegant, with a haunting bouquet, it is a wine that has been treated to every superlative. Alexandre Dumas said one should drink it kneeling and bare-headed. Recently some Montrachets have been reported to be below par and unworthy of such a great *appellation*. Nemesis rather than human error may be responsible: some vines have been affected by an incurable virus known as fan-leaf – it has been called "the Aids of Montrachet" – which results in inferior wine.

The refined, if lightweight, red and white wines from the village of St-Aubin are produced by vineyards almost as high up as those of St-Romain. Within the commune lies the charming hamlet of **Gamay**, which has a medieval castle and a partly 10th-century church. It gave its name to the grape variety that Philippe le Hardi banned from Burgundy in the 14th century, describing it as "a very evil and treacherous plant which produces a very great abundance of wine".

The last of the great Côte de Beaune *appellations*, a forceful, mostly red wine that ages well, is produced by the village of **Santenay**, which has a bustling atmosphere not found elsewhere in Côte d'Or villages, no doubt because it doubles up as a busy spa complete with a turn-of-the-century casino. Spectacular views over the vineyards are to be had from its 13th-century wooden-porched church of St-Jean, tucked under cliffs high above the village. If the building is open, do not miss the lively statues of saints within.

Côte Chalonnaise: The area south of Santenay marks the start of the **Côte Chalonnaise** *appellation régionale*. Here, the concentration of Romanesque village churches that reaches its flabbergasting apogee in the area west of Tournus begins to build up. There are four *appellations communales* in the

Chalon-sur-Saône from the river.

254

Chalonnais, strung out along or near the road south towards Cluny (D981): Rully, Mercurey and Givry, whose reds and whites rival, at their best, the lesser *appellations* of Côte d'Or; and Montagny, an aromatic white.

Rully, with its impressive 12th-century stronghold and abundance of very old houses, is a congenial village well worth visiting. The once fortified village of **Givry** was, like Rully, devastated by the plague in 1348 and sacked more than once. It is now a quietly prosperous, spacious little town with several old fountains and two fine 18th-century buildings, its *mairie* and its majestically proportioned church, which has no fewer than six cupolas. Just west of Givry is some delightful rolling countryside where vineyards are interspersed with small hedge-lined fields growing other crops. There are Romanesque churches worth visiting in the sleepy villages of **Mellecey** (which is also the site of Philippe le Hardi's country residence, the Château de Germolles), **St-Jean-de-Vaux**, **Châtel-Moron** and **Jambles** (note the unusual emblem of a crowing cockerel on the village war memorial).

A good place to sample local wines (some of which come from vineyards in Jambles) in relaxed surroundings, either on their own or with Burgundian cuisine, is the reasonably priced Maison des Vins de la Côte Chalonnaise in **Chalon-sur-Saône**. The city also boasts a tip-top restaurant that is very good value for money, Le Moulin de Martorey, housed in a delightful former water mill that is about to be engulfed by Chalon's urban sprawl.

Because of its strategic location on the River Saône at the point where it meets the Dijon-Lyon land corridor, Chalon has always been a busy trading city. Its two annual fur fairs are the relics of major medieval fairs. Tin from Cornwall in England used to be loaded on boats there and taken down the river to the Mediterranean. Stendhal noted in 1837: "Chalon seems to me full of activity, youth and life. It is maritime activity, a foretaste of Marseille."

Cathedral cloisters, Chalon.

Worth seeing in Chalon are the **Musée Denon** (a good archaeological section, 17th to 19th-century Dutch and French painting, handsome 18th-century Burgundian furniture), the former Cathedral of St-Vincent (partly Romanesque), the **Musée Nicéphore-Niepce** (Niepce, who was born in Chalon, was one of the inventors of photography) and the **Roseraie St-Nicolas** (a collection of 25,000 roses).

West to Le Creusot: The **Canal du Centre** runs from Chalon to Montchanin, a few miles from Le Creusot. Once an important industrial town, **Le Creusot** is now a quiet, clean backwater. It first began to expand in the 18th century, when Marie-Antoinette transferred her glassworks there and built the elegant **Château de la Verrerie** in 1787. Its two conical glass-making furnaces (now converted into a theatre and exhibition hall) stand incongruously in the courtyard, as though they had descended from outer space.

The château was bought in 1836 by Eugène and Adolphe Schneider. They exploited the local presence of coal and iron ore and founded an integrated industrial complex that manufactured locomotives, bridges, armour-plating and so on. Within a few years Schneider became France's biggest industrial company, partly through a shrewd reliance on paternalism: it provided its workers with medical care (in 1905 infant mortality in Le Creusot was the lowest in France) and housed them in neat little bungalows complete with gardens. Some of these in the 1865 Villedieu housing estate below the château's extensive grounds have survived the demolition squads. The massive, 21-metre (68-ft) high power hammer invented by a Schneider engineer has been placed at one of Le Creusot's crossroads as a monument to its former industrial glory. The history of Le Creusot is intelligently illustrated by the Ecomusée in the Château de la Verrerie.

As it expanded, Le Creusot hoovered up manpower from the surrounding countryside, much of which became depopulated. The long-strung-out

Sully Château; "Burgundy's Fontainebleau".

village of Couches not only helped to swell the ranks of Schneider's workers but provided plonk to assuage their thirst. It now makes more upmarket wine that qualifies for the Bourgogne *appellation*. This village, which was important in the Middle Ages, has several features of interest: the 13th-century Château de Marguerite de Bourgogne, the Templars' house, the Tour Guérin with a roof of patterned tiles (now a gîte), the 12th-century Tour Bajole, once a monastery and now a restaurant, and, outside the village, a group of five large menhirs.

To the north lies **Nolay**, a compact little town with a 14th-century covered market. Those interested in Renaissance architecture should strike out westwards to the moated **Château de Sully**, a remarkably harmonious building set in extensive grounds and described by Madame de Sévigné as "Burgundy's Fontainebleau". Here you can walk in the romantic gardens and taste the proprietor's wine. Just east of Nolay is the village of **La Rochepot**, which has a delightful 12th-century church, with a 16th-century triptych and several Romanesque capitals. Perched above it is the heavily restored 15th-century Château de La Rochepot.

The area north of Nolay marks the beginning of the other face of Côte d'Or – its little-known hinterland, which is as wild and romantic as the vineyard side is trim and materialistic. Near Nolay is the **Bout du Monde**, a valley that runs past Vauchignon between amazing cliffs up to a dead end and a waterfall. Farther north, around **Bouilland**, **Bruant** and **Arcenant**, country lanes twist and turn. On the plateau above, patches have been snipped out of the forest to make curiously bleak wheat fields.

Narrow, round-bottomed, sinuous valleys (*combes*) that look like giant bobsleigh runs sweep down to Gevrey-Chambertin, Chambolle-Musigny, Nuits-St-Georges and Beaune, slicing through the limestone of the Côte d'Or ridge; the most magical of these is the tiny **Combe Demange** that careers down from **Clavoillon**.

La Verrerie Château, Le Creusot.

The hinterland is dotted with peaceful untouristy villages: **Arcenant**, a centre of blackcurrant growing (blackcurrants replaced some vines when Phylloxera hit Côte d'Or; **Dijon** subsequently became famous for its cassis, and **Canon Kir** launched his immensely popular apéritif); and **Bouilland**, which has remained completely unspoilt despite the presence there of one of Côte d'Or's finest restaurants, the Auberge du Vieux Moulin.

A much larger village, and a very pleasant backwater in which to stay, is **Bligny-sur-Ouche**. Perhaps in memory of the fact that it was already a large seigneury in Charlemagne's time, it has a touchingly grand and outsized 19th-century *mairie*, built at a time when the village was a major centre of weaving (in the older streets, note the large openings to the cellars where the weavers worked). Its church, half-Romanesque, half-15th century, once formed part of the stronghold razed by Louis XI because Bligny had remained loyal to Marguerite de Bourgogne.

One of the most compelling religious buildings in Côte d'Or is the tiny ruined **Abbaye de Ste-Marguerite**, near Bouilland. Founded in the 11th century by the lords of Vergy, it huddles among trees near the top of a high and inaccessible little valley. It evokes more strongly than many grander and better preserved monasteries what life must have been like for the monks of a small abbey in the perilous Middle Ages. Did they, one wonders, have such a marked predilection for the wines of Burgundy as their Cistercian brothers on the plain or later prelates and popes?

The papal connection with Côte d'Or did not die when the papacy returned to Rome in 1377. In 1951, for instance, Angelo Roncalli (papal nuncio to France and Pope Jean XXIII-to-be) was persuaded to ascend the Montagne de Beaune, a hill situated just outside the town, and bless the vines stretched out before him. Did the already thrice-blessed Côte d'Or really need yet another benediction?

Left, La Rochepot.

SOUTHERN BURGUNDY

Southern Burgundy, most of which is within the Saône-et-Loire *département*, is still wine country, but once the hills of the Mâconnais are left behind other elements of the Burgundian tapestry predominate. To the west cows: the rich farmland of the Charolais is home to the famous milk-white cattle. To the east chickens: the flat plains of the Bresse accommodate such fine fowl they have their own *appellation contrôlée* and the dedicated can follow chicken trails across the country.

But above all this area is distinguished by its fine Romanesque architecture; the grand abbeys of Cluny, Paray-le-Monial and Tournus are only rivalled by the sheer number of exquisite little churches to be discovered. It provides an extraordinary opportunity for surveying an entire period of architecture and its development from the barrel vault to the soaring naves of the abbey churches. Anyone with a particular interest might choose to follow a route dictated by architectural chronology rather than geographical logic.

There is much else to see and many distractions of a more vinous nature. This is not dramatic countryside although there is a distinct thrill in seeing an entire hillside of soon-to-be-harvested vines, but it is almost always pretty and often very beautiful in a soft, mellow, almost English way. Apart from the occasional limestone crag, the contours are rounded and soft. And, however quiet and sleepy the countryside, it is never remote, never primitive. This is land that has, after all, been civilised and cultivated for centuries, by monks above all, dedicated to more than prayer, drawing the very best wine and produce from the land.

The Bresse: To the east the Burgundian Bresse (in the great regional reorganisation of 1790 the Bresse was

Preceding pages: Brionnais cow country; fast food, Burgundy-style. **Right,** a farmhouse in Bresse.

divided between three different *départements*) is distinctly different from the rest of Burgundy but well worth exploring. **Louhans** in particular has a very fine market (every Monday) where the local produce can be seen at its best, particularly a huge amount of very live livestock including the superb white-feathered Bresse chickens, fed on maize and milk; and many different breeds of rabbits. It is a pleasant town best explored when the market has closed for the day – when everyone has headed off for lunch in the many small brasseries.

The arcaded central street is part 14th-century, and is famous for its Hôtel-Dieu with its 18th-century dispensary and fine collection of pottery and glass. The Bresse is also known for its unusual "Saracen" chimneys; elaborate central chimneys like miniature Romanesque belltowers, originally above fireplaces in the middle of the room with a large hood to take away the smoke. (Saracen seems to have been a label used indiscriminately for anything of foreign origin.)

Villages such as **Romenay** and **St-Trivier-de-Courtes** have some of the best examples, and 5 km (3 miles) east of St-Trivier-de-Courtes there is a Bresse farm open to the public which has its original fireplace intact, with its open hood and "ancestors' bench" tucked in against the wall.

Local Bresse architecture still predominates: low half-timbered houses with overhanging roofs of curved tiles, where corn cobs and huge bunches of red peppers are hung to dry. Considerable effort has been made to preserve local traditions and a series of Eco-museums in various locations throughout the region including the Château of St Pierre de Bresse specialise in different aspects of Bresse life; for example, agriculture, forestry, chair-making, tile production and bread-making.

Tournus makes an ideal base for visiting the Chalonnais and Mâconnais vineyards. Its superb abbey – for some the most beautiful in Burgundy, where there is plenty of competition – predates Cluny and thus makes an excel-

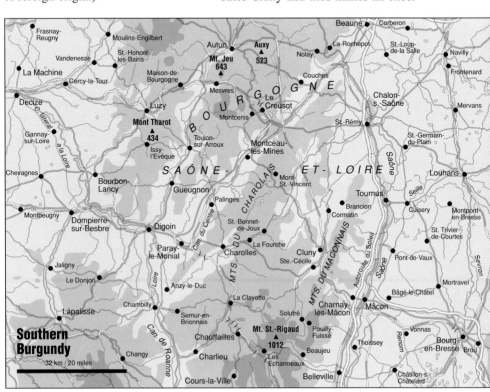

Southern Burgundy

32 km / 20 miles

lent introduction to the Romanesque trail. The old town has dozens of secret alleys, buildings set with curious gables and corbels, old shop fronts and mansions, a wealth of antique shops, and enough cafés and restaurants to make life very pleasant.

The **Abbaye St-Philibert** merits an extended visit because there is so much to see, including the bones of St Philibert himself (616–685). The best way to approach is by the west gate. Two imposing 10th-century towers (with 11th- and 12th-century additions) mark the abbey precincts, and from here the church has a distinct military look of tremendous strength with arrow slits and high thick walls, designed more for repelling invaders than welcoming pilgrims. This is not surprising considering the events leading to its construction: in 836 the monks of St-Philibert-de-Noirmoutiers fled before the Norman invaders, taking with them the bones of their saint. They tried to settle near Angers, on the Loire, but the Normans swept all before them. The

monks tried again in Messay, then in 871 reached St-Pourçain in the Auvergne. Four years later, Charles the Bold offered them the Abbey of St-Valérien at Tournus which they accepted. However, though they were safe from the invaders from the north, they had not reckoned with danger from the east and in 937 the Hungarians sacked the town and destroyed the abbey.

They quickly rebuilt, but in 1006 the building was again destroyed, this time by fire. They were a determined band, however, consecrating the present church only 13 years later. It was built before Cluny and always managed to remain independent of its powerful neighbour. You enter at the narthex, almost 1,000 years old and the most ancient part of the abbey, an anteroom crowded with huge pillars supporting the massive weight of the towers and floor above.

The narthex has its own chapel of St-Michel, on the second storey, which is of tremendous height with views up into the two towers, and can be reached by

Tournus from River Saône.

the stairway just inside the entrance. It is worth the climb for the aerial view of the nave and its magnificent black and white banded vaulting.

As you enter the nave, note the wall painting above the north entrance. From here the sight of the side aisles of unbroken columns is stunning. It is worth taking binoculars to view the superb capitals, the best of which are at the crossing in the nave. Most are very primitive carvings of strange mythical beasts and goblins.

The choir is a joy. The five apsidial chapels are all square with zigzag brickwork. In the lady chapel are the celebrated relics of St Philibert in a gold case: his thigh bones and elbows there for all to see. Be sure to visit the crypt, with its deep well and a series of slender columns supporting the choir with decorative capitals carved with foliage.

To the south of the church there is only a small surviving section of cloister but it is very calm and peaceful. It is reached from the Chauffoir, where the monks warmed their hands and their inks. Capitals taken from the belltower are exhibited here, and there are two beautiful carved figures representing St Philibert and St Valérien.

The abbey is in the northern part of the old town, famous for its historic houses. The **Rue de la République** runs the length of the town, beginning at the tourist office in the wooden frame house, Logis de la Tête Noir, dating from the 14th century, and the rest of the street ranges from 14th-century to 16th-century buildings. Note particularly the Logis de la Piguette at number 67; the buildings and arcades flanking the Place Hôtel de Ville; the 15th-century arcaded Hôtel Jean Magnon; the 17th-century turreted Hôtel de l'Escargot at number 72 and the Hôtel Delaval with 13th to 16th-century features.

At the southernmost end of the street is **Ste-Madeleine**, a 12th-century church built on the site of a Roman castrum, with a fine doorway and square tower. A stroll down the facing Rue de la Friperie brings you to the old Rue du Quatre Septembre and the

Stone carving in St-Philibert; church of St-Pierre, Brancion.

Maisons des Chapelains de la Madeleine, four 16th-century buildings. The Hôtel-Dieu has a wonderful 17th-century pharmacy, and will soon house the Musée Greuze, devoted to local artist Jean-Baptiste Greuze. Also worth a visit is the Musée Bourgignon on place de l'Abbaye with its collection devoted to local traditions, tools and costumes.

Perhaps it is the river that gives Tournus its timeless quality. The Saône is very wide at this point, with only one bridge crossing it in the town. Quiet *quais* run next to the water, used by walkers and fishermen.There is a road alongside the river, but unlike Mâcon, it has not been turned into a urban throughway; the Quai de Verdun is a quiet, tree-lined boulevard, with parking under the trees and the odd café. Boats can be taken from the Quai du Midi to Chalon-sur-Saône and Mâcon, and for river trips returning to Tournus.

The Mâconnais hills: Heading southwest towards Cluny, the route takes you through the gentle hills, verdant valleys and forests of the Mâconnais. These roads are off the main tourist route and can be very quiet. Approaching Cluny, it is possible to imagine the experience of earlier pilgrims as they arrived at the crest of a wooded hill to view their sacred objective for the first time.

But head first for **Brancion**, perched on a col overlooking two ravines. It is a charming little town within 14th-century ramparts entered through an ancient gateway. The keep and the Tour de Beaufort remain of the ruined 10th-century fortress, and there are many well-restored medieval houses. There is an especially splendid 15th-century wooden raftered market hall. At the highest point of the town is the little church of St-Pierre, also beautifully restored with a series of exquisitely coloured 14th-century frescoes. From its terrace is a breathtaking view over the surrounding countryside, and here in June the feast of St John is celebrated with a huge bonfire visible for miles.

Wine-lovers reluctant to leave the Mâconnais hills may wish to divert to the little village of **Chardonnay**, which

Chapaize, church of St-Martin.

gave its name to probably the most famous grape in the world, known from California to Australia, and responsible for all the best white wine in Burgundy. As in most villages in wine country the grapes occupy all of the valuable land, growing right up to the sides of the houses and the road. A large wine producer occupies pride of place in the village square.

Returning to the ecclesiastical trail, **Chapaize** has a very beautiful church, its lovely Lombardic square tower visible through a veil of trees as you approach. St-Martin is early 11th-century and carefully restored, all that remains of the priory founded by the Benedictine monks from Chalon. It is a fine composition of volumes and forms, very stark and simple, with walls, huge columns and ceiling all in the same warm yellow-ochre limestone so that you feel as if you are inside a great sculpture. The aisles end in charming little apsidial chapels rebuilt in the 13th century and the whole building has a very pleasing unity.

There are a number of fine châteaux to see in this region; **Sercy**, near **St-Gengoux-le-National**, has an extraordinary mixture of architectural styles including five distinctly different towers. **Cormatin**, on the D981, is a magnificent Renaissance château, built on the site of a 13th-century fortress founded by the du Blé family, and particularly famous for its richly painted 17th-century interiors.

Although nothing of the original building remains, when the moat was drained recently evidence of the corner towers was discovered. It was rebuilt by Antoine du Blé, Baron d'Uxelles, at the beginning of the 17th century. The interiors were painted for his son, Jacques, by Parisian artists; walls and ceilings are completely covered in panel paintings and gilding to extraordinary effect, complemented by period furniture. Also noteworthy are the kitchens and the arched stone staircase, one of the earliest of its kind.

In 1896 Raoul Gunzbourg, director of the Monte-Carlo opera, bought the cha-

Cormatin, painted ceiling.

270

teau and entertained, in sumptuous style, stars like Dame Nellie Melba, Caruso and Sarah Bernhardt. Then the building fell into disrepair and was bought in 1980 by private owners who have dedicated themselves to its restoration and use as an arts centre.

Beyond the moat, and its imperious black swans, the restored gardens are lovely, with a long avenue of lime trees, particularly favoured by the poet Lamartine, who was a frequent visitor to the château – so frequent indeed that Jacques's daughter, the Comtesse de Pierreclos, bore him a son. Ornamental topiary, parterres and a charming wrought-iron dovecote complete the picture of a formal Renaissance garden.

A few miles further along the D981 is **Taizé**, a small village world-famous for its international religous community visited by thousands of young people every year. Its proximity to the now defunct Cluny is supremely apposite. The community has built and filled to the rafters its own large modern church but the exquisite little Romanesque vil-

lage church nearby makes a pleasing contrast; very dark, lit only by a modern stained-glass window, and empty of chairs, just a few wooden kneeling stools on the bare stone floor.

The Romanesque trail: Cluny itself feels like a town with something missing: a vast empty space around which all the streets and buildings arrange themselves. The great abbey, once the largest building in Christendom, no longer exists but the small town which grew up around it is still there, and has expanded into the ruins.

Rues Lamartine, Mèrciere and Filaterie were all built against the massive southern enclosure wall of the abbey, with many of the old houses propped against it. The Rue Porte-de-Paris follows the north and east walls of the abbey, both ending in watchtowers, the Tour Ronde and the Tour Fabry.

The whole town was originally enclosed by fortifications and of its eight gateways, two remain: the 12th-century Porte Ste-Odile on the Promenade du Fouettin, a wide boulevard, flanked by

Cormatin panelling.

TAIZÉ

"Ah Taizé, that little springtime!" So Pope John XXIII described this ecumenical monastic community which has grown to become one of the most influential places of pilgrimage in contemporary Christianity. He always kept in regular contact with the founder of the community and subsequent popes have visited it in person, such is its importance.

It is appropriate that this should happen here, in the shadow of the once-famous but now long-dead Cluny. Every year tens of thousands of young people from all religious backgrounds visit Taizé to participate in its simple life and inspirational worship.

Founded by a Swiss pastor, Roger Schutz, when he came to the almost deserted village of Taizé in 1940, the community began as a hiding place for members of the Resistance and those escaping Nazi persecution, particularly Jews. Brother Roger, as he is known, believed that taking his Christianity seriously meant that he had to live among those who were suffering and not in neutral

Switzerland. But in 1944 the Gestapo visited Taizé and he was forced to flee to Geneva. He returned after the Liberation of France, accompanied by friends from Geneva. On Easter Day 1949 the first seven brothers made a commitment to live together in celibate community life, working to relieve suffering and to bring reconciliation between Christians. In 1962, having out-grown the tiny village church, they built the Church of the Reconciliation, which now stands centrally on the hill at Taizé.

Today there are over 90 brothers from all denominations, 30 of whom live in small "fraternities" in poor parts of the world. Both there and at Taizé they accept no gifts, surviving on what they earn by their work. This includes delightful earthenware pottery, art-work and books, all of which are sold at Taizé.

There is not a great deal to see at Taizé; it is rather a place to be experienced. At the top of the steep hill to the village is the tiny Romanesque village church, its dark interior sparsely lit with candles. The atmosphere is intense with the prayer of a few figures kneeling in the dim light. The little village occasionally feels swamped by the torrent of visitors which can sometimes amount to as many as 6,000 in one week.

The young pilgrims come from all over Europe, staying for a week at a time in simple barracks and tents, many of them returning year after year. Everyone joins in the daily life of the community, doing the chores, attending Bible studies and worship three times a day.

At the heart of it are the "worships" which take place daily, morning, lunchtime and evening. The community church is huge but even so during the summer people often spill into adjoining tents.

It is always kept dark, the only light coming from stained-glass windows and hundreds of tiny candles. Everyone sits on the floor around the altar in silence, interspersed with meditative chants and Bible readings in several different languages. These gatherings also take place in cities throughout Europe, encouraging young people to work for peace and reconciliation. It is in this way that Taizé exerts its influence, not in the building of daughter communities as Cluny once did, but in the inspiration of its worship throughout the world. **Taizé at prayer.**

lime trees, created by filling in the moat, and the Porte St-Mayeul opening onto the old road to Charolles.

Sadly the great central space of Cluny is now impossible to enter without paying for a 75-minute guided tour of the few fragments of the abbey that the 18th and 19th-century burghers of the town inadvertently left standing. The classic octagonal tower, of the south transept, with its two tiers of arcades, copied all across France, appears tantalisingly over high walls and locked gates. It is all that remains of the massive church which dominated the entire region and influenced building all over Europe.

The destruction of the abbey was not the work of a mob as is often thought; even a mob crazed with anger could not demolish a building of such great size. It took the Revolutionary army a whole week just to burn the archives. The mob did break a few statues, but it was left to the town government to destroy it totally. After the Revolution it became town property and was divided up into four lots with a road driven right through the centre of the nave to show the division. The church was bought at auction by Batonard of Mâcon, who, despite the protests of Paris and antiquarians worldwide, set up a quarry there from 1798 to 1823, selling off the dressed stones as building materials. It took more than 70 explosions to topple the 700-year-old walls.

Less than a tenth of the building remains: one of the transepts and a few column bases, around which Cluny now bases its tourist industry. Should you stay in the Hôtel de Bourgogne you will not have to look far to see the abbey – you will be sleeping right on top of it. The hotel's geranium-festooned windows follow the course of the columns of the north aisle of the nave. (One column has been excavated beneath the hotel and the base of it sits in a little cave hollowed out of the hotel wall.)

Throughout Cluny there are reminders of what lies hidden or destroyed. The whole quarter by Rue des Tanneries is in ruins, but hopefully awaiting restoration. In Rue Filaterie opposite, is the

Cluny, view of south tower.

15th-century Hospice St-Blaise, which took in poor travellers and pilgrims in the Middle Ages. It has a Gothic doorway and window lintel which have aged to a beautiful brown patina. Not everything has been ruined, however; Rue Lamartine has a number of fine Romanesque buildings with arcaded windows. There is a 12th-century house on Rue de la République and the Hôtel des Monnaies on Rue d'Avril.

The parish church of **Notre Dame** is worth a visit. Built shortly after 1100, it was enlarged and altered so that it is now largely Gothic in character. The original floor level has been revealed in the northwest corner of the nave, showing a well head and the base of the pillars, giving a good indication of its original proportions. Each arm of the transept has a beautiful rose window with ten branches. Note also the superb 17th-century woodwork. The tympanum and the narthex were destroyed during the Revolution, though parts of the springing arches remain either side of the battered 13th-century front door with its mutilated statues of Moses and Aaron. The outside walls of the nave can also be seen, thanks to the bombardment of 1944 which destroyed the houses built against it. In front of the west door is the charming Place Notre Dame with an 18th-century fountain and the 13th-century Maison des Griffons, named after its carved capitals.

The great barn-like volume of **St-Marcel-de-Cluny** is also notable, with no columns or even chairs to clutter the space. There is a 13th-century baptismal font at the entrance but most striking is the slim three-storey Romanesque 42-metre (138-ft) octagonal belltower.

Struggle up the 120 steps to the top of the 11th-century **Tour de Fromage** in the abbey walls for the excellent view. The ground floor houses the tourist information office. The abbey palaces are both standing though by no means complete. The palace of John of Bourbon was constructed in 1460 and now houses the Museum of Art and Archaeology. It originally extended by means of a fortified pavilion to the palace of

Adam and Eve capital, Cluny; interior of south tower, Cluny.

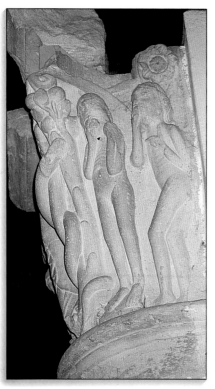

John of Amboise, built in 1500 and connected to the main gate and watchtower. Gate and pavilion were both demolished during the Revolution but the main body of the Amboise Palace remains, now the Hôtel de Ville.

The fantastic flamboyant Gothic carving on its facade is in the then fashionable Italian manner, which looks as if it was assembled as booty from other people's palaces (like the front of St Mark's in Venice). It looks out over one of the abbey lawns – open to the public and a good picnic spot. To the immediate west of the church are the abbey gates, battered but still standing. Through here passed popes and kings.

On Rue Lamartine, the 11th-century **Tour de Moulin**, the Mill Tower, rises over the steep rooftops. It has been well-restored after considerable bomb damage in World War II. Through the basement flows the stream which used to work the abbey mill, and adjoining the building is the 12th-century abbey grain store (which can be seen only as part of the abbey tour).

It is well worth visiting **Berzé-la-Ville** at this point to view the magnificent paintings, executed by the same painters as at Cluny. The **Chapelle aux Moines** is a small estate, clinging to a rock jutting out over the Saône plain, which came under the control of Cluny in 1093. It was one of 30 such farms, with attached chapels, that supplied the abbey of Cluny with food. St Hugues, then engaged in expanding Cluny, loved the place and used it as his private retreat. But it was during the time of Ponce de Melgueil, St Hugues's successor, that a team of artists were sent from the Cluny workshop to paint the interior. The entrance is unassuming, down a dark tunnel and through a farmyard, but on entering you are confronted with a truly amazing spectacle. The entire east end of the chapel is a mass of brilliant colours. After St-Savin, this is the most important collection of Romanesque paintings in France. The luminous colours and eastern technique indicate Oriental inspiration. The painted murals owe a tremendous

Berzé-la-Ville apse painting.

amount to mosaic work and the "golden gloom" of Byzantium. There are five colours in all, red, ochre, blue, gold, and violet, obtained by a red wash over blue.

A huge Christ figure dominates the half dome of the apse, surrounded by his apostles and deacons. Below the windows are a group of Byzantine-looking saints – identities unknown. The paintings are lit by a typical Cluniac arrangement of three windows in an arcade around the apse with two blind arches filled with paintings. The apsidial arch originally had a round light above it, now closed; the crossing had two windows, one above each other on either side; and finally the nave arch, where it rises above the apse, has a top window. The chapel was bought after World War II by the great Romanesque scholar, Joan Evans, and presented to the Academy of Mâcon in 1947.

The village of Berzé also has a little church, later in date, with a square tower and there are remnants of much older houses to be detected. Nearby the castle at **Berzé-le-Châtel** is like driving straight into the Duc de Berry's book of hours with vineyards planted right up the steep incline to the castle walls. It is a proper castle with the remains of a drawbridge, machicolations for pouring horrible things down on unwelcome visitors, and an ancient crooked gatehouse with two powerful towers of its own. A small formal garden with topiary and stone statues connects the two parts of the château and is the only part open to the public.

There is a beautiful drive to the east of Cluny to the archaeological site at **Azé** where there is a network of caves and an underground river, and a museum with a collection of local paleolithic remains.

Rich pastures: To the west are the **Charolais** hills, prime agricultural country, a carefully stitched patchwork of little fields divided by dry stone walls or carefully trimmed hedges dotted with *étangs*, pools of water glittering in the green-gold light. Small brown farms nestle into the folds of accommodating hills and valleys moulded by centuries of human labour. Almost every field has

Berzé-le-Chatel.

276

a couple of huge white Charolais cows with their short necks and long curved horns, ruminating comfortably, surrounded especially on damp mornings by the plump *champignons* that will eventually join them in an authentic *boeuf bourguignon.*

It is a region reminiscent of the Cotswolds in England 50 years ago: every hedgerow abuzz with small birds and in the autumn, thick with blackberries, rosehips and haws. Autumn shows its most fruitful aspect: fields full of plump corn, kitchen gardens with burgeoning fruit trees, bulging red pumpkins and clumps of tied crysanthemums, golden, purple and pink.

The Butte de Suin is an excellent orientation point on the route to Charolles, whether you stick to the main Route Nationale or preferably wander along the narrow but always well-maintained country roads that dictate a slower and more appropriate pace for this deeply rural landscape.

Suin is a tiny hamlet near the top of Suin hill, one of the mystical buttes of Charolais, which has panoramic views of rolling hills, forests and vineyards. There are two small towers, one of which is an orientation platform from which you can see a sum total of 52 belltowers. The Romanesque tower of Suin church has unusual arcading, and the fields around the church, with their 360° views, are ideal picnic spots. To the north are a number of small villages with particularly fine Romanesque churches. In the tiny village of **St-Vincent-des-Prés** the church is a bijou version of Cluny II, built between 1030 and 1063. Six huge cylinders support its barrel vault at the east end and below the tower, carved fleur-de-lys and leaves pattern the remaining west end capitals, and the apse has small fragments of the original wall paintings.

Nearby **Massy** is a classic example of the Romanesque churches found in southern Burgundy but, like so many, it has suffered some interference. In this instance there is a false ceiling which almost halves the height of the nave, and a lot of gilt and hideous statuary. It is

Prime pastureland of Charolais.

better seen from outside; the strong tower with its wonderful naïve but powerful zigzag work; the gravestones in the tiny churchyard huddled right up to the church walls; a manor house looming protectively over the church and, if you're lucky, a red squirrel scuttling down the lane.

Charolles itself is a small, sleepy, country town with tractors in the main street and very little tourism. The ruins of the château dominate the town from a bluff, approached via Rue Baudinot, a steep cobbled thoroughfare leading up through the old quarter to the stone gateway of the château.

Despite its sleepiness Charolles has had a chequered history. It was dependent on the dukes of Burgundy, four of whom held the title of Count of Charolais. Originally Charolles was independent of the king of France though it was owned at different times, through marriage or purchase, by both the house of Bourbon and the house of Armagnac. From the 13th century until the French Revolution in was also owned at various times by the kings of France, Spain and Austria.

Just inside the castle gateway, to the right, is a rusticated round tower, the 14th-century Tour de Diamants, the old town prison, so named because the stones are cut with facets. Inside the château there is little left except the 15th-century ivy-covered tower of Charles the Bold. This has remarkable woodwork on the fourth floor which is designed like a wheel with interlocking spokes. Most of the watchtowers have been levelled: pink dahlias grow in the base of one and a 1916 cannon has been placed in another for children to play on. A potager grows between the inner and outer walls of the ramparts. The terrace area has been laid out in formal flowerbeds and gives a pleasant view over the town.

Halfway down the hill, at 25 Rue Baudinot, is **L'ancien couvent des Clarisses**, a 16th-century building now used as a tourist information centre and exhibition hall. Ste Marguerite Marie Alacoque, who was born in nearby

Charolles canals.

Verosvres, lived for several years in the convent and made her first communion there in 1656. She was the founder of the cult of the Sacred Heart of Jesus (to which the local neo-Romanesque edifice is dedicated, as is Sacré Coeur in Paris). The convent roof is made of chestnut in the shape of an inverted boat and there is a good spiral stone staircase.

The slow-moving Arcone divides and flows through the town in a series of attractive algae-covered canals, meandering down the middle of a block then disappearing beneath a house, to reappear in someone's backyard, its banks and footbridges overhung with flowers. There are more than 30 bridges in the town which is sometimes known, at least in travel brochures, as "the Venice Charolaise". There is a regular market here every Wednesday and apart from the fine local beef, specialities include Charolais cheese, a long cylinder which can be made from goat's or cow's milk.

Cow culture and churches: Cow country continues south into the **Brionnais**, a quiet rural landscape of small farms and tiny villages with probably the best pastureland in France. The local domestic architecture is unpretentious, with outside staircases and wooden porches sheltering chickens and hung with drying corn. The Romanesque churches of this area are, however, superb. Though usually small, they are often exquisitely decorated with fine carvings and sculpture, a surprising development in such a backwater, due of course to the influence of Cluny. There are so many to see that a *Circuit des Églises Romanes* has been mapped out by the local tourist authority.

But first, to experience contemporary cow culture to the full, consider an early morning trip to the cattle market in **St-Christophe-en-Brionnais** held every Thursday. It starts at 5am and you really need to be there by about 8am to see any action. It claims to be the biggest weekly market in France and, for such a small place, this is no mean feat. Everywhere are huge, double-parked cattle trucks, the bellowing of cows and bulls, and throngs of red-faced farmers, all

Charolais cattle.

with flat peaked caps, wellingtons and sturdy sticks. There is a powerful reek of ammonia and rich slurry underfoot from the thousands of cattle gathered in the covered market, tethered to railings, or in the holding yard where 50 trucks at a time can unload straight into the pens. The farmers prod and pull the cattle, earnestly discussing their finer points. By 9am the enormous market café is always lost in a cloud of steam and smoke, its tables packed with rows of peak-capped farmers, each with a bottle of red wine and huge baguettes of sausage and salami.

Before embarking on the Romanesque trail of the Brionnais, **La Clayette**, where Potain cranes are made, is worth a slight detour to the east. In the middle of town is a very fine castle set on a lake, which reflects its lovely mansard roof, round turreted towers and drawbridge. It is private, but is opened on 1 June every year for visitors to pick lily-of-the-valley, considered to be lucky. Its outbuildings house a popular vintage car museum.

You can wander at will through the Brionnais looking at Romanesque churches and never see them all, so the following examples are only edited highlights. The church at **Vareilles** to the west of La Clayette, has an apse lit by three fine Romanesque windows with a blind arch either side in the manner of Cluny. Unfortunately, a nasty false ceiling has been erected in the nave, destroying its proportions. The high square tower is its pride and joy with two storeys of boldly cut arcading, contrasting nicely with the solid cylinder of the apse. The village also has some charming buildings, a typical shuttered Brionnais house with curved tiled roof, a wooden house with an open upstairs porch, and an old house which uses the original columns from the nave of the church to make a gallery.

The exterior of **St-Laurent-en-Brionnais**, just to the south, is very attractive; thick tiles on the apse and chapels look like clam shells piled on top of each other. The tower is very tall, rising three storeys above the nave. St-

St-Julien-de-Jonzy tympanum.

280

Maurice, a tiny hamlet just outside Châteauneauf, has a lovely little ruined 12th-century Romanesque church. All that remains is the square tower and semi-circular apse set in its old church-yard but this has been made into a room used for exhibitions and though the walls have massive cracks and the floor is simply gravel, the ancient structure is charming. Two miles west on the D8, at **Ligny-en-Brionnais**, are the 11th-century remains of the Abbey of St-Ligard, home of Peter the Hermit, who preached the first crusade. Going east, the D8 crosses the river Sornin to **Châteauneuf** over a Roman bridge.

St-Julien-de-Jonzy is a small hamlet dominated by the square tower of its Romanesque church, in an old church-yard overlooking open countryside and the Beaujolais mountains. The tympanum and lintel were cut from the same huge block of sandstone by an anonymous master and feature a wonderful carving of the Last Supper with everybody's feet sticking out from under a carefully modelled tablecloth. All but two of the heads were knocked off during the Revolution but the work is still very impressive. Just inside the porch, to the left of the main door, is a cow's head capital, appropriately enough, staring quizzically at the visitor. The uplifiting sense of light and space inside is caused by a tall clerestory level filled with plain glass.

One of the most charming features in the 11th-century church at **Iguerande** is the Cyclops playing the pipes of Pan who stares, with his one central eye, down from the first pillar on the left as you enter. There are many other fine carved capitals featuring foliage and geometric designs, some of them still painted in their original colours, and a medieval wall-painting extending right over the crossing and around the apse. The interior proportions of the church are very pure and simple with delightful semi-circular apsidial chapels either side of the apse in the correct Cluniac manner. Outside, don't miss the carved cornice corbels on the chevet which feature dogs, monkeys and horses.

La Clayette.

Semur-en-Brionnais is especially beguiling; a once fortified town, with part of its ramparts still remaining and an arched town gate leading to grassy footpaths and fields. The castle is small but very impressive, with flocks of black birds swooping round its squat 9th-century keep. This was the birthplace of St Hugues, the famous abbot of Cluny, and a geneology of his family, the house of Semur, is on display. The two towers were used as a prison in the 18th century and still have prisoners' graffiti on the walls, and a game carved on the window-sill of a lookout slit, by the soldiers of the watch. Steep stone steps, almost 1,000 years old and very narrow, lead to the secret dungeon and a 5-metre (18-ft) deep pit which has been luridly lit with green light.

Outside the castle is a square of shady lime trees, and a wonderful old-fashioned café, with a big fire in winter, home-made blackberry conserves served with bread and coffee, wood beamed ceiling, simple wooden tables and an importunate cat. The unmistakable aroma of Gauloises intensifies when farmers from the cattle market at St-Christophe stop on Thursday mornings for a late breakfast of wine and soup. Outside the café is a water pump with a huge iron handle that could have been made by Miró or Calder.

The church of St-Hilaire is a beautiful and celebrated example of Cluniac architecture, in particular its octagonal belfry with two storeys of Romanesque arcading, one of the best in the region. The view from the east end is remarkable with the flat planes of the tower contrasting with the semi-circles of the apse. There are tympani over both north and west doors. The interior has triforum arcading and an overhanging gallery at the west end supported by superb corbelling. This gallery is thought to be a copy of an original in the Chapel of St Michael in the abbey church of Cluny.

The church has plenty of breathing space and stands in a wide square surrounded by sympathetic architecture with plenty of turrets and towers, in-

Anzy-le-Duc fresco ceiling.

cluding the former priory and the 18th-century Hôtel de Ville.

The late 11th-century church at **Anzy-le-Duc**, once part of an important priory, is considered to be one of the finest in the Brionnais, with a three-storey Romanesque tower and particularly well preserved capitals. Its famous tympanum can now be seen in the museum at Paray-le-Monial. It is very similar to Vézelay and allows us to see how Vézelay looked before the addition of its Gothic buttresses.

Sacred Heart: Paray-le-Monial, which is at this point only a few miles to the north, is an essential element in the Romanesque jigsaw puzzle. The twinning of Paray with Wells is appropriate – both towns have the same quiet, bourgeois confidence, seemingly exempt from world events, their lives dominated by the giant churches at their centre, their rivers slow-moving and their population unhurried.

Paray-le-Monial is famous as the centre of the worship of the Sacred Heart, a cult which was started by Marguerite-Marie Alacoque, born in nearby Verosvres. As a nun in Paray, she had a divine revelation to worship the Sacred Heart of Jesus. After her beatification in 1864, the church of Sacré Coeur was built in Paris, and yearly pilgrimages to Paray have taken place ever since, establishing the town as a very important religious centre.

To get an idea of how Cluny III must have looked, visit the basilica of Paray-le-Monial (**Basilique du Sacré Coeur**) first. It was begun at the end of the 11th century and completed by 1109. It is in a beautiful setting, its impressive facade of golden stone facing the river bank and removed from whatever hustle and bustle Paray can muster.

Paray shows how daring the Romanesque Burgundian church builders could be. To get light into the church they built a very high nave, 22 metres (71 ft), crowned by a pointed barrel vault. This exerted less downward thrust than a round barrel so did not need the usual supporting vaults above the aisles to buttress it. Without the galleries above the vaults they could build

clerestory windows and illuminate the nave directly from outside. Fluted pilasters with Corinthian capitals line the nave arcade and classical details have been taken from Roman buildings such as the Roman gateway in Autun.

The glory of Paray is in the lighting of its east end. The nave terminates in a vertical wall with three lights directly over the choir which has nine clerestory windows of its own on a lower level. The ambulatory has two storeys of windows and each radiating chapel has three windows. Thus light enters the east end on four levels of elevation and in four different planes of space, a remarkable achievement for the time. Cluny III was very similar, only on a larger scale with more chapels.

The nave of Paray was not completed; only three bays join the crossing to the narthex with its two great towers, but the awkward joining of the nave to the narthex, coupled with the fact that the west door is not quite aligned to the present altar, suggest that the builders intended to demolish the 11th-century

Anzy-le-Duc capital carving.

towers and narthex, and continue their new nave to a point much closer to the river. The result is a strange, squeezed appearance from the west, with the towers frankly too close to each other, whereas the east end is expansive and confident. The towers are the oldest part of the present church, predating it by about 100 years, but they have suffered extensive rebuilding. The narthex which they house is on two floors, as in Tournus – a Burgundian speciality.

The central tower is mock Romanesque, built in the 1860s to replace an unsympathetic 18th-century dome. The community of monks the abbey was originally intended to accommodate was never more than 25 strong – its huge scale was for the glory of God and not man. However, it is providentially suitable for receiving the great crowds of Sacred Heart pilgrims who flock here every year. The **Hiéron Museum**, part of the basilica complex, houses the beautifully carved 12th-century tympanum from Anzy-le-Duc, rescued during the Revolution.

There are other fine buildings to see in Paray: the marvellous 16th-century Renaissance **Hôtel de Ville**, formerly the private mansion of Pierre Joyet who contructed it in 1525–28. The elaborate carved facade is festooned with medallions and emblems, niches, carved figures and many *coquilles St Jacques*. Note the pair of faux dormer windows on the third floor which do not actually pierce the steep roof: their top windows open to the roof tiles instead of attic rooms. Two doors to the right is a building with a remarkable row of medieval windows, each in a different style. Across from this group is the finely proportioned **Tour St Nicolas**, which is a deconsecrated church.

The old quarter of town is pretty in a restrained way, particularly the Place de la Boucherie, with low buildings set at attractive angles on wide airy streets, window boxes and newly restored fronts. In front of the church the Bourbince flows between quiet riverbanks shaded by planched trees, with ducks and swans calmly floating by.

The Central Canal passes close to Paray and local industrial production includes sandstone paving and tiles. To the north is **Montceau-les-Mines**, an industrial town which developed due to the coal mined locally. The best view of this area is to be had from the small town of **Gourdon** which overlooks Montceau-les-Mines, Le Cruesot and out as far as the Morvan.

But in Paray, we have now almost reached the Loire, and the D79 follows it for some time, making a very pleasant drive onto **Digoin**, an important pottery centre and the hub of a network of canals with a canal-bridge linking the Saône and the Loire.

A little further on is **Bourbon-Lancy** with its thermal baths and medieval buildings; it is quiet, the approach shaded by huge chestnut trees, and there are good views from the old town, high on its hill. But these are digressions from the more essential aspects of Burgundy, and, surfeited with Romanesque, it is time to return to its other main attraction; the wine country of Mâcon and Beaujolais.

Left, Cluny, south tower. Right, Paray-le-Monial; modelled on Cluny.

MÂCON AND BEAUJOLAIS

The red pantile roofs of Mâcon herald the south, the landscape becomes more rugged as the hills of Beaujolais beckon and only the most dedicated oenophile would regret exchanging the dullard contours of the Côte d'Or for more challenging vistas. Nor is the wine a poor substitute; both in Mâcon and in Beaujolais it is affordable, a realistic accompaniment to a picnic lunch rather than the revered travel objective.

Apart from the splendid monument at Brou, and a sprinkling of churches and châteaux, this region is not especially rich in architecture, and can be enjoyed most of all for its judicious combination of good wine and beautiful country. Lamartine is its spokesman; he was born here in the tiny village of Milly-Lamartine (and his legacy is fully exploited) and adored this land, writing innumerable poems singing praises to its beauty. "My eye finds a friend in all this horizon; / every tree has its history and each stone a name."

To the north, between Mâcon and Tournus, are the Mâconnais hills where most of the Mâconnais *appellation* is grown. About a third of this wine is red or rosé, based on the Gamay or Pinot Noir grape and two-thirds are white, grown from the Chardonnay grape. The main *appellations* are Mâcon Rouge, Mâcon-Villages Blanc, Pouilly-Fuissé and Saint Véran. The latter two, considered the best of the Mâcon wines, are grown on the chalky hills to the south of Mâcon itself.

The town of **Mâcon**, though an important wine centre, and a pleasant enough base for visiting the region, is not a particularly compelling tourist attraction. As the most southerly of the Burgundy towns it looks more towards Lyon than Dijon, and has always been an important regional crossroads, linking Paris with the south and looking east towards Switzerland. It was established

Preceding pages: Jarnaux Château, Beaujolais. **Left**, Mâcon, Quai Lamartine.

as a port by the Romans, though its history can be traced right back to pre-historic times, and the river has always been its *raison d'être*, with trade as its mainstay. At this point the Saône is about as wide as the Thames in London, sluggish and slow-moving; Julius Caesar observed that it was so slow he could not tell which way it was moving. There is a river walk from one end of the town to the other and at either end it widens out, with poplars and willows lining the banks. Upstream the Saône provides a wide enough basin to accommodate the French Rowing Championships. Along Quai Lamartine and Quai Jean Jaurès are terrace cafés and restaurants with a good view of the river.

The northern part of the old town of Mâcon is built over a steep hill on the west bank of the river. Sadly, many of the old over-hanging houses in the area have been demolished, and what remain are dwarfed by massive 1960s-style government buildings.

Mâcon was one of the centres of early Protestantism, and was the scene of fierce fighting during the Wars of Religion. During the French Revolution the Mâconnais took anti-clericalism to heart and did a thorough job, destroying all 14 of their Romanesque churches. Only a few fragments of the cathedral church of **St-Vincent** remain, looking as if they have suffered from a great conflagration, which they have. Any visitor coming to Burgundy in search of the beauties of the Romanesque will thus be disappointed in Mâcon. In the 1860s the citizens even had to construct a neo-Romanesque parish church, the Église St-Pierre, to cater for their own needs.

In the battered remains of St-Vincent there is a small museum of Romanesque artefacts salvaged from the rubble – mainly capitals and fragments of pillars. The tympanum is largely intact and has many interesting carved figures, otherwise all that remains of the church are the narthex, the two hexagonal towers and the portion of the nave beneath.

But churches are not everything: there is the beautiful **Place des Herbes**, where the vegetable market shelters beneath

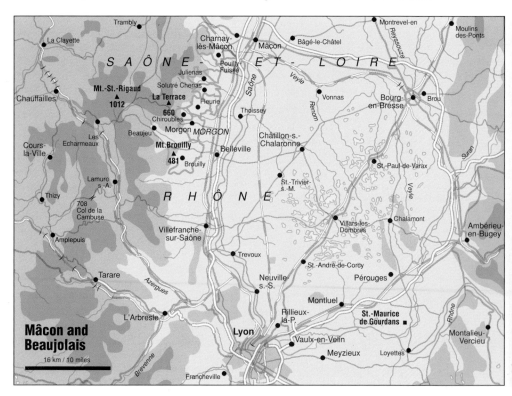

Mâcon and Beaujolais

16 km / 10 miles

two rows of leafy, shady, trees. Here on the corner of the market and the rue Dombey is the amazing **Maison de Bois**: a three-storey, 15th-century wooden house covered in the kind of elaborate carving you would normally expect to find adorning the interior; here be dragons, birds, unicorns and griffins. Monkeys and human figures pull faces and parade naked overhead. In *La revendeuse de Mâcon*, the Goncourt brothers described the building as "a large wooden sideboard that the people of Mâcon can only sneak a glance at", due to the risqué figures on the walls. The Maison de Bois now houses a reasonably priced café and makes a good place to sit and get the feel of the town.

A little further along the Rue Carnot, one of the busiest shopping streets of the town, is the **L'Ancien Hospice de la Charité**, designed and built in 1752–62 by Soufflot as a hospital and now an old people's home. The oval chapel of St-Vincent-de-Paul was designed to link directly with the hospital, to allow the sick to attend church services without having to move to the ground floor. To the right of the front door is a swivel-gate, one of the few remaining in France. It consists of a barrel built into the wall to allow desperate parents to abandon new-born babies without being seen. The child was placed in the barrel which was then swivelled to face inside. When the bell was rung the nuns ran immediately to collect the baby.

The **Musée des Ursulines** on the Rue des Ursulines is the municipal museum, housed in a 17th-century convent building. It has mainly Flemish and French paintings and porcelain, with some contemporary works, and is worth visiting for its local history material and the collection includes a particularly good exhibition on the excavations at nearby Solutré, plus examples of local pottery, wine-growing tools and Bresse furniture.

It is in Mâcon that the Lamartine trail begins; the **Hôtel d'Ozenay** at 15 Rue Lamartine is his old family house, and in the 17th-century Hôtel Senecé is housed the **Musée Lamartine**, with a collection of literary and political docu-

Risqué carvings on Maison des Bois.

ments relating to the poet. On the way out of Mâcon to the north, on Avenue de Lattre de Tassigny, is a new cultural centre and theatre complex, as well as the **Maison des Vins**, which provides an opportunity for tasting regional wine and food; look out for a wide variety of local *saucisson*, and the famously pungent *chèvre de Mâcon*. Each May, Mâcon holds a national wine fair with hundreds of different wines.

Although it's not technically in Burgundy, it would be a pity to be so close and not visit **Bourg-en-Bresse**. Head out of Mâcon to the east across the 14th-century St-Laurent bridge – a good place to get a general view of Mâcon over the river. This is true Bresse country again with its busy, bustling market gardens and low wood and red brick houses hugging the earth. Bourg (pronounced Bourk if you want to sound like the locals) is the centre of this rich agricultural region, which is especially well-known for its cattle and poultry – best seen on market days and at the annual fair. The town is most famous,

however, for the church and the monastery at **Brou**.

A sacred promise: Brou was built by Margaret of Austria to fulfil a vow made by her mother-in-law, Margaret of Bourbon, who promised to rebuild the existing small priory at Brou if her husband, Philip, Count of Bresse, recovered from a hunting accident. She unfortunately died before she could fulfil her promise and Margaret of Austria, her daughter-in-law, initiated the construction instead in 1506.

As the daughter of Emperor Maximilian, she had been a particularly unfortunate pawn in the politics of the time and by the time she was 24 had been widowed twice. She became regent of Flanders and Franche-Comté, and was a most highly respected and cultured ruler. In fulfilling the sacred promise of the earlier Margaret she hoped to avoid further disaster. She left Bourg-en-Bresse to live in Malines, near Brussels, from where she oversaw the plans, but died of an infected foot in 1530, and never saw the completion of the build-

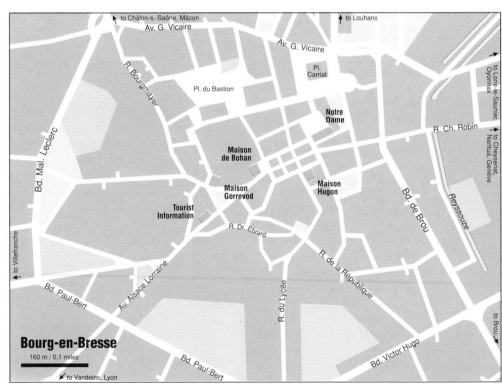

Bourg-en-Bresse

160 m / 0,1 miles

ing. The monastery and church (now deconsecrated) which houses the tombs of Margaret, her husband Philibert, and Margaret of Bourbon, was designed and constructed by Louis Van Boghem, a Flemish mason.

The church, which has recently undergone restoration work, is a fine example of flamboyant Gothic with superb carving on the facade. Within, the light from the clerestory brilliantly illuminates the soaring nave and double aisles. Note in particular the superb carving of the choir stalls and the detail of the misericords, the brilliant colours of the original stained-glass windows, and the finely carved rood screen.

Situated in the centre of the choir and the two chapels to the side, are the tombs themselves – extraordinary monuments, richly carved, with the three effigies sculpted from huge blocks of white Carrara marble that was transported all the way from Italy. True-to-life yet rather gruesome, Margaret's effigy even shows the gangrenous foot which caused her death.

Brou, misericord carving; Brou sculptures on St Philibert's tomb.

The monastery to the side of the church has three fine cloisters where the atmosphere is a world apart from the busy traffic-filled streets round about. The kitchen cloisters are the oldest part of the monastery – the remains of the former 14th-century priory. Located above the vaulted great cloisters are the monks' dormitories which now house a museum of paintings, including a portrait of Margaret of Austria by Bernard van Orley, and works by Breughl, Gustave Doré and Millet. There is also a collection of Bresse furniture and tapestries.

Perhaps most pleasing about the entire ensemble at Brou (apart from the fact that it miraculously survived the Revolution) is the way it has retained its original purpose as a monument – a glorious testimony both to its founder and to the numerous skilled artists that she employed.

Bourg-en-Bresse is a surprising town; despite its agricultural base, it feels very elegant, with luxury shops, well-dressed people and an almost Parisian ambience to its streets and cafés. Don't miss, for

LAMARTINE

Burgundy's greatest native writer, Alphonse de Lamartine (1790–1869), is revered in France as one of the greatest poets of the French Romantic movement, second only to Victor Hugo; every schoolchild studies his work. Being a somewhat humourless and high-flown figure, he was very far from the stereotype of a jolly, bibulous, down-to-earth Burgundian. But he did have a warm feeling for his homeland, the hills west of Mâcon, as is clear from many of his poems.

He was born in Mâcon, into a family of landowning minor aristocrats who owned several manor houses in the villages to its west. Here he spent much of his time, when he was not working elsewhere as a diplomat or Paris politician. Just as Rousseau influenced Wordsworth, so the bard of Grasmere in turn had an impact on Lamartine; and the significance that the French poet attached to his early environment, and to its deep effect on his character, has strong Wordsworthian echoes. In one long poem, telling of the

moon and stars, the billowing grassland, the herds on the hillsides, he says: "All these speak to me a most intimate language... these old memories that sleep deep within us, that a landscape preserves for..." Those lines are from *Milly ou la terre natale*, about the village of Milly where he spent much of his childhood ("Here is the rustic bench where my father sat"). Here is the family's old stone house, where he later wrote the first of his *Méditations* and recalled "the sweet and melancholy voices of the little frogs that sing on summer evenings".

Nearer Mâcon, just north of the N79, the handsome ochre-coloured château of Monceau was one of Lamartine's favourite homes in his middle years: here this lover of pomp lived in extravagant style as a country squire, sometimes plagued by creditors. Neither this château nor the house at Milly is open to visitors; nor is the 17th-century manor at Pierreclos, south of Milly, home of the woman who was his inspiration for Laurence in his epic poem *Jocelyn*. In Mâcon itself, his home between 1805 and 1820 still stands, at the now aptly named 15 Rue Lamartine, and the nearby Hôtel Senecé contains a museum of his souvenirs.

The Château of St-Point, west of Milly, *can* be visited. The poet received it from his father as a wedding gift in 1820, and he lived there often. It contains his bed, writing-desk and other mementoes. In the little church are two paintings by his English wife, Anna Eliza Birch, and in its chapel are his tomb and hers. In the garden, you can still see the stone bench under the lime-trees where he wrote many of the *Méditations*, and the oak-tree under which he wrote *Jocelyn*.

All this is authentic. But a notice by the pond in the park states "Le Lac" which is misleading, for Lamartine's best-known poem, *Le Lac*, is actually about the large and lovely Lac du Bourget, in the alpine foothills of Savoy, where in 1816 the young poet met the wife of a Paris doctor, Julie, and fell romantically in love. She suffered from a lung complaint, and died in Paris before she could return to meet him the next year. Just before her death, he sat on a hill above the lake and wrote his famous poem: *O temps, suspend ton vol! et vous, heures propices, suspendez votre cours!*... (O time, suspend your flight! and you, propitious hours, suspend your course!). ∎

example, Le Français, an old-style brasserie with aspidistras and velvet banquettes, tall mirrored columns and brown nicotine stained ceiling. The comfortable plumpness of its patrons attests to their consumption of large quantities of rich local dairy produce. The old buildings of the town, clustered round the Gothic church of Notre Dame, have been recently and very well restored; look out for fine Renaissance mansions and 15th-century half-timbered houses like the Maison du Bois on the corner of Rue l'Espagne and Rue du Palais, the double-jettied Maison Hugon on the Rue Gambetta and the wooden buildings on the Place des Bons Enfants.

West of Mâcon: After this detour, head west again to complete a tour of the southernmost part of Burgundy. Leaving Mâcon on the N79 in the direction of Cluny, there is what is now the suburb of **Charnay-les-Mâcon**. Continue further, over the autoroute, and the 11th-century church of Charnay can be found, away from the road, in the middle of a wide village green, originally the grave-

yard. Over the years the church has been embellished with four side chapels, a narthex and an inappropriate glazed tiled dome added to the tower. Beneath it all, however, remains a beautifully proportioned Romanesque building; the hexagonal tower rises from a square base against which is set the semi-circular apse. It is built from golden brown stone and was well restored in 1970 with the exception of the new stained-glass windows, which resemble disco lighting and make the interior too dark.

There is a small museum on the floor above the triple arches of the narthex; unfortunately, it is difficult to see very much because of the dim light, but the view of the nave is good.

In the chapel housing the font, protected by a 17th-century oak screen, the legendary Claude Brosse is buried. He was an enterprising local wine-grower, a giant of a man, who decided to take his wine to Paris in the hope of selling it to a great lord.

The journey took him 33 days; his two oxen pulling a wagon groaning with

Pierreclos Château.

two hogsheads of his best wine. In Versailles, Brosse attended Mass where his great size attracted the attention of the Sun King. Brought before Louis XIV, Brosse, a simple country man unencumbered by elaborate court etiquette, happily explained his plan. Charmed, the king tasted his wine and pronounced it far superior to the Suresnes and Beaugency normally drunk at court. The assembled nobility placed orders and the wines of Mâcon assumed the prestigious position that they hold today.

The church is the centrepiece of a pleasant rural ensemble of village houses, all in the same warm ochre stone, with a glorious view out over the golden vineyards of Pouilly-Fuissé.

The Lamartine Trail: A dedicated fan could spend a pleasant day touring the "circuit Lamartinien" and indeed it is a good a way as any to structure a visit to the area. Getting lost is certainly not a problem since every possible Lamartine connection has been diligently labelled.

South of the N79 is the tiny village of **Milly-Lamartine**, where the poet spent much of his childhood, and which inspired his early work. Sadly, Lamartine had to sell the house here 10 years before his death in order to pay off some of his debts. It is beautiful in the formal French sense: symmetrical and flanked by low outbuildings. The two cedar of Lebanon trees, planted when Lamartine returned from the East more than 170 years ago are still there, now mature and beautiful. The building is clearly identified, but is private. A statue of the poet stands at the top of the village.

The Château of **Pierreclos**, residence of the woman who inspired the heroine, Laurence, in Lamartine's epic poem, *Jocelyn*, has been restored and can be visited; see the lavish interior, kitchens, bakery and wine cellars. It is set on a wonderful site among the vineyards which come right up to its walls. It is a very attractive, classic 17th-century château with steep roofs and towers, one of which has coloured glazed tiles which catch the sun.

But probably the most authentic place to visit is the Château of **St-Point**, a

The Rock of Solutré.

little further to the west. Lamartine loved it and is buried with his wife in the little chapel. In the château his study, salon and bedroom are open, with many mementoes, portraits and letters exhibited.

By now the great Rock of **Solutré** will be a familiar sight, its great craggy outline dominating the gentle slopes of the Pouilly-Fuissé vineyards which surround it, shadowed by the smaller rock of **Vergisson** close by. This great limestone outcrop is also a famous archaeological site; since excavation began in 1866 the discoveries made there of bones and flints have helped establish the chronology of the Palaeolithic era. It was a hunting site for over 25,000 years; the bones of horses and reindeer are scattered over more than 0.8 hectares (2 acres) to a depth of 1 metre (3 feet).

However, the idea that the horses were actually driven over the cliff by their hunters has recently been discredited, and its now thought that they were slaughtered at the foot of the great rock. A fine archaeological museum has recently been established, built underground at the site. There is a path to the excavation site and on to the summit from which there are splendid views of the Saône Valley and on a clear day all the way to the Alps.

Solutré has achieved a more recent fame, due to a vow made by François Mitterrand while he was a prisoner of war in Germany, that he would climb the rock at Solutré every Whit Sunday. Actually, according to the mayor of Fuissé, Georges Burrier, the climb itself is a myth, and he often came by helicopter for a photo-opportunity. For lesser mortals, an excellent place to view Solutré is from the heights of **Grange du Bois**, a little village on the D31 which has terrific views right across the vineyards. The village itself is bisected by the boundary between the *départements* of Saône-et-Loire and the Rhône.

Circumscribed by the vine: Pouilly-Fuissé is the most highly regarded of the Mâcon wines, grown on 700 hectares (1,730 acres) divided between the villages of Pouilly, Fuissé, Solutré, Vergisson and Chaintré. It is a dry

Golden vineyards of Pouilly-Fuissé.

golden-green wine, a colour which often seems to suffuse the land itself, and it is particularly pleasing to drink *in situ*. Local restaurants plan their menus to complement the wine, and a good (expensive) Pouilly-Fuissé inevitably seems just the right choice.

Fuissé is typical of these wine villages, utterly dominated and circumscribed by the vines which grow right up to the village walls, indeed right up to the walls of the village church and the small château of Fuissé. The roads actually seem to get narrower, encroached by vines planted as tightly as possible in every available pocket of space.

The local architecture – ochre-coloured stone walls and pale terracotta tiled roofs – has a distinctly southern aspect, and worth noting are some of the fine houses of the *vignerons* with their verandas and stone colonnades. Mayor Georges Burrier is a wine-maker, as was his father before him; he explains that the area which is permitted to call itself Pouilly-Fuissé is strictly controlled. Every scrap of available land is cultivated, "No-one is ever allowed to build on wine land," emphasises Burrier.

St-Véran is close in quality to Pouilly-Fuissé, and the vineyards are situated to the north and south of Vergisson and Fuissé. In the north the *appellation* includes the villages of Davayé and Prissé, and in the south Chânes, Chasselas, Leynes, St-Amour and St-Vérand, which gave its name to the *appellation*. There are two other small *appellations*, still within the Mâcon area, **Pouilly-Loché** and **Pouilly-Vinzelles**, again producing wines very similar to Pouilly-Fuissé.

The Beaujolais Trail: From here on we have entered the **Beaujolais**, whose vines merge imperceptibly, to anyone other than a Mâcon wine-maker. Following a wine trail through France is perhaps a dangerous thing to do since once on a southern track there is wine everywhere and no particular reason to stop. Still, no wine-lover visiting Burgundy would wish to resist the temptation to add northern Beaujolais to the route, and it is officially considered (at least by Dijon) to be part of Burgundy.

Harvesting Beaujolais.

Once in Beaujolais, there is an encouraging proliferation of *vente directe* signs and *dégustations*; the casual visitor is welcomed rather more warmly to the *caveaux* than in the rest of Burgundy. That said, it is still generally assumed that you will buy wine if you are tasting, even if it is only one bottle.

The fame of Beaujolais Nouveau means that more than half today's crop is turned into *primeur* wine, made to be drunk young, and many people are thus less familiar with the fine wines of Beaujolais; a brief tour of the main *appellation* villages is the best possible way to acquaint oneself better. Nearly all Beaujolais wine is grown from the Gamay Noir à Jus Blanc, and this grape produces the best wine; the *crus* and Villages of the Haut Beaujolais, about a third of the total Beaujolais production.

The Gamay grape.

While Beaujolais is not of course comparable to the serious Burgundies, the lighter quality of its *crus* has a distinct appeal to today's market. Hachette's *Les Vins de France* describes it thus: "Beaujolais has the colour of rubies, tinged with violet. The bouquet suggests fruit and flowers and is lively, fresh, sprightly and straightforward." The wine writer Hugh Johnson confesses he finds it difficult to distinguish between most of the various *grand crus*, but adds that they all have one thing in common, "a sheer joyful smooth drinkableness which balks analysis". Needless to say, Beaujolais has inspired more poetic tributes; for example, "When one drinks Beaujolais, one wishes one had a neck as long as a swan's, to make the pleasure last longer."

What is certain is that for a wine tourist with a limited budget they provide a good opportunity to sample and buy a range of delicious and dependable wines without breaking the bank or building one's own wine cellar. You will often be served local *saucisson* to accompany the wine, especially *rosettes*, traditionally served with the wine of the same year, and *saucisson au vin*, a coarse sausage cooked, naturally, in Beaujolais. The landscape too makes a refreshing change with its wooded hills and

cultivated valleys. If approaching from the Charolais to the west, it is interesting to experience the change in the rural landscape, from rich pastureage dotted with turreted farmhouses and small discreet châteaux, up to the rounded hills of the Beaujolais vineyards with sheep and goats on the upland slopes, and little brown stone hamlets huddled within the folds of the mountains.

Beaujolais stretches for 50 km (30 miles) or so towards Lyon to the west of the Saône river. Beaujeu, once the capital, gave its name to the region but was replaced in 1514 by Villefranche-sur-Saône, which is on the boundary dividing Beaujolais into two distinct geological zones. The northern area is granite rock and the vines are grown on the hillsides. To the south limestone predominates, a golden stone, known as *pierre dorée,* which seems to give a permanently warm glow to this lovely landscape. Here the Beaujolais vineyards mingle with pine and chestnut forests on the upper slopes, and there are gentle meadows full of cows in the valleys. Wine-growing in the area since the 10th century has left a legacy of small châteaux, and the wine-making technique has contributed to a particular style of architecture; the living quarters are built over the caves and grain storehouses, with access from an exterior staircase and veranda. Often the wine is fermented on the upper floor and then poured straight into the cellar vats.

Here we are most concerned with seeking out the 10 Beaujolais *crus*, all of which are in the northern region, easily accessible from Burgundy. The *crus* consist of St-Amour, Juliénas, Moulin-à-Vent, Chénas, Fleurie, Chiroubles, Morgon, Brouilly and Côte de Brouilly, and finally Régnié, which was added only in 1988. A route which takes in some or all of these villages can be followed comfortably in a single day, allowing for frequent stops and restrained *dégustations*.

The small town of **Juliénas**, which forms part of the Juliénas appellation, is entirely typical of the region in its devotion to wine; growers selling directly to

Terracotta rooftops herald the south.

the public, shops selling local wines, as well as corkscrews, bottles in every conceivable size and other cellar equipment. Tastings are enthusiastically conducted and even the old church, replaced by a larger one, is now used as the *caveau*, the Cellier de la Vieille Église. The château of Juliénas also has famous cellars, and the château of Bois de la Salle, a former 17th-century priory is now used by the Cave cooperative. Look out for the 16th-century Maison de la Dîme, the tithe house, with its double row of arcading.

The local restaurant Coq au Vin is famous for its own special recipe for *Coq au Vin* and other local dishes, and Juliénas wine owes much of its fame to journalists on the satirical newspaper *Le Canard Enchaîné* in the 1930s. Local wine merchant, Victor Peyret, (also responsible for founding the Cellier) was a friend of the cartoonist, Henri Monnier, and often visited the Paris offices equipped with bottles of his wine, which were enthusiastically drunk and subsequently celebrated in print.

St-Amour is slightly to the north, right on the border between Mâcon and Beaujolais. It is named after a Roman soldier, St Amateur, who founded a monastery here overlooking the Saône. The *appellation* was the most recent (1946) until Regnié in 1988.

To the south it is a short drive through the hillside vineyards to **Chénas**, named originally for its oak trees, most of which have long ago been chopped down and replaced by vines. It is the smallest of the *crus* but one of the best for keeping and was known as far back as the 17th century when it was served to Louis XIII. It has been charmingly described as "a bunch of flowers in a velvet basket". Chénas has the distinction of two *grand crus* on its territory, its own and the grapes that go to make Moulin-à-Vent. A brief detour will bring you to the famous **Moulin-à-Vent**, the name given to the combined *cru* of Chénas and the nearby village of **Romanèche-Thorins**. It is the oldest *cru* in the Beaujolais, fixed in 1924, and claims, "*la grace d'un beaujolais et le prestige d'un*

Moulin-à-Vent grape gathering.

BEAUJOLAIS NOUVEAU

One of the wine trade's most spectacular marketing successes of recent years has been Beaujolais Nouveau. Its arrival in shops, bars and restaurants each year has become an "event" on the calendar. The third Thursday in November is now synonymous with the scramble to get the infant wine to Paris, London, Tokyo and other world capitals. Publicity gimmicks to promote Beaujolais Nouveau (also known as Beaujolais Primeur) have included, over the years, delivery by sports or vintage cars, microlight, elephant and rickshaw.

Enthusiasts are prepared to pay the equivalent of the cost of a bottle of Montrachet for the privilege of being the first to sample the year's vintage, whether in Beaune or at Tokyo airport. Producers and *négociants* naturally adore it; a whole year's vintage can be shifted within a matter of weeks. It is not surprising that an ever greater proportion – now about two-thirds – of all Beaujolais and Beaujolais Villages (but not the *crus*) is now marketed as Beaujolais Nouveau, and that

many other regions and countries have hopped on to the Nouveau bandwagon.

Yet often the brew offered to customers is overpriced and disappointing. A dark purplish liquid with only a hint of the characteristically Gamay nose, it hits the tastebuds like a sledgehammer, rasps the oesophagus like a breadknife and produces an instant headache. As for its taste, "bubble gum and synthetic banana" (Paul Levy) would in most cases be a fair description.

A far cry indeed from the original Beaujolais Nouveau which, until discovered by Parisians after the last war, was little known outside the cafés of Lyon. Regarded as a *petit vin bourru* (a churlish little wine), it had an alcoholic content of only 9.5°–11° and a wonderfully fruity nose. It was usually served straight from the barrel, from which the carbon dioxide still being given off by the wine could escape.

Now that Beaujolais Nouveau is no longer consumed only on the spot, fermentation of the wine has to be brought to a halt before it is bottled, otherwise there is a danger that corks may start popping unasked. But no wine naturally ceases to be active by the third week in November, just six weeks or so after the harvest. So steps are taken to ensure that it behaves itself in the bottle: in addition to the usual practice of adding sulphur dioxide to kill bacteria and unwanted yeasts, producers bombard the wine with ultra-violet rays and pasteurise it at 85°C (185°F). The traditional wine-maker's technique for clearing wine is fining or filtration, but this takes too long, so Beaujolais Nouveau is subjected to the equally efficient, but brutal, processes of centrifugation or freezing or both. Even supposing that Beaujolais Nouveau escapes this treatment, the chances of its tasting as it did in the prewar cafés of Lyon are very slender. This is simply because it is not the same wine. The massive increase in demand has resulted in the familiar old syndrome of vineyard extension and increased yields.

Fortunately, there are still some who supply discriminating bars and restaurants in Beaujolais and Lyon with the genuine product, a light-coloured wine low in alcohol and high in fruitiness, served very cool, but not chilled, direct from the barrel. It's a marvellous accompaniment to hearty, unpretentious food. ∎

bourgogne". Hugh Johnson says it is the one Beaujolais that really stands apart, and he recalls drinking it with a perfectly complementary meal of *volaille de Bresse aux morilles* and *crêpes Parmentier* (potato flour pancakes.)

The windmill itself, three centuries old and no longer working, is built on a rocky promontory with a panoramic view of vines as far as the eye can see, right across the Saône Valley. There are tasting cellars either side of the road from the path which leads to it.

The most famous son of **Romanèche-Thorins** is Benoît Raclet, a *vigneron* who in the 1830s saved the Beaujolais vineyards from the pyralid moth blight. The vines were continually devastated, until one day Raclet noticed that the vine which grew where the maid threw out the dirty water from the house, was flourishing. Raclet decided to try watering his vines with boiling water to great success. Scalding or *échaudage* then became common practice. Today the Musée Raclet exhibits the wide variety of containers used for this essential la-

bour, as well as furniture and domestic objects from the 19th century. To the east of the village is the zoo, a 10-hectare (25-acre) park full of birds and animals roaming free; the main purpose of the centre is in breeding different species, but a leisure park caters to visitors. You can also visit the Hameau de Vin, a wine museum in the old train station.

Perhaps because of its delightful name, **Fleurie** is often described as the most "feminine" Beaujolais; it is appropriate then that it has been enthusiastically promoted by one Marguerite Chabert, famous for her passionate devotion to the wine, and the first woman head of a wine cooperative in France. The Chapel of the Madonna, built in 1875, stands in protection over the vineyards.

The cave cooperative in the middle of the village, built in the 1930s, still retains its original lettering, and there are plenty of *vente-directe* outlets as well as two very welcome restaurants. Here you would do well to try the local culinary speciality, *andouillettes au Fleurie*, naturally accompanied by the local wine.

Corcelles Château.

Head west through the mountains to **Chiroubles**, where there is a bust in the village square in memory of Victor Pulliat, famous for saving the vines from Phylloxera in the 1880s, by the use of American vine stocks. From here if you continue along the mountain road to the Terrasse des Chiroubles, you will be rewarded by a magnificent view of the vineyards. A little further on, at **Fut d'Avenas**, an orientation point gives an excellent panorama of the region. The tiny village of **Avenas** has a 12th-century Romanesque church, noted for its exquisitely carved marble altar.

Once up in these beautiful mountains you may wish to follow the quiet winding roads down to Beaujeu; otherwise to complete the Beaujolais *cru* trail head back towards **Villié-Morgon** along the D18. In the village the *caveau* can be found in the middle of a delightful little park which has animal pens for deer and chickens. It was the first tasting *caveau* in the area and can be found in the spacious cellar of the 18th-century château. Morgon is a rich wine, and

considered one of the best of the *crus* for ageing. Nearby the **Château de Pizay** is famous for its topiary gardens and its *cuvage*. The **Château de Corcelles**, close to the N6, has medieval buildings and a Renaissance courtyard, and a guard room now used as a *caveau*. The château was painted by Utrillo, who once lived nearby with his mother, the painter Suzanne Valadon.

Regnié, between Morgon and Brouilly, is the most recent *cru* appellation. The village of **Regnié-Durette** is distinguished by its 19th-century church with two towers and the Domaine de la Grange Charton, built in 1820 with dwellings for *vignerons* on the upper floor with typical outside staircases, entwined by vines. It still belongs to the Hospices de Beaujeu, and its huge *cuvages* store all the local wine.

The Regnié vines flank the road from Belleville-sur-Saône to Beaujeu, along the Ardières valley, once the old wine route to Paris. Just to the south are the *appellations* of **Brouilly** and **Côtes de Brouilly**, the largest of the *crus*, domi-

Beaujeu street; Beaujeu rooftops.

nated by the rounded hill of Mont de Brouilly. At the summit of the hill, which affords good views over the Saône and south towards Lyon, is a small chapel, Notre Dame du Raisin, built in 1857. The hill is the site of an annual celebration by *Les Amis de Brouilly*, which appears to consist mainly of drinking as much Beaujolais as possible and still being able to get back down the slope.

In fact, Beaujolais is distinguished by the passion with which it is celebrated and the quantity in which it is drunk. Not just drunk either – a favourite snack is *tartines au vin*, toasted bread soaked in Beaujolais and sprinkled with sugar.

The Brouilly *appellation* includes the communes of Odenas, St-Lager, Charentay, Cercié, Quincié and St-Étienne-la-Varenne, but, strangely, there is no actual village of Brouilly. At **St-Lager** is a tasting cellar for Brouilly and Côtes-de-Brouilly. From here you can follow a *route des vins* via a number of châteaux, including the 17th-century **La Chaize**, to the west of Odenas, built from plans by Mansart, with huge gardens designed by Le Nôtre. It is most famous, however, for having the largest wine cellar in Beaujolais. One notable scion of the family was Père La Chaize, Louis XIV's confessor, after whom the famous Paris cemetery is named.

Ancient capitals: Beaujeu itself is charming, strung out along the Ardières valley, overlooked by vineyards on the steep hillsides. It is now just a small town with little evidence of its importance in the Middle Ages when it was ruled by the Lords of Beaujeu and held a commanding position on the trade route between the Rhône and the Loire. However, the Hospices de Beaujeu continues to hold its wine auction as it has done since the 12th century. Worth a visit, in the town square, is the Romanesque church of St-Nicolas, with its 12th-century rounded apse and square tower. Across from the church is the 15th-century Maison de Pays de Beaujolais, a beautiful wooden Renaissance building, with overhanging eaves and very old windows; it holds tastings and sales of local produce including wine,

Villefranche-sur-Saône market.

honey and cheese. The whole group surrounding the church is very attractive including the town hall, behind which there is a small park beside the river. The Musée Marius-Audin has a large collection devoted to regional crafts and traditions, particularly winemaking, and a doll museum. Best of all, perhaps, is the main street which looks as if time has stood still for 60 years since most of the shop fronts retain their wonderful '30s facades. Beaujeu is a good base for walkers, and many footpaths have been established through the vineyards and forests which surround it.

Villefranche-sur-Saône today merits a visit as the wine capital of the region; it is full of small cafés, rather like Lyon, where Beaujolais is drunk from the traditional *pots*. Its residents are known as *Caladois*, after the paving stones, *calades*, in front of the church of Notre Dame des Marais, which is distinguished by its oddly assymetrical frontage, Romanesque belltower and 15th-century flamboyant Gothic facade, donated by Anne de Beaujeu, daughter of Louis XI and patron of Villefranche, who made Villefranche capital of the Beaujolais in 1514. (She paid for it by fining the people of Trévoux who were caught counterfeiting coins.) The Rue Nationale has a number of fine 16th- and 17th-century houses, tall and Italianate with beautifully restored facades and courtyards. From Villefranche either return to Mâcon or continue the eternal wine trail on to the south of Beaujolais, to Lyon, and beyond.

Gabriel Chevalier, author of *Clochemerle*, and perhaps more responsible than anyone else for the image of a typical Beaujolais village, summarises the people of Beaujolais thus: "They offer their hearts in the palms of one hand… the hand, that is, that does not hold a glass." But his description of Beaujolais wine is as good a general tribute to wine as any: "The more you drink of it, the more delightful you find your wife, the more loyal your friends, the rosier your future and the more bearable mankind."

Left, Burgundy vineyards.

INSIGHT GUIDES

Travel Tips

New Insight Maps

Maps in Insight Guides are tailored to complement the text. But when you're on the road you sometimes need the big picture that only a large-scale map can provide. This new range of durable Insight Fleximaps has been designed to meet just that need.

Detailed, clear cartography
makes the comprehensive route and city maps easy to follow, highlights all the major tourist sites and provides valuable motoring information plus a full index.

Informative and easy to use
with additional text and photographs covering a destination's top 10 essential sites, plus useful addresses, facts about the destination and handy tips on getting around.

Laminated finish
allows you to mark your route on the map using a non-permanent marker pen, and wipe it off. It makes the maps more durable and easier to fold than traditional maps.

The first titles
cover many popular destinations. They include Algarve, Amsterdam, Bangkok, California, Cyprus, Dominican Republic, Florence, Hong Kong, Ireland, London, Mallorca, Paris, Prague, Rome, San Francisco, Sydney, Thailand, Tuscany, USA Southwest, Venice, and Vienna.

👁 INSIGHT GUIDES
The world's largest collection of visual travel guides

CONTENTS

Getting Acquainted

The Place 310
Climate 310
The Economy 310
Government 310
The People............................311

Planning the Trip

What to Bring........................311
Entry Regulations..................311
Customs 311
Animal Quarantine 312
Health 312
Emergencies.........................312
Currency 312
Public Holidays 312
Getting There 313
By Air/Sea/Train 313
By Channel Tunnel 314
By Bus/Car............................314
Language Courses 315
Disabled Travellers...............315

Practical Tips

Emergencies..........................316
Weights & Measures 316
Business Hours 316
Media 316
Postal Services 317
Telecommunications 317
Embassies/Consulates 317
Tourist Offices.......................318

Getting Around

Public Transport 318
Private Transport...................319
On Foot 320
Hitchhiking............................320
By Boat 321

Where to Stay

Bed & Breakfast....................322
Self-Catering/Gîtes...............322
Camping 322
Hotels 323

Eating Out

Restaurants 328
Wine 333
Wine Tasting 334

Outdoor Activities

Excursions 336

Sites

Places of Interest 336
Museums & Art Galleries.......336

Festivals & Nightlife

Live Arts/Diary of Events 342
Nightlife 343

Shopping

Shopping Areas.....................343
Markets 344
Buying Direct 345

Sport

Participant Sports..................345
Spectator Sports 347

Language

Words & Phrases...................347

Further Reading

General/Other Insight Guides.352

Art/Photo Credits...................354
Index......................................355

Getting Acquainted

The Place

Area: 31,600 sq. km (12,198 sq. miles)
Capital: Dijon
Population: 1,607,000
Language: French
Time zone: One hour ahead of Greenwich Mean Time (GMT)
Currency: Franc and Euro
Weights and measures: metric
Electricity: 220/230 volts and 50 cycles
International dialling code: 00 33

Special Interest

Burgundy is renowned world-wide for its wines and its annual wine auctions are extremely popular with the trade and tourist alike. It is also a noted centre of gastronomy. Another big draw for visitors is the vast network of waterways, some 1,200 km (745 miles) of rivers and canals are given over almost entirely to leisure pursuits.

Indeed lovers of the great outdoors will find much to attract them to the region; the vast Morvan Park offers all kinds of activities in addition to the expected rambling trails and wildlife.

Culturally Burgundy offers a wide range of treasures; early Gallic and Roman sites, Romanesque monasteries and chapels, Gothic abbeys, medieval châteaux, magnificent Renaissance mansions and superb art collections.

Climate

Burgundy enjoys a pleasant climate, which rarely reaches extremes; summer can be very hot with occasional showers, while winter is cold, but not damp. Autumn, when it is bright and sunny but not too hot for touring, is often considered to be the best time to visit. However, early morning mists may put a damper on some sightseeing. In the Morvan, where the altitude climbs to over 600 metres (1,970 ft), expect mountain conditions.

The Economy

Without a doubt, wine is the principal product of the region, with just over 27,500 hectares (67,953 acres) of vineyards, mostly in the east of Burgundy. Agriculture too is very important, with the Charolais cattle being the pride of the local farmers. The Bresse poultry, bred in the south of the region have the rare distinction of carrying an *appellation contrôlée*.

In the west, the Morvan has its own industry, mostly related to forestry, including sawmills, the production of charcoal, Christmas trees and quality furniture.

Other good sources of income for the region are stone quarrying (much of Paris was built with the white stone of Burgundy) and the allied manufacture of cement; as well as ceramics, in particular decorative tiles and pottery.

Government

Although nominally part of France, Burgundy largely retained its independence until the reign of Napoleon I. In recent history France has been ruled by a very centralised form of government, but under the socialists (1981–86) the Paris-appointed *préfets* lost a great deal of their power, as the individual *départements* (or counties) gained their own directly elected assemblies for the first time, giving them far more financial and administrative autonomy.

Although each *département* still has a *préfet*, the role is now much more advisory. The *préfecture* is based in the county town of each *département*: Bourg-en-Bresse in Ain, Dijon in Côte d'Or, Nevers in Nièvre, Lyon in Rhône, Mâcon in Saône-et-Loire and Auxerre in Yonne (strictly speaking, Rhône and Ain form part of the Rhône Valley region but they are included for the purposes of this guide). These offices handle the majority of matters concerned with the social welfare of their citizens.

Each French *département* has a number which is used as a handy reference for administrative purposes – for example it forms the first two digits of the postcode in any address as well as the last two figures on vehicle licence plates. Burgundian *département* numbers are as follows: Ain – 01, Côte d'Or – 21, Nièvre – 58, Rhône – 69, Saône-et-Loire – 71, Yonne – 89.

Each *département* is divided into a number of disparately sized *communes* whose district councils control a town, village or group of villages under the direction of the local mayor. *Communes* are responsible for most local planning and environmental matters. Decisions relating to tourism and culture are mostly dealt with at regional level, while the state still controls education, the health service and security.

France first became a Republic in 1792 after the abolition of the monarchy. Constitutional change

Useful Websites

General:
www.bourgogne-tourisme.com
www.burgundy-tourism.com
Transport:
www.sncf.fr
www.britrail.co.uk
www.eurostar.co.uk
www.raileurope.com
Accommodation:
www.chatotel.com (châteaux and independent hotels)
www.fuaj.org (youth hostels)
www.relaischateaux.fr
www.campingfrance.com
www.gites-de-france.fr
Restaurants:
www.bottin-gourmand.com
www.calvacom.fr/savoy
Weather:
www.meteo.fr

resulted in the establishment of the Second, Third, Fourth and the current Fifth Republic, which was instituted when General Charles de Gaulle became Prime Minister in 1958. The President, who holds a powerful office, is elected for a term of seven years. He (to date the President has always been a man), appoints the Prime Minister as head of government.

Parliament is made up of two houses: the National Assembly and the Senate. The major political parties are: the Partie Communiste Français (PCF), and the Partie Socialiste (PS), both belonging to the left. On the right there are two parties: Rassemblement pour la République (RPR) and the Union pour la Démocratié Française (UDF).

The People

The region enjoyed early prosperity due to its position as a major cross-roads for trade routes. It continued to thrive after the Roman invasion, as can be seen from the well-preserved remains. Later, around the 10th century, Burgundy came under the powerful influence of the abbey at Cluny and its satellites.

The Burgundians' fortunes were revived under the great dukes of Burgundy (the House of Valois), the first of whom, Philip the Bold, ruled the region from 1364 for 40 years. The Duchy of Burgundy then extended much further than the present region, encompassing what was later to become Belgium and Holland. It was Philip who brought the artists from Flanders that gave much of the local architecture its particular decorative style.

The last duke, Charles, who died in 1477, was largely responsible for the fall of the Duchy, when most of Burgundy's territory was added to the French kingdom. He continually antagonised King Louis XI, so after the duke's death, the king added most of the territory to his kingdom, except for a small area which Charles's daughter Mary took with her to the House of Hapsburg on her marriage to the Emperor Maximilian I.

Planning the Trip

What to Bring

CLOTHING

Seasonal clothing is needed; it is always wise to pack a light raincoat. Good walking shoes are essential.

MAPS

A first essential in touring any part of France is a good map. The Institute Géographique National (IGN) is the French equivalent of the British Ordnance Survey and their maps are excellent; those covering the region are listed below:

Red Series (1:250,000, 1 cm to 2.5 km) sheet no. 108 covers the whole region at a good scale for touring.

Green Series (1:100,000, 1 cm to 1 km) are more detailed local maps – sheet nos 28, 29, 36 and 37 cover most of the region, although you may need nos 21 and 22 for the extreme north and west of the region and no. 43 for southern Saône-et-Loire and Beaujolais.

There is also a special map no. 306 at the same scale as the Green Series covering the **Morvan regional park**.

Also available from IGN are the highly detailed 1:50,000 and 1:25,000 scales, which are ideal for walkers. For planning your route, IGN 901 covers the whole of France at a scale of 1 cm to 10 km and is regularly updated.

The **Michelin** regional maps are published at a scale of 1:200,000 (1 cm to 2 km); the whole of Burgundy is covered in two sheets – no. 238 for the west and 245 for the east and centre, and on four

more detailed sheets at the same scale: nos 65, 66 (north), 69 and 70 (south).

Michelin also publish town plans, as do **Blay**, but local tourist offices often give away their own town plans free of charge. Michelin's Route Planning Map 911 shows motorways and alternative routes and other travel advice.

Good map sources include: **Stanfords International Map Centre**, 12–14 Long Acre, Covent Garden, WC2E 9LP tel: 020-7730 1354; **The Travel Bookshop**, 13 Blenheim Crescent, London W11 2EE, tel: 020-7229 5260; website www.thetravelbookshop.co.uk. Also notable is **World Leisure Marketing**, 11 Newmarket Court. Derby, DE24 8NW, tel: freephone 0800-838080 fax: 01332-573 399 – which is the IGN agent and offers a mail-order service.

Entry Regulations

To visit France, you need a valid **passport**. All visitors to France require a **visa** except citizens of EU countries, Andorra, Monaco, the USA, Canada and Switzerland. If you are in any doubt about entry regulations, check with the French consulate in your country – the situation may change from time to time. If you intend to stay in France for more than 90 days, then you should have a *carte de séjour* (again from the French consulate); this also applies to EU citizens until restrictions are relaxed.

Customs

All personal effects may be imported into France without formality (including bicycles and sports equipment). It is forbidden to bring into the country any narcotics, pirated books, weapons and alcoholic liquors that do not conform to French legislation. In theory, since 1993, customs barriers within Europe for alcoholic drinks and tobacco have practically ceased to exist – duty-free allowances ceased June 30 1999. However, there are still recommended allowances, which are shown below. These can be exceeded, provided that proof is shown that the goods bought are for personal consumption (such as a family wedding) and not for resale. If in doubt, check with your local customs office. (In the UK: HM Customs and Excise, Dorset House, Stamford Street, London SE1 9NG, tel: 020-7928 3344 or any Excise enquiry office.)

Customs Allowances

Recommended allowances for EU citizens over 18 years old are: 10 litres of spirits or strong liqueurs, over 22 percent vol., 20 litres of fortified wine, 90 litres wine (of which no more than 60 litres may be sparkling wine), 200 cigars, 400 cigarillos, 800 cigarettes, 110 litres beer and 1 kilo tobacco. For US citizens, the duty-free allowance is: 200 cigarettes, 50 cigars or 3 lb tobacco; 1 US quart of alcoholic beverages and duty-free gifts worth up to $100.

Animal Quarantine

Animal quarantine laws are about to be changed in Britain and anyone wishing to take their pet abroad should contact the Ministry of Agriculture. However, at present it is still not advisable to take animals to France from the UK because of the six months' quarantine required by the British authorities on your return. For further details, contact the French consulate in your country. Once you are in continental Europe, you can travel between countries as long as you have a valid vaccination certificate for your pet.

Health

The International Association for Medical Assistance to Travelers (IAMAT) is a non-profit-making organisation, which anyone can join, free of charge (although a donation is requested). Benefits include a membership card, entitling the bearer to services at fixed IAMAT rates by participating

physicians, and a Traveller Clinical Record, a passport-sized record completed by the member's own doctor prior to travel. A directory of English-speaking doctors belonging to IAMAT and on call 24 hours a day, is published for members' use. IAMAT offices: US: 417 Center Street, Lewiston NY 14092, tel: 716-754 4883.

EU nationals should check before leaving for France that they qualify for subsidised treatment under the EU. (Most British nationals do: check with the Department of Health and acquire from them the form **E111**.) The E111 does not cover the full cost of any treatment so you may find it worthwhile to also take out private insurance.

Note: For minor ailments you can consult a pharmacy (recognisable by its green cross sign), where the pharmacist has wider "prescribing" powers than chemists in the UK or US. They are also helpful in cases of snake or insect bites and identifying fungi.

If you need to see a doctor, expect to pay around FF110 for a simple consultation, plus a pharmacist's fee for whatever prescription is issued. The doctor will provide a certificate called a *feuille des soins*, which you need to keep to claim back the majority of the cost (around 75 percent) under the EU agreement. You have to attach the little stickers (*vignettes*) from any medicine prescribed to the *feuille* to enable you to also claim for that.

Refunds have to be obtained from the local *Caisse Primaire* (ask the doctor or pharmacist for the best address).

The standard of treatment in French hospitals is generally high, and you should be able to find

Emergencies

In cases of medical emergency, either dial 15 for an ambulance or call the **Service d'Aide Médicale d'Urgence** (SAMU), which exists in most large towns and cities – numbers are given at the front of telephone directories.

someone who speaks English to help you. Or you may prefer to try to get to either the American Hospital at 63 boulevard Victor-Hugo, 92292 Neuilly, tel: 01 46 41 25 25; or the British Hospital Hortford, 3 rue Barbes, 92300 Levallois, tel: 01 46 39 22 22 both just outside Paris. Show the hospital doctor or authorities your E111 and you will be billed (once you are back home usually), for approximately 25 percent of the cost of treatment.

Currency

The **Franc** is divided into 100 **centimes** – a 5-centime piece being the smallest coin and the FF500 note the highest denomination bill.

Banks displaying the "*Change*" sign will change foreign currency and, in general, at the best rates (you will need to produce your passport in any transaction). If possible avoid hotel or other independent bureaux which may charge a high commission. **Credit cards** are widely accepted, but Visa is by far the most common and can now be used in hypermarkets and many supermarkets. Access (MasterCard/Eurocard) and American Express are also accepted in some establishments. **Eurocheques**, used in conjunction with a cheque card, drawn directly on your own bank account, can be used just like a cheque in the UK and are commonly accepted. Apply for these, or if you prefer, **travellers' cheques**, from your own bank, a couple of weeks before your departure.

Credit cards and cashcards from many European banks can be used to obtain cash from cashpoint machines outside banks, using a pin number.

Public Holidays

A list of major public holidays is given below. It is common practice, if a public holiday falls on a Thursday or Tuesday, for French business to *faire le pont* (literally, bridge the gap) and have the Friday or Monday as a holiday as well.

Details of closures should be posted outside banks a few days before the event but it is easy to be caught out, especially on Assumption Day, which is not a holiday in the UK.

- **New Year's Day**: 1 January
- **Easter Monday** (but not Good Friday)
- **Labour Day**: Monday closest to 1 May
- **Ascension Day**
- 8 May to commemorate the end of World War I
- **Whit Monday** (Pentecost)
- **Bastille Day**: 14 July
- **Assumption Day**: 15 August
- **All Saints' Day** (Toussaint): 1 November
- **Armistice Day**: 11 November
- **Christmas Day**: 25 December

Useful Numbers

Air France:
UK, tel: 08 02 80 28 02
US (New York), tel: 212-247 0100
Canada (Montreal), tel: 514-147 5087
Ryan Air Dublin, tel: 18 44 44 00
American Airlines, tel: 01 69 32 73 07
Continental, tel: 01 42 99 09 09
Delta, tel: 01 47 68 92 92
TWA, tel: 01 49 19 20 00
United, tel: 01 41 40 30 30

Getting There

BY AIR

Air France: Direct flights go to Lyon, just south of the region, from Heathrow (Air France has a fly-drive option on this route) and Manchester (Air Littoral, bookable through Air France). **Ryan Air** have a daily flight to Lyon–St Etienne (including Sundays) from Stansted Airport. Geneva Airport gives easy access to southern Burgundy.

Air France operates a rail package with flights available from 5 airports around the UK to Paris, then onward by train to Dijon, Nevers or Mâcon – via Paris-Gare de Lyon.

Travellers from America and other countries can catch direct flights to Paris, Lyon and Geneva, although a charter flight to London, then onward from there may work out cheaper.

There are regional flights to and from Dijon with **Proteus Airlines**, tel: 04 77 36 77 47/ 04 72 22 88 66.

Regional Airlines connects Dijon with Clermont Ferrand, Rouen, Rennes, Nantes, Poitiers, Limoges, Pau, Angoulême, Bordeaux, Toulouse, Marseille and Toulon, tel: 03 80 67 22 84. Dijon Airport, tel: 03 80 67 67 67.

Other low-price charter flights can be obtained through "bucket shops" – check the national press and the internet for offers.

Students and young people can normally obtain discounted charter fares through specialist travel agencies in their own countries. In the UK try **Campus Travel**, 52 Grosvenor Gardens, London SW1W 0AG, tel: 020-7730 3402, for your nearest branch. Campus is part of the international group USIT, whose main US address is: The New York Student Centre, 895 Amsterdam Avenue, New York, NY 10025, tel: 212-663 5435.

BY SEA

Several **ferry services** operate from the UK, Eire and the Channel Islands to the northern ports of France. All of these services carry cars as well as foot passengers. **Hovercraft** crossings are fast, but more dependent on good weather than the ferries. The **Seacat catamaran** service offers the quickest crossing but, like the hovercraft, it can carry only a limited number of cars.

The port of **Calais** offers the fastest access by motorway to the region; other good alternative ports to travel via are the ports of Boulogne and Dunkerque.

Brittany Ferries: there are sailings from Portsmouth to St-Malo and from Plymouth and Cork (Eire) to St-Malo or Roscoff. Alternative crossings are Portsmouth to Caen in Normandy, or by their cheaper Les Routiers service from Poole to Cherbourg, tel: 0990 360 360.

Hoverspeed operates hovercraft and catamarans from Dover to Calais and Folkestone to Boulogne (crossing time is approximately 30 minutes). Details from Hoverspeed Ltd, Marine Parade, Dover CT17 9TG, tel: 01304-240241.

North Sea Ferries connect travellers from the north of England and Scotland to France, via their Hull–Zeebrugge route. Situated 55 km (35 miles) from the French border, Zeebrugge gives relatively good access to the region. Contact the company at King George Dock, Hedon Road, Hull HU9 5QA, tel: 01482-795141.

Cunard Lines: New York–Southampton–New York, tel: 1-800 5-CUNARD.

BY TRAIN

For visitors travelling from Paris, the train is a fast, efficient way to reach the region, especially with the high-speed express trains (TGV). All services leave from Paris-Gare de Lyon. The principal destinations in the region are Dijon, Mâcon, Nevers, Beaune and Chalon-sur-Saône. Car and bicycle hire is available at most main stations – as a package with your rail ticket if you prefer.

TGV

Approximate journey times on the super-fast TGV are as follows:
- Paris (G. de L.) to Auxerre = 2 hours
- Paris (G. de L.) to Dijon = 1 hour 40 minutes (There is also a TGV service running direct from Charles de Gaulle airport.)
- Paris (G. de L.) to Macon = 1 hour 40 minutes, five times a day
- Paris (G. de L.) to Nevers = 2–2½ hours, 13 times a day
- Also to Dijon from Lille TGV = 2 hours 50 minutes, once a day
- Lyon to Dijon 1 hour 50 minutes once a day
- Marseille to Dijon = 5–5½ hours
- Metz to Dijon = 3 hours

Tickets may be booked for through journeys from outside France. In the UK, tickets, including those for ferry travel, can be booked from any national railway station. Rail travel centres can supply details of services in continental Europe, or these can be obtained by contacting the National Rail International Enquiries, International Rail Centre, Victoria Station, London SWI, tel: 020-7834 2345. Students and young people under 26 can obtain a discount. **Eurotrain**, tel: 020-7730 3402, offers 30 percent off standard two-month return tickets for those under 26.

French Railways has a telephone service, Rail Shop, in London to provide an instant booking service. The lines, however, are usually very busy and a little patience is required. The service includes ferry bookings, discounted tickets for young people, a *Carte Vermeil* for senior citizens, which gives a generous discount on tickets and **Eurodomino** rail passes (*see below*). Lines are open Monday to Friday from 8am to 8pm and Saturday from 9am to 4pm, tel; 0990-300 003 for information as well as reservations.

For reservations and information in France, contact the **SNFC** (Société Nationale des Chemins de Fer de France) website at www.sncf.fr or tel: 08 36 35 35 35.

Prior **reservation** is essential for travel on TGVs. Any rail ticket bought in France must be validated by using the orange automatic date-stamping machine at the entrance to the platform. Failure to do so may incur a surcharge. French railway stations will accept Visa and most credit cards.

Rail Passes: There are several rail-only and rail combination passes available to foreign visitors. These must always be bought before departing for France. In the UK a **Eurodomino Pass** offers unlimited rail travel on any 3, 5 or 10 days within a month. This can also be purchased in conjunction with an Air France rail ticket.

Reductions in France: For those aged between 12 and 25 years,

there is a 25 percent reduction on proof of age; for those over 60, proof of age also entitles you to a 25 percent reduction in fares. There are various other reductions available for families travelling together where there are children under 12 or 16 years of age. Ask at the railway station for more details.

Visitors from North America have a wide choice of passes, including Eurailpass, Flexipass and Saver Pass which can be purchased in the US, tel: 212-308 3103 (for information) and 800-223 636 (reservations). Similar passes are available to travellers from other countries, although the names of the tickets and the conditions attached to them may vary slightly.

BY CHANNEL TUNNEL

The **Channel Tunnel** offers fast, frequent rail services from London (Waterloo) to Lille (2 hours) and London (Waterloo) to Paris (Gare du Nord – 3 hours). The Eurostar service offers high-speed connections via Lille. **Le Shuttle** takes cars and their passengers from Folkestone to Calais on a simple drive on-drive off system. The journey time through the tunnel is about 35 minutes. No tickets are needed – you just turn up and take the next service. Le Shuttle runs 24 hours a day, all year round, with a service at least once an hour through the night. Enquiries in UK, tel: 0990-353535.

BY BUS

Eurolines Coaches have overnight services from London (Victoria) to Dijon. There are daily departures in summer, thrice-weekly the rest of the year. The ticket includes the ferry crossing (via Dover) and National Express coaches have connections with the London departures from most major towns in the UK. For details contact: Eurolines UK, 52 Grosvenor Gardens, London SW1W 0AU, tel: 020-7730 8235 or your local Eurolines office.

BY CAR

The A6 motorway from Paris takes you right through the centre of the region via Auxerre and Beaune down to Mâcon. It connects with the A31 to Dijon at Beaune. From Calais you can travel by motorway right through (A26/A5, which joins the A31 north of Dijon).

If speed is not of the essence, and you intend to make the drive part of your holiday, follow the green holiday route signs to your destination – these form part of a national network of *bison futé* routes to avoid traffic congestion at peak periods. You will discover gorgeous parts of France you never knew existed and may therefore be more likely to arrive relaxed.

The first weekend in August and the public holiday on the 15 are usually the worst times to travel, so avoid them if you can. For further details about driving in France, *see Getting Around.*

Special Facilities

CHILDREN

In France generally, children are treated as individuals, not just appendages. It is pleasant to be able to take them to **restaurants** (even in the evening) without heads being turned in horror at the invasion. It has to be said, however, that French children, being accustomed to eating out from an early age, are on the whole well behaved in restaurants, so it helps if one's own offspring are able to understand that they can't run wild.

Many restaurants offer a **children's menu**; if not they will often split a *prix-fixe* menu between two children. If travelling with very young children, you may find it practical to order nothing specific at all for them but just to request an extra plate and give them tasty morsels to try from your own dish. French meals are usually generous enough to allow you to do this without going hungry yourself, and you are unlikely to encounter any hostility from *le patron* (or *la patronne*).

Most **hotels** have family rooms so that children do not have to be separated from parents; a cot (*lit bébé*) can often be provided for a small supplement, although it is a good idea to check availability if booking in advance.

Although family leisure activities in the region are somewhat limited, there are a few parks offering a variety of amusements. Of particular note are La Toison d'Or in Dijon (also a major commercial centre and good for shopping), the water park at Quétigny, also in Côte d'Or, and the Touro-Parc leisure park at Romanèche-Thorins (Saône-et-Loire). The best area for family holidays is the Morvan which offers plenty of outdoor pursuits.

The tourist offices in each *département* also organise events for unaccompanied children, including stays in *gîtes d'enfants* or on farms. For further information, contact the tourist office or the Loisirs Accueil service in the individual *départements*.

STUDENTS & YOUNG PEOPLE

Students and young people under the age of 26 can benefit from cut-price travel to France and rail cards for getting around the region – for details *see Getting There*.

If you wish to stay in the region for a prolonged amount of time, it may be worth finding out about an exchange visit or study holiday. Several organisations exist to provide information or arrange such visits. In the UK, the Central Bureau for Educational Visits and Exchanges, Seymour Mews House, Seymour Mews, London WIH 9PE, tel: 020-7486 5101, produces three books: *Working Holidays* (note that opportunities in the region are fairly limited; however, the grape harvest is still a big draw for young people and employment opportunities are listed here); *Home from Home* (listing a wealth of useful information about staying

with a French family) and *Study Holidays*, which gives details of language courses in the region.

The following agencies specialise in helping young people to arrange their holidays in France and will help you with a youth card:

UFCV (Union Française des Centres de Vacances et de Loisirs)
10 Quai Charente, 75019 Paris
Tel: 01 44 72 14 14
Fax: 01 40 34 53 49
Organises cultural, sporting and leisure holidays for young people from 4 to 18 years old.
Campus Travel
Tel: 020-7730 3402
STA (London)
Tel: 020-7937 9921
STA (Australia)
Tel: 03-347 6911
CUTS (Canada)
Tel: 416 979 2402
CIEE (Council on International Educational Exchange)
205 E. 42nd Street
New York
NY 10017
Tel: 212-661 1414.
American Council for International Studies Inc.,
19 Bay State Road
Boston
Mass. 02215
Tel: 617-236 2051
Youth for Understanding International Exchange,
3501 Newark Street NW
Washington DC 20016
Tel: 202-966 6800

Language Courses

Accueil des Jeunes en France
119 Rue St-Martin
75004 Paris
Tel: 01 42 77 87 80
Fax: 01 42 77 70 48
Offers French study programmes, inexpensive accommodation (and accommodation with a family) and tours for individuals or groups.
Centre des Échanges Internationaux
104 Rue de Vaugirard
75006 Paris
Tel: 01 45 49 26 25
Sporting and cultural holidays and educational tours for 15 to 30 year

olds. This is a non-profit-making organisation.

Once in France, students will find a valid student identity card is useful in obtaining discounts on all sorts of activities, including admission to museums and galleries, the cinema and theatre. Reductions may sometimes be allowed by proving your status with a passport.

Further Details

- **CIDJ** (Centre d'Information et de Documentation Jeunesse)
  101 quai Branly
  75740 Paris Cedex 15
  Tel: 01 44 49 12 25
  Fax: 01 40 65 02 61
- **Loisirs de France Jeunes** (for information on holiday centres for children and teenagers)
  30 rue Godot-de-Mauroy
  75009 Paris
  Tel: 01 47 42 51 81
  Fax: 01 42 66 19 74

Disabled Travellers

Most less able travellers will want to book **accommodation** in advance rather than arriving "on spec". Most of the official list of hotels (available from the FGTO or the regional tourist office – *see Useful Addresses*) include a symbol to denote wheelchair access, but it is always advisable to check directly with the chosen hotel as to exactly what facilities are available.

Balladins is a chain of newly-built, budget-priced hotels throughout France, which all have at least one room designed for disabled guests and restaurants and all other public areas are accessible. For a complete list contact: Hotels Balladins (Hotels et Compagnie Nuit d'Hotel Balladins Climat de France Relais Bleus), 7 rue Cap Horn, 91940 Les Ulis, tel: 02 69 29 32 00, fax: 02 69 07 93 89.

An **information sheet** aimed at disabled travellers is published by the French Government Tourist Office; this lists accommodation suitable for the disabled (including wheelchair users) across France but if you have specific needs it is best to double check when booking.

The following organisations all offer advice and publish booklets specifically for handicapped people wanting to take various kinds of holiday in France:

Association des Paralysés de France
Service Information
17 boulevard August Blanqui
75013 Paris
Tel: 01 40 78 69 00
CNFLRH (Comité Nationale Francais de Liaison pour le Readaption de Handicapés)
236 bis, rue de Tolbiac
75013 Paris
Tel: 01 53 80 66 66
Fax: 01 53 80 66 67
E-mail: cnrh@worldnet.net

For information on access to **museums** contact the Direction des Musées de France, Service Accueil des Publics Spécifiques, 6 rue des Pyramides, 75041 Paris Cedex, tel: 01 40 15 35 88.

SNCF (French Rail) and the Gîtes de France organisation both publish practical guides for travellers with reduced mobility.

The *Michelin Red Guide France*, for hotels and their *Camping-Caravanning – France* both include symbols for disabled welcome.

RADAR (The Royal Association for Disability and Rehabilitation), 12 City Forum, 250 City Rd. London EC1V 8AF, tel: 020-7250 32222, has some useful information for tourists, and France's sister organisation – CNFLRH (the Comité National Français de Liaison pour la Réadaptation des Handicapés – for address, see above) – offers a good information service .

SATH (Society for the Advancement of Travel for the Handicapped), 347 5th Avenue, Suite 610, New York, tel: 212-447 0027, fax: 212-725 8253, web: www.sath.org/index.html).

Emergency Numbers

- Ambulance 15
- Police (police) 17
- Fire brigade (pompiers) 18

Practical Tips

Emergencies

To report a crime or loss of belongings, visit the local *gendarmerie* or *commisariat de police*. Telephone numbers are given at the front of local directories, or in an emergency, dial 17. If you lose a passport, report first to the police, then to the nearest consulate. If you are detained by the police, ask to telephone the nearest consulate for a member of the staff to come to your assistance.

For lost credit cards, notify the authorities immediately on the following telephone numbers:
American Express
Tel: 01 47 77 72 00
Visa/Carte Bleue
Tel: 08 36 69 08 80
Diner's Club
Tel: 01 49 06 17 50

Weights & Measures

The metric system is used in France for all weights and measures, although you may encounter old-fashioned terms such as livre (roughly 1 lb weight – 500 grams) still used by small shop-keepers.

As a kilometre is ⅝ of a mile – a handy reckoning whilst travelling is to remember that 80 km = 50 miles.

Business Hours

Office workers normally start early – 8.30am is not uncommon – but often stay at their desks until 6pm or later. This is partly to make up for the long lunch hours (from noon or 12.30pm for two hours), which are still traditional in banks, shops and other public offices. Many

Temperature

Temperatures are always given in celsius (centigrade). To convert to fahrenheit, see below:

0°C	=	2°F
10°C	=	50°F
15°C	=	59°F
20°C	=	68°F
25°C	=	77°F
30°C	=	86°F

companies are beginning to change to shorter lunchbreaks as employees appreciate the advantages of getting home earlier in the evening.

Banks are normally open 8.30am–noon and 1.30–4.30pm or 5pm, Monday–Friday. Some banks also open on Saturday morning.

Media

NEWSPAPERS

Regional newspapers, such as *Le Progrès*, *Le Bien Public*, *Les Dépêches* and *Le Courrier*, contain national and international as well as local news, and have a far higher standing in France than their counterparts in the UK and are often read in preference to the **national dailies** such as *Le Monde*, *Libération* and *Le Figaro*. British and American dailies, notably *The Times* and the *International Herald Tribune*, are also available in major towns and cities.

TELEVISION

Viewers in the region can receive the two main national channels **TF1** (commercial) and **Antenne 2** (state-owned but largely financed by advertising), as well as **FR3**, which offers regional programmes. **Cable TV** provides access to BBC channels.

RADIO

France Inter is the main national radio station (892 long wave), it broadcasts English-language news twice a day in summer (generally 9am and 4pm). There is fairly good reception for BBC Radio 4, especially in the north of the region.

Postal Services

Post Offices – *Postes* or PTTs – are usually open Monday–Friday 9am–noon and 2–5pm, Saturday 9am–noon (opening hours are posted outside). Inside major post offices, individual counters are marked for different requirements – if you just need stamps, go to the one marked *Timbres*. If you need to send an urgent letter overseas, ask for it to be sent *par exprès*, or by *Chronopost*, which is fast, but costly.

For a small fee, you can arrange for mail to be kept *poste restante* at any post office, addressed to **Poste Restante**, Poste Centrale (for main post office), then the town post code and name, eg. 21000 Dijon. A passport is required when collecting mail.

Stamps (*timbres*) are often available at tobacconists (*bureaux de tabacs*) and other shops selling postcards and greetings cards. Letters within France and most of the EU cost FF3.

Telegrams can be sent during post office hours or by telephone (24 hours). To send a telegram abroad dial 0800 33 44 11.

Fax and photocopying facilities are often available at major post offices and *maisons de la presse* (newsagents) and many supermarkets also now have coin-in-the-slot photocopiers.

Telecommunications

The French telephone system is now one of the best in the world. That is not to say that you can be guaranteed to find telephone boxes (*cabines publiques*) that are always operational, but most are.

Telephone numbers have been rationalised to ten figures, given in sets of two, e.g. 01 23 45 67 89.

International calls can be made from most public booths, but it is often easier to use a booth in a post office – ask at the counter to

use the phone, then go back to settle the bill – although you have no indication of how much the call is going to cost until the end.

Coin-operated phones take most coins, and card phones are now very common and simple to use. It is worth purchasing a phone card (*une télécarte*) if you are likely to need to use a public call box, as most have now been converted to cards. **Cards** are available from post offices, stationers, railway stations, some cafés and *bureaux de tabacs*. If you use a phone (not a public call box) in a café, shop or restaurant you may be surcharged.

To make an **international call**, insert the money (if necessary), dial 00, then dial the country code (*see box below*), the area code (omitting any initial 0) and the number.

Dialling Codes

International dialling codes:
Australia 61
Canada 1
Ireland 353
UK 44
US 1
Useful numbers:
● Directory enquiries 12
● Operator services 13

If using a US credit phone card, dial the company's access number: **Sprint**, tel: 00 00 87; **AT&T**, tel: 00 00 11; **MCI**, tel: 00 00 19. NB: The computerised **Minitel** system of telephone directories is currently under review, and may no longer be available in post offices.

If you need to make a phone call in rural areas or small villages with no public phone, look for the blue plaque saying *téléphone publique* on private houses. This means the owner is officially required to allow you to use the phone and charge the normal amount for the call.

You cannot **reverse charges** (call collect) within France but you can to countries which will accept such calls. Go through the operator and ask to make a **PCV** (pronounced "pay-say-vay") call. Telephone calls can only be received at call boxes

displaying the blue bell sign. The cheapest times to call are weekdays 7.30pm–8am and after 1.30pm on Saturday.

Doing Business

Business travel is now such an important part of the tourist economy that the French Government Tourist Office in London and Chicago (*see list overleaf*) has a department set up to deal exclusively with business enquiries. They help organise hotels, conference centres and incentive deals for any group, whether large or small.

For general information about business travel and facilities contact the regional tourist offices (*see Tourist Offices*). Another good source of business information and local assistance are the Chambres de Commerce et d'Industrie in the individual *départements*. Here you can obtain details about local companies, assistance with the technicalities of export and import, interpretation/translation agencies and conference centres – indeed, most chambers of commerce have conference facilities of some kind themselves. The main Chambres de Commerce et d'Industrie in Dijon are found under the umbrella of the Chambre Régionale de Commerce et d'Industrie, 68 rue Chevreul, 21000 Dijon, tel: 03 80 65 91 00.

Embassies/Consulates

In most cases, the nearest consular services are in Paris.
USA Embassy: 2 avenue Gabriel 75008 Paris, tel: 01 43 12 22 22
Australia: 4 rue Jean Rey, 75015 Paris, tel: 01 40 59 33 10
British Embassy: 35 rue du Faubourg St-Honoré, 75008 Paris, tel: 01 42 66 91 42
Canada: 35 avenue Montaigne, 75008 Paris, tel: 01 4059 33 00
Eire: 14 rue Rude 75016 Paris, tel: 01 44 17 67 00

Tourist Offices

UK
French Government Tourist Office
178 Piccadilly
London W1V 0AL
Tel: 0891-244 123
Fax: 020 7493 6594
A French travel centre for
information, books and guides is
also now open at 178 Piccadilly
(email: piccadilly@mdlf.demon.co.uk;
website: www.franceguide.com).

USA
Air France/Maisons de France
New York:
444 Madison Ave
16th Floor
New York
NY 10020
Tel: 212-838 7800
Fax: 212-838 7855
Los Angeles:
9454 Wilshire Boulevard
Suite 715 Beverly Hills
Los Angeles
CA 90212-2967
Tel: 310-271 2693
Fax: 310-276 2835.

France
Maison de la France
20 avenue de l'Opéra
75001 Paris
Tel: 01 42 96 70 00
Fax: 01 42 96 70 71

Burgundy
Comité Régional de Tourisme de
Bourgogne
12 boulevard de Brosses
21000 Dijon
Tel: 03 80 50 90 00/
03 80 30 59 45

DÈPARTEMENTAL TOURIST OFFICES

Ain
34 rue Général Delestraint
BP78
01002 Bourg-en-Bresse Cedex
Tel: 04 74 32 31 30

Côte d'Or
Hôtel du Département
BP1601

21035 Dijon Cedex
Tel: 03 80 63 66 92

Nièvre
3 rue du Sort
58000 Nevers
Tel: 03 86 36 39 80
Fax: 03 80 49 90 97

Rhône
Office de Tourisme
Place Bellecour
BP2254
69214 Lyon Cedex 02
Tel: 03 78 42 25 75
Fax: 03 78 37 02 06

Saône-et-Loire
389 avenue de Lattre de Tassigny
71000 Mâcon
Tel: 03 85 21 02 02

Yonne
Maison du Tourisme
1–2 Quai de la République
89000 Auxerre
Tel: 03 86 72 92 00

SERVICES RÉSERVATION LOISIR ACCUEIL

Nièvre
Service de Réservation Loisirs
Accueil du Nivernais-Morvan
3 rue du Sort
58000 Nevers
Tel: 03 86 59 14 22

Yonne
1–2 quai de la République
89000 Auxerre
Tel: 03 86 72 92 10

Getting Around

Public Transport

BY BUS

Details of routes and timetables are
generally available free of charge
either from bus stations (*gares
routières* – typically situated close
to train stations – or from local
tourist offices.

BY TRAIN

Information on services is available
from stations (*gares SNCF*). The
region is well served by trains
north–south en route to or from
Paris; getting across the region
east to west by train is not so easy.
   If you intend to travel extensively
by train it may well be worth
investing in one of the rail passes
available before leaving home (*see
Getting There for further details*).
These tickets can be used on any
journey, otherwise individual tickets
need to be purchased. However,
some discounts are available, e.g.
the *Carte Couple* for married
couples travelling together on off-
peak services, so it is worth
investigating your options at the
station. Any children under four
years travel free; those from four to
12 years travel for half fare.

Ticket Validation

All tickets purchased at French
stations have to be put through
the orange machines, marked
compostez votre billet, at the
stations to validate them before
boarding the train.

Private Transport

BY CAR

You should always carry your **driving licence**, vehicle's **registration document** and valid **insurance** – third party is the minimum and a green card from your insurance company is strongly recommended.

Additional insurance cover, which can include a get-you-home service, is offered by a number of organisations including the British and American Automobile Associations and Europ-Assistance, Sussex House, Haywards Heath, West Sussex, RH16 1DN. For information, tel: 01444-442211; emergency breakdown, tel: 01444-442500.

Automobile Club Secours, 20 avenue Maronniers, 93400 St-Ouen, tel: 0800 08 07 06; fax: 01 40 10 84 07.

Roads & Speed Limits

Speed limits are 130 km/h (80 mph) on motorways, 110 km/h (68 mph) on dual carriageways, 90 km/h (56 mph) on national and *département* roads. The speed limit for built-up areas is 50 km/h (31 mph). You have to pay tolls on French motorways, which can prove costly over a long distance.

Highway Code

The minimum age for driving in France is 18. Foreigners are not permitted to drive on a provisional licence. Full or dipped **headlights** must be used in poor visibility (including during heavy rain) and at night. Sidelights are not sufficient unless the car is stationary. Beams must be adjusted for right-hand-drive vehicles, but yellow tints are not compulsory.

Wearing **seat belts** (front and rear if fitted) in cars, and crash helmets on motorcycles, is compulsory. **Children** under 10 are not allowed in the front seat unless the car is fitted with a rear-facing safety seat or if it has no rear seat.

Priorité a la Droite

Until recently, priority on French roads was always given to vehicles approaching from the right, except where otherwise indicated. Nowadays, on main roads, the major road will normally have priority, with traffic being halted on minor approach roads with one of the following signs:

• *Cedez le passage* – give way.
• *Vous n'avez pas la priorité* – you do not have right of way.
• *Passage protégé* – no right of way.

However, care should be taken in smaller towns and in rural areas where there may not be any road markings (watch out for farm vehicles), in which case you will be expected to give way to traffic coming from the right. Note that in determining priority a driver may flash his or her headlights to indicate that he or she has priority.

Priority is always given to emergency services and also to vehicles from public utility (e.g. gas electric and water) companies. A yellow diamond sign indicates that you have priority, the diamond sign with a diagonal black line indicates that you do not.

Fines

Heavy on-the-spot fines are given for traffic offences, such as speeding, and drivers can be stopped and breathalysed during spot checks. If you do not have enough cash, you will be required to pay a deposit or you will be given a ticket to be presented at a local police station. Police are fairly visible on the main roads of France during the summer months.

For information about road conditions, telephone the *Inter Service Route* line on 08 36 69 20 00 (a recorded announcement in French and not always terribly clear) or tune into the local radio station (frequencies are often indicated on signs beside roads and *autoroutes*). During the holiday season, traffic reports and advice on major routes will follow the news on television.

The French **drink-driving limit** is 50 mg alcohol per 100 ml of blood. This can mean that as little as just one glass of beer can take you up to the limit.

Fuel

Unleaded petrol (*essence sans plomb*) is now widely available in France.

Breakdowns

If you are driving your own car, then arrange for breakdown insurance with a free phone number. In France most car insurance policies include a breakdown service. If you are hiring a car check the number to call before you drive away. The emergency breakdown services (*touring secours*) can be reached from the emergency telephones.

Car Hire

Hiring a car is expensive in France. Some fly/drive deals work out reasonably well if you're only going for a short visit – and it is best to arrange hire in the UK or US before leaving for France. There are car hire desks at all major railway stations (or within walking distance of the station) and all airports. Offices of the major car hire companies are listed below. The driver must be at least 21 years old and some companies will not hire to people under 26. You must have had a full driving licence for at least a year.
Avis: Central reservation office, tel: 01 46 10 60 60; provincial office, tel: 0800 32 53 25.
Budget: Central reservation office, tel: 08 00 10 00 01.
Europcar: Central reservation office: tel: 01 30 43 82 82.
Hertz: Central reservation office, tel: 01 39 38 38 38; provincial office, tel: 0800 05 33 11.

Routes

Following a tourist circuit or route is a sure way of getting to see the major sites of a region. Tourist offices will help with suggestions, but probably the most important is the **Route des Ducs de Bourgogne**, which covers much of the region from Auxerre and Châtillon-sur-Seine in the north, down to Chalon-sur-Saône in the southeast. It takes in many of the important ducal châteaux such as Ancy-le-Franc, Bussy-Rabutin and Tanlay, as well as some important religious buildings such as Fontenay.

In the far northeast of the region around Auxerre you can follow the **Route Historique des Trésors de La Puisaye**, which includes the churches of La Ferté-Loupière and Toucy as well as some major secular buildings such as the Châteaux de St-Fargeau and La Bussière.

Part of the **Route Historique Buissonière**, which goes from Paris right down to Lyon, can be traced through Burgundy, on a direct north-west-south-east axis from Auxerre to Paray-le-Monial, taking in the sites at Vézelay, and Château-Chinon, among others on the way.

BY MOTORCYCLE OR MOPED

Rules of the road are largely the same as for car drivers. The minimum age for driving machines over 80cc is 18. GB plates must be shown and crash helmets are compulsory. Dipped headlights must be used at all times. Children under 14 years are not permitted to be carried as passengers.

On Foot

There are countless opportunities for exploring the region on foot – perhaps the most obvious is the unspoilt Morvan regional park right at the heart of Burgundy. The **Tour du Morvan**, taking in most of the major lakes, is an ideal circuit of around 220 km (135 miles). Alternatively, you can follow the GR13 footpath from Auxerre to Autun. All the main footpaths in France form part of the national network of long distance footpaths (**Sentiers de Grandes Randonnées** or GR). The major footpaths in the region outside the Morvan are the GR7 in the east of the region, passing near Dijon and continuing on to Cluny; part of the GR2 from Châtillon-sur-Seine to Dijon; and the GR3 which follows the path of the

Loire along the western edge of the region, taking in Nevers. Another suggested tour in the north is the **Tour de La Puisaye** – in author Colette's country.

Hitchhiking

With sensible precautions, hitchhiking can be an interesting and inexpensive way to see France. Would-be hitchhikers may be discouraged by the difficulty of getting a lift out of the Channel ports, so it may be worth taking a bus or train for the first leg of your journey. Hitching is forbidden on motorways, but you can wait on slip roads or at toll booths. **Allostop** is a nationwide organisation that aims to connect hikers with drivers (you pay a registration fee and a contribution towards the petrol). For further details, tel: 01 53 20 42 43 (Paris) or 08 03 80 36 66 (Paris and all regions).

The French Ramblers' Association, Fédération Française de la Randonnée Pédestre (FFRP), publishes Topoguides (guidebooks incorporating IGN l:50,000 scale maps) to all of France's footpaths but they are available only in French. Titles available for Burgundy include Nos 032 Tour de Morvan, 022 Tour de La Puisaye, 352 Sentier de la Loire (covering the GR3), 125 Sentier Île de France-Bourgogne for the GR13, No. 201 Sentier de la Seine et de l'Yonne for the GR2 and 710 Sentier Vosges-Pyrénées which covers the GR7. These guides are available in good bookshops in the region, or in case of difficulty contact the Centre d'Information Sentiers et Randonnées, FFRP, Centre d'Information Sentiers et Randonnées, 14 rue Riquet, 75019 Paris, tel: 01 44 89 93 90/93; fax: 01 40 35 85 67.

In the UK try **Stanfords** (see Maps, page 311). A good basic guide for serious walkers is Rob Hunter's book Walking in France,

published by Oxford Illustrated Press. The IGN Blue series maps at a scale of 1:25,000 are ideal for walkers, and sheet No. 306 Morvan Regional Park, although less detailed, is also useful. (See Maps, page 311 for stockists)

Each département has its own ramblers' organisation which arranges a variety of activities throughout the year, with guided walks taking a day, a weekend or more, as well as walks with a particular theme – flora or wildlife, for example.

Parc Naturel du Morvan, Maison du Parc, St-Brisson, 58230 Montsauche, tel: 03 86 78 70 16.

Comité National des Sentiers de Grande Randonnée, 64 rue de Gervorie, 75014 Paris, tel: 01 45 45 31 02.

WALKING HOLIDAYS

Various walking holidays with accommodation either in hotels or under canvas are available. Some are organised through package tour operators in the UK, others can be booked through the French tourist offices and other local organisations. The Service Loisirs Accueil in both Nièvre and Côte d'Or (See Tourist Offices, page 318) offer walking holidays, and a selection of other operators are:

Association Les Quatre Chemins, 33 Grand-Rue-Chauchien, 71400 Autun, tel: 04 85 52 07 91. Walking and other activity holidays in the Morvan.

Horizon Aventure, 5 Place Jacques Prévert, 21000 Dijon, tel: 03 80 30 38 64.

Ramblers Holidays, Box 43, Welwyn Garden City, Herts AL8 6PQ, tel: 01707-331133. Sight-seeing holidays by coach and foot, half board, nine days with up to about four hours walking a day.

Club Adventure, 18 rue Seguier 75006 Paris, tel: 01 44 32 09 30. Organises walks with your luggage transported for you.

By Boat

Possibly one of the most popular ways of discovering Burgundy is on board a **narrowboat** or one of the other craft that can be hired on the region's many navigable canals and rivers. Situated at the watershed of France's three great rivers, the Seine, Loire and the Rhône, served by a network of canals and complemented by the rivers Saône, Yonne and Seille, Burgundy offers almost 1,200 km (745 miles) of waterways, now barely used by commercial traffic. The **Canal du Centre** is the only one which has a significant amount of business traffic but not enough to disturb its tranquil scenery.

The **Canal de Bourgogne** is the longest, connecting the River Yonne in the north to the Saône in the south. It also has the greatest number of locks. Devotees of canal architecture will wish to incorporate into their trip the aqueduct at Briare. This remarkable edifice, with foundations laid by the company of the engineer, Eiffel, was built in 1896 to connect the Briare and the Loire lateral canals. A masterpiece of engineering, 664 metres (2,180 ft) long and now mainly used by pleasure boats, it was built to enable freight to be carried all the way from the Channel to the Mediterranean. The Briare canal was built by Sully in the early 17th century and served as a prototype for all France's later canal-building.

There are several options available for holidays afloat. Small boats for just two people or narrowboats accommodating 12 can be hired from several operators; these are fully equipped for self-catering. Boats can be hired for a weekend or longer and even if you have never navigated before, you will feel confident after a minimum of instruction (foreigners require no permit or licence).

Several companies in the UK offer "package" holidays afloat including travel arrangements. A selection is given below:

Abercrombie and Kent Ltd
Sloane Square House
Holbein Place
London SW1W 8NS
Tel: 020-7730 9600
Blakes Holidays
Wroxham
Norwich NR12 8DH
Tel: 01603-784131
fax: 01603-782871
Crown Blue Line
8 Ber Street
Norwich
Norfolk NR1 3EJ
Tel: 01603-630513
Fax: 01603-664298
French Country Cruises
54 High Street East
Uppingham
Rutland LE15 9PZ
Tel: 01572-821330
Hoseasons Holidays Abroad
Sunway House
Lowestoft NR32 3LT
Tel: 01502-500555
Fax: 01502-500532

Agencies in the US include:
Abercrombie and Kent Ltd
1420 Kinsington Road
Oak Brook
Illinois 60521 2106
Tel: 800-323 7308

If you prefer to book direct in France, try the **Service Loisirs Accueil** in the individual départements (*see Tourist Offices, page 318*) or contact one of the following companies (this is just a selection of the many operators):
Bourgogne voies navigables
SRLA Yonne
3–4 Quai de la République
89000 Auxerre
Tel: 03 86 52 18 99
This firm acts as an agent for many smaller operators.
Locaboat Plaisance
Quai du Port-au-Bois
89300 Joigny
Tel: 03 86 91 72 72
Fax: 86 62 42 41
Crown Blue Lines
Le Grand Bassin
11401 Castelnaudry
Tel: 68 23 17 51
Fax: 68 23 33 92
Operates 120 boats in three centres. (In Britain call 01603 630513; in the US call the toll-free number: 800 355 9394)

Maps of the Waterways

If you are navigating for yourself, a map or guide to the waterway is essential. These are often provided as part of a package deal, otherwise you will need to take your own. **Crown Blue Line** produce large-format map-guides for their own clients, which are now available to the public; their titles for Burgundy are CBL2 Bourgogne-Franche-Comté and CBL3 Loire Nivernais. **ECM** map-guides are well-produced strip maps with all navigation aids, boating services and tourist information. There are several titles for the Burgundy region. **Vagnon** map-guides are also very good, with some colour photography. All these, and a selection of general publications about French waterways, are available by mail order from Compass Books (*see Maps, page 311*).

Where to Stay

Bed and breakfast accommodation (*chambres d'hôte*) is fairly widely available in private houses, often on working farms, whose owners are members of the Fédération Nationale des Gîtes Ruraux de France. All such accommodation is inspected by a local representative of the Fédération to ensure that standards are maintained in accordance with its "star" rating (which in fact is shown by ears of corn on a scale of one to four). Bookings can be made for an overnight stop or a longer stay. Breakfast is included in the price and evening meals – usually made with local produce and extremely good value – are often available.

Staying with a family in this way provides an ideal opportunity to get to know the local area and its people more intimately. Brochures of all recognised Gîtes-Chambres d'hôtes are available from Gîtes de France organisation in each *département*; some are bookable through the Gîtes de France office at The Brittany Centre, Wharf Rd, Portsmouth, PO2 8RU, tel: 0990-360360, or Maison de Gîtes de France, 59 rue St. Lazare, 75009 Paris, tel: 01 49 70 75 75.

B&B Abroad offer a straightforward bed-and-breakfast service, which can include ferry bookings if desired. They book accommodation at either a single destination or various stops around the region. Contact: 5 World's End Lane, Green St Green, Orpington, Kent BR6 6AA, tel: 01689-857838; fax: 01689 850931. B&B (France) publishes *Le B&B* (with l'Association Francaise B&B France); for further details, contact

94–96 Bell Street, Henley-on-Thames, Oxon RG9 1XS, tel: 01491-578 803; fax: 01491 410806. **Café-Couette**, tel: 01 42 94 92 00, offers a selection of B&B addresses in Paris and the provinces.

For B&B on a slightly grander scale, try **Château Welcome**, PO Box 66, 94 Bell Street, Henley-on-Thames RG9 1XS, tel: 0491-578803. They organise stays in privately-owned châteaux, where an evening meal is often also served.

In Canada: book through Tours Chanteclerc, 65 Rue de Brésoles, Montréal, Québec H2Y 1V7, tel: 514-845 1236, and 100 Adelaide Street West, Toronto, Ontario M11 1S3, tel: 416-867 1595.

If you don't want to book in advance, look out for signs along the road (usually in the country) offering *chambres d'hôtes*. You will be taking pot luck, but you may be delighted by the simple farm food and accommodation on offer.

COTTAGES & GÎTES

France offers what is probably the best network of self-catering holiday cottages anywhere in Europe. The Fédération des Gîtes Ruraux de France was set up in the 1960s with the main aim of restoring rural properties (by means of offering grants to owners) on the condition that these properties would then be let as cheap holiday homes for the less well-off town and city dwellers. These **gîtes** (literally: a place to lay one's head) are an inexpensive way of enjoying a rural holiday in regional France. The properties range from simple farm cottages to grand manor houses and châteaux.

The properties are all inspected by the Relais Départemental (the county office of the national federation) and given an "épi" (ear of corn) classification. The gîtes are completely self-catering (in many cases expect to supply your own bedlinen), but most have owners living nearby who will tell you where to buy local produce (and if on a farm, often provide it).

Note that some of these properties will be off the beaten track and a car, or at least a bicycle, is usually essential. Bicycles can often be hired locally or even from gîte owners. Car hire is expensive, but some fly/drive packages still make this a relatively inexpensive way to visit Burgundy.

CAMPING

There is a good choice of campsites in the region, many of them near lakes or rivers. The *Comité Régional du Tourisme* (*see Tourist Offices, page 311*) produces a list of all recognised sites, with details of star-rating and facilities. The sites can get booked up in high season, so do consider advance booking. Members of the Camping Club or Camping and Caravanning Club of Great Britain may make use of their booking services. The *Michelin Camping/Caravanning Guide* lists sites that accept (or insist on) pre-booking. The Camping Service at 69 Westbourne Grove, London W2 4UJ, tel: 020-7792 l944, can book sites either from their own brochure of ★★★ and ★★★★ sites or independent sites and will also book ferries.

Campsites, like hotels, have official classifications from one-star (minimal comfort, water points, showers and sinks) to four-star luxury sites which allow more space to each pitch, and offer above-average facilities. The majority of sites are two-star.

If you really like to get back to nature, and are unimpressed by the modern trappings of hot water and electric power, look out for camp-sites designated *Aire naturelle de camping*, where facilities will be absolutely minimal and prices to match. These usually have a maximum of 25 pitches.

Some farms also offer "official" sites under the auspices of the Fédération Nationale des Gîtes Ruraux – these are designated

Camping à la ferme. Facilities are usually limited but farmers are only allowed to have six pitches.

Packaged camping holidays are becoming increasingly popular with British holiday makers and are ideal for overseas visitors too, as all the camping paraphernalia is provided on the site. Companies have couriers on the sites to help with any problems. Interestingly, where such companies have taken over sections of existing sites, facilities have improved to meet the demands of their customers and so benefit all campers.

For information on Burgundy's campsites, write to the Camping Service, 69 Westbourne Grove, London W2 4UJ, tel: 020-7792 1944, the regional tourist office, or enquire at a French Government Tourist Office. A selection of package operators is listed below:

Canvas Holidays
12 Abbey Park Place
Dunfermline KY12 7PD
Tel: 01383 621000

Eurocamp Travel
Hartford Manor
Greenbank Lane
Northwich
CWH 1HW
Tel: 01565 626262

Solaire Holidays
1158 Stratford Road
Hall Green
Birmingham B28 8AF
Tel: 0121 778 5061

The Caravan and Camping Service
Tel: 020 7792 1944
Fax: 020 7792 1956
This organisation can book sites from their own brochure of ★★★ and ★★★★ sites or some others, and also book ferries. A camping *carnet* is useful – some sites will not accept a booking without one.

USEFUL READING & FURTHER CONTACTS

The *French Federation of Camping and Caravanning Guide* (FFCC) lists 11,600 sites nationwide and shows which sites have facilities for disabled campers. Available from Deneway Guides, Chesil Lodge,

West Bexington, Dorchester DT2 9DG, tel: 01308-897 809.

Michelin Green Guide – Camping/Caravanning France is very informative and lists sites with facilities for the disabled.

For further details on where to camp, contact the Camping and Caravanning Club, Greenfields House, Westwood Way, Coventry, CV4 8JH, tel: 01203-422 024, or the Caravan Club, East Grinstead House, East Grinstead, West Sussex RH19 1UA, tel: 01342-316101.

YOUTH HOSTELS

Holders of accredited Youth Hostel Association (YHA) cards may stay in any of Burgundy's hostels. Contact the following for more information: Fédération Unie des Auberges de Jeunesse (FUAJ), 27 rue Pajol, 75018 Paris, tel: 01 44 89 87 27; fax: 01 44 89 87 10. The federation is affiliated to the International Youth Hostel Federation. You can also contact the Ligue Française pour les auberges de jeunesse (LFAJ), 38 bvd Raspail, 75007 Paris, tel: 01 45 48 69 84; fax: 01 45 44 57 47.

In Britain: The British Youth Hostel Association (YHA) publishes the *International Youth Hostel Handbook*, which includes all the hostels in Burgundy and is available from the YHA by post from 8 St Stephen's Hill, St Albans, Herts, tel: 01727-845 047 or in person from 14 Southampton Street, London WC2E 7H7, tel: 020-7836 8541, and 174 High Street, Kensington, London W8 7RG. The London office also handles membership queries, tel: 020 7836 1036.

In the US: apply to American Youth Hostelling International, PO Box 37613, Dept USA, Washington DC 20013/7613, tel: 202-783 6161.

Gîtes d'Etape also offer hostel accommodation and are popular with ramblers and horse riders – some offer stabling. All official gîtes d'étape come under the auspices of the *Relais Départementaux des Gîtes Ruraux (see Self-Catering*

Cottages, page 322). They are a popular form of inexpensive accommodation particularly in the national parks. Prices are similar to youth hostels and you do not have to be a member of any organisation to use them.

Hotels

Hotels are plentiful in the main towns of the region and along the main highways, but those tucked away in the smaller country villages are often the best. All hotels in France conform to national standards and carry ★-ratings, set down by the Ministry of Tourism, according to their degree of comfort and amenities. Prices are charged per room, rather than per person.

Hotels are required to show their menus outside the hotel and details of room prices should also be visible either outside or in reception, as well as on the back of bedroom doors. It is possible for a hotel to have a ★ rating, with a ★★ restaurant. This is ideal if you are on a budget and more interested in food than fading wallpaper or eccentric plumbing.

When booking a room, it is normal to look at it first; if it doesn't suit you, ask to be shown another, as rooms can vary hugely in the same building. Supplements may be charged for an additional bed or a cot (*lit bébé*). You may be asked when booking if you wish to dine, particularly if the hotel is busy – preference should not, but may be given to hungry customers as there is not a lot of profit in letting rooms alone. The simple request, *On peut dîner ici ce soir?* will confirm that the restaurant in the hotel is open – many are closed out of season on Sunday or Monday evenings.

Lists of hotels can be obtained from the French Government Tourist office in your country or from the regional tourist offices in Burgundy. The *Logis et Auberges de France* guide is also an invaluable guide to reasonably-priced family-run hotels offering a friendly welcome and good local cuisine. It can be used to book hotels before travelling (for the central reservation office in Paris, tel: 01 45 84 83 84). Some tourist offices will make hotel bookings for you, for a small fee.

Several other hotel chains and associations offer central booking facilities. These range from the very cheap and simple groups such as the Balladins chain, which has almost 100 modern ★ hotels, to the Concorde group of 28 ★★★★ and de-luxe hotels. A list of central booking offices is given below.

Mercure, Reservations: tel, 0803-88 33 33; UK office, Resinter tel: 020-8283 4500/4580; fax: 020-8283 4650.

Campanile, Reservations: 21 Avenue Jean-Moulin, 77200 Torcy, tel: 01 64 62 46 46/0149 78 01 45; fax: 01 64 62 46 61. With 225 ★★ to ★★★★ hotels; UK office, Red Lion Court, Alexandra Road, Hounslow TW3 1JS, tel: 020-8569 6969; fax: 020-8569 4888.

Climat de France: 5 rue Cap Horn, 91943 Les Ulis, tel: 01 64 62 48 88 150. ★★ hotels; UK office, Voyages Vacances Int., 34 Saville Row, London W1X 1AG, tel: 020-7287 3181.

Concorde Hotels: 35–37 Grosvenor Gardens, London SW1W 0BS, tel: 0800-181 591/020-7630 1704; fax: 020-7630 0391.

Formule 1, Reservations: 35 rue Dr Babinski 93400 Saint-Ouen, tel: 01 49 21 90 75; fax 01 49 21 90 79 178. ★ budget-priced hotels, offering a booking service from one hotel to another in the chain.

Ibis Reservations: 91021 Evry, tel: 08 03 88 22 22. With 170 ★★ hotels; UK office, Resinter, 1 Shortlands, London W6 8DR, tel: 020-8283 4500; fax: 020-8283 4650.

Minotels Great Britain, 37 Springfield Road, Blackpool FY1 IP2, tel: 01253-292 000; fax: 01253-291 111.

The prices given are per person, per room, per night

Budget   Under FF300
Moderate Under FF700
Luxury   Over FF700
CC = credit cards
CB = Carte Bleue

List of Hotels

The following is a selection of good hotels in Burgundy to suit all budgets. Hotels are listed by area.

YONNE

Arcy-sur-Cure
Hôtel des Grottes ★
RN6, 89270
Tel: 03 86 81 91 47
Fax: 03 86 81 96 22
Small hotel on the main road, with its own garden, convenient for visitors to the famous caves. CC: Visa, MasterCard. Closed: Wednesday out of season and 10 December–25 January. Budget.

Auxerre
Hôtel Les Clairions ★★
RN6 direction Paris
89000 Auxerre
Tel: 03 86 94 94 94
Fax: 03 86 48 16 38
Member of both the Logis and Charme Hôtel chains. Situated on the RN6, 2 km (1 mile) from the town centre; facilities include a swimming-pool and tennis courts in the garden. Has rooms suitable for the disabled. CC: Amex, Diners, Visa, MasterCard. Moderate.

Le Moulin des Ruats ★★★
Vallée du Cousin
89200 Auxerre
Tel: 03 86 34 97 00
Fax: 03 86 31 65 47
Small hotel in a converted watermill overlooking the river, with a garden. Several rooms have terrace views. There is a restaurant offering imaginative menus. Fully equipped rooms overlooking garden or river, some with terrace. CC: Diners, Visa, MasterCard. Closed: Monday

evening out of season; 15 November–15 December and 15 January–15 February. Moderate.

Hôtel Normandie ★★
41 Boulevard Vauban
89000 Auxerre
Tel: 03 86 52 57 80
Fax: 03 86 51 54 33
An attractive 19th-century country house hotel, a few minutes from the centre of Auxerre, with rooms overlooking garden or terrace. Gym, Sauna, 24-hour room service menu. Close to old town centre. CC: Amex, Diners, Visa, MasterCard. Moderate.

Parc de Marechaux ★★★
6 Avenue Foch
89000 Auxerre
Tel: 03 86 51 43 77
Fax: 03 86 51 31 72
Centrally located 19th-century townhouse with traditional decor and views over park. No restaurant. CC: AE, Diners, CB. Moderate.

Avallon
Le Relais Fleuri ★★★
Route Saulieu (RN6)
89200 Avallon
Tel: 03 86 34 02 85
Fax: 03 86 34 09 98
Comfortable hotel just off the motorway, with a garden, outdoor heated swimming pool and tennis courts. Fully-equipped rooms, overlooking garden or park, some accessible for the disabled. Restaurant with traditional cuisine. CC: Amex, Diners, Visa, MasterCard. Moderate

Château de Vault-de-Lugny ★★★★
89200 Vault de Lugny
Tel: 03 86 34 07 86
Fax: 03 86 34 16 36
Country mansion built in the 16th century, in its own gardens just outside town. The restaurant uses its own home-grown produce. Closed 11 November to 19 March. Private parking. Tennis. CC: Amex, CB. Moderate.

Chablis
Hostellerie des Clos ★★★★
18 rue Jules Rathier
89800 Chablis
Tel: 03 86 42 10 63
Fax: 03 86 42 17 11

Hotel in elegant 12th-century building with own shady garden and dining terrace, surrounded by own Chablis vineyards. Restaurant with regional cuisine and good wine list. CC: Visa, MasterCard. Closed: 20 December–10 January plus Wednesday, and Thursday lunchtime out of season. Moderate.

Joigny
Hôtel à la Côte Saint-Jacques ★★★★
14 Faubourg de Paris
Tel: 03 86 62 09 70
Fax: 03 86 91 49 70
One of France's top restaurants has its own hotel, a luxury Relais et Châteaux establishment, beside the Yonne with gardens, terraces and indoor swimming pool. CC: Amex, Diners, Visa, MasterCard. Closed: January. Luxury.

Mailly-Le-Château
Hôtel le Castel ★★
Place de l'Église
89660 Mailly-le-Château
Tel: 03 86 81 43 06
Fax: 03 86 81 49 26
Small village hotel with tree-shaded garden and imaginative menus. CC: Visa, MasterCard. Closed: Wednesday and from 15 November to 15 March. Budget.

Montbard
Hôtel de l'Écu ★★★
7 rue August-Carré
21500 Montbard
Tel: 03 80 92 11 66
Fax: 03 80 92 14 13
Family-run Logis de France hotel in a cosy old stone building, close to the Burgundy Canal. Fully equipped rooms, two restaurants. CC: Amex, Diners, Visa, MasterCard. Moderate.

St-Père-sous-Vézelay
Hôtel l'Espérance ★★★★
89450 St-Père-sous-Vézelay
Tel: 03 86 33 39 10
Fax: 03 86 33 26 15
Hotel and celebrated restaurant in a delightful setting , with some rooms in a converted mill. CC: Amex, Diners, Visa, MasterCard. Closed: January; restaurant closed Tuesday and Wednesday lunch. Luxury.

Hôtel la Renommée ★
RN6 89450 St-Père-sous-Vézelay
Tel: 03 86 33 21 34
Fax: 03 86 33 34 17
A small hotel for those on a budget. Quiet, spacious rooms with views of the church and hills: Closed: Wednesday and November. Budget.

Sens
Hôtel de Paris et de la Poste ★★★
97 rue de la République
89100 Sens
Tel: 03 86 85 17 43
Fax: 03 86 64 48 45
Centrally located hotel with a good restaurant, conservatory and flowery terrace. CC: Amex, Diners, Visa, MasterCard. Moderate

Tonnerre
Hôtel l'Abbaye St-Michel ★★★★
89700 Montée de St-Michel
Tel: 03 86 55 05 99
Fax: 03 86 55 00 10
A 10th-century Benedictine abbey in its own parkland, with beautifully restored and frescoed rooms. Meals served on shady terrace or in vaulted dining room. CC: Amex, Diners, Visa, MasterCard. Closed: 1 January–8 February. Luxury.

Vézelay
Résidence Hôtel le Pontot ★★★
Place du Pontot
89450 Vezelay
Tel: 03 86 33 24 40
Fax: 03 86 33 30 05
Fortified medieval building in centre of town, close to the Basilica. With enclosed garden, stone-flagged, antique-furnished rooms and an elegant salon. Breakfast in the garden on warm days. No restaurant. Booking 30 days in advance and reservation – fee required. CC: Amex, Diners, Visa, MasterCard. Closed 15 October–30 April. Moderate/luxury.

MORVAN & NIÈVRE

Autun
Hôtel St-Louis et De La Poste
6 Rue de l'Arbalète
71400 Autun
Tel: 03 85 52 01 01

Fax: 03 85 86 32 54
This handsome old coaching inn which once accommodated Napoleon and Josephine, has a quiet inner courtyard and rooms elegantly decorated with period furniture. CC: Amex, Diners, Visa, MasterCard. Closed: 22 December–28 January. Moderate.

Pouilly-en-Auxois
Château de Chailly
Tel: 03 80 90 30 30
Fax: 03 80 90 30 00
Magnificently restored château, one of Burgundy's most exclusive hotels, favoured for politicial retreats. Every imaginable facility including swimming pool, gardens and two luxury restaurants. CC: Amex, Diners, CB. Closed 12 December–20 January. Expensive.

Lormes
Hôtel Perreau ★★
8 rue d'Avallon
58140 Lormes
Tel: 03 86 22 53 21
Fax: 03 86 22 82 15
Prettily decorated Logis de France hotel in the centre of town, with restaurant serving regional cooking. Closed: Sunday evening and Monday out of season, and February. Budget.

Nevers
La Folie ★★
Route des Saulaies
58000 Nevers
Tel: 03 86 57 05 31
Fax: 03 86 57 66 99
Modern family-run, Logis de France hotel restaurant with fully-equipped rooms, shady terrace, outdoor pool and tennis court. CC: Visa, MasterCard. Closed: 16 December– to 5 January. Budget.

Saulieu
Résidence La Côte d'Or ★★★★
2 rue d'Argentine
21210 Saulieu
Tel: 03 80 90 53 53
Fax: 03 80 64 08 92
The hotel of Bernard Loiseau's famous restaurant, an 18th-century post-house with rooms full of antique furniture and paintings

overlooking gardens and courtyard. Top low-fat cuisine. CC: Amex, Visa, Diners, MasterCard. Closed: 19 November–22 December. Luxury.

Hôtel de la Poste ★★★
1 rue Grillot
21210 Saulieu
Tel: 03 80 64 05 67
Fax: 03 80 64 10 82
Converted 17th-century post-house with sound-proofed rooms and own restaurant. CC: Amex, Diners, Visa, MasterCard. Moderate

CÔTE D'OR

Aloxe-Corton
Villa Louise
21420 Aloxe-Corton
Tel: 03 80 2646 70
Fax: 03 80 26 47 16
Converted 17th-century mansion next to famous wine château. Open fires, elegant rooms, garden, marble bathrooms. No restaurant. CC: Visa, MasterCard. Moderate.

Beaune
Hôtel le Cep ★★★★
27 rue Maufoux
21200 Beaune
Tel: 03 80 22 35 48
Fax: 03 80 22 76 80
A comfortable old 16th-century hotel in a Renaissance mansion, elegantly decorated with private garden and courtyard, right in the centre of town. CC: Amex, Diners, Visa, MasterCard. Luxury.

Hôtel Central ★★★
2 rue Victor Millot
21200 Beaune
Tel: 03 80 24 77 24
Fax: 03 80 22 30 40
Well located hotel close to the Hospices de Beaune, with car parking. Lovely cosy bar with open fire and good restaurant with regional specialities and extensive wine list. CC: Visa, MasterCard. Closed: January and Wednesday from November to end March. Moderate.

Hôtel le Home ★★
138 Route de Dijon
21200 Beaune
Tel: 03 80 22 16 43
Fax: 03 80 24 90 74

This small cosy hotel has comfortable rooms and a pleasant garden and is handy for the town centre. CC: Amex, Visa, MasterCard. Moderate.

CHALON-SUR-SAONE

Hôtel St-Georges ★★★
32 avenue Jean Jaurès
71100 Chalon-sur-Saone
Tel: 03 85 48 27 05
Fax: 03 85 93 23 88
Convenient for the station; comfortable rooms and a fine restaurant. CC: Amex, Diners, Visa, MasterCard. Moderate.

Hôtel St-Jean
24 Quai Gambetta
71100 Chalon-sur-Saone
Tel: 03 85 48 45 65
Fax: 03 85 93 62 69
Quiet, welcoming hotel in a former mansion, situated beside the river. Beautiful views. No restaurant. CC: Visa, MasterCard. Budget.

Couches
Hôtel des Trois Maures ★★
Place de la République
71490 Couches
Tel: 03 85 49 63 93
Fax: 03 85 49 50 29
Family-run Logis de France hotel in a renovated old post-house with garden in centre of the village. Restaurant serves traditional Burgundy specialities and wine. CC: Amex. Closed: Monday out of season and February. Budget.

Dijon
Hôtel Ibis Central ★★
3 Place Grangier
21000 Dijon
Tel: 03 80 30 44 00
Fax: 03 80 30 77 12
Minitel: S2100CENT
Recently modernised rooms (some

suitable for disabled visitors) in an old house in a very central location. Excellent restaurant. CC: Amex, Diners, Visa, MasterCard. Moderate.

Hôtel le Jacquemart ★★
32 rue Verrerie
Tel: 03 80 60 09 60
Fax: 03 80 60 09 69
Very inviting, quiet and friendly hotel in the old quarter. Booking advised. No restaurant. CC: MasterCard, Visa. Budget.

Hôtel du Palais ★★
23 rue du Palais
Tel: 03 80 67 16 26
Fax: 03 80 65 12 16
Especially good for travellers on a limited budget, centrally situated, quiet, pleasant and comfortable. CC: Visa. Closed: 24 December–1 January. Budget.

Hôtel Sofitel La Cloche ★★★★
14 Place Darcy
Tel: 03 80 30 12 32
Fax: 03 80 30 04 15
One of Dijon's most prestigious hotels with an excellent restaurant serving a delicious regional menu. CC: Amex, Diners, Visa, MasterCard. Luxury.

Hostellerie Châpeau Rouge ★★★★
5 rue Michelet
21000 Dijon
Tel: 03 80 50 88 88
Fax: 03 80 50 88 89
Fine hotel in the centre of Dijon with a popular restaurant specialising in Burgundian cuisine. Thirty air-conditioned rooms. CC: AE, Diners, CB. Moderate.

Dracy-le-Fort
Hôtel le Dracy ★★★
71640 Dracy-le-Fort
Tel: 03 85 87 81 81
Fax: 03 85 87 77 49
Minitel: S7164DRAC
Comfortable hotel, set in its own grounds (where meals may be taken) with a swimming-pool and tennis court. Good restaurant CC: Amex, Diners, MasterCard, Visa. Moderate.

Gevrey-Chambertin
Hôtel les Grands Crus ★★★
Route des Grands Crus
Tel: 03 80 34 34 15
Fax: 03 80 51 89 07

Stands in a quiet spot with a lovely garden, surrounded by the famous vineyards. No restaurant. CC: Visa, MasterCard. Closed: 5 December–25 February. Moderate.

Meursault
Les Magnolias
8 rue Pierre Joigneau
21190 Meursault
Tel: 03 80 21 23 23
Fax: 03 80 21 29 10
An 18th-century mansion with a tranquil courtyard and spacious bedrooms. No restaurant. Twelve rooms, including some for non-smokers. Private parking. Closed 1 December–1 March. CC: Amex, CB. Moderate

Nuits-St-Georges
Hostellerie la Gentilhommière ★★★
Route Meuilley Ouest
Vallée de la Serrée
Tel: 03 80 61 12 06
Fax: 03 80 61 30 33
Modern, pleasant and comfortable hotel with a separate restaurant in a former hunting lodge with great food. CC: Amex, Diners, Visa, MasterCard. Closed: mid-December to mid-January. Moderate.

SAÔNE-ET-LOIRE & BEAUJOLAIS

Bagnols
Château de Bagnols ★★★★
69620 Bagnols
Tel: 04 74 71 40 00
Fax: 04 74 71 40 49
Immensely luxurious château hotel with landscaped gardens and fine gourmet restaurant. Closed Tuesday evening and Wednesday from 3 April to 2 May and 2 November–20 December. CC: Amex, Diners, CB. Luxury.

Bourbon-Lancy
Grand Hôtel ★★★
Place d'Aligre
Tel: 03 85 89 08 87
Fax: 03 85 89. 32 23
Traditional, quiet hotel in a spa town. CC: Visa, MasterCard. Closed: 25 October to 1 April. Budget.

Bourg-en-Bresse
Hôtel Terminus
19 rue A. Baudin
Tel: 04 74 21 01 21
Fax: 04 74 21 36 47
Comfortable hotel in the local Charme Hôtel chain. In lovely grounds and handy for the station. No restaurant. CC: Amex, Diners, Visa, MasterCard. Moderate.

Charolles
Hôtel de la Poste
2 avenue de la Libération
71120 Charolles
Tel: 03 85 24 11 32
Fax: 03 85 24 05 74
Comfortable town hotel with good bar and restaurant, and a charming garden. CC: Amex, MasterCard, Visa. Budget.

Chervinges
Château de Chervinges
Chervinges
69400 Villefranche-sur-Saône
Tel: 03 74 65 29 76
Fax: 03 74 62 92 42
An 18th-century farmhouse 4 km (2½ miles) out of Villefranche, within view of Beaujolais vineyards. Swimming-pool, tennis court and restaurant offering gastronomic cuisine. CC: Amex, Diners, Visa, MasterCard. Closed: Sunday and Monday out of season and from 2 to 20 January. Moderate/luxury.

Cluny
Hôtel Bourgogne ★★★
Place de l'Abbaye
71250 Cluny
Tel: 03 85 59 00 58
Fax: 03 85 59 03 73
A 19th-century mansion built over the remains of Cluny abbey. The house has a central courtyard and garden and a popular restaurant well known for its Burgundy cuisine. CC: Amex, Diners, Visa, MasterCard. Closed: 16 November–9 March. Moderate.

Hôtel de l'Abbaye ★★
Avenue Charles de Gaulle
Tel: 03 85 59 11 14
Fax: 03 85 59 09 76
Good value Logis de France hotel. CC: Amex, Diners, CB. Closed: 23 January to 12 February. Budget.

Louhans
Hostellerie du Cheval Rouge ★★
5 rue d'Alsace
71500 Louhans
Tel: 03 85 75 21 42
Fax: 03 85 75 44 48
Family-run hotel with comfortable rooms and restaurant. CC: Visa, MasterCard. Closed 24 December to 10 January and 15 to 22 June. Budget.

Mâcon
Hôtel Terminus ★★
91 rue Victor Hugo
71000 Mâcon
Tel: 03 85 39 17 11
Fax: 03 85 38 02 75
Comfortable hotel and restaurant with private swimming-pool and garden. CC: Amex, Diners, Visa, MasterCard. Budget.

Grand Hôtel de Bourgogne ★★
6 rue Victor Hugo
71000 Mâcon
Tel: 03 85 38 36 57
Fax: 03 85 38 65 92
Centrally located, charming hotel with good restaurant, part of the Interhôtel chain. CC: Amex, Diners, Visa, MasterCard. Moderate.

Hôtel du Nord ★★
313 Quai Jean Jaurès
71000 Mâcon
Tel: 03 85 38 08 68
Fax: 03 85 39 01 92
This moderately-priced hotel is by the river. No restaurant. CC: Amex, Visa, MasterCard. Budget.

Marcigny
Les Récollets ★★★
Place du Champ de Foire
71110 Marcigny
Tel: 03 85 25 05 16
Fax: 03 85 25 06 91
This charming house on the edge of the little market town was once a convent. It is now a cosy guest house with 9 rooms, open fires, home-baked brioches, hand-made chocolates and generally homely atmosphere. No restaurant. Open all year round. Moderate.

Paray-le-Monial
Hostellerie des Trois Pigeons
2 rue Dargaud
71600 Paray-le-Monial

Tel: 03 85 51 03 77
Fax: 03 85 81 58 59
Minitel: S7160HOPI
Hotel set in its own garden, with some rooms suitable for disabled visitors. CC: Amex, MasterCard. Closed: 30 November–1 March. Budget.

Hôtel aux Vendanges de Bourgogne ★★
5 rue Denis Papin
71600 Paray-le-Monial
Tel: 03 85 81 13 43
Fax: 03 85 88 87 59
Family-run Logis de France hotel restaurant. CC: Visa, MasterCard. Closed 4 January–4 February and Mondays out of season. Budget.

Replonges
Hôtel la Huchette
Route de Bourg-en-Bresse
RN79
01750 Mâcon
Tel: 03 85 31 03 55
Fax: 03 85 31 10 24
Elegant country hotel with swimming-pool in lovely grounds on the main road just outside Mâcon. CC: Amex, Diners, Visa, MasterCard. Closed: Monday out of season and 25 October–15 November. Moderate.

Tournus
Hôtel de Greuze ★★★★
5–6 Place de l'Abbaye
71700 Tournus
Tel: 03 85 51 77 77
Fax: 03 85 51 77 23
Fine old hotel opposite the abbey. No restaurant. CC: Amex, Diners, Visa, MasterCard. Closed 21 November–10 December. Moderate/luxury.

Hôtel le Rempart
2 avenue Gambetta
71700 Tournus
Tel: 03 85 51 10 56
Fax: 03 85 51 77 22
Elegant hotel near the abbey with some rooms suitable for disabled visitors. Excellent restaurant offering regional dishes. CC: Amex, Diners. Moderate.

Villefranche-sur-Saône
Hôtel Plaisance
96 avenue de la Libération

69652 Villefranche-sur-Saône
Tel: 04 74 65 33 52
Comfortable, air-conditioned and well-kept France Accueil hotel. CC: Amex, Diners, Visa, MasterCard. Closed: 24 December–2 January. Moderate.

Hôtel Newport
avenue de l'Europe
69652 Villefranche-sur-Saône
Tel: 04 74 68 75 59
Fax: 04 74 09 08 90
Hotel and restaurant set in pleasant grounds – meals may be taken outside. CC: Amex, MasterCard, Visa. Closed: 23 to 31 December.

Where to Eat

Burgundy's Best

Burgundy – home to such delights as *boeuf bourguignon, escargots de Bourgogne* and *oeufs en meurette* (poached eggs in red wine) and the capital of mustard-based sauces – enjoys world renown for its fabulous cuisine. The following list includes its most famous restaurants and recommends a selection of less expensive establishments that are very good value. Many are located within hotels, so we indicate where accommodation is also available. Booking is always advisable.

Passionate foodies may be interested in a gastronomic holiday at the American **La Varenne** Cooking School. High-level courses are given in English. For further information, contact the school at **Château du Fëy**, 89300 Villecien, tel: 03 86 63 18 34; fax: 03 86 63 01 33, or La Varenne, Box 25574 Washington DC 20007, tel: 202-337 0073; fax: 703-823 5438.

Restaurants

YONNE

Joigny
La Côte Saint-Jacques
14 Faubourg de Paris
Tel: 03 86 62 09 70
For pure luxury and some of the most exciting food around, such as *croustillant de pieds de porc, tourteau et pâtes fraîches au basilic* (pig's feet with crab, pasta and basil). There's also exquisite traditional cooking including *boeuf bourguignon* and homemade blood sausage with silky mashed potatoes. Expensive. Closed: 2 January–27 February. CC: Visa, Amex, Diners. Accommodation available.

Auxerre

Restaurant Jean-Luc Barnabet
14 quai de la République
Tel: 03 86 51 68 88
The menu in this former coaching inn features several luxuries as well as more down-to-earth fare: warm foie gras in pastry with cabbage; sea bass with oysters; river perch; sweetbreads and *pièce de boeuf au gamay d'Irancy* (a lighter version of *boeuf bourguignon*). Expensive. Closed: Sunday evening, Monday and 23 December–7 February. Expensive. CC: Visa, Eurocard.

Le Jardin Gourmand
56 Boulevard Vauban
Tel: 03 86 51 53 52
Pierre Boussereau changes his menu seven times a year, and always produces imaginative and zesty food. Good examples include rabbit with honey and rosemary, poached chicken with mushroom and celery risotto and spicy pears in puff pastry. Moderate. Closed: Tuesday and Wednesday, 21 March–5 April and 29 August–20 September. CC: Visa, CB, Amex.

Chevannes

La Chamaille
4 Route de Boiloup
Tel: 03 86 41 24 80
In a thoroughly romantic spot in the countryside, the creative chef makes good use of local products, e.g. *pithiviers de pigeon au fumet d'Irancy* (squab with Irancy wine sauce and puff pastry). Moderate. Closed: Monday, Tuesday and mid-January–mid-February. CC: Visa, Amex, CB. Accommodation available.

Chablis

Hôstellerie des Clos
18 rue Jules Rathier
Tel: 03 86 42 10 63
Michel Vignaud's contemporary menu is expertly tuned to the seasons and the surrounding Burgundy landscape. In autumn, for example, there's wild squab paired with quince, veal kidneys with verjuice and grapes, chicken in Chablis wine sauce or *fricassée d'escargots*. Moderate, CC: All except Diners. Accommodation also available.

Prix-fixe Menus

By law, menus must be displayed outside any establishment. Most places offer a *prix-fixe* menu – a set meal at a particular price, sometimes also including wine. Otherwise you order separate items from *la carte*. Ordering a prix-fixe menu is nearly always the best value for money, unless you really only want one dish.
● **Cheap:**   from 100FF
● **Moderate:** from 180FF
● **Expensive:** over 200FF
NB: There are usually cheaper menus available at lunchtime, when most French people eat their biggest meal of the day.

Au Vrai Chablis
Place du Marché
Tel: 03 86 42 11 43
This village bistro, complete with zinc-covered bar, is a fine place for sampling Burgundy's sturdy cooking – snails, eggs in red wine sauce, *andouillette*, and, of course, the local Chablis, served here by the glass. Cheap. Closed: Monday evening and Tuesday, December to February. All CCs.

Vincelottes

Auberge les Tilleuls
Tel: 03 86 42 22 13
An unassuming spot for homemade terrines, *coq au vin d'Irancy*, ham in Chablis sauce as well as seasonal dishes such as wild boar. Moderate. Closed: Wednesday evening and Thursday. Open every day from Easter to the end of September. All CCs. Accommodation available.

Nitry

La Beursaudière
Chemin de Ronde
Tel: 03 86 33 62 51
At this folkloric institution, energetic waitresses in regional costume serve up platters of wonderful Burgundy soul food: poached eggs in red wine, rabbit baked in the bread oven, and melting Époisses cheese on country bread. Moderate. Open: daily. Last dinner orders taken at 10pm. All CCs.

THE HEARTLAND

Vezelay

L'Espérance
St-Père-sous-Vézelay
Tel: 03 86 33 20 45
Marc Meneau delivers some of the most delicious food in the Burgundy countryside, drawing on the finest local ingredients. His contemporary dishes include *ambroisie de volaille* and *turbot en croute* with lobster butter. Closed Tuesday and February. Last dinner orders taken at 10pm. All CCs accepted. Accommodation available.

Avallon

Moulin des Ruats
Vallée du Cousin
Tel: 03 86 34 97 00
A secluded, enchanting spot – especially in summer when tables are set up by the stream – for contemporary dishes such as *fricassée d'escargots en soupe de champignons* (snails with mushroom sauce) and banana tart with ginger. Moderatc. Closed: Monday and mid-November–mid-February. All CCs accepted. Accommodation available.

Ste-Magnance

La Chènevotte
Route Nationale 6
Tel: 03 86 33 14 79
The Luciani family runs this homely, flower-filled restaurant, offering heirloom recipes: *terrine maison*, *foie gras*, *escargots de Bourgogne* and delicious duck with cider. Moderate. Closed: Tuesday evening and Wednesday. Last dinner orders taken at 10.30pm. All CCs accepted.

Smoking Laws

It is a new law in France to have separate eating areas for smokers and non-smokers. However, this must be one of the most commonly flouted laws in existence and many French still like to puff constantly throughout a meal.

Epoisses
Ferme-Auberge La Garande
Jeux-lès-Bard
Tel: 03 80 96 74 51
Near the village of Époisses, which gives its name to the pungent Burgundian cheese washed with the local *marc de Bourgogne*, Robert and Jacqueline Charlut welcome guests to their country *auberge*, serving products from the farm. This is the place to sample *oeufs en meurette* (poached eggs in red wine), farm-raised poultry and lamb, and, of course, Époisses cheese. Moderate. Open: Saturday and Sunday. Open durnig the week by reservation only. Last dinner orders taken at 8.30pm. Reservations required. All CCs.

Semur-en-Auxois
Café-Restaurant des Minimes
39 rue de Vaux
Tel: 03 80 97 26 86
Try this savvy village bistro for a good salad, leek or onion tart, and a Burgundy standby such as *boeuf bourguignon* or *oeufs en meurette*. Closed: Sunday evening and Monday. Last dinner orders taken 10.30pm. Menus: moderate. All CCs accepted.

Flavigny-Sur-Ozerain
La Grange des Quatre Heures
Soupatoires
Place de l'Église
Tel: 03 80 96 20 62
Marie-Françoise Couthier prepares generous farm cooking in this converted barn-restaurant, run by a farmers' cooperative. Among the offerings on one four-course menu are two terrines and several choices of tarts, roast chicken or chicken simmered with vegetables, rabbit stew, a seasonal vegetable, cheese, dessert, wine and coffee. Cheap. Open all week. Closed: November to 1 March. All CCs accepted.

Vitteaux
La Rochefontaine
Ste-Colombe-en-Auxois
Tel: 03 80 49 60 12
"We don't have freezers here," explains Madame Aubertin. Based

Tipping

The majority of restaurant bills include a service charge; if in doubt, ask "Le service, est-il compris?" In any case, it is common to leave a small additional tip for the waiter if service has been good. Remember to address waiters as "Monsieur" – never "garçon", and waitresses as "mademoiselle" or "madame" (according to age). On the subject of tipping, it is customary (although not obligatory) to tip taxi drivers 10 percent.

on her list of reservations for each meal, this farmer's wife makes up a single, special menu and sets aside just so many fresh chickens and goat's-milk cheeses for her guests. Specialities include *oeufs en meurette* and *terrine maison de foie de volaille*. Cheap. Open: weekends. Closed: January and February. Reservations required. All CCs.

NIÈVRE

Quarre-Les-Tombes
Auberge de l'Atre
Les Lavaults
Tel: 03 86 32 20 79
In an old stone house in the Parc Régional du Morvan, Francis Salamolard cooks with the park's bounty: trout with wild herbs, Charolais beef with forest mushrooms, tarts packed with the fruit of low-bush blueberries. Moderate. Closed: Tuesday dinner and Wednesday, first week in December, end of January and beginning of March. All CCs accepted.
Auberge des Brizards
Les Brizards
Tel: 03 86 32 20 12
Francine and Jérôme Besancenot's old-time *auberge*, set alongside a stream in the Morvan forest, this makes a peaceful retreat and the perfect spot to sample regional fare: *crapiaud de blé noir* (a local pancake), blood sausage, *civet de*

canard au sang (duck stew thickened with blood) and pheasant with cabbage. Cheap. Closed: Monday and 6 January–10 February. Last dinner orders taken 10.30pm. All CCs.

Saulieu
La Côte d'Or
2 rue d'Argentine
Tel: 03 80 64 07 66
This great landmark to French gastronomy (the legendary Aléxandre Dumaine was chef here) is today one of France's most luxurious hotel-restaurants. Bernard Loiseau's food is stark but satisfying: e.g. *panaché d'abats de veau à la purée de truffes* (veal escalope and sweetbreads served with the best mashed potatoes), frogs' legs with garlic purée and perch in red wine and shallot fondue. Expensive. Open every day, all year round. All CCs. Accommodation available.

Arnay-Le-Duc
Chez Camille
1 Place E.-Herriot
Tel: 03 80 90 01 30
Down the road from the Maison Régionale des Arts de la Table, a museum dedicated to the art of eating, is Chez Camille, a solid, old-fashioned hotel-restaurant. Here, in an enclosed garden, Armand Poinsot offers classic cooking from the Burgundian repertoire: *jambon persillé à l'Aligoté* (ham in parsley sauce), *rissoles d'escargots aux pâtes fraîches et aux champignons* (snails with fresh pasta and mushrooms) and *truffière de charolais*, prepared with Burgundy's fine beef. Moderate. Open: daily. CC: Visa, Amex, Diners. Accommodation available.

Autun
Le Chalet Bleu
3 rue Jeannin
Tel: 03 85 86 27 30
In this small-town restaurant, Philippe Bouché prepares imaginative cuisine with strong regional roots at prices to applaud. Even the FF110 menu offers plenty

of choice, including eggs in red wine sauce with Burgundy snails, and hare served with wine-poached pears and a celery mousse. Moderate. Closed: Monday dinner, Tuesday. Open all year round. All CCs except Diners.

Dijon

Restaurant Jean-Pierre Billoux
14 Place Darcy
Tel: 03 80 38 05 05
Jean-Pierre Billoux's elegant cooking includes *terrine de pigeonneau à l'ail* (squab terrine with garlic); *blanc de pintade au foie de canard et aux cèpes* (guinea fowl with duck liver and wild mushrooms) as well as several Burgundy classics. Very conveniently situated Expensive. Closed: Sunday dinner, Monday. CC: Visa, Amex. Accommodation also available (Hôtel de la Cloche).

Restaurant Thibert
10 Place Wilson
Tel: 03 80 67 74 64
For truly wonderful upscale dining, try Jean-Paul Thibert's *petits choux verts farcis aux escargots* (cabbage stuffed with snails) and *assiette de lapin* (confit of rabbit leg with squid and celery, roast saddle of rabbit, and stuffed cabbage rolls) and river perch. Menus: moderate. Closed: Monday lunch and Sunday. All CCs except Amex.

Le Chabrot
36 rue Monge
Tel: 03 80 30 69 61
Christian Bouy's wine bar-restaurant particularly specialises in salmon (the menu lists no fewer than 15 salmon dishes), but you can also try hearty regional favourites, including the rare *consommé chabrot* (doused with red wine) and *filet de canard au pain d'épice* and Burgundian wine by the glass. Cheap. Closed: Monday lunch and Sunday and 15–20 August. Last dinner orders taken 10.30pm. CC: Visa.

Coum' Chez Eux
68 rue Jean-Jacques Rousseau
Tel: 03 80 73 56 87
A friendly, funky spot (the menu is in comic-strip form) for a simple omelette or a daily special from the Morvan: ham hock and lentils, *la*

potée morvandelle (pork and vegetable stew), *boeuf gros sel* (boiled beef), and *lapin sauté morvandiotte* (rabbit stew). Cheap. Closed: Sunday. Open all year round. Last dinner orders taken 10.30pm. All CCs.

COTE D'OR

Marsannay-la-Côte

Les Gourmets
8 rue du Puits-de-Têt
Tel: 03 80 52 16 32
This is the place where local vintners take their clients and Burgundy wines are flattered by the creative dishes of Joël Perreaut: *tarte fine au saumon fumé* (smoked salmon tart) and *daube de lapin en lasagne* (rabbit with fresh pasta). Moderate. Closed: Sunday evening, Monday, first week in January and last two weeks in February. All CCs.

Fixin

Chez Jeannette
7 rue Noisot
Tel: 03 80 52 45 49
Set in a hamlet among vineyards, this modest hotel-restaurant offers classic regional specialities and wonderful local cheeses. Cheap. Open all week; closed 22 November–22 December. All CCs.

Gevrey-Chambertin

Rôtisserie du Chambertin
Rue du Chambertin
Tel: 03 80 34 33 20
A Burgundy landmark with inspired regional cooking: carp with sorrel sauce, a lighter version of *coq au vin*, and frogs' legs with parsley sauce. Expensive. Closed: Sunday dinner, Monday, first three weeks in February and first two weeks in August. CC: Visa, MasterCard.

Ternant

La Ferme de Rolle
Hameau de Rolle
Tel: 03 80 59 50 39
At their rural bistro near Gevrey-Chambertin, Didier and Martine Chevalier serve up all the Burgundian favourites: e.g., *salade*

à la gratinée d'Époisses, snails, *coq au vin*, and pears in red wine, as well as wood-fired *grillades* of beef, pork and lamb, plus wild boar in season. Cheap. Open all year round but *jours de fermeture* (days when closed) are subject to change. Strictly by reservation only. All CCs.

Prix-fixe Menus

- Cheap: from 100FF
- Moderate: from 180FF
- Expensive: over 200FF

Bouilland

Le Vieux Moulin
Tel: 03 80 21 51 16
The young Jean-Pierre Silva finds inspiration for his sophisticated, eclectic food within the classic Burgundian repertoire and beyond it: *estouffade de jeunes poireaux*, *jambonnette de grenouille en meurette* (leeks and frogs' legs in red wine sauce) and *turbot aux épices* with *compôte d'oignons* (turbot with spices and onion jam). Expensive. Closed: Wednesday, Thursday lunch and January. CC: Visa, Eurocard. Accommodation available.

Chagny

Lameloise
36 Place d'Armes
Tel: 03 85 87 08 85
At Lameloise, one of Burgundy's finest tables, you can still taste perfect *haute cuisine bourguignonne*, including *raviolis d'escargots de Bourgogne dans leur bouillon d'ail doux* (snail ravioli in garlic-infused broth) and *pigeon de Bresse en vessie* roasted with truffles. Menus: expensive. Closed: Wednesday, Thursday lunch, 23 December–27 January. Reservations recommended. All CCs. Accommodation available.

Chalon-Sur-Saône

Le Moulin de Martorey
Saint-Rémy
Tel: 03 85 48 12 98
Jean-Pierre Gillot redefines the Burgundy classics and invents new ones with such dishes as snails in

red wine with deep-fried oyster mushrooms, rabbit sausage and fillet with verjuice sauce and *fondant au Guyaquil et pralin feuilleté* (chocolate with praline). Moderate. Closed: Sunday dinner, Monday and Tuesday lunch. All CCs.

LE MACONNAIS

Sennecey-Le-Grand
Ferme-Auberge de Malo
Etrigny
Tel: 03 85 92 21 47
For a Burgundian snack of *charcuterie* or an omelette and a glass of wine, try this heartwarming *auberge*. If you order ahead, Jacqueline Goujon will also prepare more substantial fare such as a simple roast chicken (or in cream sauce), *civet de porc* (pork stew), and peaches in Aligoté wine. Cheap. Open weekends from Easter to November. Last dinner orders taken 8pm, 8.30pm July and August. No CCs.

Montpont-En-Bresse
Les Plattières
Ste-Croix-en-Bresse
Tel: 03 85 74 80 70
On a typical half-timbered Bresse farmstead, sample homemade pâté and light cheese tart, or ring ahead and settle into a serious meal featuring René Perrin's Bresse chicken. Cheap. Open weekends only. Last lunch orders taken 1pm. Reservation only. No CCs. Accommodation available.

Vernoux
Ferme-Auberge du Colombier
Tel: 03 74 30 72 00
Catherine Debourg sets a superb table with *salade bressane* (warm chicken liver salad), chicken in cream sauce, *gratin dauphinois* and *tarte bressane* (cream and sugar tart hot from the bread oven), while the star ingredients – chickens and turkeys – scratch in the barnyard. Competition for a table here can be fierce, so book ahead. Cheap. Closed: half of January and Monday, Tuesday and Wednesday. No CCs.

La Clayette
Ferme-Auberge de Lavaux
Châtenay-sous-Dun
Tel: 03 85 28 08 48
At this restored farmhouse, feast on *poulet à la crème* (chicken in cream sauce), *canard aux olives* (duck with olives, in April and October) and the *gâteau de foies de volaille* (chicken liver mousse). Cheap. Closed: Tuesday and 1 November to Easter. All CCs. Accommodation available.

Prix-fixe Menus

- **Cheap:** from 100FF
- **Moderate:** from 180FF
- **Expensive:** over 200FF

Châteauneuf
La Fontaine
Tel: 03 85 26 26 87
Don't miss the remarkable talents of Yves Jury on display in this excellent value village restaurant. His intelligent, earthy food exemplifies the best of contemporary French cooking: fricassee of snails, artichokes and cabbage, oxtail with pleurotte mushrooms and rich chocolate cake with liquorice custard sauce. Moderate. Closed: Tuesday evening, Wednesday and Sunday evening from October to April. CC: Visa, CB.

Mailly
La Maillerotte
Tel: 03 85 84 00 50
While Annik Costa watches over the dining-room at this simple inn, Dominique Costa tends to the stove, preparing the local Charolais beef, wild boar, fish or *lasagne aux escargots*. Cheap. Closed: Tuesday and January. All CCs. Accommodation also available.

BEAUJOLAIS

Vonnas
Restaurant Georges Blanc
Tel: 04 74 50 90 90
For an outstanding dining experience with attentive service, a comfortable setting, and brilliant food: *crêpe parmentière au saumon et caviar* and Bresse chicken with garlic and foie gras. Expensive. Closed: Monday and Tuesday lunch, 1 January–11 February. All CCs. Reservations recommended. Accommodation available.
L'Ancienne Auberge
Place du Marché
Tel: 04 74 50 90 50
Georges Blanc's bistro annexe with fashionable and soothing fare: homemade sausage with lentils in Beaujolais, sautéed frogs' legs, *crème brûlée*. Moderate. Closed: January, otherwise, open every day Last dinner orders taken 10pm. All CCs. Reservations recommended.

Bourg-en-Bresse
Le Français
7 avenue Alsace-Lorraine
Tel: 04 74 22 55 14/47 02
A cavernous, old-fashioned late-19th-century brasserie with pleasantly tacky décor and a menu studded with regional specialities including local rosette sausage and Bresse chicken. Cheap. Closed: Saturday lunch, Sunday, the last three weeks in August and the last week in December. CC: Visa, Amex, Eurocard.

Montmerle-sur-Saône
Hôtel-Restaurant du Rivage
12 rue du Pont
Tel: 04 74 69 33 92
With tables set out under shady trees and an inviting menu, this family-run establishment makes a very pleasant stop for local *charcuterie*, *petite friture* (tiny fried fish) and sweetened fresh cheese with cream. Cheap. Closed: Sunday evening, Monday and for 10 days in March. CC: Visa, Amex, Eurocard. Accommodation available.

Chenas
Restaurant Les Platanes de Chenas
Tel: 03 85 36 72 67
Shady summer dining in the garden; favourite local dishes include *andouille sausages de chenas* and turbot with shallots. Moderate. Closed: Tuesday evening and Wednesday. CCs: Visa, Amex, Diners, Eurocard.

Fleurie
Auberge du Cep
Place de l'Église
Tel: 04 74 04 10 77
Feast on some of the best of the region's fare including *andouillette* sausage in Beaujolais, Bresse chicken with cream and morels, and *crayfish en ragoût.* Moderate. Closed: Sunday, Monday and mid-January–mid-February and school holidays. All CCs except Diners.

Tarare
Restaurant Jean Brouilly
3 rue de Paris
Tel: 04 74 63 24 56
A *maison bourgeoise* in a park on the edge of town, for modern food with a regional twist: perch-pike and lobster *pauchouse,* a variation of the local fish stew, and *filet de sole au vin de Brouilly.* Moderate. Closed: Sunday, Monday, February and three weeks in August. All CCs.

Wine

THE BURGUNDY APPELLATION

The area known as Greater Burgundy (*Grande Bourgogne*) includes: Chablis and the Auxerrois, Côte de Nuits and Côte de Beaune (which together make up Côte d'Or), the Chalonnais, the Mâconnais and Beaujolais. Roughly half its total annual output of about 2.5 million hectolitres (330 million bottles) consists of Beaujolais. Greater Burgundy is not a major wine-making region in volume terms, accounting for a bare 10 percent of the total French production.

BURGUNDY

The appellations (in ascending order of quality) are:

Appellation régionale
This term covers wine from vineyards that qualify for the Burgundy appellation. It accounts for 52 percent of total Burgundy production. There are two types of appellation régionale:

1) Wine made from a specific grape variety or varieties
● Bourgogne: (red) Pinot Noir; (white) Chardonnay.
● Bourgogne Grand Ordinaire (BGO): (red) Gamay; (white) Chardonnay and Aligoté.
● Bourgogne Passe-Tout-Grains: (red) Gamay and Pinot Noir.
● Bourgogne Aligoté: (white) Aligoté.
● Crémant de Bourgogne: (white) Chardonnay and Aligoté.
There also exist rosé versions of Bourgogne, BGO, Bourgogne Passe-Tout-Grains and Crémant de Bourgogne, made with various blends of the grape varieties permitted for the whites and reds.

2) Wine produced in a specific Burgundy area
These wines include: Petit Chablis, Bourgogne Côtes d'Auxerre, Bourgogne Irancy, Bourgogne Hautes-Côtes de Nuits, Bourgogne Hautes-Côtes de Beaune, Bourgogne Côte Chalonnaise, Bourgogne Aligoté de Bouzeron, Mâcon, Mâcon-Supérieur and Mâcon-Villages. Principal grape varieties permitted: Pinot Noir, Chardonnay.

Appellation communale
Wine from 35 specific communes. It accounts for 35 percent of total Burgundy production. Any wine with the mention "*villages*" after its name is an *appellation communale,* with the notable and confusing exception of Mâcon-Villages (an *appellation régionale*). Eg.: Chablis, Gevrey-Chambertin, Givry, Côte de Beaune-Villages (a blend of wines from various Côte de Beaune *communes* entitled to the *appellation communale*). Principal grape varieties permitted: Pinot Noir, Chardonnay.

Appellation prèmier cru
Wine from over 400 specially classified vineyards (or *climats*) located in certain *appellations communales.* The name of the vineyard usually appears on the label. It accounts for 10 percent of total Burgundy production. Eg.: Chablis Premier Cru Fourchaume, Fixin Premier Cru Les Arvelets, Rully Premier Cru Margotey. Principal grape varieties permitted: Pinot Noir, Chardonnay.

Appellation grand cru
Wine from Burgundy's top vineyards (or *climats*) located in a handful of *appellations communales.* It accounts for 3 percent of total Burgundy production. Because of the prestige of the vineyards, the *appellation grand cru* mentions only the name of the vineyard, not the *commune(s)* in which it is located, except in the case of Chablis. Eg.: Chablis Grand Cru Vaudésir, Montrachet, Romanée-Conti. Principal grape varieties permitted: Pinot Noir, Chardonnay.

List of grands crus:
Grand cru/Commune(s)

Chablis
● Les Clos (white)/Chablis
● Vaudésir (white)/Chablis
● Valmur (white)/Chablis
● Blanchot (white)/Chablis
● Preuses (white)/Chablis
● Grenouille (white)/Chablis
● Bougros (white)/Chablis

Côte de Nuits
● Chambertin (red)/ Gevrey-Chambertin
● Chambertin-Clos-de-Bèze (red)/ Gevrey-Chambertin
● Latricières-Chambertin (red)/ Gevrey-Chambertin
● Charmes-Chambertin (red)/ Gevrey-Chambertin
● Mazoyères-Chambertin (red)/ Gevrey-Chambertin
● Mazis-Chambertin (red)/ Gevrey-Chambertin
● Ruchottes-Chambertin (red)/ Gevrey-Chambertin
● Chapelle-Chambertin (red)/ Gevrey-Chambertin

Wine Categories

Greater Burgundy is divided into two different categories: **Burgundy** (all *appellations* except Beaujolais) and **Beaujolais.**

● Griotte-Chambertin (red)/
Gevrey-Chambertin
● Clos de la Roche (red)/
Morey-St-Denis
● Clos St-Denis (red)/Morey-St-Denis
● Clos des Lambrays (red)/
Morey-St-Denis
● Clos de Tart (red)/Morey-St-Denis
● Bonnes-Mares (red)/
Morey-St-Denis, Chambolle-Musigny
● Musigny (red)/Chambolle-Musigny
● Clos de Vougeot (red)/Vougeot
● Grands-Echezeaux (red)/
Flagey-Echezeaux
● Echezeaux (red)/Flagey-Echezeaux
● Richebourg (red)/Vosne-Romanée
● Romanée-St-Vivant (red)/
Vosne-Romanée
● Romanée-Conti (red)/
Vosne-Romanée
● Grande Rue (red)/Vosne-Romanée
● La Romanée (red)/Vosne-Romanée
● La Tâche (red)/Vosne-Romanée

Côte de Beaune
● Corton (red)/Aloxe-Corton, Ladoix-
Serrigny
● Corton-Charlemagne (white)/
Aloxe-Corton, Ladoix-Serrigny,
Pernand-Vergelesses
● Montrachet (white)/Puligny-
● Montrachet, Chassagne-
Montrachet
● Chevalier-Montrachet (white)/
Puligny-Montrachet
● Bâtard-Montrachet (white)/
Puligny-Montrachet, Chassagne-
Montrachet
● Bienvenues-Bâtard-Montrachet
(white)/Puligny-Montrachet
● Criôts-Bâtard-Montrachet (white)/
Chassagne-Montrachet

BEAUJOLAIS

Beaujolais is a red wine made from
a single grape variety, Gamay. The
appellations (in ascending order of
quality) are:

Beaujolais
Wine from any vineyard that
qualifies for the Beaujolais
appellation. It accounts for about
half of total Beaujolais production,
and three quarters of Beaujolais
Nouveau.

When to Drink

The locals will tell you that no
decent Burgundy should be drunk
until it is at least 4 years old.
And beware – it is rare to find a
bargain in Burgundy. Even in the
hypermarkets you are unlikely to
find a drinkable Burgundy for less
than FF50.

Beaujolais-Villages
Wine from 39 specific *communes*. It
accounts for about a quarter of
total Beaujolais production, and one
quarter of Beaujolais Nouveau.

Crus
Wine from the 10 named Beaujolais
growths, which are: Brouilly,
Chénas, Chiroubles, Côte de
Brouilly, Fleurie, Juliénas, Morgon,
Moulin-à-Vent, Régnié and St-Amour.
The *crus* account for about a
quarter of total Beaujolais
production. None is sold as
Beaujolais Nouveau.

Glossary of Wine Terms

AOC – Appellation d'origine contrôlée.
Guarantee of origin of wine
cave – wine cellar
caveau – wine cellar open to public
cave coopérative – collectively run
wine-making enterprise
chaptalisation – adding sugar to
increase fermentation and alcoholic
strength
climat – Small section of vineyard
with its own geological and climatic
conditions
cru – a specific vineyard
cuve – wine vat
dégustation – wine tasting
fining – clarifying the wine
*INAO – Institut National des
Appellations d'Origine* organisation
controlling the AOC system
maceration – soaking and
separating the grapes
must – grape juice before
fermentation
négociant – term used mainly in
Burgundy for shipper or wine
merchant who buys wine in bulk for
storage and re-sale

Phylloxera – aphid which destroyed
many French vineyards in 19th
century
primeur – wine ready for early
drinking, particularly Beaujolais.
tastevin – shallow silver cup used
for tasting
vendange – grape harvest
vigneron – wine grower
vignoble – vineyard
vin de garde – wine for maturing
(Source: *The Wines and Vineyards
of France*. Viking)

Wine Tasting

Many cellars are open to the public
for tours, tastings and sale of wine.
The following organisations
disseminate information about
wines and viticulture, organise
courses and produce lists of cellars
open to the public:
**Bureau Interprofessionelle des Vins
de Bourgogne**
12 Boulevard Bretonnière
BP150m
21200 Beaune
Tel: 03 80 25 04 80
Fax: 03 80 25 04 90
also at 389 avenue de Lattre de
Tassigny, 71000 Mâcon
Tel: 03 85 38 20 15
Le petit Pontigny
1 rue de Chichee
89800 Chablis
Tel: 03 86 42 42 22
**La Maison des Vins de la Côte
Chalonnaise**
Promenade Ste-Marie
71100 Chalon-sur-Saône
Tel: 03 85 41 64 00
Fax: 03 85 41 99 83
Tastings for groups of six or more.
**Union Interprofessionnelle des Vins
du Beaujolais**
210 boulevard Vermorel
69400 Villefranche-sur-Saône
Tel: 04 74 65 45 55
    Some tourist organisations in
the region offer **wine tours** and
holiday courses, mostly lasting a
weekend. For further information,
contact the professional bodies or
tourist offices and Loisirs Accueil
services in the départements (*see
Tourist Offices, page 318*).
    The UK company, **Ablaster &
Clarke** offers short holidays

(4 nights), based in a 3-star hotel in Beaune, touring the vineyards led by an acknowledged British authority on the wines of the region; also individual tours arranged. Additional information is available from: Clarke House, Farnham Road, West Liss, Hampshire GU33 6JQ. Tel: 01730-8933444; fax: 01730-892888.

Listed below is a selection of wine cellars open to the public for tours, tastings and sales. Some require appointments to be made, but many are open to visitors at most reasonable times.

Some cellars offer free visits and tastings, while others make a charge (typically between around FF15 to FF40 per person).

Temperatures

Ideal temperatures for drinking Burgundy:
- Superior white Burgundy: 58–60°F (14.5–15.5°C)
- Ordinary white Burgundy: 48–50°F (9–10°C)
- Red Burgundy: 58–61°F (14.5–16°C)
- Beaujolais: 53–56°F (11.5–13.5°C)

CHABLIS

Domaine de Château Long Depaquit
45 rue Auxerroise,
89800
Tel: 03 86 42 11 13
Fax: 03 86 42 81 89
Wine-tasting with English spoken for the linguistically shy.

COTE D'OR

Beaune
Cave des Hautes-Côtes
Route de Pommard
21200
Tel: 03 80 25 01 00
Fax: 03 80 22 87 05.
Open: Monday–Saturday
Cave des Cordeliers
6 rue de l'Hôtel-Dieu
21200
Tel: 03 80 25 08 20

Fax: 03 80 25 08 21
Tastings in a Franciscan friars' convent. Open: daily.
Caves Exposition de la Reine Pédauque
2 Faubourg St-Nicolas
21200
Tel: 03 80 22 23 11
Fax: 03 80 22 70 20
Exhibition cellar of the main vintages of Burgundy.
Maison Patriarche Père et Fils
7 rue du Collège
21200
Tel: 03 80 24 53 78
Fax: 03 80 24 53 11
Burgundy's biggest cellars.

Buxy
Cave des Vignerons de Buxy
71390
Tel: 03 85 92 03 03
Fax: 03 85 92 08 06.

Meursault
Château de Meursault
21190
Tel: 03 80 26 22 25
Fax: 03 80 26 22 76
Situated only a few miles from Beaune; fine 19th-century cellars where you can try the wines produced on the estate.

Nuit-St-Georges
Cave Moillard-Grivot
21700
Tel: 03 80 62 42 20
Fax: 03 80 61 28 13
On the RN74. Open: daily. English spoken.
Morin Père et Fils
9 quai Fleury,
21700
Tel: 03 80 61 19 51
Fax: 03 80 61 05 10
Visits to an 18th-century cellar. Open: daily.

Vougeot
La Grande Cave
RN74, 21640
Tel: 03 80 62 87 13
Fax: 03 80 62 82 46
Tasting of "grands vins" in fine ancient cellars. Open: daily.

MÂCON & BEAUJOLAIS

Chardonnay
Cave de Chardonnay
71700 Chardonnay
Tel: 03 85 33 22 85
Fax: 03 85 33 26 46
English spoken.

Igé
Cave Co-opérative d'Igé
71960 Igé
Tel: 03 85 33 33 56
Fax: 03 85 33 41 85

Viré
Château de Viré
71260 Viré
Tel/fax: 03 85 33 10 12
Open: daily. English spoken

LOIRE

Pouilly
Landrat et Guyollot
Les Berthiers
58150 St-Andelain
Tel: 03 86 39 11 83
Fax: 03 86 39 11 65
Open: daily. English spoken

Outdoor Activities

Excursions

TOURIST TRAINS

Little tourist trains offer a good means of seeing the local countryside at a slower pace than by express. They are ideal for family outings, particularly if they give children the chance to ride on a real steam train.

The Ouche Valley
The Ouche Valley railway runs a steam train on the former "fisherman's" track from Dijon to Epignac. Trains leave Bligny-sur-Ouche station. The trip lasts 60 minutes on Sunday, mid-May to mid-October. Information and booking: ARVO, 4 rue Pausmont, 21200 Beaune, tel: 03 80 22 86 35.

River Ouche & the Burgundy Canal
From Plombières-lès-Dijon, you can take a round trip on a diesel train, known as the "petit train de la Côte d'Or". It follows the River Ouche and the Burgundy Canal. The trip lasts 90 minutes and runs from 1 July to 15 September. Details from APOTCO Gare de Plombières-Canal, 21370 Plombières-sur-Dijon, tel: 03 80 45 88 51.

The Serein Valley
Discover the Serein Valley on the P'tit Train de l'Yonne, a 45-minute ride between Noyers-sur-Serein and Avallon. Sundays and public holidays, May to September. For reservations tel: 03 86 33 93 33.

Le Creusot
The Combes railway offers a one-hour ride around the city of Le Creusot, weekends from May to October. For further details, tel: 03 85 55 26 23.

IN THE AIR

There is a surprisingly large number of companies offering balloon trips in the area; some even offer ballooning holidays. Here are a few suggestions:

Air Escargot
Remigny
71150 Chagny
Tel: 03 85 87 12 30
One hour trips or hotel packages.

Air Aventures
Avenue du Général-de-Gaulle
21320 Pouilly-en-Auxois
Tel: 03 80 90 74 23
Mostly luxury holiday breaks of four days, but also introductory flights arranged.

Bombard Balloon Adventures
Château de Laborde 21200
Meursanges
Tel: 03 80 26 63 30
Information and booking also direct in the US from: 6727 Curran Street, McLean, Virginia 22101-6006. Tel: 703-448 9407 or toll free 800-862 8537; fax 703-883 0985.

HORSE-DRAWN CARRIAGES

Some riding centres offer trips lasting an hour or more, in carriages or traps. Full-day trips often include meals in the price. You may have to have a minimum number to make up a party. Some trips can be booked by the Service Reservation Loisirs Accueil (see Tourist Offices, page 318) or from the Tourist Office in Tonnerre, 10 rue du college, tel: 03 86 55 14 48.

Sites

Places of Interest

"Rich" is an adjective that is often used to describe Burgundy and it is certainly rich in its cultural heritage. It has come under the influence of many civilisations through the centuries: the Romans and Greeks, and the early Christians, and this is now reflected in the sumptuous collections in its many museums and art galleries. All its famous sons (and daughters) – Canon Kir, Vauban, Larousse and Colette – are fêted, mostly at their birthplaces.

Museums & Art Galleries

Most museums charge an entrance fee – expect to pay around FF15–30 per person (reductions usually given for children, the elderly and students – on production of a card). Most museums close for lunch, normally from noon till 2.30pm and nearly all of them close on public holidays. Opening times given may be subject to change. Municipal museums are normally closed on Mondays, national museums on Tuesdays.

YONNE

Arcy-sur-Cure
Les Grottes
Open: daily March–Nov
Tel: 03 86 81 90 63.

Ancy-le-Franc
Château d'Ancy-le-Franc
89160 Ancy-le-Franc
Tel: 03 86 75 14 63
Guided visits daily 15 April–11 Nov. Also Musée de l'Automobile et de l'Hippomobile. Entrance fee.

Auxerre
Musée St Germain
Tel: 03 86 51 09 74
Open: every day except Tuesday.
Entrance fee.
Musée Leblanc-Duvernoy
9 bis, rue Egleny
Tel: 03 86 52 44 63
Open: every afternoon, except
Tuesday and public holidays.
Entrance fee. Ticket includes entry
to the crypts of St-Germain Abbey.
**Conservatoire de la Nature Paul-
Bert**
5 boulevard Vauban
Tel: 03 86 51 51 64
Open: daily (weekends afternoons
only). Free entry.

Avallon
Musée de l'Avallonnais
Place de la Collégiale
Tel: 03 86 34 03 19
Open: 1 May–30 Oct; closed
Tuesday. Entrance fee.
See also the **Costume Museum**
6 rue Belgrand
Open: every day 19 April–1 Nov
Tel: 03 86 34 19 95.

Chablis
Maison de la Vigne et du Vin
Syndicat d'Initiative
28 rue Auxerroise
Tel: 86 42 42 22
Open: daily, except Wednesday and
Thursday in December

Druyes-les-Belles-Fontaines
**Château des Comtes d'Auxerre et
de Nevers**
Info from: Les Amis du Château de
Druyes, 11 rue Chanzy, 89560
Druyes-Les-Belles-Fontaines. Tel: 03
86 41 51 71
Château open every afternoon
throughout July and August, all year
round for groups by appointment
and some weekends. Entrance fee.

Escolives-St-Camille
Important archaeological site
Tel/fax: 03 86 53 39 09
Open: every day from April–Oct, rest
of year by appointment except
Mondays. Free entry. Info: Société
archéologique d'Escolives, Le
Moulin, 9 rue Raymond Kapps.

Laduz
Musée Rural des Arts Populaires
Tel: 03 86 73 70 08
Open April–Nov. Afternoons only
April, May and October. Entrance fee.

Noyers-sur-Serein
**Donation Yankel Museum of Naive
Art**
Tel: 03 86 82 83 72
Includes modern collections
Open: daily from June–Sept;
afternoons at the weekend for the
rest of the year. Entrance fee.

Pourrain-les-Vernes
Musée de la Guerre 1939–45
Atelier Sontrop
Les Vernes
89240 Pourrain
Tel: 03 86 41 13 27
Entrance fee.

Pontigny
Pontigny Abbey
Info: Les Amis de Pontigny. B.P.6.
89230 Pontigny. Tel: 03 86 47 54 99
Guided visits all year round by
appointment through Les Amis.
Closed to the public during
services. Entrance fee.

Ratilly
Château de Ratilly
Tel: 03 86 74 79 54
Open: every afternoon, mornings in
July–Sept. Closed: Sunday
Nov–March.

St-Amand-en-Puisaye
Château Musée du Gres
Tel: 03 86 39 63 15
Open weekends and public hols
from 1 April–30 June. Daily except
Tuesday from 1 July–30 October.
Entrance fee.

St-Fargeau
La Ferme du Château
Tel: 03 86 74 05 67
Open: daily 1 April–11 Nov. Entry
free to park, entrance fee into
museum.
**Guedelon, Construction of
Medieval Château**
89170 Saint-Fargeau
Tel: 03 86 74 19 45
www.guedelon.org
Open April–Nov. Daily except

Wednesday. July–Aug: daily.
Entrance fee.
Parc naturel de Boutissaint
Tel: 03 86 74 18 18
A natural wildlife reserve with deer
etc. roaming freely. Open: daily
8am–8pm. **Château:** son-et-lumière
presentations in summer (*see Live
Arts*). Open: daily April–mid-Nov. Tel:
03 86 74 05 67. Entrance fee.

St-Leger-Vauban
Maison Vauban
Tel: 03 86 32 26 30
Open: daily 25 March to 5
November. Entrance fee.

St-Père-Sous-Vézelay
Fontaines Salées
Tel: 03 86 33 37 31/36
Open: daily 1 April–2 November.
Entrance fee.

St-Sauveur-en-Puisaye
Musée Colette
Tel: 03 86 72 85 10.
Open 1 April–31 Oct. Closed
Tuesday. Open weekends out of
season. Entrance fee.

Saints
Le Moulin Vanneau
Saints-en-Puisaye
Tel: 03 86 45 59 80
Former water mill, surrounded by
meadows, plus a farm museum and
old inn. Open every afternoon 1
April–30 Oct.

Sens
Musée & Treasury
Tel: 03 86 64 46 22
Open: daily all year but afternoons
only on Monday, Thursday and
Friday from 1 Oct–31 May. Free
entry on first Sunday of month.
St-Étienne, Guided visits April–Sept.
Further information and bookings
from tourist office.

Taingy
Aubigny
Tel: 03 86 52 38 79
Guided visits of underground stone
quarries, afternoons April–Sept.
Entrance fee.

Tanlay
Renaissance Château
Tel: 03 86 75 70 61
Open: April–mid-Nov. Closed: Tuesday.
Entrance fees to château and park.

Tonnerre
Ancien Hôpital
L'Hôtel Dieu et Musee Hospitalier
Tel: 03 86 54 33 00
Open: weekends and public hols.
April–Oct. Daily except Tuesday, 1
June–30 Sept.

Vézelay
Basilique Ste-Madeleine
Tel 03 86 33 26 73
Open year round, daily.

Villiers-St-Benoît
Musée d'Art Régional
Rue Paul-Huillard
Tel: 03 86 45 73 05
Open: every day except Tuesday, 1
Feb–15 Dec except some public hols.

NIÈVRE

Bibracte
Mont-Beuvray, major archaeological
site and museum; **site** tel: 03 85
86 52 35, open: all year round;
**museum: Centre Archéologique
Europeen and Musée de la
Civilisation Celtique**, tel: 03 86 78
69 00. Open daily all year round,
except Tuesday September–June.

Château-Chinon
Musée du Septennat
6 rue du Château
Tel: 03 86 85 19 23
Open: daily, 5 Feb–31 Dec. Closed
Tuesday. Entrance fee.
Costume Museum
Tel: 03 86 85 18 55
Open: daily, 5 Feb–31 Dec. Closed
Tuesday. Entrance fee.

Clamecy
**Musée d'Art et d'Histoire Romain
Rolland**
avenue de la Republique
Tel: 03 86 27 17 99
Open: every day except Tuesday.
Also closed Sunday out of season

Cosne-sur-Loire
Musée de la Loire
Place de la Résistance
Tel: 03 86 26 71 02
Open: every day except Tuesday.

Donzy
Ecomusée de la Meunerie
Rue André Audinet
Tel: 03 86 39 39 46
Open: every afternoon, 1 June–30
Sept; weekends May and October.
Info. from APSMM. Entrance fee.

Guerigny
Forges Royales de la Chaussade
Tel: 03 86 37 01 08
Open afternoons 4 July–19 Sept
except Tuesday.

La Machine
Musée de la Mine
1 Avenue de la République
Tel: 03 86 50 91 08
Open: mid-June–mid-Sept, except
Tuesday, otherwise just Sunday
afternoons or by appointment.
Closed: Nov– March. and some
public holidays.

Magny-Cours
The ultra-modern **motor racing
circuit** near Nevers is open to the
public every afternoon all year
round. Free of charge. Training
sessions are available on Renault
or Porsche cars. For information,
tel: 03 86 21 82 01.

Nevers
Musée Municipal
16 rue St-Genest
58000 Nevers
Tel: 03 86 71 67 90
Open every afternoon except Tues.
All day from 2 May–30 Sept and at
weekends and on public holidays.
Entrance fee.

St-Brisson
Herbularium, situated in the
Morvan Regional Park (by the
Maison du Parc). Open: daily. Free
entry.
Maison du Parc du Morvan
Tel: 03 86 78 79 00
Musée de la Résistance en Morvan
Maison du Parc Naturel Régional du
Morvan

Tel 03 86 78 79 06
Open: every afternoon, July–mid Sept.

Tamnay-en-Bazois
Musée des Metiers du Monde Rural
Tel: 03 03 86 84 06 18/03 86 84
05 66
Open afternoons 1 June–1 Oct.
Otherwise weekends and Easter.
Entrance fee.

COTE D'OR

Alise-Ste-Reine
Site of Alésia
Tel: 03 80 96 10 95
Museum and view over the
battleground of Alésia (52 BC).
Open: March–Nov. Entrance fee.

Arny-le-Duc
**Maison Régionale des Arts de la
Table**
Anciens Hospices St-Pierre
15 rue St-Jacques
Tel: 03 80 90 11 59
Open: daily 1 April– 31 Oct
10am–6.30pm. Entrance fee.

Arnay-sous-Vitteaux
Zoo de l'Auxois
Tel: 03 80 49 64 01
Open: daily 10am–sunset. Entrance
fee.

Beaune
Musée du Vin de Bourgogne and
Hotels des Ducs de Bourgogne,
both rue d'Enfer
Tel: 03 80 22 08 19
Closed: Tuesday, Dec–March. Open
9.30am to 6pm. Entrance fee.
Hôtel-Dieu
Tel: 03 80 24 45 00
Open daily. all year round. Entrance
fee.
Musée des Beaux Arts
Rue de L'Hôtel de Villc
Tel: 03 80 24 56 92
Open 1 April–1 Nov and weekend of
Vente des Vins. Entrance fee.
Archéodrome, just south of Beaune
(at the A6 Beaune-Tailly motorway
services or via the D18 to Tailly,
then D23 to Merceuil), tel: 03 80
26 87 00.

Bèze

Caves and boat ride along the underground river. Open: daily May–Sept, weekends only in April and October, tel: 03 80 75 31 33. Entrance fee.

Buffon

Buffon Forges
Tel: 03 80 92 10 35
Open: every day from 1 April–30 Sept except Tuesday. Rest of year by appointment. Entrance fee.

Bussy-Rabutin

Château du Comte de Bussy
Tel: 03 80 96 00 03
Open: every day from 1 April–30 Sept except 1 May and from 1 Oct–31 March except Tuesday, Wednesday and public holidays.

Châtillon-sur-Seine

Musée Archéologique
7 rue du Bourg
Tel: 03 80 91 13 19 (tourist office) and 03 80 91 24 67 (*musée*)
Home of the massive *Vase de Vix*.
Closed: Tuesday, except from mid June–mid Sept.

Chênove

The 18th-century wine presses of the Dukes of Burgundy. Open: every afternoon from mid-June–30 Sept, rest of year by appointment only, tel: 03 80 52 51 30. Free entry.

Cîteaux

Cîteaux Abbey, the 19th-century church is all that is open to the public. Video presentation about the life of the monks. Closed: Sunday mornings, tel: 03 80 62 15/ 03 80 61 11 53.

Dijon

Musée des Beaux Arts
Place de la Ste-Chapelle
Tel: 03 80 74 52 70
Closed: Tuesday. Entrance fee.
Musée d'Art Sacré
15 rue Ste-Anne
Tel: 03 80 44 12 69
Closed: Tuesday. Entrance fee.
Musée de la Vie Bourguignonne
17 rue Ste-Anne
Tel: 03 80 44 12 69
Closed: Tuesday. Entrance fee.

Musée Archéologique
5 rue du Docteur Maret
Tel: 03 80 30 88 54
Closed: Tuesday. Entrance fee.
Musée d'Histoire Naturelle
1 Avenue Albert 1er
Tel: 03 80 76 82 76
Closed all day Tuesday and Saturday and Sunday morning.
Jardin Botanique
Jardin de l'Arquebuse
1 avenue Albert Premier
Tel: 03 80 76 82 84
Free entry
Amora Mustard Factory Museum
More information from the *Syndicate d'Initiative*, 48 Quai Nicholas Rolin.
Tel: 03 80 44 44 52.
Open all year round by rendezvous.
Closed Tuesday and Saturday mornings. Entrance fee.
Musée Magnin
4 rue des Bons Enfants
Tel: 03 80 67 11 10
Closed Monday. Entrance fee.
Musée Rude
8 rue Vaillant
Tel: 03 80 74 52 70
Open 1 June–31 Oct daily except Tuesday. Free entry.
Chatreuse de Champmol
Tel: 03 80 42 48 48
Under restoration at time of printing.

Epoisses

Medieval fortress
Tel: 03 80 96 40 56
Closed: Tuesday. Entrance fee.

Fixin

Musée Noisot
Tel: 03 80 52 45 62
Open: afternoons Wednesday, Thursday, Saturday and Sunday, April–mid-Oct.

Fontenay

Abbaye de Fontenay
Tel: 03 80 92 15 00
Open all year round. Entrance fee.

Gevrey-Chambertin

Fortress
Tel: 03 80 34 36 13
Open all year round except public hols. Entrance fee.

Lantilly

Château
Tel: 03 80 97 11 57
Open 1 July–30 Sept; closed: Tuesday. Entrance fee.

Molesme

Molesme Abbey
Tel: 03 80 81 44 47
Open: Easter–1 Nov by appointment, weekend afternoons in May and every afternoon throughout July and August except Tuesday. Entrance fee.

Nuits-St-Georges

Musée Archéologique
Tel: 03 80 61 13 10
Open: May–Oct daily except Tuesday. Entrance fee.

Reulle-Vergy

Musée des Arts et Traditions des Hautes-Côtes
Tel: 03 80 61 40 95
Open: every day by appointment otherwise Sundays and public hols.

Saulieu

Musée François Pompon
Parvis de la Basilique
Place Docteur. Roclore.
Tel: 03 80 64 19 51
Closed: Tuesday. Entrance fee.

Semur-en-Auxois

Tour de l'Orle d'Or
Tel: 03 80 97 11 95
Open July and August and rest of year for groups by appointment. Entrance fee.
Musée Municipal
Rue Jean-Jacques-Collenot
Tel: 03 80 97 24 25
Open every afternoon except Tuesday and on public holidays.

Seurre

Ecomusée du Val de Saône
Rue Bossuet
Tel: 03 80 21 09 02
Open: 1 May–30 Sept. Closed on Monday. The rest of year open by appointment only. Entrance fee.

Vougeot

Château du Clos de Vougeot
Tel: 03 80 62 86 09
Open everyday all year except 24,

25, 31 December and 1 January.
Entrance fee.

SAÔNE-ET-LOIRE

Autun
Musée Rolin
3 rue des Bancs
Tel: 03 85 52 09 76
Closed: Tuesday and public
holidays. Open 2 Jan–30 Sept.
Entrance fee.
Musée Lapidaire
10 rue St-Nicolas
Tel: 03 85 52 35 71
Gallo-Roman architecture. Closed
Tuesday, public holidays and Feb.
Free entry.
Musée d'Histoire Naturelle
14 rue St-Antoine
Tel: 03 85 52 09 15
Closed: Monday, Tuesday and
public holidays. Open afternoons
only from Oct–June. Entrance fee.

Axe
Les Grottes/Musée Archéologique
Tel: 03 85 33 32 23
Caves and museum open: daily 1
April–30 Sept, Sundays only in
October. Entrance fee.

Berze-la-Ville
**Chapelle Priorale du Château des
Moines**
Tel 03 85 33 66 52
Closed Nov–March.

Berze-le-Chatel
Medieval castle
Tel: 03 85 36 60 83
1 July–31 Aug. Entrance fee.

Blanzy
Musée de la Mine at des Hommes,
Info. tel: 03 85 68 22 85
Open: afternoons Saturday, Sunday
and public holidays, 15 March–14
Nov (every afternoon 1 July–15
Sept).

Bourbon-Lancy
Bourbon-Expo
Rue du Docteur Pain
Tel: 03 85 89 00 10
Open: Wednesday–Friday all day 1
July–31 Aug, mornings only Tuesday
and Saturday, closed Sunday. Rest

of year open Tuesday morning and
Saturday. Free entry.

Chalon-sur-Saône
Musée Denon
Place de l'Hôtel de Ville
Tel: 03 85 48 01 70
Closed: Tuesday and public
holidays. Entrance fee
Musée Nicéphore Niepce
28 Quai des Messageries
Tel: 03 85 48 41 98
Closed: Tuesday. and some public
holidays. Entrance fee.

Charolles
Musée René Davoine
Tel: 03 85 88 36 01
Open: 2 May–30 Sept. Closed:
Tuesday. Information from the
tourist office. Entrance fee.

La Clayette
Musée de l'Automobile
Château La Clayette
Tel: 03 85 28 22 07
Open all year round every day
except Tuesday. Entrance fee.

Cluny
**Ancienne Abbaye St-Pierre et St-
Paul**
Guided tours, tel: 03 85 59 12 79
Musée d'Art et d'Archaeologie
Palais Jean de Bourbon
Tel: 03 85 59 23 97
Open all year round, closed on
some public holidays. Entrance fee.

Cormatin
Château
Tel: 03 85 50 16 55
Open Easter–1 Nov. Entrance fee.

Le Creusot
Ecomusée
Château de la Verrerie
Tel: 03 85 55 01 11
Closed Tuesday. Only open on
afternoons at the weekend and on
public holidays.

Couches
**Château de Marguerite de
Bourgogne**
Tel: 03 85 45 57 99
Open: Sundays and public holidays
during April, May and September. All
day every day July and August.

Afternoons only June and
September. Entrance fee.

Dicy
La Fabuloserie
Tel: 03 86 63 64 21
Open: every afternoon during July
and August and weekends only from
Easter until 1 Nov. Entrance fee.

Ecuisses
La Maison du Canal
Tel: 03 85 78 92 22
Open: Easter–end-Oct. Entrance fee.

Louhans
Hôtel-Dieu et Apothicairerie
Rue du Capitaine Vic
Tel: 03 85 75 54 32
Guided visits. Thursday and
Saturday only from 1 Oct–28 Feb.

Mâcon
Musée des Ursulines
5 rue des Ursulines
Tel: 03 85 39 90 38
Closed Tuesday.
Musée de la Tour du Moulin,
Open afternoons from March–Nov;
open all day throughout July and
August. For details, tel: 03 85 39
90 38.

Montceau-les-Mines
Musée de la Mine (Mining Museum)
34 rue du Bois Clair, Blanzy
Tel: 03 85 68 22 85
Open 15 March–15 Nov. Saturday,
Sunday and public holidays (every
afternoon from 1 July–15 Sept).
Musée des Fossiles (Fossil
Museum)
76 Quai Jules-Chagnot
Tel: 03 85 57 38 51
Open afternoons (except Mondays)
1 June–15 Sept, otherwise
afternoons on Wednesdays and
every 1st Sunday in the month.
Entrance fee.

Montbard
**Musée des Anciennes Ecuries de
Buffon**
Rue du Parc Buffon
Tel: 03 80 92 01 34
Open every day except Tuesday.
Fine Arts Museum
Tel: 03 80 92 09 02
Open afternoons from 1 April–31

Oct (all day from 1 June30 Aug).
Entrance fee.
Archaeological Museum
Tel: 03 80 92 01 34
Open all year round. Closed
Mondays from April–September and
Fridays and Saturdays from
Oct–March. Entrance fee.

Paray-le-Monial
Musée d'Art Sacrée
"Le Hiéron", 28 Rue de la Paix
Currently under restoration.
Musée de la Faïence Charolaise
Prieuré Bénédictin, Avenue Jean-
Paul II
Tel: 03 85 81 10 92
A particularly fine collection of
porcelain dating from 1836 to the
present day. Also on show is an
exhibition of moulds and tools, plus
drawing and documents. Open 1
May–1 Nov. Closed Tuesday.
Entrance fee.

Pierreclos
Château de Pierreclos
Tel: 03 85 35 73 73
Open every day. Entrance fee.

Pierre-de-Bresse
**Ecomusée de la Bresse
Bourguignonne**
Château de Pierre
Tel: 03 85 76 27 16
Open: every afternoon, also
mornings June–Sept. Entrance fee.

Rancy
A branch of the Ecomusée de la
Bresse Bourguignonne, dedicated
to the craft of chair-making and
cane work. Open: Sunday afternoons,
May–Sept, tel: 03 85 76 27 16
(Château de Pierre).

Romanêche-Thorins
Hameau du Vin. For lovers of wine.
For details, tel: 03 85 35 22 22.

Sagy
Department of the **Ecomusée de la
Bresse Bourguignonne** based in the
village communal house. Tours of
seven water mills, plus displays of
the technical development of
hydraulic mills. Contact: the Château
de Pierre, tel: 03 85 76 27 16.
Open all year round by appointment.

St-Martin-en-Bresse
**Branch of the Ecomusée de la
Bresse Bourguignonne,** with
exhibitions on the Bresse forest
and woodcrafts. Open: May–Sept
every afternoon except Tuesday.
Information, tel: 03 85 76 27 16
(Château de Pierre).

Semur-en-Brionnais
Château
Saint-Hugues
Tel: 03 85 25 13 57
Open: every day from 1 April–1 Nov.

Solutre
Musée de la Préhistoire
Tel: 03 85 35 85 24
Open every day from 1 February–30
Nov and 1 June–30 Sept, otherwise
closed Tuesday and public holidays.
Entrance fee.

St-Point
Château d'Alphonse de Lamartine
Tel: 03 85 50 50 30
Open: March–mid-Nov. Closed:
Wednesday all day and Sunday
mornings and public holidays.

Sully
Château de Sully
Tel: 03 85 82 10 27
Entrance fee. Grounds open Easter
to October; guided visits of interior,
afternoons June–Sept and rest of
year by appointment.

Tournus
**Musée Bourguignonne de Perrin de
Puycousin.** Reconstructed interiors
and scenes from traditional
Burgundian life; plus Napoleonic
souvenirs of the Tournus soldier,
Jean-Marie Putigny. Open: daily,
except Tuesday, 1 April–1 Nov, tel:
03 85 51 29 68. Entrance fee.

Verdun-sur-le-Doubs
Musée du Blé et du Pain. A branch
of the Ecomusée de la Bresse
Bourguignonne, depicting the story
of wheat and bread through the
ages. Open May–Sept every
afternoon except Tuesday, tel: 03
85 76 27 16 (Château de Pierre).

Architectural Terms

- *chancel* – altar, sanctuary and
choir
- *narthex* – porch
- *nave* – central space of church,
often flanked by aisles
- *transept* – wings of the
cruciform at right-angles to the
nave
- *apse* – half-domed or vaulted
semi-circular recess at east end
- *apsidal chapels* – chapels
radiating from the apse
- *chevet* – semi-circular east end
often with attached apses
- *ambulatory* – aisle running
round east end behind the
sanctuary
- *tympanum* – recessed space
above a doorway, triangular or
semi-circular and ornamented
- *lintel* – horizontal beam over
door or window
- *pilaster* – rectangular column
attached to the face of a wall
- *capitals* – top of a column,
often elaborately carved
- *clerestory* – row of windows
above the aisle roof lighting the
nave
- *triforium* – arcade of windows
above the arches of the nave
- *retable* – ornamental screen
behind the altar
- *corbel* – supporting bracket

AIN

Bourg-en-Bresse
Musée de Brou
63 Boulevard de Brou
Tel: 04 74 22 83 83.

St-Trivier-de-Courtes
La Ferme de la Fôret (Forest Farm),
Courtes
Tel: 04 74 30 71 89
Open: daily mid-June–mid-Sept, also
Sunday between Easter and
October.

Festivals

Live Arts

Son-et-lumière displays are now a popular way of presenting historical events; in Autun, for example, there is an **historical Gallo-Roman show** at the ancient Roman theatre, the largest of its kind in the world. Performances normally start at 10pm and there are several shows in July and August. For information contact the local tourist office.

Another impressive setting for a sound and light show is the Hôtel-Dieu in Beaune which tells the story of **the creation of the famous Hospices.** Performances in English and French, from Easter until October. Information and booking, *Office de Tourisme*, Beaune.

The **historical pageant** at the Château de St-Fargeau uses 600 local "actors" and 50 horses and it has an audience capacity of 6,000. Tickets also include entry to the château's farm, reconstructed in local style. Information and booking: Château de St-Fargeau.

La Clayette (Saône-et-Loire) is the setting for the Chantemerle Theatre Company's son-et-lumière presentations in July and August. For further information enquire at the tourist office.

A musical interpretation of the life of **Bernadette Soubirous** (St Bernadette of Lourdes) who died in Nevers, takes place at dusk on the banks of the Loire in Nevers, Friday and Saturday, 23 June–30 August.

The Legend of the Magic Ring tells the history of Burgundy at La Rochepot in July. Information from Beaune tourist office as above.

The Cultural Affairs department of Dijon Town Hall publishes a monthly programme of events, the main venues being the Grand Théâtre (for plays, opera and musical programmes), the Atheneum (mostly music and dance), the Centre Arts et Loisirs Fontaine-d'Ouche and the Salle des Jacobins which both put on a variety of performances. Dijon has a full cultural programme all year round; summer visitors can enjoy outdoor events during the Estivade. Beaune too presents outdoor performances at the Hospices during its summer music festival. Listed here are brief details of events throughout the region. For more details, contact the local tourist offices.

Diary of Events

January
Festivals of St Vincent, patron saint of wine growers, take place in a different village each year.

March
Chalon-sur-Saône: Saône-et-Loire. Carnival, with the "Goniots" people in fancy dress (sometimes held in February).
Nevers: Nièvre, Foire de Nevers. Annual Fair.
Nuits-St-Georges: Côte d'Or. Wine Sale of the Hospices (sometimes held in April).

April
Nevers: Nièvre. Porcelain Festival (odd-numbered years).

May
Dijon: Côte d'Or. Antiques Fair.
Mâcon: Saône-et-Loire, Foire des Vins de France. Wine Fair.
Saulieu: Côte d'Or, Journées gourmandes du Grand Morvan. Local Produce Fair.

June
Auxerre: Yonne. Festival de Jazz.
Beaune: Côte d'Or. Music Festival (continues into July).
Chalon-sur-Saône: Saône-et-Loire. Balloon Festival.
Dijon: Côte d'Or. Été Musicale – Music Festival.
Donzy: Nièvre. Festival de Musique.
Esolives Ste-Camille: Yonne. Foire aux Cerises – Cherry Fair.

St-Jean-de-Losne: Côte d'Or. Grand Pardon des Mariniers – Boatmen's Annual Festival.

July
Anzy-le-Duc: Saône-et-Loire. Été Musical – Summer Music Festival.
Autun: Saône-et-Loire. Musique en Morvan.
Chalon-sur-Saône: Saône-et-Loire. Festival National des artistes des rues – street performers everywhere in the town.
Dijon: Côte d'Or. L'Estivade – all kinds of arts and music events throughout the summer, some out of doors.
Flagy: Saône-et-Loire. Flagy-Mâcon Festival – what started as the "smallest theatre festival in the world" has now gained considerable prestige and national support.
Meursault: Côte d'Or. Festival des Grands Crus – Music Festival.
Vézelay: Yonne, Pélerinage de la Madeleine – religious pilgrimage and music concert.

August
Bouhans: Saône-et-Loire. Fête de la Balme – centuries old fair, created in 1645, originally just a sale of horses, now also a cattle market, plus lively entertainment.
Clamecy: Nièvre. Fête des Vaux d'Yonne.
Cluny: Saône-et-Loire. Festival des Grands Crus – "Les Grandes Heures" – five classical music concerts under the vaults of the abbey cloister.
Étigny: Yonne. Fête des Moissons – Harvest Festival.
Glux-en-Glenne: Nièvre. Fête de la Myrtille – Bilberry Fair.
St-Honoré-les-Bains: Nièvre. Fête des Fleurs – Flower Festival.
Saulieu: Côte d'Or. Fête du Charolais – Festival of Charolais Cattle.

September
Alise-Ste-Reine: Côte d'Or. Martyr de Ste-Reine – Religious Festival.
Cosne-sur-Loire: Nièvre. Foire de la Saint Michel.
Dijon: Côte-d'Or. Folkloriades Internationales et Fêtes de la Vigne – International Folk and Wine

Festival (some events in Beaune). Also in Dijon the start of the winter music concert season.

Gevrey-Chambertin: Côte d'Or. Festival des Grands Crus "Musique au Chambertin"; Fête du Roi Chambertin – Wine prize-giving.

Joigny: Yonne. Foire aux melons et oignons – Produce Fair.

Sully: Saône-et-Loire. Fête de la Chasse et de la Nature – Festival of Hunting and Nature at Château de Sully.

October

Auxerre: Yonne. Montgolfiades – Hot-air Ballooning Festival.

Dijon: Côte d'Or. Foire Internationale et Gastronomique – starts at the end of October and continues well into November.

Nevers: Nièvre. Salon des Fleurs et des Animaux – Flower and Animal Show.

St-Léger-sous-Beuvray: Saône-et-Loire. Foire aux Marrons – Chestnut Fair.

November

The most important event in November is "Les Trois Glorieuses" – three days dedicated to wine, the third weekend in November.

Clos de Vougeot: Côte d'Or. The Chapter meeting;

Beaune: Côte d'Or, Vente des Vins – the famous auction at the Hospices de Beaune;

Meursault: Côte d'Or, Paulée – Wine Festival.

Other wine festivals around the region are the Fête de Vin Bourru in Nuits-St-Georges, Côte d'Or; the Fête du Vin in Chablis, Yonne and the Fête du vine de l'Auxerrois in St-Bris-le-Vineux, Yonne.

Nevers: Nièvre, Concours agricole – Agricultural Show.

December

Dijon: Côte d'Or. Salon de l'artisanat d'art et du cadeau – Art and Crafts Fair.

Marcigny: Saône-et-Loire. Foire aux dindes et aux oies – Poultry Fair (turkeys and geese).

Nightlife

For most evening entertainment you need to be in the major towns such as Dijon or Beaune, although in summer there are concerts, son-et-lumière displays etc. right across the region. If you take young children to such displays, note that they often start quite late, around 10pm.

Santenay (Côte d'Or) at the heart of the region, 20 km (12 miles) south of Beaune, boasts a **Casino**, open every night except Monday.

For something more out of the ordinary, and absolutely typical of the region, it is possible to attend initiation ceremonies at some of the wine-drinking brotherhoods. Of particular interest is the **Confrérie des Chevaliers du Tastevin** which holds its initiation ceremonies at the beautiful Clos de Vouget Château, midway between Beaune and Dijon. Small groups of visitors are admitted on prior request; information from the Côte d'Or departmental tourist office (*see Tourist Offices, page 318*).

In the main, though, nightlife in rural Burgundy, as in country areas everywhere, is limited to a local level – small bars, cafés and restaurants, village hops, harvest festivals and other gatherings. Do not expect bars to be open very late in the country.

Everybody celebrates on the **14 July** – even the smallest villages often have their own **fireworks** displays, and nearly all towns and villages in France have a **summer fête**. If you are staying in a *gîte* or other family accommodation you are likely to be warmly encouraged to join in the festivities.

Information about nightclubs, cinemas and other entertainment is available from the tourist offices, or at your hotel.

Shopping

Shopping Areas

Over the past couple of decades most major towns in France have made the sensible decision to keep the town centre for small boutiques and individual shops. Many of these areas, such as in Beaune and Dijon, are pedestrianised and attractive (although beware – some cars ignore *voie piétonnée* signs). Large supermarkets, hypermarkets, furniture stores and do-it-yourself outlets tend to be grouped on the outskirts of the town, mostly designated as a *Centre Commercial*.

These centres, although aesthetically quite unappealing, are fine for bulk shopping for self-catering or for finding a selection of wine to take home at reasonable prices. The biggest selection of such stores in Burgundy is on the southern outskirts of Dijon. But for gifts and general window-shopping the town centres are far more interesting. It is here that you will find the individual souvenirs that give a taste of the region, alongside the beautifully dressed windows of delicatessens and *pâtisseries*.

China-lovers can have a field day in Nevers, which is full of shops selling **faïence**. Only three small factories remain, Du Bout du Monde (10 rue de la Porte du Croux); Georges (20 rue Bovet); and Bernard (1 Rue Sabatier).

Practical Information

Food shops, especially bakers, tend to open early; boutiques and department stores open from 9am, but sometimes not until 10am. In town centres, just about everything closes from noon until 2.30 or 3pm apart from the department stores which usually stay open. Most shops close in the evening at 7pm. Out of town, the hypermarkets are usually open all day until 8 or even 9pm. Most shops are closed Monday mornings and large stores generally all day. If you want to buy a picnic lunch, remember to buy everything you need before midday. Good delicatessens (*charcuteries*) have a selection of delicious ready-prepared dishes, which make picnicking a delight.

CLOTHING

Most shops are happy to let you try clothes on (*essayer*) before buying. Children's clothes sizes, in particular, are rather on the small side compared with British and US age ranges. The charts below will help you find the right size to try:

Sizes

WOMEN
Dresses/suits/coats

● France	38	40	42	44	46	48
● UK	30	32	34	36	38	40
● US	8	10	12	14	16	18

Blouses/pullovers

● France	28	40	42	44	46	48
● UK, US	30	32	34	36	38	40

Shoes

● France	36	37	38	39	40	40
● UK	3	4	5	6	7	8
● US	3	6	7	7.5	8	9

Stockings

● France	1	2	3	4	5
● UK, US	8.5	9	9.5	10	10.5

MEN
Suits/sweaters/coats

● France	32	34	36	38	40	42
● UK	33	34	35	36	37	38
● US	42	44	46	48	51	54

Shoes

● France	41	42	43	44	45	46
● UK	8	9	10	11	12	13
● US	8	8.5	9.5	10	10.5	11

Socks

● France	39–40	40–41	42	42–43	43–44
● UK, US	10	10.5	11	11.5	12

Hats

● France	53	54	55	56	57	58
● UK, US	6½	6⅜	6¾	6⅞	7	7⅛

Markets

The heart of every French town is its market; they mostly start early in the morning and close at midday. The French themselves usually visit early to get the best of the produce. In a region which prides itself on the quality of its food production, it is hardly surprising that even local markets are seen as very serious events. There is a whole series of special fairs and auctions for instance in Charolles (Saône-et-Loire), mostly devoted to the sale of their famous Charolais cattle. Similarly, the Bresse region, whose chickens carry their own *appellation contrôlée*, has regular poultry markets. The lovely old town of **Louhans**, for example, has a market every Monday where the poultry has pride of place among the 200 stalls which offer all kinds of wares.

Other particularly interesting markets include the following:
Autun (Saône-et-Loire); Wednesday and Saturday in the Champ de Mars.
Auxerre (Yonne); Tuesday.
Avallon (Yonne); Wednesday and Friday.
Bourg-en-Bresse (Ain); Wednesday, plus livestock market on Tuesday afternoons.
Beaune (Côte d'Or); Saturday.
Chagny (Saône-et-Loire); Sunday market with bric-à-brac and local produce.
Chalon-sur-Saône (Saône-et-Loire); by the cathedral on Friday and Sunday, with fruit, vegetables and bric-à-brac.
Dijon (Côte d'Or); Friday and Sunday best days, also open Tuesday and Saturday.
Donzy (Nièvre); Saturday is best, also Thursday.
Joigny (Yonne); Saturday.
Louhans (Saône-et-Loire); Monday.
Mâcon (Saône-et-Loire); extensive Saturday market on Lamartine promenade and the quayside.
Marcigny (Saône-et-Loire); the Monday market, which is noted for its poultry, was instituted by a charter in 1266.
St-Christophe-en-Brionnais (Saône-et-Loire) dates back to the 16th century; in the autumn up to 4,000 heads of cattle are sold each week.
St-Honoré-les Bains (Nièvre); Thursday is best; also open and Saturday.
Sens (Yonne); Monday.
Villefranche-sur-Saône (Rhône) the town's covered market in its famous old halls is held on Friday, Sunday and Monday.
Villeneuve-sur-Yonne (Yonne); Friday.

There are also antique and craft fairs and *marchés exceptionnels*, held at various times during the year, such as harvest time. Some of the most important, such as wine sales, are listed in the *Diary of Events*, for others check with the local tourist office for details.

Buying Direct

You may be tempted by all the signs you see along the road for *dégustations* (tastings). Many wine producers and farmers will invite you to try their wines and other produce with an eye to selling you a case, or, for instance, a few jars of pâté. This is a good way to try before you buy and can sometimes include a visit to a wine cellar. Sometimes farm produce is more expensive to buy this way than in the supermarkets – do not forget that it is home-produced and not factory-processed. For a selection of wine cellars open to the public, *see Wines, pages 333–5.*

EXPORT PROCEDURES

On most purchases, the price includes TVA (VAT or Valued Added Tax). The base rate varies and can be very high on luxury items. Foreign visitors can claim back TVA; worth doing if you spend more than FF4,200 (FF2,000 for non-EC residents) in one place. Ask the store for a *bordereau* (export sales invoice). This must be completed to show (with the goods purchased) to customs officers on leaving the country (pack the items separately for ease of access). Then mail the form back to the retailer who will refund the TVA in a month or two. Certain items purchased (e.g. antiques) may need special customs clearance.

If you have a complaint about any purchase, return it in the first place to the shop as soon as possible. In the case of any serious dispute, contact the local Direction Départementale de la Concurrence et de la Consommation et de la Répression des Fraudes (*the telephone directory will have the number*).

Sport

Facilities

You are likely to find opportunities for most sports within the region. Most medium-sized towns have swimming-pools and even small villages often have a tennis court, but you may have to become a temporary member to use it – enquire at the local tourist office or *mairie* (town hall) which will also provide details of all other local sporting activities.

It seems to be a quirk of the French tourist industry that they do not always take full advantage of their facilities. Even though there may be good weather in early summer and autumn, open-air swimming-pools and other venues often limit their seasons to the period of the school holidays.

Participant Sports

WATERSPORTS

Although land-locked, the region offers some opportunities for water sports, on man-made or natural lakes (particularly in the Morvan Regional Park), or sometimes on safe stretches of a river. Often called a *Base de Loisirs*, these centres offer all kinds of leisure activities, not just water sports. They often have a café, bar or even a restaurant and picnic areas.

Many offer tuition in the various sports available – canoeing, wind-surfing etc; most fees are charged at an hourly or half-hourly rate. Where boating and windsurfing are allowed, equipment is often available for hire, or you may take your own.

Listed below are the main *Bases de Loisirs* in the region, with details of their facilities/activities:

Nièvre

Châtillon-en-Bazois: Base Nautique de l'Étang de Baye. Sailing, windsurfing, canoeing and fishing; as well as mountain biking, volleyball and horse-riding. Accommodation and restaurant available on the site. Open: April–September.

Decize: At the end of the Nivernais canal, the Stade Nautique offers good facilities for watersports, also for bathing.

Lormes: Base Nautique de Chaumeçon. A beautiful lake in the west of the Morvan Park, which connects by means of the River Cure to the Lac du Crescent to the north. Sailing and canoeing, campsite and other accommodation. Open: April–October.

Étang du Goulot, sailing and windsurfing.

Montsauche-les-Settons: Base Nautique des Settons. Leisure centre on the Settons Lake, at the heart of the Morvan Park. Swimming, sailing, windsurfing, water-skiing and canoeing, plus riding, tennis and mini-golf. Campsite and other accommodation available. Open: April–October.

Pannecière: Centre Nautique de Pannecière, in the Morvan Regional Park, sailing and windsurfing. Open: weekends only from lst June, daily in July and August.

Cote d'Or

Auxonne: Water sports on a stretch of the River Saône; also bathing.

Dijon: Base Nautique du Lac Kir, 21370 Plombières-les-Dijon. Canoeing and other amenities, including a restaurant on the Chanoine Kir reservoir.

Nuits-St-Georges: *Plans d'eau de Saule-Guillaume.* Windsurfing and other water sports.

Pontailler-sur-Saône: Leisure centre and campsite on a stretch of the River Saône; various water sports and bathing; also good for fishing.

Saulieu: Lac de Chamboux, in the Morvan Regional Park, is the HQ of the Club Nautique de Saulieu – sailing possible.

Semur-en-Auxois: Lac du Pont, reservoir, 3 km (2 miles) south of town. Water sports and bathing.

Saône-et-Loire

Autun: Centre de Loisirs du Moulin du Vallon, a large man-made lake located on the outskirts of town with safe bathing, fishing, sailing and windsurfing; also facilities for horse-riding, golf and mini-golf, tennis and climbing.

Chalon-sur-Saône: Pleasure boating and other water sports on a stretch of the River Saône.

Gigny-sur-Saône: Lac de Laives leisure centre. Sailing and other water sports, near Chalon-sur-Saône.

Mâcon: Excellent boating facilities on a stretch of the River Saône.

Ain

Montrevel-en-Bresse: Montrevel-Malafretaz leisure centre, all kinds of sporting activities as well as water sports at this large site. Camping possible. For information, tel: 03 74 25 48 74 (tourist office).

Thoissey: All kinds of water sports and bathing on a stretch of the River Saône; campsite.

Rhone

Cublize: Lac des Sapins, large man-made lake between Amplepuis and Thizy. Water sports include canoeing, sailing, pedalos and bathing; also horse-riding, mountain bikes and mini-golf. Snack bars, restaurants, camping and wooden chalets also on the site.

Villefranche-sur-Saône: A large lake, right next to the municipal campsite on the Route de Riottier, offers supervised bathing, angling and other sporting activities.

Both the Côte d'Or and the Nièvre Loisirs Accueil services offer **courses** and **all-in holidays** in canoeing and other water sports. In the latter case, these are mostly on the River Loire where there is an annual canoe rally. For more details on canoeing, contact the **Canoë-Kayak Club de France**, 47 quai Ferber, 94360 Bry-sur-Marne, tel: 01 45 81 54 26. Call the Maison du Parc for details on the Morvan Park waterways.

ANGLING

With its wealth of waterways and lakes, fishing is a popular activity in the region. Before casting your line, you must obtain a permit from the appropriate tourist office, or from *bureaux de tabac* during the season – look out for the *Certificates de Pêche* notices. For further information, contact: **Pêche en France**, tel: 03 22 35 34 70.

CYCLING

To take your own *vélo* to France is easy – they are carried free on most ferries and trains – or you can rent cycles for a reasonable price; main railway stations usually have them for hire and you can often arrange to pick up at one station and leave the bike at another. Alternatively try enquiring at a bicycle retailers/repairers or ask at the tourist office.

Some youth hostels rent cycles and also arrange tours with accommodation in hostels or under canvas. For details, contact the YHA (*see Where to Stay, page 323*).

"Packaged" cycling holidays are offered by various organisations with camping or hotel accommodation. The advantage to this is that your luggage is normally transported for you on to your next destination. The Nièvre Loisirs Accueil service offers a six-night tour of the upper Loire Valley.

It is advisable to take out **insurance** before you go. Advice and information can be obtained from **The Touring Department**, Cyclists Touring Club, Cotterell House, 69 Meadrow, Godalming, Surrey GU7 3HS, tel: 01483-417217. Their service to members includes competitive insurance, free detailed touring itineraries and general information sheets about France while their tours brochure often lists trips to the region, organised by members. The club's French counterpart, **Fédération Française de Cyclotourisme**, is at 8 rue Jean-Marie-Jégo, 75013 Paris, tel: 01 45 80 30 21.

Also very comprehensive is the new IGN 906 Cycling France map which gives details of routes, cycling clubs and places to stay (*see Maps, page 311*).

MOUNTAIN BIKING

Once again, the Morvan attracts many devotees of the sport, its hilly landscapes providing ideal routes. Starting from St-Saulge in the Nièvre, the Centre National VTT has marked out 550 km (340 miles) of trails. The organisations listed under *Cycling* all offer holidays or try Nièvre Loisirs Accueil.

Mountain bikes (known in French as VTT – *Vélo Tout Terrain*) and protective gear can be hired locally, try the local tourist office, or cycle/repair shops.

HORSE-RIDING

Some 220 riding centres across France offer riding holidays under the auspices of the syndicat National au Tourisme Equestre who operate a charter of quality. For information, contact Fédération des Randonneurs Equestres, 16 rue des Apennins, 75017 Paris, tel: 01 42 26 23 23.

GOLF

The regional tourist boards have joined forces with the French Golf Federation in an effort to promote golf. General information can be obtained from the Comité Régional au Tourisme (*see Tourist Offices, page 318*) or the FFG – the Fédération Française de Golf, 69 Avenue Victor Hugo, 75783 Paris Cedex 16, tel: 01 45 02 13 55.

HANG-GLIDING

Ecole de Vol Libre du Poupet. St-Thiebald 39110 Salins-les-bains, tel: 03 80 26 63 30.

HOT-AIR BALLOONING

Bourgogne tour incoming, 14 rue du Chapeau Rouge, 21000 Dijon, tel: 03 80 30 49 49.

SPELEOLOGY

For caving and potholing contact: Fédération Française de Spéléologie 130 rue St-Maur, 75011 Paris, tel: 01 43 57 56 54.

CANOEING

Fédération Française de canoe-kayak, 87 quai de la Marne, 94340 Joinville-le-Pont, tel: 0248 89 39 89 or the Comité de l'Yonne de canoe-kayak, ev. Yver prolongée 89000 Auxerre, tel: 03 86 52 13 86.

Spectator Sports

The Dijon-Prenois **motor racing** circuit stages the Formula 3 French Championship, the Grand Prix Historique, and the European Lorry Grand Prix, among other races.

In Nièvre, the Grand Prix Formula 1 race takes place in July at the Magny-Cours racing circuit, which in March stages the World Superbike Championship. For more details of these and other events at the track, tel: 03 86 21 20 74.

In the Morvan in August is the *Grand Prix Cycliste International*, held during the *Fête du Morvan*.

Semur-en-Auxois stages some prestigious **horse races**; in particular the *Course des Chausses et des Damoiselles*, and the oldest horse race of them all (1639), the *Fête de la Bague*, both in May. More information from the Maison du Tourisme. Other races (with official betting) takes place in mid-July and mid-August at Vitteaux, near Dijon.

Water jousting and other unusual water sports are on display in Clamecy (Nièvre) in July and at Coulanges-sur-Yonne in August.

Details of these and other local sporting events can be obtained from the nearest tourist office.

Language

French is the native language of more than 90 million people and the acquired language of 180 million. It is a Romance language descended from the Vulgar Latin spoken by the Roman conquerors of Gaul. It still carries the reputation of being the most cultured language in the world, and the most beautiful. People often tell stories about the impatience of the French towards foreigners not blessed with fluency in their language. In general, however, if you attempt to speak in French, they will be helpful.

Since much of our vocabulary is related to French, thanks to the Norman Conquest, travellers will often recognise many helpful cognates, such as *hôtel, café* and *bagages*. You should be aware, however, of some misleading "false friends" (*see page 248*).

Language

Standard French is spoken in the region. The local accents should not cause any problems of understanding for anyone with a reasonable grasp of the language. Harsh sounds tend to be softened – Auxerre, for example, becomes Ausserre. Most people are very willing to try and communicate with visitors whose French is limited.

Words & Phrases

How much is it? *C'est combien?*
What is your name? *Comment vous appelez-vous?*
My name is... *Je m'appelle...*
Do you speak English? *Parlez-vous anglais?*

I am English/American *Je suis anglais/américain*
I don't understand *Je ne comprends pas*
Please speak more slowly *Parlez plus lentement, s'il vous plaît*
Can you help me? *Pouvez-vous m'aider?*
I'm looking for... *Je cherche*
Where is...? *Où est...?*
I'm sorry *Excusez-moi/Pardon*
I don't know *Je ne sais pas*
No problem *Pas de problème*
Have a good day! *Bonne journée!*
That's it *C'est ça*
Here it is *Voici*
There it is *Voilà*
Let's go *On y va. Allons-y*
See you tomorrow *A demain*
See you soon *A bientôt*
yes *oui*
no *non*
please *s'il vous plaît*
thank you *merci*
(very much) *(beaucoup)*
you're welcome *de rien*
excuse me *excusez-moi*
hello *bonjour*
OK *d'accord*
goodbye *au revoir*
good evening *bonsoir*
here *ici*
there *là*
today *aujourd'hui*
yesterday *hier*
tomorrow *demain*
now *maintenant*
later *plus tard*
this morning *ce matin*
this afternoon *cet après-midi*
this evening *ce soir*

On Arrival

I want to get off at... *Je voudrais descendre à...*
Is there a bus to the Louvre? *Est-ce qui'il ya un bus pour le Louvre?*
What street is this? *A quelle rue sommes-nous?*
Which line do I take for...? *Quelle ligne dois-je prendre pour...?*
How far is...? *A quelle distance se trouve...?*
Validate your ticket *Compostez votre billet*
airport *l'aéroport*
train station *la gare*

bus station *la gare routière*
Métro stop *la station de Métro*
bus *l'autobus, le car*
bus stop *l'arrêt*
platform *le quai*
ticket *le billet*
return ticket *aller-retour*
hitchhiking *l'autostop*
toilets *les toilettes*
This is the hotel address
C'est l'adresse de l'hôtel
I'd like a (single/double) room...
Je voudrais une chambre (pour une/deux personnes) ...
....with shower *avec douche*
....with a bath *avec salle de bain*
....with a view *avec vue*
Does that include breakfast? *Le prix comprend-il le petit déjeuner?*
May I see the room? *Je peux voir la chambre?*
washbasin *le lavabo*
bed *le lit*
key *la cléf*
lift/elevator *l'ascenseur*
air conditioned *climatisé*

On the Road

Where is the spare wheel? *Où est la roue de secours?*
Where is the nearest garage? *Où est le garage le plus proche?*
Our car has broken down *Notre voiture est en panne*
I want to have my car repaired *Je veux faire réparer ma voiture*
It's not your right of way *Vous n'avez pas la priorité*
I think I must have put diesel in the car by mistake *Je crois que j'ai mis du gasoil dans la voiture par erreur*
the road to... *la route pour...*
left *gauche*
right *droite*
straight on *tout droit*
far *loin*
near *près d'ici*
opposite *en face*
beside *à côté de*
car park *parking*
over there *là-bas*
at the end *au bout*
on foot *à pied*
by car *en voiture*
town map *le plan*
road map *la carte*
street *la rue*

Basic Rules

It is worth trying to master a few simple phrases before holidaying in France. The fact that you have made an effort is likely to get you a better response. More and more French people like practising their English on visitors, especially waiters and the young. Pronunciation is the key; they really will not understand if you get it very wrong. Remember to **emphasise each syllable**, but not to pronounce the last consonant of a word as a rule (this includes the plural "s") and always to drop your "h"s. Whether to use **"vous"** or **"tu"** is a vexed question; increasingly the familiar form of "tu" is used by many people. However it is better to be too formal, and use "vous" if in doubt. It is very important to be polite; always address people as **Madame** or **Monsieur**, and address them by their surnames until you are confident first names are acceptable. When entering a shop always say, "Bonjour Monsieur/ Madame," and "Merci, au revoir," when leaving.

square *la place*
give way *céder le passage*
dead end *impasse*
no parking *stationnement interdit*
motorway *l'autoroute*
toll *le péage*
speed limit *la limitation de vitesse*
petrol *l'essence*
unleaded *sans plomb*
diesel *le gasoil*
water/oil *l'eau/l'huile*
puncture *un pneu de crevé*
bulb *l'ampoule*
wipers *les essuies-glace*

The Alphabet

Learning the pronunciation of the French alphabet is a good idea. In particular, learn how to spell out your name.
a=ah, **b**=bay, **c**=say, **d**=day **e**=er, **f**=ef, **g**=zhay, **h**=ash. **i**=ee, **j**=zhee, **k**=ka, **l**=el, **m**=em, **n** =en, **o**=oh, **p**=pay, **q**=kew, **r**=ehr, **s**=ess, **t**=tay, **u**=ew, **v**=vay, **w**=dooblah vay, **x**-=eex, **y** ee grek, **z**=zed

Shopping

Where is the nearest bank (post office)? *Où est la banque/Poste/ PTT la plus proche?*
I'd like to buy *Je voudrais acheter*
How much is it? *C'est combien?*
Do you take credit cards? *Est-ce que vous acceptez les cartes de crédit?*
I'm just looking *Je regarde seulement*

Have you got...? *Avez-vous...?*
I'll take it *Je le prends*
I'll take this one/that one *Je prends celui-ci/celui-là*
What size is it? *C'est de quelle taille?*
Anything else? *Avec ça?*
size (clothes) *la taille*
size (shoes) *la pointure*
cheap *bon marché*
expensive *cher*
enough *assez*
too much *trop*
a piece *un morceau de*
each *la pièce (eg ananas, 15F la pièce)*
bill *la note*
chemist *la pharmacie*
bakery *la boulangerie*
bookshop *la librairie*
library *la bibliothèque*
department store *le grand magasin*
delicatessen *la charcuterie/ le traiteur*
fishmonger's *la poissonerie*
grocery *l'alimentation/l'épicerie*
tobacconist *tabac (can also sell stamps and newspapers)*
markets *le marché*
supermarket *le supermarché*
junk shop *la brocante*

Sightseeing

town *la ville*
old town *la vieille ville*
abbey *l'abbaye*
cathedral *la cathédrale*
church *l'église*
keep *le donjon*
mansion *l'hôtel*
hospital *l'hôpital*

town hall *l'hôtel de ville/la mairie*
nave *la nef*
stained glass *le vitrail*
staircase *l'escalier*
tower *la tour (La Tour Eiffel)*
walk *le tour*
country house/castle *le château*
Gothic *gothique*
Roman *romain*

Time

At what time? *A quelle heure?*
When? *Quand?*
What time is it? *Quelle heure est-il?*
● Note that the French generally use the 24-hour clock.

Romanesque *roman*
museum *la musée*
art gallery *la galerie*
exhibition *l'exposition*
tourist *l'office de*
information *tourisme/le*
office *syndicat d'initiative*
free *gratuit*
open *ouvert*
closed *fermé*
every day *tous les jours*
all year *toute l'année*
all day *toute la journée*
swimming pool *la piscine*
to book *réserver*

False Friends

False friends are words that look like English words but mean something different.
le car motorcoach, also railway carriage
le conducteur bus driver
la monnaie change (coins)
l'argent money/silver
ça marche can sometimes mean walk, but is usually used to mean working (the TV, the car etc.) or going well
actuel "present time"
(la situation actuelle the present situation)
rester to stay
location hiring/renting
personne person or nobody, according to context
le médecin doctor

Dining Out

Table d'hôte (the "host's table") is one set menu served at a set price. **Prix fixe** is a fixed-price menu. **A la carte** means dishes from the menu are chosen and charged separately.

breakfast *le petit déjeuner*
lunch *le déjeuner*
dinner *le dîner*
meal *le repas*
first course *l'entrée/les hors d'oeuvre*
main course *le plat principal*
made to order *sur commande*
drink included *boisson compris*
wine list *la carte des vins*
the bill *l'addition*
fork *la fourchette*
knife *le couteau*
spoon *la cuillère*
plate *l'assiette*
glass *le verre*
napkin *la serviette*
ashtray *le cendrier*

Breakfast and Snacks

baguette **long thin loaf**
pain **bread**
petits pains **rolls**
beurre **butter**
poivre **pepper**
sel **salt**
sucre **sugar**
confiture **jam**
oeufs **eggs**
...à la coque **boiled eggs**
...au bacon **bacon and eggs**
...au jambon **ham and eggs**
...sur le plat **fried eggs**
...brouillés **scrambled eggs**
tartine **bread with butter**
yaourt **yoghurt**
crêpe **pancake**
croque-monsieur **ham and cheese toasted sandwich**
croque-madame **...with a fried egg on top**
galette **type of pancake**
pan bagna **bread roll stuffed with salad Niçoise**
quiche **tart of eggs and cream with various fillings**
quiche lorraine **quiche with bacon**

First course

An *amuse-bouche, amuse-gueule* or appetiser is something literally to "amuse the mouth", served before the first course

anchoiade **sauce of olive oil, anchovies and garlic, served with raw vegetables**
assiette anglaise **cold meats**
potage **soup**
rillettes **rich fatty paste of shredded duck, rabbit or pork**
tapenade **spread of olives and anchovies**
pissaladière **Provençal pizza with onions, olives and anchovies**

Emergencies

Help! *Au secours!*
Stop! *Arrêtez!*
Call a doctor *Appelez un médecin*
Call an ambulance *Appelez une ambulance*
Call the police *Appelez la police*
Call the fire brigade *Appelez les pompiers*
Where is the nearest telephone? *Où est le téléphone le plus proche?*
Where is the nearest hospital? *Où est l'hôpital le plus proche?*
I am sick *Je suis malade*
I have lost my passport/purse *J'ai perdu mon passeport/porte-monnaie*

Meat and Fish

La Viande **Meat**
bleu **rare**
à point **medium**
bien cuit **well done**
grillé **grilled**
agneau **lamb**
andouille/andouillette **tripe sausage**
bifteck **steak**
boudin **sausage**
boudin noir **black pudding**
boudin blanc **white pudding (chicken or veal)**
blanquette **stew of veal, lamb or chicken with a creamy egg sauce**
boeuf à la mode **beef in red wine with carrots, mushroom and onions**
à la bordelaise **beef with red wine and shallots**
à la Bourguignonne **cooked in red wine, onions and mushrooms**
brochette **kebab**
caille **quail**

canard **duck**
carbonnade **casserole of beef, beer and onions**
carré d'agneau cassoulet **rack of lamb stew with beans, sausages, pork and duck, from the southwest**
cervelle **brains (food)**
chateaubriand choucroute **thick steak with sauerkraut, bacon and sausages from the Alsace region**
confit **duck or goose preserved in its own fat**
contre-filet **cut of sirloin steak**
coq au vin **chicken in red wine**
côte d'agneau **lamb chop**
daube **beef stew with red wine, onions and tomatoes**
dinde **turkey**
entrecôte **beef rib steak**
escargot **snail**
faisan **pheasant**
farci **stuffed**
faux-filet **sirloin**
foie **liver**
foie de veau **calf's liver**
foie gras **goose or duck liver pâté**
gardiane **rich beef stew with olives and garlic, from the Camargue**
cuisses de grenouille **frog's legs**
grillade **grilled meat**
hachis **minced meat**
jambon **ham**
lapin **rabbit**
lardon **small pieces of bacon, often added to salads**
magret de canard **breast of duck**
médaillon **round meat**
moelle **beef bone marrow**
mouton navarin **stew of lamb with onions, carrots and turnips**
oie **goose**
perdrix **partridge**
petit-gris **small snail**
pieds de cochon **pig's trotters**
pintade **guinea fowl**
Pipérade **Basque dish of eggs, ham, peppers, onion**
porc **pork**
pot-au-feu **casserole of beef and vegetables**
poulet **chicken**
poussin **young chicken**
rognons **kidneys**
rôti **roast**
sanglier **wild boar**
saucisse **fresh sausage**
saucisson **salami**
veau **veal**

Poissons **Fish**
Armoricaine **made with white wine, tomatoes, butter and cognac**
anchois **anchovies**
anguille **eel**
bar (or *loup*) **sea bass**
barbue **brill**
belon **Brittany oyster**
bigorneau **sea snail**

Table Talk

I am a vegetarian *Je suis végétarien*
I am on a diet *Je suis au régime*
What do you recommend? *Qu'est-ce que vous recommandez?*
Do you have local specialities? *Avez-vous des spécialités locales?*
I'd like to order *Je voudrais commander*
That is not what I ordered *Ce n'est pas ce que j'ai commandé*
Is service included? *Est-ce que le service est compris?*
May I have more wine? *Encore du vin, s'il vous plaît?*
Enjoy your meal *Bon appétit!*

Bercy **sauce of fish stock, butter, white wine and shallots**
bouillabaisse **fish soup served with grated cheese, garlic croutons and** *rouille*, **a spicy sauce**
brandade **salt cod purée**
cabillaud **cod**
calmars **squid**
colin **hake**
coquillage **shellfish**
coquilles Saint-Jacques **scallops**
crevette **shrimp**
daurade **sea bream**
flétan **halibut**
fruits de mer **seafood**
hareng **herring**
homard **lobster**
huître **oyster**
langoustine **large prawn**
limande **lemon sole**
lotte **monkfish**
morue **salt cod**
moule **mussel**
moules marinières **mussels in white wine and onions**
oursin **sea urchin**
raie **skate**

saumon **salmon**
thon **tuna**
truite **trout**

Légumes **Vegetables**
ail **garlic**
artichaut **artichoke**
asperge **asparagus**
aubergine **eggplant**
avocat **avocado**
bolets **boletus mushrooms**
céleri **grated celery**
rémoulade **with mayonnaise**
champignon **mushroom**
cèpes **boletus mushroom**
chanterelle **wild mushroom**
cornichon **gherkin**
courgette **courgette/zucchini**
chips **potato crisps**
chou **cabbage**
chou-fleur **cauliflower**
concombre **cucumber**
cru **raw**
crudités **raw vegetables**
épinard **spinach**
frites **chips, French fries**
gratin dauphinois **sliced potatoes baked with cream**
haricot **dried bean**
haricots verts **green beans**
lentilles **lentils**
maïs **corn**
mange-tout **snow pea**
mesclun **mixed leaf salad**
navet **turnip**
noix **nut, walnut**
noisette **hazelnut**
oignon **onion**
panais **parsnip**
persil **parsley**
pignon **pine nut**
poireau **leek**
pois **pea**
poivron **bell pepper**
pomme de terre **potato**
radis **radish**
roquette **arugula, rocket**
ratatouille **Provençal vegetable stew of aubergines, courgettes, tomatoes, peppers and olive oil**
riz **rice**

Non, non, garçon

Garçon is the word for waiter but is never used directly; say *Monsieur* or *Madame* to attract his or her attention.

salade Niçoise **egg, tuna, olives, onions and tomato salad**
salade verte **green salad**
truffe **truffle**

Fruits Fruit

ananas **pineapple**
cavaillon **fragrant sweet melon from Cavaillon in Provence**
cerise **cherry**
citron **lemon**
citron vert **lime**
figue **fig**
fraise **strawberry**
framboise **raspberry**
groseille **redcurrant**
mangue **mango**
mirabelle **yellow plum**
pamplemousse **grapefruit**
pêche **peach**
poire **pear**
pomme **apple**
raisin **grape**
prune **plum**
pruneau **prune**
Reine claude **greengage**

Sauces Sauces

aioli **garlic mayonnaise**
béarnaise **sauce of egg, butter, wine and herbs**
forestière **with mushrooms and bacon**
hollandaise **egg, butter and lemon sauce**
lyonnaise **with onions**
meunière **fried fish with butter, lemon and parsley sauce**
meurette **red wine sauce**
Mornay **sauce of cream, egg and cheese**
Parmentier **served with potatoes**
paysan **rustic style, ingredients depend on the region**
pistou **Provençal sauce of basil, garlic and olive oil; vegetable soup with the sauce.**
provençale **sauce of tomatoes, garlic and olive oil.**
papillotte **cooked in paper**

Puddings Dessert

Belle Hélène **fruit with ice cream and chocolate sauce**
clafoutis **baked pudding of batter and cherries**
coulis **purée of fruit or vegetables**
gâteau **cake**
île flottante **whisked egg whites in**
custard sauce
crème anglaise **custard**
pêche melba **peaches with ice cream and raspberry sauce**
tarte tatin **upside down tart of caramelised apples**
crème caramel **caramelised egg custard**
crème Chantilly **whipped cream**
fromage **cheese**
chèvre **goat's cheese**

In the Café

If you sit at the bar (le zinc), drinks will be cheaper than at a table. Settle the bill when you leave; the waiter may leave a slip of paper on the table to keep track of the bill. The French enjoy bittersweet aperitifs, often diluted with ice and fizzy water.

drinks les boissons
coffee café
...with milk or cream au lait or crème
...decaffeinated déca/décaféiné
...black/espresso express/noir
...American filtered coffee filtre
tea thé
...herb infusion tisane
...camomile verveine
hot chocolate chocolat chaud
milk lait
mineral water eau minérale
fizzy gazeux
non-fizzy non-gazeux
fizzy lemonade limonade
fresh lemon juice served with sugar citron pressé
fresh squeezed orange juice orange pressé
full (eg full cream milk) entier
fresh or cold frais, fraîche
beer bière
...bottled en bouteille
...on tap à la pression
pre-dinner drink apéritif
white wine with cassis, blackcurrant liqueur kir
kir with champagne kir royale
with ice avec des glaçons
neat sec
red rouge
white blanc
rose rosé
dry brut
sweet doux

sparkling wine crémant
house wine vin de maison
local wine vin de pays
Where is this wine from? De quelle région vient ce vin?
pitcher carafe/pichet
...of water/wine d'eau/de vin
half litre demi-carafe
quarter litre quart
mixed panaché
after dinner drink digestif
brandy from Armagnac region of France Armagnac
Normandy apple brandy calvados
cheers! santé!
hangover gueule de bois

On the Telephone

How do I make an outside call? Comment est-ce que je peux téléphoner à l'exterieur?
I want to make an international (local) call Je voudrais une communication pour l'étranger (une communication locale)
What is the dialling code? Quel est l'indicatif?
I'd like an alarm call for 8 tomorrow morning. Je voudrais être réveillé à huit heures demain martin
Who's calling? C'est qui à l'appareil?
Hold on, please Ne quittez pas s'il vous plaît
The line is busy La ligne est occupée
I must have dialled the wrong number J'ai dû faire un faux numéro

Days of the Week

Monday lundi
Tuesday mardi
Wednesday mercredi
Thursday jeudi
Friday vendredi
Saturday samedi
Sunday dimanche

Capitalisation

Days of the week, seasons and months are not capitalised in French.

Seasons

spring *le printemps*
summer *l'été*
autumn *l'automne*
winter *l'hiver*

Months

January *janvier*
February *février*
March *mars*
April *avril*
May *mai*
June *juin*
July *juillet*
August *août*
September *septembre*
October *octobre*
November *novembre*
December *décembre*

Numbers

0 *zéro*
1 *un, une*
2 *deux*
3 *trois*
4 *quatre*
5 *cinq*
6 *six*
7 *sept*
8 *huit*
9 *neuf*
10 *dix*
11 *onze*
12 *douze*
13 *treize*
14 *quatorze*
15 *quinze*
16 *seize*
17 *dix-sept*
18 *dix-huit*

Slang

métro, boulot, dodo nine-to-five
syndrome
McDo McDonald's
branché trendy (literally
"connected")
C'est du cinéma It's very unlikely
une copine/un copain friend/pal
un ami friend but **mon ami**,
boyfriend; also **mon copain**
un truc thing, "whatsit"
pas mal, not bad, good-looking
fantastic! fantastic! terrible!

19 *dix-neuf*
20 *vingt*
21 *vingt-et-un*
30 *trente*
40 *quarante*
50 *cinquante*
60 *soixante*
70 *soixante-dix*
80 *quatre-vingts*
90 *quatre-vingt-dix*
100 *cent*
1000 *mille*
1,000,000 *un million*
*Note that the number 1 is often
written as an upside down V and the
number 7 is usually crossed.*

Further Reading

General

Ardagh, John. *France Today.*
London: Secker and Warburg. Up-to-
date, hefty tome on modern France.
Cole, Robert. *A Traveller's History
of France.* London: The Windrush
Press. Slim volume for background
reading.
Hamilton, Ronald. *A Holiday History
of France.* London: The Hogarth
Press. Illustrated guide to history
and architecture.
Braudel, Fernand. *The Identity of
France.* London: Fontana Press.
Wells, Patricia. *The Food Lover's
Guide to France.* London: Methuen.
The best restaurants, food shops
and markets in France, plus
regional recipes.
Busselle, Michael. *Burgundy – Wine
Lover's Regional Guide.* London:
Pavilion. Photographer's guide to
the vineyards and countryside of
Burgundy.
Sutcliffe, Serena. *The Wines of
Burgundy.* London: Mitchell Beazley.
Pocket guide to the appellations
and châteaux of Burgundy.
Pomerol, Charles (ed). *The Wines
and Winelands of France.* London:
Robertson McCarta. Guide to the
wine regions of France, paying
particular attention to the geology
and science of the subject, plus
itineraries and history.
Johnson, Hugh and Duijker,
Hubrecht. *Wine Atlas of France.*
London: Mitchell Beazley. Well-
illustrated atlas, concentrating on
wine and vineyards, but also
supplementary information on
history, architecture and culture.
Parker, Robert. *Burgundy.* London:
Dorling Kindersley.
Dunlop, Ian. *Burgundy.* London:
Hamish Hamilton. Traces the
architectural development of the
region from 1000–1789.
Bourgogne Romane. Zodiaque
Press. Romanesque architecture.

Other Insight Guides

Apa Publications has more travel guide titles in print than any other guide book publisher, with over 200 *Insight Guides*, more than 100 *Pocket Guides* and over 200 *Compact Guides*.

Insight Guide: France is the major book in the French series covering the whole country, with features on food and drink, culture and the arts as well as a broad picture of the nation. Other Insight Guide titles cover **Alsace**, **Brittany**, **Corsica**, the **Côte d'Azur**, the **Loire Valley**, **Normandy**, **Paris** and **Provence**.

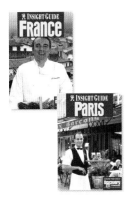

Insight Pocket Guides are written by host authors who show you the best of the places they know well. The books are designed in a series of day trips and excursions, and are particularly useful for people with only a short time to make the most of their visit. Titles include **Alsace**, **Brittany**, **Corsica**, the **Côte d'Azur**, the **Loire Valley**, **Paris** and **Provence**. Complete with pull-out map.

Compact Guides are the handiest guide books around. These inexpensive, full-colour mini-encyclopaedias give you the best routes of the region with a star-rated system of all the sites worth seeing, plus all the practical information you will need for your stay. Titles include **Brittany**, **Burgundy**, **Normandy**, **Provence** and **Paris**.

ART & PHOTO CREDITS

All photography by Lyle Lawson except for:
David Ashkam: Spectrum 104
Attilio Ru 85
Bibliothèque Municipale, Dijon 44, 46
Bibliothèque Municipale, Valenciennes 37
Bibliothèque Nationale, Paris 51, 63
J. H Breuil 84
Château de Versculles 55
Peter Graham 112
Denis Hughes-Gilbey 118, 119
Barry Miles 274
Musée de Beaux Arts, Dijon 62, 65
Musée Carnavalet, Paris 1, 22
Musée de Chantilly 226
Musée de Cluny 53/54
Musée de Rheims 35
Jean-Paul Nacivet: Spectrum 102/103, 247
Spectrum 48, 86, 87, 93, 111
George Taylor/Apa 2
Yannick Vetillard 212
Vienna O.N.B. 67

Cover photographs: all by George Taylor except front cover and bottom spine

Map Production Colourmap Scanning Ltd (inside flap maps) and Berndtson & Berndtson Publications (all other maps)

Cartographic Editor **Zoë Goodwin**
Production **Stuart A Everitt**
Cover Design **Tanvir Virdee**
Picture Research **Hilary Genin**

Index

Numbers in italics refer to photographs

a

Alésia 38, *26*, 185
Alexander III, Pope 140
Alise-Ste-Reine 38, 185–186
Ancy-le-Franc, Château de 150–151
Anzy-le-Duc 283
Apremont-sur-Allier, Château de 215
Arcenant 259
architecture 43–48, 140, 264, 283
Arcy-sur-Cure 162
Arleuf 204
Armançon, River 147
Arras, Jean d' 150
Autun 195, 206–209
Auxerre *73*, 144–147
Auxey-Duresses 252–253
Auxois, L' 195, 196
Auxonne 236
Avallon 87, 174–175
Avenas 304

b

ballooning 180
Beaujeu 305, 307
Beaujolais Nouveau 106, 298, 302
Beaujolais wine 104–107, 298–305
Beaujolais, Le 298, 300
Beaune 248, 249–251
Bénigne, St 223
Béregovoy, Pierre 86, 210
Bernadette, Saint 95, 213
Bernard, St 23, 35, 95, 140, 151, 169, 182–184
Berzé-la-Ville 275–276
Bevin, Ernest 247
Bèze 235–236
Bibracte 26, 206
Bligny-sur-Ouche 259
Bouilland 259
Bourbilly, Château de 177
Bourbon-Lancy 284
Bourg-en-Bresse 121, 292–295
Brancion 269
Braudel, Fernand 240
Bresse, La 264–269
Bretonne, Réstif de la 26, 157
Brionnais, Le 279
Brosse, Claude 107, 295–296

Brou 71, 292
Brouilly 304–305
Brunhilde 33, 36, 236
Buffon, Comte de 76, 78, 162, 179–182
Burgundy wines 104–114, 124, 242
Burgundy, dukes of 55–66, 119, 226
Bussy-Rabutin, Château de 74, 75, 76, 186–187
Bussy-Rabutin, Roger de 25, 74, 75, 186–187

c

Canal de Bourgogne 196, 202
Canal de Briare 144, 202
Canal du Nivernais 202
canals 202
caves 162
Chablis town 154–155
Chablis wine 107, 109, 155–156
Chailly-sur-Armançon 197
Chalon-sur-Saône 98, 255–256
Chambolle-Musigny 243
Chanceaux 188
Chapaize 270
Chardonnay 269
Charité-sur-Loire, La 214–215
Charlemagne 35, 43
Charles the Rash 61–66
Chârnay-les-Macon 295
Charolais hills 276–277
Charolles 278–279
Chartreuse de Champmol 56, 225, 233–234
Chassagne-Montrachet 254
Chastenay, Manoir de 162
Château-Chinon 89, 204
Châteauneuf 196
Châtel-Censoir 161
Châtel-Moron 255
Châtillon-en-Bazois 210
Châtillon-sur-Seine 185
Chaumard 203
cheese 120, 177, 196
Chenôvre 242
Chénas 301
Chevalier, Gabriel 93, 307
Chitry-le-Fort 160
Cîteaux Abbey 23, 95, 120, 245–246
Clamecy 97, 98
Clayette, La 280
Clochemerle 93, 100, 307
clog-making 96, 173, 201
Clos de Vougeot 96, 99, 100, 108, 244–245

Cluny 44, 50–51, 271–275
Cocteau, Jean 155
Colette 22, 24, 26, 139, 141–143
Commarin 196
Confrérie des Chevaliers du Tastevin 88, 100, 108, 244, 248
Cormatin, Château de 270–271
Cosne-sur-Loire 215
Côte Chalonnaise 254–256
Côte d'Or 22, 87, 240–254
Côte de Beaune 247–254
Côte de Nuits 242–247
Couches 98, 257
Coulanges-la-Vineuse 159
cowboys 95, 205
Cravant 160–161
Creusot, Le 38, 79, 256–257
Cure, River 160, 162

d

Decize 216
Delors, Jacques, 198
demography 93
Depardieu, Gérard 88, 184
Desjardins, Paul 153
Digoin 284
Dijon 73, 56, 86, 87, 100, 120, 221–234
  Archaeological Museum 224
  culinary capital 226
  environs 234–236
  history 222
  Notre Dame 224
  old town 228
  Palais des Ducs 227
  St-Bénigne 223
  St-Philibert 224
Druyes-les-Belles-Fontaines 161
Dumaine, Alexandre 124, 125

e

Edmund, St 153
Eiffel, Gustave 25
Eliot, T. S. 153
Époisses 36, 176–177
Erasmus 251
Escolives-Ste-Camille 158–159
Eudes III, Duke 232

f

faïence 143, 210, 212
farming 88
Ferté-Loupière, La 144
festivals 95, 98, 100, 179, 229
Fête de la Bague 98, 179

Fête de la Madele ine 95
Fête de la Vivre 98
Fisher, M.F.K. 119, 221, 233
Fixin 242
Flavigny-sur-Ozerain 169, 187–188
Fleurie 303
Fontaine-Française 236
Fontaines-Salées 173
Fontenay Abbey 120, 182–184
food 26, 87, 119–125
forestry 88, 96
Frederick III, Emperor 62–65
Fuissé 298

g

Gainsbourg, Serge 172, 173
Gamay 254
gastronomy 119, 221, 233
Gevrey-Chambertin 242
Gide, André 153
Givry 255
Gorges de la Canche 206
Gregorian chant 50
Grivot, Abbé Denis 208
Gueugnon 93

h

Harding, Stephen 23, 151
history 31–88
    Capetian rule 35
    Carolingian Renaissance 35
    Celts 31
    Louis XI of France 61–66
    decisive dates 38–39
    Enlightenment 76
    foundation of Burgundy
    Napoleonic wars 78
    Postwar development 86–88
    Revolution 77
    Roman occupation 32
    Romanesque tradition 43–48
    the Frondes 75
    Treaty of Senlis 71
    Valois dukes 55–61
    Wars of Religion 72–73
    World War I 83
    World War II 83–86
Hoffmann, Ernst 243, 247
Hospices de Beaune 100, 244,
    248, 253
Hugues, St 50, 275, 282

i

Iguerande 281
industry 79, 87
Irancy 160

ironworks 78–79, 181
Is-sur-Tille 235
Île-sur-Serein 176

j, k

Jambles 255
James, Henry 22, 26
Joan of Arc 38, 214, 216
John Paul, Pope 95
John the Fearless 57–59
John XXIII, Pope 272
Johnson, Hugh 299, 303
Joigny 141
jousting 60
Juliénas 300–301
Kir, aperitif 25, 83, 222, 259
Kir, Canon 25, 83, 86, 222, 259
Knights Templar 173–174

l

Lac de Pannecière 203
Lac des Settons 203
Lacarrière, Jacques 100, 157
Lamargelle 235
Lamartine, Alphonse de 21, 24,
    79, 271, 289, 291, 294,
    296–297
Langton, Stephen 153
Lantilly, Château de 179
Larousse, Pierre-Athanase 25, 152
Ligny-de-Châtel 154
Ligny-en-Brionnais 281
Louhans 266
Louis XI 38, 61–66, 232, 250
Louis XIV 74, 75, 107, 247, 296
Lux 235

m

Mâcon town 289–92, 294
Mâcon wine 107, 289
Mailly-de-Château 161
Malaparte, Curzio 104
Malaparte, Curzio 104
Malraux, André 208
Mann, Thomas 153
Margaret of Austria 292–293
Margeurite de Bourgogne 71,
    147–148, 257
markets 233, 279
Marsannay-la-Côte 60, 242
Massy 277
Maulnes, Château de 149–150
Mellecey 255
Meneau, Marc 97, 173
Mérimée, Prosper 170
Meursault 253

migration 87, 205
Miller, Henry 86, 221
Milly 21, 79, 289, 294, 296
Mirebeau 236
Mitterrand, François 21, 83, 85,
    86, 89, 93, 198, 204, 297
Monceau-les-Mines 284
Mont Beuvray 206
Montbard 179–182
Montereau 139
Montgolfier brothers 180, 183
Monthelie 252
Montréal 73, 98, 175–176
Morey-St-Denis 243
Morris, Jan 221
Morvan, Le 87, 89, 96, 98, 195,
    199–209
Moulin-à-Vent 301
mustard 120, 231, 232

n

Nallet, Henri 86, 88, 94, 148
Napoleon 78, 236, 243
Nevers 73, 95, 210–214
Niepce, Nicéphore 25, 79, 87, 256
Nièvre, La 86, 87, 195–216
Nivernais, Le 195, 209
Nolay 257
Noyers 156–157
Nuit-sous-Ravières, Château de
    151
Nuit-St-Georges 104, 247

p

pain d'épices 120, 231, 232
Paray-le-Monial Abbey 48, 95,
    283–284
Parker, Robert 104
Pernand-Vergelesses 249
Philip the Bold, Duke of Burgundy
    55–57, 225
Philip the Good, Duke of Burgundy
    59, 60, 61, 120, 227
Philip VI, King 232
Philippe Auguste, King 169
Pierre-Perthuis 173
Pierre-Qui-Vire Abbey 23, 98, 120,
    199
Pierreclos 294, 296
politics 83, 86
Pommard 251
Pontaubert 174
Pontigny Abbey 120, 151
pottery 143, 211, 212
Pouilly-en-Auxois 196
Pouilly-Fuissé wine 297
Pouilly-sur-Loire 215

provincial life 93–100
Puisaye, La 22, 141–144, 215
Puligny-Montrachet 253–254
Pulliat, Victor 304

q, r

Quarré-les-Tombes 200
Raclet, Benoît 303
Rance, Patrick 120
regionalism 99
Regnié-Durette 304
Reigny 162
religion 23, 95
Resistance 84–85 199, 200, 272
restaurants 119, 141, 144, 147,
    154, 155, 173, 174, 197, 200,
    203, 233, 255, 259, 267, 301
Reulle-Vergy 259
Rochepot, La 257
rock-climbing 160, 161
Rogny-les-Sept-Écluses 144
Rolin, Nicolas 208, 250
Romanèche-Thorins 301, 303
Romanesque trail 43–48, 271,
    279, 280–283
Romenay 266
Rosières 236
Rude, François 77, 228
Rully 255

s

Sacy 157–158
St-Amand-en-Puisaye 143
St-Amour 301
St-Bris-le-Vineux 159–160
St-Christophe-en-Brionnais
    279–280
St-Fargeau 143
St-Florentin 147
St-Jean-de-Vaux 255
St-Julien-de-Jonzy 281
St-Laurent-en-Brionnais 280
St-Maurice 281
St-Père 96, 172–173
St-Philibert Abbey 46, 48,
    267–268
St-Pierre-le-Moûtier 215
St-Point 296–297
St-Romain 112
St-Romain 253
St-Sauveur-en-Puisaye 22, 142,
    143
St-Seine-l'Abbaye 234–235
St-Triver-de-Courtes 266
St-Vincent-des-Prés 277
Sambin, Hugues 75, 229, 230,
    231

Sancerre 215
Santenay 254
Saône-et-Loire 87
Saulieu 197–199
Savigny-lès-Beaune 249
Schneider, Eugène and Adolf 39,
    79, 256
Schutz, Roger 23, 39, 272
Scott, Sir Walter 61–62
Seine, Sources de 188
Semur-en-Auxois 178–179
Semur-en-Brionnais 282
Sens 140
Sercy Château 270
Serein, River 151
Seurre 251
Sévigné, Madame de 21, 74, 75,
    177, 178, 257
Sluter, Claus 24, 224, 225, 228,
    233, 236
snails 122
Solutré, Rock of 21, 89, 297
Suin 277
Sully, Château de 257
superstition 99
Surgy 161

t

Taizé 23, 39, 95, 271, 272
Talant 234
Talmay, Château de 236
Tanlay, Château de 73, 148–149
Thomas à Becket 140, 151, 169
Til-Châtel 235
Tonnerre 88, 94, 147–148
Toucy 152
tourism 87
Tournus 46, 48, 266–269

v

Valois dukes 38, 55–66, 226
Vareilles 280
Vase de Vix 31, 185
Vault-de-Lugny 174
Vausse, Prieuré de 182
Vaux 100, 158
Vercingétorix 26, 32, 38,
    185–186, 206
Vermenton 162
Vézelay 48, 169–172
    Basilique Ste-Madeleine
        169–171
    town 95, 97, 171–172
vignerons 112
Villefranche-sur-Saône 307
Villié-Morgon 304
Villiers-St-Benoît 144

Vincenot, Henri 21, 24, 26, 99,
    122, 196, 216
Viollet-le-Duc, Eugène 170, 251
Volnay 252
Voltaire 249
Vosne-Romanée 246

w, y

Wagner 32, 36
walking 160, 174, 198, 307
waterways 22, 202
Weyden, Roger van der 24, 159,
    228, 251
wine auctions 100, 248
wine classification 109–111
wine confraternities 99, 108
wine festivals 100, 253
wine routes 158, 240, 298
wine-growers 96, 109, 112, 113
wines 88, 104–114, 124, 215,
    242–249, 251–255,
297, 299
Yonne, département 87, 139–162
Yonne, River 139, 160

✳ INSIGHT GUIDES

The world's largest collection of visual travel guides

Insight Guides – the Classic Series that puts you in the picture

Alaska	China	Hong Kong	Morocco	Singapore
Alsace	Cologne	Hungary	Moscow	South Africa
Amazon Wildlife	Continental Europe		Munich	South America
American Southwest	Corsica	Iceland		South Tyrol
Amsterdam	Costa Rica	India	Namibia	Southeast Asia
Argentina	Crete	India's Western	Native America	Wildlife
Asia, East	Crossing America	Himalayas	Nepal	Spain
Asia, South	Cuba	India, South	Netherlands	Spain, Northern
Asia, Southeast	Cyprus	Indian Wildlife	New England	Spain, Southern
Athens	Czech & Slovak	Indonesia	New Orleans	Sri Lanka
Atlanta	Republic	Ireland	New York City	Sweden
Australia		Israel	New York State	Switzerland
Austria	Delhi, Jaipur & Agra	Istanbul	New Zealand	Sydney
	Denmark	Italy	Nile	Syria & Lebanon
Bahamas	Dominican Republic	Italy, Northern	Normandy	
Bali	Dresden		Norway	Taiwan
Baltic States	Dublin	Jamaica		Tenerife
Bangkok	Düsseldorf	Japan	Old South	Texas
Barbados		Java	Oman & The UAE	Thailand
Barcelona	East African Wildlife	Jerusalem	Oxford	Tokyo
Bay of Naples	Eastern Europe	Jordan		Trinidad & Tobago
Beijing	Ecuador		Pacific Northwest	Tunisia
Belgium	Edinburgh	Kathmandu	Pakistan	Turkey
Belize	Egypt	Kenya	Paris	Turkish Coast
Berlin	England	Korea	Peru	Tuscany
Bermuda			Philadelphia	
Boston	Finland	Laos & Cambodia	Philippines	Umbria
Brazil	Florence	Lisbon	Poland	USA: Eastern States
Brittany	Florida	Loire Valley	Portugal	USA: Western States
Brussels	France	London	Prague	US National Parks:
Budapest	Frankfurt	Los Angeles	Provence	East
Buenos Aires	French Riviera		Puerto Rico	US National Parks:
Burgundy		Madeira		West
Burma (Myanmar)	Gambia & Senegal	Madrid	Rajasthan	
	Germany	Malaysia	Rhine	Vancouver
Cairo	Glasgow	Mallorca & Ibiza	Rio de Janeiro	Venezuela
Calcutta	Gran Canaria	Malta	Rockies	Venice
California	Great Barrier Reef	Marine Life ot the	Rome	Vienna
California, Northern	Great Britain	South China Sea	Russia	Vietnam
California, Southern	Greece	Mauritius &		
Canada	Greek Islands	Seychelles	St. Petersburg	Wales
Caribbean	Guatemala, Belize &	Melbourne	San Francisco	Washington DC
Catalonia	Yucatán	Mexico City	Sardinia	Waterways of Europe
Channel Islands		Mexico	Scotland	Wild West
Chicago	Hamburg	Miami	Seattle	
Chile	Hawaii	Montreal	Sicily	Yemen

Complementing the above titles are 120 easy-to-carry Insight Compact Guides, 120 Insight Pocket Guides with full-size pull-out maps and more than 60 laminated easy-fold Insight Maps